Editor in Chief

Harriet Plyler

Executive Editor

Jill Hurst

Principal Contributors

Anthony Nemecek

John Wallis

Alice Fishburn

Introduction by Rowena Boddington, Director, Advising & Marketing, US-UK Fulbright Commission, EducationUSA.

Cartoon Illustrations

Tim Sanders

Cover Design

David Preston

Front cover: University of Washington, Syracuse University. Back cover: University of the South (Sewanee)

With thanks to Kathryn Behringer, Patricia Blumenthal, Jim Bock, Rowena Boddington, Janice Chalmers, Annie Cheek, Christopher Cheek, Jamie Dunn, Dustin Daniels, Tara Eames, Caroline Edwards, Harry Edwards, Margaret Gandy, Susan Gowland, Susan Hamlyn, Denise Hart, Marva Hall, Theresa Hare, Regine Henrich, Eleanor (Daisy) Hill, Rosie Hodgart, Charlotte Hollingshead, Emma Hurst, Janet Irons, Shannon Javitz, Tiffany Alison Kirkland, Jacquelin Linn, Katja Lips, Shari Lord, Ralph Lucas, David Mannion, Alexander McClean, Joshua Murray, Emily Nelson, Parker Oliver, Kathleen Paul, Eileen Penman, Michelle Placek, the Countess of Ronaldshay, Chelsea Ryder, Nancy Machles Rothschild, the Sutton Trust, Thomas Turnbull, Chaffee Viets, Bill Visick, Janette Wallis, Sarah Weitzke, Lauren Welch, Connor Wilson, Joe Winkleman; international contributors (online version) Vanessa Bertagnole, Charles Baker, Pongpong Chua, Lydia Halls, Damara Klaasen, Thompson Plyler, Cassie Symes, Sean Thornton, Simon Sweeney and Alex Warren.

Universities in the USA

Also worth considering...

... and we can help

About This Book

This guide is written by students for students, with substantial input by university experts (credited and quoted throughout) who wrote or contributed to the articles in the first half of the book.

In choosing which schools to write about, we have considered a wide range of criteria. We have looked at vast state universities and small liberal arts colleges. We have examined institutions on the East Coast, on the West Coast and those scattered in between. We have looked at places that produce artists and places that produce nuclear scientists. We have looked at the oldest of American colleges and at those that are only just beginning to make a splash.

We have selected colleges and universities we think will or should interest British students, and while this book covers only a small and fairly elite percentage of the total, we think we have provided a good cross section of most of the different types available.

There are certain qualities that the institutions we have chosen have in common. We have tried to cover universities that combine good academic reputations with sizeable international populations. Many of them offer financial aid, in one form or another, to international applicants. Most are a reasonably straight shot from Heathrow or Gatwick.

These reviews are not filled with facts and statistics. All those technical details – the skeletal outline of a university – are available online and you should certainly study them.

What is not available online is the real feel of a university: the experiences people have there, what makes it hard, what makes it fun, what makes it worth travelling thousands of miles to get there. In short, the everyday life of its students, and their unvarnished opinions – warts and all.

We hope the guide is helpful to you, not as a comprehensive list of the places you should consider, but as an insight into the workings of some of the top institutions in the US and how to find one that's the right fit for you.

We have personally visited all the universities that feature in the guide (except in rare cases, where noted), and have spoken with the people studying there. Our reviews are based almost entirely on the opinions and knowledge of these students. Often, they're a little too far off piste for the comfort of various uni marketing departments. We think that this gives you an authentic sense of what to expect and where you would feel most comfortable, but it also means that our findings should be taken with a pinch of salt.

We also welcome feedback, whether on the university reviews or the articles: email us at editor@goodschoolsguide.co.uk.

One thing that became apparent to us as we compiled it, and that we hope we will communicate to you, is that your choice of university should be difficult precisely because there are so many great options. We hope that picking a university abroad will be one of those good hard decisions, the kind where you can't really go wrong, and that your eventual choice will be as rewarding as you deserve it to be.

Finally, close students of *Uni in the USA* might notice that we have begun taking advertisements. It's important to note: only institutions and resources selected for review or listing are allowed to advertise in any of *The Good Schools Guide* publications (print or online versions, UK or international), including *Uni in the USA*; no one can pay to be in any of our guides.

Best of luck with your search.

Introduction to the First Edition of Uni in the USA, 2004

I have a confession to make. I owned a pair of Harvard pyjamas as a child. There are pictures of me looking charming in them and reading Beatrix Potter. My indoctrination in the merits of an American education may well have started at this point, although I am certain I held out for a good many years.

But finally, having spent the better part of my teenage years ignoring parental suggestions, I ploughed my way through my SATS as well as my A Levels, submitted my applications and found myself on a plane to Boston. Now, in my final year at Harvard, I am the recipient of an education that has been considerably harder than Peter Rabbit but just as rewarding. And as the deadly date of graduation creeps ever nearer, I find myself thinking back over the decisions that got me here.

Try as I might, I don't think I can blame the pyjamas. Even the skilled psychological tactics of my parents were not the deciding factor. Instead I realised I simply couldn't get what I wanted from England. I had no idea what I wanted to do with my life and the thought that, aged 18, I would be limited to one academic subject for the next three years gave me claustrophobia. America, on the other hand, refused to let me confine myself. I had to take a variety of courses – in three years here I have studied physics, Chinese politics and musical theory while majoring in history and literature.

I was given the freedom to choose what I wanted to do and the flexibility to go back and correct any initial mistakes (did I really think I wanted a degree in Classics?). The American education offered me the chance both to explore and to specialise – an option that many undecided students in the UK are simply not aware of.

I jumped at the chance to write this book because it gave me the opportunity to dispel several of the myths that persist about college in America. Try as we might, we Brits can often not refrain from viewing education on that side of the pond with a certain amount of disdain. The thought that I, a quintessentially British girl in both birth and education, would want to throw in my lot with a bunch of Americans came as a nasty surprise to many of my friends and teachers.

But what school teachers particularly fail to recognise is that today American universities are some of the most successful and prosperous around. Indeed, when the Times Higher Educational Supplement recently ranked the top ten universities in the world, seven American schools were among them – and by the time you get down to Durham University you have dropped below another 36 US unis on the way. British applicants have begun to wake up to this reality. I am the second generation in my family to go to Harvard, but I am the first to find myself surrounded by Brits who have chosen the same track.

Many refuse to even consider the USA option because they believe it is simply too expensive for them. But the rise of tuition fees in England is slowly forcing people to look across the Atlantic. The excellent financial aid and bursary programmes in place at most American universities ensure that many British students can afford to go, regardless of their educational background or economic status.

Most students will graduate with less debt than their British contemporaries. Not every part of the American educational system has been wonderful. I have worked harder at Harvard than ever before in my life. I have undergone culture shock, missed my friends and family and developed an increasingly bizarre way of speaking. I have also made a dent in the bank balance of several very special people. But none of these obstacles would stand in my way if I had to choose my college path all over again. America has offered me something I couldn't find in England – a freedom to explore both academically and personally, and a chance to make friends with people who I would never have met back home.

This book is designed to answer all the questions you might have about the American college system. It will tell you who to see, what to ask and when to do it by. It looks at a selection of the many excellent schools and tries to give you an idea of what life would be like for you on the inside. But most of all, we hope, it will inspire you to at least consider the idea of America as you begin to make those nerve-wracking decisions about what you actually want from life.

Alice Fishburn
Editor, *Uni in the USA*
Harvard
Boston, Massachusetts, 2004

Why the USA? A word from the Fulbright Commission

The Fulbright Commission offers an advisory service for students who are interested in studying in the USA. This service is a component of EducationUSA, which provides objective, accurate, and comprehensive information and advice to individuals and organisations, but does not endorse or rank any college or university, or any services provided by third-party companies

Considering uni in the USA? You're in good company. The USA is the top destination for international students worldwide. In fact, 11,600 British students chose the States for their studies in 2015-2016; attendance at the annual Fulbright USA College Day has grown to over 4500, and traffic on the UK-US Fulbright website has increased to a million visitors a year.

The US–UK Fulbright Commission is delighted to work alongside *Uni in the USA* to promote study in the US and to host events throughout the year to assist students and schools with this process. Fulbright's advisory service is part of the EducationUSA network and is designated by the US State Department as the UK's official source of information on US higher education.

In addition to our website on applying to American universities (www.fulbright.org.uk), we offer seminars for students and parents, a training seminar for schools and our USA College Day fair in London, attended by more than 170 American universities each autumn. *Uni in the USA* complements our work, by offering you detailed information on specific American universities you may be considering from British students just like you.

As you read this publication, you will see there are many benefits to studying in the USA, but don't just take our word for it. Each summer the Fulbright office teams up with the US Embassy in London to survey British students as they apply for their student visas. Here are the top reasons they tell us they've chosen to study in the States.

Choice of a wide range of universities: There are more than 4,500 US institutions offering undergraduate degrees, from the prestigious Ivies and 'public Ivies' to liberal arts institutions and community colleges. With such a wide range of universities and degrees on offer, there is bound to be one that is a great fit for you. American universities are also known for their high quality of education around the world, occupying the top spots in most every world university league table.

Liberal arts approach and focus on undergraduate teaching: Not sure what you want to major in? You can apply to US universities as 'undecided' about your major. Under the 'liberal arts philosophy', you will take classes from a variety of subjects during the first 1–2 years before specialising in your major field. Students who already know what they want to study can complete a 'double major' – degrees in two academic fields – often completed within the normal four years of study. Moreover, students can expect a high level of undergraduate instruction, with at least 15 contact hours per week.

Experience American college life: In the States, learning is not confined to the four walls of the classroom. US universities are known for their vibrant campus life. Cheer your university's football (American, that is) team to victory or play intramural sports yourself. Join a club – there are hundreds to choose from. Become a leader in student government, raise funds for local charities through your sorority or fraternity, or write for the university newspaper. Act or sing in the campus arts programme or volunteer in the community. There are so many ways to get involved in American college life. This is not only a fun addition to your studies, but also a way to build up transferable skills for your CV.

Take advantage of funding opportunities: Many students are able to fund their studies through scholarships from US universities and external funding bodies. Funding is offered to students based on merit, extracurricular achievement, financial need, talent and/or personal characteristics, such as country of origin, field, gender or ethnicity. If you look hard enough, there may be a scholarship out there for you.

Internationalise and strengthen your CV: Studying and working abroad can make you stand out in the job market when you return to the UK. According to a Council for Industry and Higher Education (CIHE) survey of 230 UK companies, one in three employers valued job applicants with international study experience, while 65% of employers favoured applicants with overseas work experience. International students in the US have the opportunity to gain work experience during their studies and to work in the US for up to one year after graduation on the Optional Practical Training scheme. Students in the sciences and engineering may stay on for even longer.

Regardless of what draws you to the USA, Fulbright and *Uni in the*

USA look forward to helping you. We believe that studying abroad changes lives and changes countries – for the better. So, congratulations on getting this far in your journey and good luck!

Rowena Boddington
Director, Advising and Marketing
US–UK Fulbright Commission – EducationUSA
www.fulbright.org.uk

Background on American Universities: Read This First!

Making the decision to apply to a US university for your undergraduate course can be exciting if a bit daunting. Besides the prospect of narrowing down your choices from the more than 4500 US colleges and universities, of which approximately 2,000 offer undergraduate degrees (four years), you still have to deal with the complicated applications, money questions, prospect of culture shock and completely mysterious terminology – let alone the translations from English to American.

Dealing With the Terminology

Learning how Americans define their universities is an important part of the application process. Failure to suss the semantics can land you in trouble. For example, rather than referring to the delights of your 'uni', you will constantly be talking about your 'school', causing some confusion among grandparents who thought you had passed your A-levels. Here we explain some of the terminology of the US university system.

Accreditation

Accreditation has to be your biggest consideration when looking at US universities, not only to ease credit transfer, but also to ensure recognition of your degree when you come back to the UK. It is vital to make sure that your university is accredited by a body recognised by the Council for Higher Education Accreditation (CHEA) in Washington DC. If the school or university is not accredited by one of these agencies, there may be problems with recognition and acceptance of your qualification both within the US and in the UK. Check the *Uni in the USA* website www.uniintheusa.com to see CHEA's database of recognised postsecondary institutions and programmes.

The Ivy League

(Harvard, Princeton, Yale, Brown, Columbia, Penn, Dartmouth, Cornell)

The Ivy League schools are the Holy Grail of the US college admissions process – the American equivalent of Oxbridge. But while these elite colleges enjoy some of the best reputations in America, the famous title actually started out as little more than the name of a sports division (and not even a particularly good one). No one, however, dares dispute the academic excellence of the Ivies. Each school is remarkably different but all are situated on the East Coast and all enjoy stellar reputations.

Ivy League graduates are at the top of the tree in finance, media and politics (among other areas), and most of them never shut up about how their glory years in the most prestigious colleges got them where they are today. In fact, there is a plethora of universities in America that more than rival the Ivy League, but society finds it hard to resist that old East Coast arrogance and these colleges remain among the most popular around (and most difficult to get into).

College

In the US, 'college' and 'school' are used interchangeably with 'university'. 'College' always refers to higher education. A university is technically made up of more than one college (eg: it may have a College of Arts and Sciences plus a College of Engineering) or, confusingly, 'school' (as in the University of Florida School of Engineering).

Liberal Arts

Many US universities follow a liberal arts curriculum, but few can actually label themselves liberal arts colleges. This epithet applies only to a select group of mostly superb schools that pride themselves on the instruction of the undergraduate. As a result, they tend to have smaller campuses and fewer irritating grad students hanging around stealing the professors' attention.

Liberal arts programmes are designed to give you a broad and basic education rather than prepare you for a professional career. As a result you will normally be expected to come up to scratch in a range of academic disciplines. This ensures that at the end of four years, you emerge as a well-rounded individual. Most liberal arts colleges are private schools and Williams, Amherst and Swarthmore are often recognised as three of the top options. But students who want the breadth of a variety of courses need not confine their search to those colleges that are officially 'liberal arts'. The majority of undergraduate programmes at good universities insist their students take a broad base of courses.

Public Schools/State Universities

Don't get confused. When you hear people refer to public schools, they don't mean the Eton and Harrow equivalents of America but rather the institutions that are supported by the state and open to all members of the public (which actually makes more sense if you think about it). These schools have names like Penn State or the University of Indiana and the majority of the student body hail from within that state, something that allows them to pay reduced fees.

Public/state universities tend to be huge in size and some of them are absolutely excellent (e.g. UCLA and UVA). Be warned, though – standards vary immensely and if you are an out-of-state candidate, competition is generally fierce.

State vs Private Universities (and which are cheaper?)

In the United States private universities make up 75% of all institutions. However, 75% of US students attend the remaining 25% – the state universities. State universities are founded and subsidised by state governments to provide a less expensive higher education to residents of their state. For example, if a resident of Ohio attends Ohio State University, his fees will be much lower than those of anyone from out of state. However, the fees for non-residents, while much higher, are still less than private university fees. With student bodies of 20,000 plus, state universities admit a wider range of students than private universities.

Unfortunately, the economic incentive that US students have for attending their 'state' universities does not exist for non-US citizens. There will be little, if any, financial aid available to international students.

Private universities are funded by a combination of fees, grants, endowments and gifts from alumni. They are usually much smaller and, as a result, much harder to get into. However, they are also far more likely to be able to provide financial assistance to international students.

Community Colleges

Another option, and one which may be appealing for both late developers and those struggling economically, is the community college. Community colleges, also known as junior colleges, are similar to the FE sector in the UK. They provide two-year courses leading to an Associate's degree – very similar to an HND. As a rule, admissions criteria are much more flexible, many not even requiring an admissions test, such as the SAT. They are also much, much cheaper and thus attractive to those on a tight budget.

Many students elect to attend a community college for the first two years of their degree and then transfer to a four-year institution, similar to topping up an HND. In fact, many community colleges have agreements with prestigious universities that will guarantee acceptance upon successful completion of the two year course.

For students who have, perhaps, not yet proved themselves academically, the community college route offers an opportunity to demonstrate their capabilities and save a lot of money. For some international students, the community college may make the transition to the American system more comfortable, as a more gradual means of acclimatising to the American style of assessment.

The downside to community colleges is that they tend to attract older students, many of whom might be balancing classes, homework and full time jobs and/or families, so it may be more difficult to find a satisfying social group or peers with spare time. The college also may not have the resources to provide special support for international students, and may not offer the total 'living' experience provided by four-year institutions – many do not cater for housing, etc.

If you are considering a community college, find out what agreements they have with four-year institutions and what sort of support they offer international students, both academically and socially, before you make any decisions.

If you are considering a community college, find out what agreements they have with four-year institutions and what sort of support they offer international students, both academically and socially, before you make any decisions.

Uni in the US vs Uni in the UK: What's the Difference?

The greatest difference between Bachelor degrees in the US and BAs in the UK is summed up by two words: 'liberal' and 'arts'. If you feel that nothing but three years of physics is right for you, then stay at home. If you know what you're good at but want to explore a hundred other things as well, then the US may be just what you need. Have no idea? Head to America and put off those daunting decisions for a little while longer.

Students at a liberal arts college or a university with a strong liberal arts programme – most of the ones covered in this guide – can take classes in a wide variety of courses before zeroing in on a specialist subject. Even if you plan to major in engineering, you will usually have to take courses in the humanities and social sciences; history majors will be required to courses in maths and science subjects and so forth. The end result? A flexible education that enables you to carry on exploring academically throughout your undergraduate career.

This philosophy is one of the most striking differences between UK and US degree programmes. For some students, the thought of having to take a subject that they may have gratefully left behind at GCSE level will be unappealing, but the US system believes in urging everyone to explore a varied curriculum before allowing them to commit to a major area of focus.

This system also makes the US degree far more flexible for those students who are unable to make up their minds. For the most part, any 'class' (American lingo for 'course module') taken to fulfil the liberal arts core can also be used to fulfil graduation requirements. It is thus perfectly possible to start out as a history major and change to Spanish, without losing any time.

Transfer Students

What's more, should you decide to transfer to a different university, you can bring what you have already completed with you – rather than having to start over. Obviously, there will be instances when you cannot transfer directly because courses will differ from university to university, but for the most part universities are co-operative and accept transfer credits.

There's plenty of single-minded education on offer in the US too – although the best of it is often postgraduate-only. Large universities tend to comprise colleges of arts and sciences and several 'professional' (i.e. career-orientated) schools, such as business, agriculture, medicine, law and journalism. Institutes of technology have a scientific emphasis.

Tinker, Tailor, Doctor, Lawyer

Med School

If you are one of those noble characters who has known from the cradle that you have a vocation for mending broken bodies or diagnosing ingrown toenails, then you may regard the American medical school system as a serious waste of time. There are hardly any courses for undergraduates seeking a medical degree in the United States (with the exception of a couple, such as the combined courses at Northwestern).

Instead, would-be doctors must go through their college career as pre-meds, combining the courses that will set them on track to med school with those that give them a liberal arts education. Though frustrating for many, this approach does guarantee a wider base of knowledge and means you are not exposed to the gore and pressure of the medical system at the tender age of eighteen.

But being a pre-med is no easy task. The requirements are fairly painful and, if you plan to carry on in the US system, you will have to take your MCATs while studying for your undergrad degree. This dreaded nine-hour exam is a multiple choice stamina test that is mandatory for entry into the many excellent American medical schools.

The advantage of this system is that if you are presently considering medicine as a career option, but are by no means set on it, you get an extra three years of broad education while you make up your mind. The disadvantage is that pre-meds work harder than most other students and still have to jump through the extra hoop of applications at the end of the four years.

Even then, you are chancing your arm if you intend to stay on in the US for your postgraduate medical studies. Fewer than one half of 1% of students in US medical colleges are international students. This is because medical schools are typically mandated to serve the healthcare needs of the state where they are based, so they are unwilling to divert funds to educate foreigners. Fewer than half of US medical schools even entertain international applications.

Therefore, even if you hold an appropriate undergraduate degree, the likelihood of acceptance is virtually nil. Worse, if you are accepted, there is almost no financial aid for international medical students and many of the medical schools that do accept international students require that those students place in escrow the equivalent of one to four years' tuition and fees (US$50,000-US$250,000).

Those still set on a US medical education should be aware that once you have completed your medical studies in the UK, it is quite possible to enter the US for your residency/clinical practice stage. Contact the Fulbright Commission or the relevant universities/ med schools for additional information.

Law School

Would-be lawyers in America find themselves in a similar situation. There is no actual undergraduate law degree. Instead, the students designate themselves (you guessed it) pre-laws and round off their college career with the LSAT exam to apply to postgraduate law schools. Those set on a legal career do not have the same college-imposed requirements as their medical peers, but they do have to suffer the slings and arrows of important grad school applications and tests in the midst of what should be the final fun fling of their collegiate years.

For students wanting to study law, the prospects of graduate study in the US after earning an LLB in the UK are bright. If it is your goal to practise law in the US, following your LLB, you can apply to do a one-year LLM (Master of Laws) in the US and may be able to take the qualifying bar exam in several states. As each state sets its own requirements, and they change frequently, it is best to consult with the Fulbright Commission first.

Degree of Difficulty

An American education is hard work. Your friends back home will spend much of their first year sitting in the pub, while you spend it trekking back and forth to the library. The fact that most of these universities operate under the principle of continuous assessment means that goofing off for semesters at a time is not an option.

Instead, practically everything you do in a class will influence the eventual status of your degree. Exams (usually at least two per term), tests (sometimes unannounced), essays or written assignments, problem sets, laboratory reports, laboratory practicals, class attendance and discussion participation may all be used to determine your final grade. While you get a chance to laugh at the Brits back home when they all start panicking about finals, you will have spent four years working much harder than they have on a day-to-day basis.

US colleges do not come cheaply and you should expect to get your money's worth in terms of hours of class. There's none of that 'six hours of tuition a week, attendance optional if you have a hangover' stuff here. Students should expect to attend at least twelve hours of lectures a week with quality professors. Attendance at several smaller sessions (something akin to tutorials) will also be required.

And falling behind on that massive reading load really isn't a possibility if you hope to keep your grades up. Courses are marked as a percentage, then translated to the letter grade scale as follows (with some minor variations): 100–90% = A; 89–80% = B; 79–70% = C; 69–60% = D; 59–50% = F = fail. (Some systems use E for fail.) Competition for those As tends to be fierce, so prepare yourself for four years of hard work.

There is one easier option available to the lazier variety of student. This is to take a course on a pass/fail basis rather than for a letter grade. Most universities have become wise to this easy option, however, and there may well be a limit to the number of courses a student can take by this method. The option also may not be available if the course is required for the student's major. The system works well, however, for students who want to experiment in different fields but don't want a potentially low grade to risk their treasured GPA.

However hard you work, you can rest assured you are not the only person putting in long hours. While America expects a lot from its students, it also expects its professors to teach well. Students are able to assess their lecturers' performance at the end of each course and access to members of the faculty is generally less restricted than in Britain. America prides itself on the unity of its academic communities and professors are normally fairly involved in undergraduate education.

But don't be a shy and retiring Brit about it. US students have been trained from an early age to go out there and introduce themselves to that scary person lecturing at them. Learn to do likewise and you will benefit hugely.

Credits and Courses

American undergraduate degrees allow you a variety of options. Students usually experience a wide variety of courses before selecting a major on which to focus. It is also possible to create your own unique programme of study. Every course you take each semester earns a specified number of credits (also termed 'hours' or 'units'). You get your degree when you have completed the appropriate number of credits (normally after four years of full-time study). Don't worry, though – most US colleges have an advising system in place that allows students to discuss the courses they will take during the academic year with a tutor. This ensures that nothing vital gets overlooked.

It is not uncommon for students to take longer than four years to complete their degrees. This often happens if they take less than a full-time course load per term owing to academic or financial reasons. Students can also adjust their workloads between terms – taking five courses in one semester and only three in the next. Courses taken in the first two years are known as lower division courses and those in the final two years as upper division courses.

The individual courses that make up the degree programme can be divided into the following types:

Core courses: These provide the centre of the degree programme. Students take a variety of courses drawn from maths, English, humanities, sciences, social sciences, foreign languages and foreign cultures. Core requirements vary from college to college but are the base of the liberal arts culture and a valuable part of the American system.

Major courses: A major is the subject on which a student chooses to concentrate. Most students major in one subject; however, some colleges offer the option of pursuing a double major with a related subject. Of the total number of courses required for the completion of a degree, a quarter to a half will be spent collecting credits for your major.

Minor courses: A minor is a subject in which a student may choose to take the second greatest cluster of courses. The number of courses required for a minor tends to be half the number of major courses. Minors are a great way of pursuing a secondary interest, in such fields as languages or the arts.

Elective courses: These courses may be chosen from any department and often have little to do with a student's major. They help make up the total number of credits required to graduate and also offer the student the chance to really explore everything their university has to offer. As a result, they can be one of the most fun parts of an American degree.

What is a GPA?

Instead of a degree classification, students complete their degree with a Grade Point Average (GPA). A cumulative Grade Point Average is the GPA for all courses taken throughout the degree programme. This number is what prospective employers look at, and during job-hunting season, you will see your classmates frantically trying to calculate their total.

To work out your GPA, you assign a numerical value to each letter grade you achieved (most universities use four for an A, three for a B and so on, but a few, purely to confuse, score an A as five and so on down).

You then multiply this number by the number of credits the course is worth to give total grade points for the course (i.e. a three hour course (that typically does meet three hours a week) is worth 3 credits x your grade).

Add all these up and divide by the total number of credits for all the courses you have taken and hey presto! there are your average grade points per credit – your GPA. A GPA of 4.0 is the highest; this suggests all your grades are As. A GPA of 3.0 means that your average is a B and so on.

Incidentally, this is the same system used in American high schools, so all American students will be entirely familiar with it. It is a key measurement on university applications from US students (Brits have national exams instead – so we substitute A Levels for GPA as an indication of how well we've done at school).

Most universities will also offer some sort of honours degree (in the UK this comes free with the BA, like an Oxbridge MA). In the US, to qualify for an honours degree you must acquire additional credits or write an honours thesis. Precise details depend on the university and/or academic department, so make sure you find out about it early in your college career. There may well be different levels of honours: summa cum laude, magna cum laude and cum laude, in descending order of distinction, based on your GPA and the honours extras.

The Academic Calendar

The academic year will be slightly different for each university/ college but will normally run from early September to the end of May. It may be divided into two terms of 18 weeks called 'semesters', or the university may have 'quarters' or 'trimesters' which are about 12 weeks in length. Additionally, universities often provide six to eight-week summer terms, but these are optional. Many students attend if they wish to decrease their course load during the regular terms, or simply make up for lost ground.

There are at least two main holidays during the academic year: a two to four-week break over Christmas and a one-week Spring Break somewhere between early March and mid-April.

English students should, however, beware. America offers none of the 'three long holidays a year' system that so many British universities enjoy. The Christmas break is fairly short and Easter does not exist. The one-week Spring Break, which college students treat as a big excuse for drunkenness and debauchery, can leave you more exhausted than relaxed, and the haul from January to May is a long one.

American summer holidays are huge but most of your contemporaries will be using them for work experience. Relaxation does not figure largely in the American calendar – occasional breaks for Presidents' Day or Thanksgiving are the most time off you can really expect in the academic term – something to bear in mind if you are someone who enjoys his leisure time.

Culture Shock

Love America one minute? Hate it the next? For students concerned about the normality of their reaction to American life, there is an answer. Sociologist Gregory Trifonovitch has studied the experiences of students transplanted to another culture and outlined the four stages of cultural adjustment.

1. The Honeymoon Stage: Upon arrival everything is wonderful. The Americans are so friendly, everyone loves your accent and the price of jeans is half that at home. You love your adopted country and it seems to love you. Until...

2. The Hostility Stage: Suddenly everything is a little too strange. Where are your friends? Why is there no pub? What on earth are people talking about? This is the stage at which Trifonovitch believes most international students experience frustration and depression, due mostly to the difficulties of settling into a new environment. The tendency is to lash out at the new surroundings – think phone calls home outlining the stranger habits of the 'bloody Americans'. This is the point at which you must make sure you are meeting lots of new people, developing those initial connections into real friendships and talking to friends or counsellors about any problems you are having.

3. The Humour Stage: Suddenly one day you wake up and you know how to deal with being a Brit in America. Mistakes are no longer irritating. They are funny. Suddenly you like being the outsider.

4. The Home Stage: Eventually you are a veteran. Despite your misgivings, you start defending American foreign policy to your English friends in much the same way you defend the British Empire to your American ones. You have become culturally ambidextrous – a true transatlantic traveller.

A Shared History?

Everyone considering applying to a US university should understand that the experience will have its ups and its downs. There will be good friends who open your eyes to a whole new cultural awareness. And, yes, there will be bad times when you feel like banging your head against the wall and screaming, 'Get me out of here!'

Always, there will be the constant reminders that you are, in essence, different from these people. It may be the evening when everyone gets drunk and decides to sing the theme tunes from their favourite childhood television shows. When you start to sing *Neighbours* or *Robot Wars*, they'll suddenly go blank and you'll shudderingly realise these English (or Australian) classics never quite made it across the pond. Or it may be the time you try to remind everyone about that great single that Ash released and the time you tried to sing it on a pub table after your GCSE results.

Again, although there may be a few indulgent smiles, the vast majority of Americans will be sitting there thinking 'Poor crazy English kid'. The sad truth is that, no matter how assimilated you become, the trends, jokes and cultural history of your childhood and adolescence will always be a mystery to Americans. However, when you really think about it, how much of your time at college do you really want to spend discussing that romance in *Hollyoaks* or the names of all four Teletubbies?

Fellow Brits

At the majority of these universities you will discover a significant number of international undergraduates. In those first baffled days as you grapple with registration, visa snags and the mysteries of the American language, it is all too easy to fall in with those you most closely identify with – your fellow countrymen.

After all, they share a common background, a similar accent and, given the minute scale of Britain, mutual geographical and social history. And, chances are, they're just as bemused by Americans as you are. These people can become your extended siblings – friends with whom to make sense of an alien environment and who can help you to assimilate. Just because you have decided to make the move out of Britain does not mean you should slam the door on all its other exports. To have a truly international university experience, you need to foster your links with the past at the same time as embracing the future.

Yet it is also important you do not isolate yourself from the American community. If you are surrounded solely by Brits or Europeans from day one, it can be difficult to make contact with actual Americans – an integral part (unsurprisingly) of the American educational experience. Remember: the natives of your new country do not all share the same background and the chances are many of them will feel as lost as you.

Getting to know roommates and classmates who come from places you would never be able to pinpoint on a map is essential and the most rewarding thing you can do. Of course, there will always be Brits available to form an emergency support system but, at the vast majority of these colleges, there will be too few of them to provide a full social circle, even if you wanted them to. Americans will come to form the major body of your friends and, whatever your angst, you must turn to them from the beginning.

The Dating Game

Does absence makes the heart grow fonder? The start of freshman year always sees a significant handful of loyal souls clinging to the relationships that have defined their teenage years. As the year progresses, however, many of these relationships fall by the wayside.

Leaving a 'significant other' back home is not an easy task to pull off. The social/drunken/hormonal atmosphere of university means the relationship will be severely tested and, even if the one drunken slip doesn't zap it, the mileage probably will. There is also the undeniably irritating, but also undeniably true, parental dictum – 'too serious, too young'. College is, after all, a time to get out there and try new things – so don't tie yourself down or you might end up resenting that one true love.

This is not to say that long-distance relationships don't work. After all, America has some pretty bizarre dating rituals and some people just feel more comfortable sticking to what they know. But it pays to consider the options before you swear eternal devotion and get on that plane.

How Do You Define 'Dating'?

Remember those high-school movies? The ugly ducking turns into a swan, the jock discovers his heart, the whole thing comes together in one great romantic climax on prom night... American fact or Hollywood fiction? It's difficult to tell but, whatever the answer, one truth stands out – dating in the United States is a whole new experience. Of course, as in Britain, it is difficult to generalise about relationships across the range of universities.

Students who head for one of the more relaxed and less academic schools will discover dating scenarios that are totally different from the insanely introspective and esoteric relationships that define some of the Ivy Leagues. Think *Road Trip* versus *Love Story*. But there are some crucial elements to American romance that seem to go across the board.

First of all, there is the definition of the word 'dating'. In Britain its meaning is clear: you're going out. But in America you can quite easily be routinely seeing the same person, yet have absolutely no idea what the dating status of your relationship actually is. Let alone if it even has one!

There comes a point when casual dating evolves into monogamous dating and it still isn't quite a relationship but doesn't allow relationships with anyone else but... well, you get the idea. Americans seem to be born with an embedded cultural chip enabling them to understand all of this stuff, but Brits are frequently left bemused.

Secondly, the date itself is a somewhat different experience. This may be due to the alcohol restrictions in this country. Somehow in Britain, pubs, bars and clubs lend themselves to drunken encounters that sometimes develop into something more memorable. In America, however, the most used phrase is 'Let's have coffee'. It makes no difference if neither of you actually likes coffee – the formalities have to be preserved. No wonder Starbucks is so popular!

Even getting to the coffee stage is something to be proud of. One Swarthmore male observes 'students are either about to get married or hardly together... the lifestyle and lack of privacy are not conducive to steady "going out".' Forget any rules of relationships you may have learnt at home.

Do not expect to go on dates alone – everyone continues to travel as a pack. Do not expect a call on day three. Americans tend to be far more assertive than your average Brit. (Although if you are the kind of person who has a little Old World reticence, rest assured it could work to your advantage!) And if you get stuck – for goodness sake, ask an American, not an international student, for advice.

The Dating Game if You're Interested in Men...

Perhaps the whole debacle can be best summed up in the words of a frustrated friend who studied in America (capitals her own):

'The "dating" KILLED ME. What I really like about European guys is they tend to tell you whether they like you or not. Then I came to North Carolina and went on a date with this guy. The movie ended and he drove me home. Nothing happened. Then he didn't call again for about a week. Then we went out to dinner and to the beach. Then he drove me home. STILL nothing happened. Then he didn't call for a few days. Then we went out again... AND THIS WENT ON FOR A MONTH OR TWO... I didn't know how to deal

with the whole situation any longer so I got him drunk and ONLY THEN something happened... and all the other girls from America were telling me not to stress as nothing seemed wrong!!! But HOW CAN SOMEONE KIND OF BE YOUR BOYFRIEND?! HE IS EITHER YOUR BOYFRIEND OR HE IS NOT YOUR BOYFRIEND.'

With the introduction of countless dating apps like Tinder and Bumble, this situation is (unfortunately for Brits) far from abnormal and will continue to be. But as American men mature, their games disappear and you can end up walking along the Brooklyn Bridge hand in hand, content to know you're at least on the way to relationship road.

The Dating Game if You're Interested in Women...

American women have, for the most part, been brought up to believe that it pays to take a more assertive attitude towards dating. Women are not backward about coming forward on college campuses (probably because they have to make a stand just to cut through the American boys' deeply relaxed attitude).

Our Swarthmore man: *'The author's right about the direct nature of American women – they single you out and tell you that they like you – but I also think this applies to American guys as well. I have another friend who's an international student at Swarthmore, and when we're at parties we sometimes like to just observe the American kids interacting – we both agree that they are about as subtle as a bull in a china shop. Sometimes, it feels like you're 12 again, because the inter-sex (or same-sex, to be fair) interactions are just devoid of any conversational finesse (for kids who are so smart) and seem to be fuelled by loud music and alcohol. By contrast, interactions between English men and women at college age really can be very subtle. I've got mates who have gone for months at a time trying to get with a girl they like without letting the girl figure it out. The American way saves a lot of confusion, but just doesn't seem as satisfying. However, I am biased!'*

The straightforward nature of the American girl can be great. You know that she likes you, she singles you out, it's good for your ego. At the same time, many English gentlemen begin to feel they are losing control. After all, they have been taught it is polite to hold doors open and pay for meals. Ultimately, however, these differences seem to work themselves out – and the long tradition of young American girls falling in love with distinguished English gents suggests you may well be in with a chance of enjoying a functional relationship on the other side of the Atlantic!

Your secret weapon

British students have one secret weapon in their mission to conquer Americans – their accent. It is undeniably true that when the English open their mouths, Americans swoon. It may have something to do with Prince Harry or Emma Watson, but the average Yankee will initially seem more than receptive to your suave English charm. So all of your dreams about the sun-kissed, liberated American, schooled in the arts of high-school seduction and just waiting for their happy ending, may very well come true.

(Note: Just don't utter a resounding cry of "You're SO fit!" as a compliment here – no one will have any idea what you're talking about.)

Fraternities (or 'Greeks')

When you tell your British friends you are planning to attend an American university, it is more than likely that at least one of them will look at you with pity and mutter something disparaging about fraternities. These Greek societies have been much parodied in Hollywood movies, most famously in the iconic *Animal House*, and remain the thing most Brits commonly associate with US universities. In truth, while the majority of American college girls do not live in sororities that specialise in naked pillow-fights, and most American boys do not swallow goldfish as part of their initiations, the Greek system is still alive and kicking on a large number of American campuses.

These social groups (often named after random Greek letters – Sigma Alpha Epsilon and so on) are particularly dominant in Southern and state universities, but exist across the United States. On many campuses, they form an integral part of the social life, offering the students privately owned buildings where it is possible to party (and drink) in relative peace. They also offer alternative accommodation for their members – frequently seen as a welcome alternative to the university dorms.

Although some of them remain hugely secretive and exclusive, many universities have insisted that any Greek house on campus open its doors to all students. For whatever reason, fraternities and sororities (for girls, and somewhat more civilised than the fraternities) have become much more integrated into the college life than they used to be (and certainly much more so than the mysterious secret societies at Yale, UVA or UNC).

Scandals do, however, continue to hang over these Greek institutions. Accusations of sexual assault, drunken casualties and the 'hazing' (which has on rare but tragic occasions gone horribly wrong and resulted in a fatality) that takes place during rush and initiation seasons, when the frats are recruiting more members, are rife. Widely associated with but not exclusive to fraternities, it's common knowledge that sexual assault is far more likely to happen at college than in other environments. The most shocking statistic is that apparently 25% of women will be assaulted before they graduate.

It's not clear whether this is a bigger problem at US colleges than at UK universities (perhaps due to fraternity culture, or different attitudes towards women, or possibly even the higher drinking age) but it makes sense to at least be aware of the dangers. On a more positive note, there is all sorts of work going on to combat these problems, much of it student-driven.

As far as you are concerned, most of the schools mentioned in this guide are not dominated by the Greek societies (although the majority have active chapters on campus), and nowadays most college students find their social life extends in other directions. However, if you are hell bent on being the next Iota Gamma, it pays to do your research before signing your life away. After all, you don't want to become the next John Belushi.

Pubs and Prohibition

The majority of Brits spend their college days enveloped in a haze of alcohol that oils the wheels of their social lives, cushions their academic crises and whips up their weekends, weeks, evenings and even the odd morning. Not so their American neighbours. In the good old US of A you can use a shotgun almost as soon as you can carry it, drive a car from the age of 16 and kill for your country before you even consider university. Yet, until your 21st birthday, a glass of wine with dinner or a pint of beer at a football game remains a criminal offence in most states.

Almost all American students think these laws ridiculous, and all Europeans certainly do. Yet the laws remain and their effects are widely felt. Not only is it an impediment to normal socialising, it also means that far more importance is attached, in the freshman year particularly, to underage drinking. This can be disturbing for Brits who suddenly feel fourteen again, hiding their vodka bottles under the bed.

Fake IDs, although obviously illegal, are used by the majority of US students to lubricate their first couple of years. Those lucky enough to have older brothers or sisters often nab their IDs. Be warned, however. Arrests happen frequently enough for actual concern and there are horror stories among international students of offenders being deported. The stories may be fictitious, but it is certainly not uncommon for IDs to be confiscated and even handed to the police.

Of-age Brits should also be aware that their English driving licence is not considered by many of the more pedantic East Coast bartenders to be a sufficient form of identification. It pays to have a colour photocopy of your passport with you at all times. This also helps to clear up the issues of reversed dates (that whole month/day, day/month thing can be a nightmare).

Certain areas are infinitely more difficult than others. Unsurprisingly Puritan New England suffers the most. In some states it is still illegal to buy alcohol on Sundays, and dry towns (a concept that would appal the average Brit) are not uncommon. Those interested in hitting the biggest nightspot of them all will be relieved to learn that the majority of bars in New York City are considerably more relaxed.

No Smoking Please

It is easy to spot the Europeans on winter nights at East Coast American universities. While everyone else is tucked up in their dorm rooms, watching four feet of snow pile up around the windows, the Europeans are sitting on their doorsteps, shivering in an inadequate coat, and frantically trying to warm themselves by the heat of a much needed cigarette.

They can only find this nicotine solace outdoors because legislation across most of the United States has banned smoking in restaurants, bars and clubs (as well as the more obvious offices and dorm rooms). Americans, particularly those of the educated variety, are frequently militant anti-smokers and for Brits with a pack-a-day mentality, this can come as a rude surprise.

Certain areas of the States are much more draconian than others – in California, for example, the only cigarettes you are likely to come across are those chain-smoked by the odd Hollywood actress in a bid to expunge all food from her diet. But although America as a whole is rapidly becoming a no-cigarette zone, stressed-out students are one sector of the population who can be relied on to boost sales. Smoking comrades are always around; the problem lies in finding somewhere to light up.

BTW for those of you Brits who are die-hard smokers, a word of warning: calling a cigarette a 'fag' is NOT a good idea unless you are given to provoking multiple misunderstandings, embarrassment and lectures on political correctness! (In the US, 'fag' is a very derogatory term for a male homosexual.)

Just Don't Inhale – and you too can Become President

Drug-taking among university students in America is really little different from drug-taking among their contemporaries in Britain. Some do it all the time, some never touch the stuff. The range of drugs is also pretty similar – rich, spoilt kids do cocaine, everyone else smokes pot and the experimental ones swallow any pill going. If there is one small difference, it is the fact that marijuana is probably even more popular among students in the US than it is in the UK – no doubt the explanation behind candidate Bill Clinton's famous denial.

The reason for this is probably because alcohol is so much harder to come by for under-21s in America, and it is often easier to smoke a joint than be chucked out by bar after bar on a Saturday night. Since the joys of Woodstock and the Swinging Sixties, pot has never really relinquished its place as drug of choice for students eager to escape reality.

However, this is not to say the American bureaucracy is willing to overlook a bunch of stoned students. Drug laws, while changing in some states, can be pretty tough and, in case you need reminding, as an international student you are particularly liable for harsh punishment. Universities are normally willing to turn a blind eye to the first minor drug offence but, as with alcohol, if you are going to indulge, you need to keep your wits about you and be careful not to get caught.

Definitely, definitely do not drive under the influence of anything. In some college towns, fines and legal fees for DUI (Driving under the influence) cases are a growth industry...and you will not enjoy the company of your fellow inmates all night in the local lockup.

If you are an athlete or going through the recruiting process for any moneymaking finance jobs, you should be warned that random drug testing is one of the perils of the process and something that has succeeded in dashing the hopes of many an ambitious stoner.

Work-out Nation

Many Americans like to say their nation is fat in the middle and thin around the edges. This is certainly a country of extremes and personal health is most definitely one of them. International students are frequently shocked by the sheer volume of food that people consume in the US. No one goes to the movies without buying a bucket of drink and a barrel of popcorn, and even the nicer restaurants will slap half a cow on your plate and call it a steak.

While obesity is a humongous problem in Middle America, college students normally need only worry about the dreaded 'freshman 15' (the just over a stone that students are rumoured to gain in their first year). Once your mind and stomach have grown accustomed to the size of your plate, you will notice another thing – American students are obsessed with working out. It rivals only their dating rituals for most baffling personality trait. While students also play all the sports English universities do, they continue to regard the gym as a sort of second home. Jogging to them is like oxygen.

You may well become sucked into this lifestyle – in fact, it may become the penance for the size of your meals. But be warned, if you are one of the brave souls who manages to withstand the onslaught of comments about your lack of gym attendance, you will be marked down as slightly unnatural. After all, doesn't everyone want to run eight miles a day?

Cold Hard Cash

As far as banking practicalities go, never put your faith in the effectiveness of international monetary transactions. Although English bank cards work in most American ATMs, there is no point in draining your Lloyds account, incurring extra charges and constantly having to calculate the dollars/pounds exchange. By far the best option is to set up an American bank account. As students return to school, all the banks compete to offer the best possible options and it is easy to get a good deal. Getting an American credit card is important, too, especially for those who plan to stay on in the United States. Building up a credit history will help you later when you need to start paying for that mortgage or car.

Note: Your school will probably have a way for you to pay your tuition and fees by credit card. It might be worthwhile to try to make those payments with a card that gives you air miles.

If you have to transfer large sums of money (or cheques) between countries, make sure you give it plenty of time. Banks often impose long waiting periods before they clear cheques or wired funds and this could prove catastrophic if your rent is due the next day.

Finally, a couple of other financial points. America is a nation that expects heavy tipping (to compensate for its remarkably low minimum wage). If you are paying for dinner or taking a taxi, leaving around 20% is considered normal. The traditional Brit who tips at 10% is treated with considerable disdain and won't necessarily be welcomed back.

And for those of you who are struggling with all those coins – here's a breakdown: 1 dollar = 100 cents; 1 quarter = 25 cents (the big coins, size of a 10p and with fun state facts on them); 1 dime = 10 cents (this is really confusing, they're the small ones – like 5ps); 1 nickel = 5 cents (bigger than the dime but less valuable); 1 penny = 1 cent (borrowed from the English).

Hitting the Road

You're in the States and an open road in the land of opportunity stretches before you. A small piece of advice: get on it.

It is all too easy to downsize to your own little campus and spend four years languishing in an obscure corner of New England, Chicago or California. This familiar haven in a terrifyingly vast land (that actually boasts ranches the size of Britain) will always feel like a secure American home for you. Don't let it trap you. Presumably you chose to come to the States because you have either some sort of wanderlust or a sense of adventure (or, in the worst case scenario, a real hatred of the UK). Going to university in such a unique environment should not kill your travel itch. Give it free rein and make all your British friends truly jealous.

Your travels are made that much easier by the fact that your American friends will be falling over themselves to show you around their hometowns. The colleges in this book are not only popular with international students, they also take Americans from all corners of the 50 states. Unless you select your friends using geographical criteria, the chances are that you will end up knowing people 'from California to the New York Island'. And on such random American holidays as Thanksgiving, the great American hospitality kicks in for the poor abandoned Brit. Accept all invitations, exploit all the long weekends you get and break out into as many of the 50 states as you possibly can.

The road trip remains a remarkable part of the American youth experience and one highly recommended to any Brit who can jump on board. If you have a friend with a car, you're set. The sole problem lies with your own driving. Not only do you face the challenges of driving on the wrong side of the road, you will also probably find you are too young to hire a car. If you fail totally in chartering your own set of wheels, the ubiquitous Greyhound bus is more than adequate for the intrepid traveller.

Choosing a University

Selecting a university that is thousands of miles away, perhaps without the opportunity to visit beforehand, will worry even the most enthusiastic of students. Fortunately, thanks to the internet you can get a good feel for an institution without adding to Branson's millions. Many universities provide virtual tours of their campuses, and give you a clear description of student life and the services available to international students.

Additionally, many US university representatives visit the UK on a regular basis and attend the College Day USA fairs in London that take place in late September/early October. See www.fulbright.org.uk for further information.

Academic Considerations

What is it you really want to study? If you have specific requirements, will the university you are looking at be able to satisfy your needs? US universities are often pretty flexible – many will allow you to design your own course within the academic resources they offer. But can you handle the requirements that they do have? Investigate.

If you plan on studying a field that will have a professional examination or required affiliation once you return to the UK, ask the UK professional body how the US degrees you are looking at will be viewed. For the most part there are few problems, but you may be required to take additional coursework or sit an examination and it is best to know this in advance.

How will a US university view your UK qualifications? Each in its own way (although some of them have been reading our newspapers decrying the value of A-levels and may need some persuasion). Most, however, will give you credit for your A-level, IB or Pre-U credentials, which can then be used to decrease the length of time needed to complete the degree. Many UK students find that an entire year can be 'waived' in this way. However, as each US university is entitled to set its own policies on credits awarded, it should be investigated before you apply.

Because there is such variety among US universities, it is essential when looking for an appropriate institution that you consider the difficulty of gaining admission. All universities will publish their general criteria. Look at that information carefully. You don't want to spend the time and money applying if your chances of getting in are hopeless. While US universities are extremely flexible and will look at each student individually, if your qualifications, SAT results etc. are below the standard they normally want, the likelihood is that you won't get in. However, with so many accredited universities from which to choose, there is almost certainly a university out there that will be the right match for you!

How is the university you are looking at rated? Unlike the UK, there is no official ranking system in the US. There are several ranking 'providers' (see the Reference Section) and each will use different criteria. They can be helpful in the initial stages of selection. Look closely at what is actually being measured and how, before placing too much value on their determinations. All ranking systems provide a very limited picture of what is on offer: beware of allowing them to limit your choice of university.

Lifestyle Considerations

In addition to cost, there are many other factors you need to think about, including location, size, social life and student services.

The United States is geographically diverse. Before choosing a university, it is important for you to consider what type of climate suits you best. You may have enjoyed your Easter break in Florida, but are you prepared for the summer heat or lack of winter? Or you may think you like snow, but are you prepared to have to shovel your way across campus in -40°F while studying in Buffalo?

Do you prefer an urban or rural setting? While it may be exciting to think of yourself in a great city, the costs of living there are often much higher – will your budget stretch? Also bear in mind that students in large cities may feel more socially isolated than those who choose a rural school. Conversely, a college that is miles away from any city may have more campus-based activities, but you may find that not being able to escape to a nearby city induces claustrophobia and that relying upon the university for socialising is too restrictive.

If you attend a very small college, will seeing the same 500 people every week be too insular for you? Will you feel like a number if you are one of 60,000 at a large public university?

There are no right or wrong answers. Investigate each university and be honest about what type of environment you will be comfortable in. Take a critical look at the university's office for international students and at the number of such students in attendance. While many enjoy being the lone 'foreigner' and having to fend for themselves, others find comfort in having a well-run place to go when homesick or confused and others with whom to share the same dilemmas.

More about Choosing a Uni...

John Wallis has expanded on this tricky process and turned it into practically another small book. Rather than add heft to this one, we've made it available as a pdf, free to *Uni in the USA* readers. To receive it, register on www.uniintheusa.com and sign up for "Choosing a University in the USA", and emails with short updates about various parts of application admissions process. You already own the book, so ignore the occasional sales pitch, but the facts included will be useful.

Applications

OK, you've short listed the unis you want to apply to. You roughly know which are sure things, which are fall-back safety schools and which are a definite reach. Now what?

First, contact the universities directly or access their websites to obtain information and application materials. Most of them will use the 'Common Application Form', which will allow you to complete one application online and send it electronically to all the schools you are interested in. However, unlike UCAS, even if you use the Common App and fill it out only once, you will be required to submit it to each university individually (usually with the school's own supplemental application) and pay a fee to each one (currently about $75).

The Common App will ask you for personal data, grades etc – but the biggest challenge will likely be the personal essay. You are given several choices for topics, so there is usually plenty of flexibility, and you only have to choose one of them.

These essays tend to be in response to a vaguely worded question about your values, your interests or your most significant experiences and while the whole thing may seem a bit pretentious, their importance should NOT be underestimated. In your essay, make sure you reveal things that are unique, interesting and informative about yourself. Pick something you're interested in – the essay will read much better if you have some conviction when you're writing it.

Be aware – this is a key part of your application so think about it carefully and bring out your best writing skills. (And make sure other people read it through for typos, grammar and other suggestions before you send it off.)

In addition to the Common Application, some universities also have a supplemental application with questions about your specific interest in their school and your qualifications – often requiring a short essay in response. Unlike the UCAS form, on which you do not discuss individual institutions, US universities will want to know why you want to attend their school in particular.

Americans tend not to be reticent about their personal achievements, so don't hold back out of any false or British modesty. Make sure your prospective university really knows about how wonderful you are, how much you want to attend their school and what a great addition you will be to their student body.

It is crucial you take your time over these Supplemental Application essays as they are often the deciding factor in admission. Each university is trying to suss out if you will fit in and, if the hard data (test scores/grades) are not quite at the required standard or if the competition is hot, your essays could sway the decision. Again, each college will be looking for candidates that suit them, so remember to target these essays individually.

There are many organisations such as EducationUSA and Petersons that provide essay review services and, depending on your circumstances, these may be worth the cost. American publishers have also cottoned on to the anxious parent markets, selling books with titles like *100 Successful Harvard/Yale/ Stanford College Essays*.

Harvard has published a helpful section on their website called Application Tips, which is obviously geared towards their own application process, but can't hurt as you look at applications for other unis.

Recommendations (References)

Most universities will ask for at least one reference, the 'counsellor' reference which is written by a careers advisor, headteacher, housemaster etc. This reference is similar to UCAS, although it should not focus on a particular course, but rather suitability in general for higher education. It is 'all about' you and should address academic performance, extra-curricular activities and personal qualities. (We've provided some guidelines below.)

Additionally, most schools will ask for at least one academic reference, sometimes more. The academic reference should come from a teacher who has taught you for at least a year and, if possible, in a core academic subject–English, history, foreign language, maths or sciences. Some schools such as MIT will demand a maths/science referee and a humanities referee.

These references, unlike the counsellor reference, should focus on the student's performance in class: academic ability, performance, ability to work independently and as a member of the group, how the student deals with setbacks, etc. While it is fine to mention outside activities if the teacher is aware, it is not the focus.

These references are very important and it is crucial you make sure your referee knows the drill. While some admissions officers appreciate British understatement, you are competing for a place against American students whose references will tend to be flagrantly positive, so it is wise to give the person you ask some guidance. Here are some guidelines you should share with the person who is writing your 'counsellor' reference.

For Counsellor Referees

(What to Include in the Student's Recommendations)

Be assertively affirmative. US referees focus tightly on achievements and blur less desirable qualities. Make a list with your student of all the main reasons they wish to study in the US and draw upon it.

If necessary, explain discrepancies in grades, i.e. those due to ill health or personal problems. This will make the student's own explanation more credible.

Include all extra-curricular activities. Admissions officers badly want students who will contribute to campus life, not just excel in a main topic of study. Five As at AS Level are great but that position in the school orchestra could prove just as valuable.

Highlight the student's personality. Many applicants with less than perfect marks have been accepted by top-rated institutions because they will contribute to the diversity of the student body, be a team-player or an enthusiastic member of campus.

Try to offer a class ranking. Most US high schools assign their students to various percentiles based on academic ability. You can be inventive and selective: for example, a student in the top 40% of his year group may be in the top 3% for his favourite subject. Consider using the ranking in the last GCSE year if students leaving have made the AS rankings a steeper slope to climb. (In other words, when students finish GCSEs, fewer from the group progress to sixth form—the cream rises to the top, so competition increases significantly. The student could have been number 10 in a class of 100, but then if only the top 20 progress to A-Level, he might find himself at the 50% mark versus the 10% mark).

Don't hold back. US referees often use highly descriptive, dramatic language. Paint an honest portrait in full colour and remember that in the US a reference is viewed as a marketing tool. You should try to do the same.

Examples of References

In order to demonstrate some of the (not so) subtle differences between references, the Fulbright Commission has created a student-written summary of their qualifications and activities, together with two supporting references, one UK-style, the other US-style. Each takes its national style to the extreme, but we hope they will show you the way to making your reference more US-friendly.

Joe Normal has GCSE results of A* in English Literature; A in English Language and History; B in Maths, Science, Art and IT; C in French and Music; 30 D in D&T. At AS he has A in English Literature, B in History, C in Art and Biology. He is predicted A in English Literature, B in History, C in Art at A2.

Joe plays football for his school team. Last year he played in the city finals, where his team lost the championship. He plays the clarinet in the school wind band. His work group in GCSE Science won a regional award for their energy-efficient car design. Over the summer holidays he participated in a week-long art workshop organised by his school for local children. He recently completed his silver Duke of Edinburgh Award, hoping to take the Gold before leaving school. He won a Promising Young Writers Award for a short story written as part of his GCSE coursework.

The US universities he is applying to (majoring in English) are Middlebury, Harvard, NYU, Mount Holyoke, College of William and Mary, and Northeastern.

Example of a UK-Style Reference

Joe Normal is a very likeable student with a solid future ahead of him. He interacts well with his classmates and seems to be quite popular among his peers.

Academically, he achieves decent marks and has good relationships with his teachers, although he could be more focused on deadlines. He should have a great future in the study and application of English, which is by far his favourite subject and the field he is most gifted in.

Joe demonstrates a certain willingness to participate in school events such as music concerts, and recently supervised a group of six young children engaged in various art-based activities on one of our summer schemes. His work with the Duke of Edinburgh Awards scheme also proves his ability to overcome challenges.

I would have no reservations in recommending Joe for your institution and am sure he will become a considerable academic asset.

Example of a US-Style Reference

It has been an absolute pleasure to work with Joe Normal, who ranks among the top 10% of students within his A-level classes. He is the best student in a competitive and enthusiastic English class, and has even won a publisher's Young Writers Award for one of the pieces he produced. His passion for the subject shines through, as does his commitment to learning in an academic setting.

Joe stands out as a popular team player, both in his school work and extracurricular activities, taking his soccer team to the city championships, and winning a science award for a group project on environmental awareness. While working towards his Duke of Edinburgh Silver Award he endured a two-day mountaineering expedition, returning with much praise for the challenge, and is anticipating another such trek for his soon-to-be-completed Gold Award.

He is keen to participate by playing his clarinet at regular wind band concerts and has recently taken time out of his school holiday to volunteer with the art department, supervising workshops for local children.

Joe's teachers speak highly of him and all predict he will be extremely successful in a US institution, where his academic talents can continue to flourish, and his love of adventure will be greatly rewarded. I do not hesitate to give my strongest recommendation that he join '.........' University and am certain you will be rewarded with an exemplary new student.

Transcripts

Your school will need to provide a transcript of your academic record from Year 10 to the present. This is not something that is customary in the UK and most schools will have to create this document from scratch. Make sure you explain the situation to your teachers in good time and show them the following explanation for the sake of clarification.

A US transcript typically consists of a list of grades that high school students have received in every class in which they have ever been enrolled. The following notes are based on suggestions from US university admissions officers and administrators. Use them as a guide only – read the application information or contact the admissions office for each individual university to learn about specific requirements.

A Special Note to Teachers and Careers Advisers

US universities are less interested in students' final exam results than in the subjects they have taken over the past four years and how their performance has changed over time. A US transcript lists courses taken by semester with the grades for each course. (Most US schools divide the school year into two semesters, as opposed to the UK three-term system.) If possible, admissions officers appreciate a similar document from UK schools for the sake of comparison.

For many schools, this will be a tedious exercise involving trawling through dusty student records. Please do your very best – it makes a real difference to your student's chances, and US universities really do want a clear picture of how a student has done in every term in every subject over the past four years.

If your school does not give grades on a term basis, any type of evaluatory mark is acceptable. Include a note explaining the grading system used. An example of this might be: 'Each mark reflects an individual instructor's assessment of the student's coursework, including homework, tests, class participation and final examinations. Each grade is on a scale of A to F, where A is excellent, C is satisfactory and F is failing.' After the internal marks, set out the examination results obtained over that period – and not just the main ones: CLAIT and RSA, too. Then list the other, non-examined courses pursued – Enrichment, General Studies or whatever. Don't leave anything out.

These documents should be on official school letterhead, with a school stamp of certification if possible.

A Special Note to Applicants

If you have certified copies of your qualifications (GCSEs, etc.), enclose them with your application. If you do not, you need to obtain copies from each of the examining boards in plenty of time. Also bear in mind you should get a transcript from all secondary schools or sixth form colleges you have attended.

Interviews

Although interviews are rarely mandatory for admission into any American university, they are often recommended and are an excellent way of finding out about the place in which you are planning to spend the next four years. Interviews for international students can function in two ways:

If you are embarking on the grand college trip (a whistle-stop tour around multiple colleges in a few days), you should try to meet with people in the admissions offices while you're on campus. They'll be impressed that you're organised enough to make the effort and it is a good chance to get any questions about the place cleared up while you're still on site. If personal interviews aren't available you should still attend the tours and information sessions for applicants. These people have got selling their institution down to a fine art and it would be a shame to miss out on the spiel.

The other and more common way of interviewing is via the alumni systems many colleges have set up. American universities believe that no one is more qualified to represent their institution than one who has been there and survived. The majority of the top universities recommend these interviews and, since their alums tend to be flung far and wide, there are normally many eager Americans in London just waiting to find the perfect Brit for their alma mater.

Preparation for these interviews need not be extensive – although wearing the colour of your intended school is one possible starting point! In general, these alumni are as intent on selling their school as they are on screening you and this is the best time to ask all those questions the many guides on your bookshelves have left uncovered.

In most cases these interviews have very little sway in the application process but are a great opportunity to form one more bond with the school and find out what you really want to know. Don't stress about them too much, just comb your hair, put on your best English manners and be prepared to talk about why you're interested in America, and what you hope to get out of your university experience there.

And in case you're wondering, the university will make sure that its interviewers in Britain get in touch with you. So don't start pestering them; every adequate applicant will get an interview, but sometimes matching up assignments can take a while.

Financial Statement

Most universities will require you to complete a financial statement. Do this carefully as it will be used to determine your eligibility for financial assistance. Do not worry that it may affect the decision to accept you – it will not. At undergraduate level, the decision to offer a place is completely separate from an offer of financial aid. US universities' admission decisions are based on merit, not ability to pay.

Deadlines

Meet your deadlines! US universities will not accept late applications unless they have 'rolling admissions', meaning they accept students on a first-come, first-served basis. Most deadlines occur between January and February, although they can be as early as November and as late as March. You must send your university everything they ask for, all of it in perfect order (follow the instructions very carefully) well before the deadline.

When submitting your application electronically (e.g. via the Common App website) make sure you know the deadline for pushing 'send'. If you are sending by snail mail, the date posted counts for nothing; if you are close to a deadline and must use the postal system, send your application by an express service that will require a signature on delivery.

The good news of your acceptances will generally arrive by April.

Early Decision/Early Action

Students who have planned well in advance and are keen to attend a particular university may wish to consider some form of early application. There are now three options: Early Action, Early Decision I, and Early Decision 2. These options are not available at all universities, though, so check each school's website to determine their policy.

Early Action (EA) is a non-binding plan that requires students to submit their applications in early autumn (usually around 1 November), in advance of the 1 January deadline for Regular applications. Notification of acceptance is made by late December, but students have until 1 May to accept or reject the offer. The advantage is you will know much earlier and can plan accordingly. The disadvantage is that candidates who apply this way tend to be much stronger and rejection is more likely than in the regular admission pool.

A student can often apply under Early Action to more than one university, but check with each school you are interested in; some may specify that, if you submit an Early Action application to them, then you cannot apply EA to other unis.

Early Decision 1 (ED1) follows the same timetable as Early Action, but is a binding plan. By applying this way, you have made a commitment, should you be accepted, to attend the university. For this reason, you can only choose one university to apply as an Early Decision candidate. Reneging on an offer of admission could mean that no other university will admit you, so make sure your heart is absolutely set on this college before you send off the forms.

Early Decision 2 (ED2) is similar – a single application and binding commitment to attend the university, if admitted – but the application deadline is later (usually 1 January, in line with Regular applications). Students are notified of the ED2 decision by mid-February. If the answer is positive, students must withdraw all other applications. This is important because, unlike ED1 when they haven't submitted any others, students often forget or think they can wait to find out what happens. If they don't withdraw other applications, they risk losing the ED2 offer and damaging their school's reputation.

Students with Additional Needs

America makes students with additional needs very welcome, and strong (rather stronger than in the UK) laws ensure they are not discriminated against. If you have any type of disability or Special Educational Needs, make sure you tell the university from the start and that they can accommodate you. While most US universities are very adept at catering for disabled students and can normally provide an array of services, there may be additional costs. Contact the university's student services division for further information. As you will have to provide evidence of your disability, and the requirements differ from the UK, it is wise to start asking two years before you plan to enrol.

Good news – if you receive some form of test accommodation for a learning disability (e.g. extra time), then you may be able to get the same or similar accommodation approved for the US university entrance exams, the SAT and the ACT (covered in the section below). It can take several months to process this request and involves a lot of documentation, so you should start the process at least 6 months before you sit the test.

Basic Academic Requirements

The least you need to apply to a US university is five GCSEs, or Scottish Standard Grades, at C or above in core subject areas, including English and maths – a hurdle you will leap lightly over. This is not to say that at the age of 16, laurelled with five Cs, you will be welcomed with open arms by Harvard. Naturally, the better the uni, the better your grades need to be.

All universities normally want a student to be 18 and above, unless there are very unusual circumstances, and most universities will want to see post-16 attainment, too: generally two to three A-levels or equivalent (International Baccalaureate (IB), Scottish Highers, BTEC, GNVQs, AVCEs). The best universities won't open your application if you haven't gone further than GCSEs.

All of these will be considered, but it is important to check with individual universities to see what their minimum standards for admission are. IB in particular is well understood. In rare cases you may need to pay to have your qualifications evaluated – see the Reference Section for companies that will do this.

Most students will be applying at the beginning of the second year of sixth form for a place the following autumn term. Because of this, universities will scrutinise GCSE and AS/Highers results together with predicted A2/IB/ Highers marks. However, unlike British universities, acceptance will not be dependent on your A2 etc. results – these are reported too late to impact acceptance in the US. Don't think this allows you to do nothing for your final year. Your final grades *will* be reported eventually and you don't want to get off on the wrong foot. Or have your offer withdrawn at the last minute (it's happened)!

You also have to face the challenge of the SAT exam or its cousin, the ACT.

Entrance Exams

Most universities will require you to take an admission test as part of the application process, either the SAT Reasoning test or the ACT. Registration and reporting is done online: the SAT details are on the College Board website (www.collegeboard.org) and the ACT details are found at www.actstudent.org. More competitive universities may also want you to take SAT Subject Tests (known as SAT IIs until 2004). More about these later in the book.

Here is a departure from the norm of which you should be aware: it is not a common practice, but some schools (e.g. NYU) are now accepting predicted marks from external exams (A-levels, IB, etc) in place of SAT/ACT scores. If you opt to rely on your exam predictions to get you in, then it's very important that you deliver on the results. Offers can be withdrawn if performance fails to meet expectations! While US schools tend to be far more flexible than those in the UK, the possibility does exist to lose your offer if you don't match predictions.

Dealing with the SAT and ACT Exams

Don't worry too much. You are an international student and, despite the official line, colleges will not expect you to do as well in these standardised exams as Americans. Any American with the hope of applying for a prestigious college has been in training for the SAT or ACT (or both) for years, coached through courses, put through numerous practices and schooled to within an inch of their lives.

Universities understand that our academic background does not, for the most part, incorporate standardised testing. The average British student writes his way through school – essays for GCSE, more essays for AS levels, yet more essays for A-levels – and is less familiar with ticked boxes and filled bubbles – the standardised testing process of SATs and ACTs. Providing GCSE, AS-level, and A level (or IB or Pre-U) predictions are of a sufficiently high standard, slightly lower scores on these American exams are, if not discounted, partially excused.

The tendency amongst many Brits is to dismiss such multiple choice testing as ridiculous. However, for the indefinite future, most international students with aspirations to American colleges will have no option but to submit to these exams, regardless of their academic background.

Competition for the prestigious American universities to which most British students aspire is fierce, and standardised testing is a significant hurdle that all must leap. You will need scores of over 600 (out of a possible 800) in each of the two sections of the SAT for your application to even be considered at the top institutions (and most Ivy League schools are looking for scores of over 700, or a total of 1400+ across the two sections). For the ACT, this hurdle for the top tier schools is a 32 (out of a possible 36).

As entrenched as the SAT and ACT are, they are nonetheless continually trying to be more relevant. The SAT just went through a complete overhaul - the inaugural sitting was in spring 2016 – and the ACT is also tweaked on a regular basis. Most of the changes attempt to level the playing field (especially for students who can't afford private test-prep tuition) and make the assessment more in line with the basic skills and knowledge that universities want students to have.

Among the more selective colleges and universities (a small but influential slice of American higher education), there's a tension between improving entrance exams and reducing their importance in the admissions process. A growing number of institutions are now test-optional, no longer requiring SAT or ACT scores – some 850+ according to FairTest (www.fairtest.org/university/optional).

The Cold Hard Facts

Plan ahead! Here's what you need to do...

Advance Registration: You need to register at least two months in advance of the exam date, possibly earlier if you want a seat at a particular testing centre close to home. (And, trust us, you don't want to travel too far – the test starts early in the morning.) Seats do fill up rather quickly so don't wait until the last minute. For the SAT, register online at www.collegeboard.org; for the ACT, go to www.actstudent.org.

The process is lengthy but simple and reserves you a seat and paper for a specific date. (Note: the College Board test registration process involves a seemingly endless number of pages asking all sorts of questions about your background and interests. For the most part, you do not have to answer these – just click on 'Continue' at the bottom of each page whenever you want to skip them.)

Payment: There is a charge for taking these exams – approximately $90 USD, including international fees, for the SAT or the ACT. This can be paid online when registering.

Location: SATs are offered four times a year at a surprisingly large number of places around the UK so it's pretty easy to find a near-ish test centre. All sites are listed on www.collegeboard.org . The ACT is administered five times a year and is building a base in the UK, but at this point is only offered at 17 locations (and not all sittings are offered at each site). The locations and dates are listed on www.actstudent.org.

Timing: Unless you are aiming for a nervous breakdown, don't take these tests at the same time you're sitting your secondary school exams. (Also, you cannot take the SAT Reasoning Test and SAT Subject Tests on the same day.) The SAT Reasoning Test and the ACT are challenging for many Brits, and it's best to find out what they're like early on, especially since you can take each test more than once. You should start to prepare for it the year after your GCSEs and, ideally, take it for the first time in the spring of your lower 6th year (Year 12 of 13).

With standardised tests that are administered around the world, there is always a concern about sharing information - and there have recently been some serious problems. In an attempt to curb the security breaches, as of spring 2017, there are fewer SAT test dates at all international sites. It's now offered in October, December, March and May. The ACT is still offered in September, October, December, April and June.

Note: the SAT Reasoning test in May is the only sitting throughout the year when students outside the US (that's you) can request a full "Question & Answer Service". This means that, in addition to the usual online score report, you can receive by mail a copy of the full test booklet (all the actual questions) and a report including your answers and the correct ones. Be sure to request this if you sign up for May – it's part of the registration process and costs less than $20. It will be invaluable as a study tool for any subsequent sittings.

Repeats, re-sits and re-grading

You can take SATs and ACTs repeatedly with no penalty – a situation many A level students long for. Even better, there has been a change in how many exam sittings students have to show colleges on their applications. Universities used to be notified of all the SAT grades you had ever achieved, not just the sparkling 1600 (a maximum 800 in both areas) you got in your latest attempt, so it looked distinctly strange if your early scores fell out of the range your university hoped to see.

Since 2009, students have been able to use Score Choice on the College Board website to choose the SAT test sitting dates they wish to have sent to a school – unless the uni has specifically requested that all sittings be reported. In either case, however, schools will look at your best score for each section (Reading/Writing and Math), even if each personal best was achieved on a different date (e.g., best Reading/Writing in October testing, best Math in December).

All scores from each of those dates will appear, but colleges do tend to count the top score for each section. This is often referred to as your 'Super Score'. Of course, if there is a huge gap between your best and worst in one section, nothing can stop the admissions office from raising an eyebrow, but supposedly they accept the best scores as an indication of what you're capable of achieving.

For the ACT, you can select the test date results that you want sent to universities, and they will not release any others. But they will send all scores from that date as a set; there is only one composite score reported for each sitting. So you cannot combine individual subject scores from different sittings to create a composite 'super score' for the ACT.

Now although ACT says they only report the test date that has been designated by the student, there is nothing to stop the university from asking for others (ditto for the SAT).

Caveat about the above: unis change admissions requirements all the time, so this information could change before the ink is dry. It cannot be repeated enough: check and recheck requirements for the unis you're interested in.

Despite all of the above re-testing opportunities, it is much better to invest time in practising beforehand – there are lots of test preparation materials, prep courses and tutors available. (See the Reference Section and our recommendations on practice materials.) Common sense should tell you when to quit. Some Brits find that one attempt is, in fact, enough to secure a satisfactory grade, while others take it three times.

Getting the Results

The dreaded results are available by phone or on the web around three weeks after the exam. When you register for the exam, you have the option of sending your scores directly to colleges of your choice. If you don't know where you wish to apply, just leave this blank. When you make up your mind later, it's easy to go online again and send the official copy of the results to the colleges you are looking at. But if you have your heart set on a particular college from the word go, sending the scores directly will save you time and trouble (and possibly fees) at a later date.

Don't worry about losing your results – they will be stored online indefinitely, as long as you have an ACT or SAT account.

What's new with the SAT?

A brand new version of the test was launched in May 2016 in the UK and is meant to be more aligned with the content you're studying in school and with the skills that universities want you to have. It's still a very long multiple-choice test covering Reading, Writing and Math – but the structure is markedly different. For one thing, the previous version had three subscores; the revised test now has only two: one for Reading/Writing combined and one for Math. The score range for each of the two sections is 200 to 800, which are added together for a composite score ranging from a dismal 400 to a perfect 1600 (versus the previous maximum of 2400).

As before, there is an essay, but now it's optional (at the end of the test) and scored separately. Some universities may still require that students submit an essay score, so if this is the case make sure you have taken the essay portion at least once.

There are also changes in content. The Math section of the new SAT focuses more heavily on algebra and data analysis, and less on geometry. It also includes a few advanced concepts not seen on the earlier SAT (largely pre-Calculus), along with some questions that ask you to apply mathematical reasoning to situations in business, science or the social sciences. There are two multiple-choice Math sections: one is 55 minutes and allows the use of a calculator, and the other is 25 minutes and must be completed without a calculator.

There is one Reading section (65 minutes) comprised of long

passages to analyse (similar to the old SAT), but one of the biggest changes is the addition of 'evidence-based reading' questions. The student is first asked to answer a question about the passage and then to locate the line from the text that supports the answer.

Vocabulary will no longer be tested in stand-alone sentences, but

is now presented in the context of passages (and – hallelujah! – will not include so many of the old arcane, obscure SAT words).

The Writing section will test many of the same concepts covered on the old SAT – so make sure you know how to properly use verbs, pronouns, punctuation and idioms. But, in a departure from the old version of the test, you will have to edit full passages and choose words that best capture an author's tone or argument.

For the optional essay, students will be given a reading passage and asked to analyse the author's evidence and arguments.

Good news – there will no longer be "negative grading", meaning there is now no penalty if you want to guess (just don't do this on every question).

Even more good news – the College Board has recently partnered with the US-based Khan Academy to offer free online test prep. Practice questions and video tutorials are available on the College Board website.

The Format of the ACT Exam

The ACT is a multiple-choice exam that measures English, Mathematics, Reading and – unlike the SAT – Sciences Reasoning. It also has an optional Writing (short essay) section. It's given five times a year at several locations throughout the UK but the number of sittings at each test centre may vary, so be sure to check the ACT website (www.actstudent.org) well in advance of the test to determine which sites are available for the date you have in mind (or vice versa).

On each of the four ACT test sections (English, Math, Reading, Science) you will receive a raw score. This raw score will be converted to a scaled score from 1 to 36, and your combined score will be the average of your four scaled scores. Thus the highest you can get is a 36, which is equivalent to a 1600 on the SAT. While there are always exceptions, the very best unis will be looking for a 32 or higher.

Importantly, not all unis require a Writing score, but the most selective schools will designate 'ACT with Writing'. The Writing score range is from 2-12, and this is not averaged into the composite score for the other subjects on the ACT. In autumn 2015, the Writing section (short essay) shifted focus from classic persuasion to more argumentative in nature. This latest version asks students to evaluate multiple perspectives and write about whether and why they agree in whole or in part with any of them.

Like the revised SAT, the ACT does not penalize you for wrong answers. This doesn't mean you should always rush through all the questions – make sure you give them the time they deserve – but it does mean that you should leave an answer for every question.

SAT Reasoning Test or ACT : Which is best for you?

With a very few exceptions, US universities accept both these tests and treat them the same. In their current formats, the ACT is broader than the SAT Reasoning Test, covering more ground with less depth, and will be more in tune with your own education. That said, the SAT is the more common test for international students to take (probably through the broader selection of testing centres).

There are many similarities between the ACT and the SAT: both tests are standardised around the globe, largely multiple-choice format, offered on Saturday mornings throughout the year, and are about 4 hours long. Also, both accommodate disabilities and can be re-taken multiple times.

Now that the new SAT is in place, there are additional similarities with the ACT – there is no penalty for wrong answers and the essay component will be optional (previously this was only true for the ACT).

However, there continue to be some key differences between the ACT and the SAT: the topics covered (the ACT adds Science Reasoning), the scoring range and method, and the greater availability of test centres for the SAT. If you're trying to decide between them, you should try a test for each and see which one of the two you are most comfortable with. Sample tests and questions are available on SAT and ACT websites.

This might help you make that decision: because the ACT is more content based than the SAT, US universities that have Subject Test requirements will fully or partially waive this requirement for students who take the full ACT (including the Writing section). Check each school's website for details.

(Caveat about the above: unis change admissions requirements all the time. It cannot be repeated enough: check and recheck requirements for the unis you're interested in).

SAT Subject Tests

You cannot take the SAT (Reasoning Test) and SAT Subject Tests on the same day. Most students take the Subjects when they are at the peak of their knowledge of the subject (e.g. after an AS-level course). The exception to this plan is if you plan to take a Subject Test in one of your GCSE subjects and won't be studying it at A-level; in this case you may want to take the SAT Subject Test soon after your GCSE course is done.

Subject Tests cover a wide range of subjects and are more akin to A-levels – while still, amazingly, being multiple choice. Each one lasts an hour and you can take up to three different subjects at the same sitting. They are more clear-cut than their A-level equivalents, much shorter, and involve less preparation for Brits who are used to concentrating on one subject at a time. If your university requires you to take the Subject Tests, check their website to see how many they want and whether there are required subjects you must sit or if you have free choice in what to take. Most of the better US universities will require two of these, though some students will take three, just to show off. The score range for each test is 200 to 800.

There are 20 Subject Tests including: Literature, US History, World History, Math Level 1, Math Level 2, Biology E/M, Chemistry, Physics, French, French with Listening, German, German with Listening, Spanish, Spanish with Listening, Modern Hebrew, Italian, Latin, Japanese with Listening, Korean with Listening and Chinese with Listening.

Scheduling the SAT Subject tests requires a bit of advance planning. They're currently being offered in October, November, December, May and June – however, not all subjects are offered at each sitting. So do check the College Board website early in the process. Note: there is only one sitting of languages 'with listening'– in November. Also, in some of these languages the standard will be set by US native speakers, and in others the curriculum may not be what you have covered in the UK – so do your homework.

The SAT Subject tests are based on curricula and subject matter taught in US schools, which can make it difficult for a UK student to pin down suitable Subject Tests to sit. For example, an A level Biology syllabus may have a very different focus from that of high school AP biology. History presents even more of a problem – Tudors and Stuarts have little place even in the World History exam.

Your best bet may to go for the English literature exam and the Math 1, since there is some overlap with the material covered on the SAT Reasoning test. It is also useful to do a language exam (though the questions may be more grammatically based than you are used to). Here's another reason to consider a language Subject test: many universities have a foreign language requirement, and sometimes a high enough score on the Subject Tests will enable you to skip it. Taking French, Spanish, or even Latin can help you kill two birds with one stone.

Before you choose your SAT Subject tests, you can see a summary of the content and some sample questions on collegeboard.org. Once you decide on a subject, the best way to prepare is by taking several sample tests. There are study guides and resource websites for each subject (listed in the Reference section and available from Amazon) so you can work through these in your own time at home.

Fear Not

As the number of Brits interested in applying to US schools has risen, so have the resources available on this side of the pond to help make sure you achieve your personal best. It is quite feasible to prepare for the SAT or ACT on your own using a range of readily available study guides (see Reference section); there are also a variety of other options for students who decide they need coaching. These range from hours of one-to-one customised tuition to group courses offered on weekends and school holidays.

In reality, you may find the best way of improving your scores is simply to practise multiple-choice tests in timed conditions. So buy a guide with a number of different sample tests and back-of-the-book answers, grab a stopwatch and get down to work. Or do one of the free online sample tests offered on the ACT website (www.actstudent.org) and the SAT website (www.collegeboard.org), which also has details about how to download an app for the 'SAT Question of the Day'. If you start this series of daily questions early enough, you will have seen just about everything the test covers by the time you take it!

Words to the Wise

Get these exams out the way. There are two reasons for this. Firstly, if you are a Shakespeare buff who gladly burnt all your maths textbooks after the rigours of GCSEs, the compulsory math section of the SAT or ACT may inspire panic.

Don't let it. Face this dreaded test – and the additional tutoring you may require – as soon as possible after the actual maths GCSE. In this way you can put your extensive knowledge of quadratic equations to good use before it is gone forever. Just don't forget your calculator.

Secondly, even if your heart is set on the US, your A-level exams are still important – to you, to your parents, and to American universities. You do not want to be taking these US uni exams at the same time as AS/A-levels, vital coursework or mock examinations. As the SAT and ACT exams are offered so regularly, it is easy to schedule them for a relatively fallow period. And once you've done them, you'll have the reassuring knowledge that you have at least have some solid exam results behind you as you head into the A-levels.

Take a timed practice test in advance. Three hours of checking boxes (actually, filling in bubbles) is very different from three hours of essay writing. It may feel as if you have masses of time but it rushes past deceptively quickly.

In The Test Room

People customarily arrive with around 25 different pencils, rubbers, sharpeners, etc. Truckloads of stationery may be excessive but do make sure you have a few spares. And in case you're wondering what on earth a no. 2 pencil is – an HB will suffice. You will be allowed to use a graphing calculator in the Maths section. (A guide to acceptable models is provided on the test websites.)

Most importantly, do not forget your picture ID – they won't let you into the test room without it.

Once you've started your exam, you've got to keep going. Each question is worth the same number of points, so there is no sense in spending hours on one problem, only to run out of time on five you could have knocked off easily.

With a few exceptions, each section of the test gets harder as you move through it. If you are faced with a question you think you can't answer, try to eliminate the options that are definitely wrong. This will narrow down your choice. Go with your instincts. If your instincts have chosen this precise moment to vanish, move on. Just make sure you leave the corresponding bubble blank.

When you're taking these multiple choice tests, make sure you don't make the fatal mistake of accidentally skipping a question and carrying on regardless. Filling out half of your answers in the wrong bubble is ridiculously easy to do and will be catastrophic for your score. As you go, check to be sure that your answers are in line with the questions.

If English is Not Your Native Language

You may have to take the Test of English as a Foreign Language (TOEFL). It doesn't make sense, but could be required even if you have spent years studying in the UK. If this is the case, go to www.toefl.org for further information.

Money, Money, Money

America might proclaim itself the 'land of the free', but there is no getting around the fact that an American education is anything but. Until recently, tuition fees in Britain had always looked fairly lightweight alongside the hefty cheques American parents have been forced to write for their children's education. The exorbitant cost of a good American college was enough to dissuade most Brits from even considering the option.

Now, of course, things are changing dramatically in the UK: most universities now charge £9,000 per year for tuition. But it's of crucial importance to realise that that UK figure does not include anything else, just tuition. So accommodation, food, books etc go on top. When you start adding up the additional costs, the disparity between the UK and US total can be surprisingly small.

The good news is that the amounts advertised by American unis are 'all-inclusive'. Amazingly, this one important fact seems to be little known in the UK, or perhaps just not believed. When a uni states that international students will need $60,000, that number is for EVERYTHING – tuition, books, accommodation, food, insurance etc. Some also incorporate the cost of one round trip ticket into the figure as well.

It is a frequently held misconception that every international student at an American college comes equipped with their own million-dollar trust fund. This is miles from the truth. A first-rate education abroad is becoming an ever more achievable option for British students of all backgrounds.

One of the reasons American universities have thrived is due to their remarkable management of financial resources. Universities like Harvard have bank balances that rival the largest American corporations and exceed those of many a developing country. Alumni from all over the nation pour money back into their alma maters and boards of savvy businessmen make sure their colleges are never short of funds. All this financial acumen allows for the generous subsidies and financial aid packages that enable students from even the most disadvantaged backgrounds to attend the college of their dreams.

The Sum Total...

Although the uni may publish an all-in annual cost, you need to work out a rough estimate yourself because the total costs will vary greatly, from $15,000 (for some state schools) to $70,000 (for some private colleges) per academic year. Many universities now have a good calculator built into their websites.

Tuition and fees are usually based on a nine-month academic year that runs from September to May. Tuition is the charge for instruction, while fees tend to cover services such as use of the library and student health service. American universities require students to purchase a lot of textbooks and these can be expensive. It is not unusual to have a book bill of $200 – $400 per semester. There are also supplies, travel costs and other personal expenses to consider.

And then there's the cost of life on campus. Obviously, this will vary depending on location and personal lifestyle, but most universities publish guidelines in the $5,000 – $12,000 range. In places such as New York and Boston, living on baked beans may be your only option to keep within budget.

And How to Deal With All That...

Brits at university in the US do not have the LEA option of a government-subsidised student loan, since they're ineligible for both US Federal Aid (FAFSA) and UK student finance. In the long-term this is a great benefit, leaving you debt-free once you're out in the real world. In the short-term though, you are deprived of the chance of blowing all your money in the pub (if they had pubs), or on that cute pair of shoes, then living hand-to-mouth for the rest of the year. You will be living hand-to-mouth all year round anyway.

One solution is to get a job – but if you are not a US citizen or green card holder, then you're limited, by visa restriction, to only 20 hours of work per week and it must be on campus. Competition for these jobs can be tough and preference is given to students receiving aid. We have to be clear: you can NOT work off campus during term. Another solution is to negotiate with your parents before the start of the academic year and agree on a loan with them – one that can be adjusted in either direction once you have gauged just how expensive campus life really is.

The main source of financial assistance for UK students, after family contributions, will be the university itself. Many, but not all, give help to international students. We haven't published a comprehensive list of grants and scholarships here (it would be out of date by the time it came off the press), but we do publish links and lists of grants and scholarships on uniintheusa.com. There are also financial aid resources in the References and Links section of this book.

At the time of writing, only about six schools are completely (officially) 'need blind' for international students (which means applications are considered and qualified students admitted regardless of ability to pay): Amherst, MIT, Harvard, Yale, Princeton and Dartmouth.

However, many others do their very best and are very generous. The point is that students must do their homework on scholarships– and a ton of paperwork.

During the application process, you will have to submit information that will enable the university to assess your family's financial situation. They then work out how much you can reasonably be expected to contribute to the cost of your education.

Many US universities will not charge you more than that amount. For example, if the university reckons the family contribution ought to be £200 a year – that may be all you will have to pay for your tuition and fees. Not all universities are so generous, but you will be surprised how many are. And for the athletes among you, there's always the option of a sports scholarship (see 'Athletic Scholarships' section).

Grants

A grant is the sum a university or private foundation gives towards the cost of your education. A grant may also cover living expenses, depending on your circumstances, and any other needs. Grants can be given on the basis of need, merit or a combination, and some will allow you to use the money in the best way you see fit.

Again, for piles of information on this, check our References and Links section of this book for scholarship information, or go to the Paying for US Uni page on www.uniintheusa.com and click on Scholarships for International Students.

Loans

Some universities offer loans to international students. It may also be possible to arrange a loan in the UK before you go — rare, but not unheard of. Additionally, if you have a US citizen who would act as a co-signer, many US banks and financial companies will grant loans to international students. Just remember, if you do take this option, bang! goes coming away from university debt-free.

Scholarships

Instead of printing out all the possible loans, we decided it would be easier for you to click around through the resources and links on the *Uni in the USA* website www.uniintheusa.com. That's where you can also register if you want us to send you our (free) giant doc "University Scholarships for International Students...How to Find Them and How to Apply", and emails with short updates about various parts of the application process. You already own the book, so ignore the occasional sales pitch, but the facts included will be useful.

Working On and Off Campus...

Unlike the hallowed halls of Oxford and Cambridge, where work of a nonacademic or pint-lifting variety is all but outlawed, American universities positively encourage their students to work outside classes. The love affair with capitalism that has propelled America so far in the world is instilled at an early age and many of your classmates will have been mowing lawns or working in shops for years. The expense of the American college system, and the stipulations of most financial aid plans, mean that many students need to find paid employment if they are to pay their way through school.

The bad news is that, as an international student, you cannot just walk into any place with a 'Help Wanted' sign, do your shift and pick up a pay cheque. The good news is that your international visa allows you to work on campus (although not off) after you have applied for a social security card – in itself a lengthy and frustrating process. (NB: Earnings from this work cannot be counted as a source of income for the official finance statements mentioned in the Applications section.)

Once you've got your hands on one of these, you have the freedom to take whatever university job you can find and earn money for it legally. Most universities have an employment office that helps students to find work in the libraries, laboratories or administration of the college – jobs that are usually set aside just for students.

The real problems start if you want to work off-campus in the US through the summers. Many students aim to do this and if you are one of them you need to plan ahead. Getting a job is a cinch in comparison with getting permission to take it. Some international students choose to do unpaid volunteering jobs or internships as a way around the problem. However, for those who need or want the money there are other, lengthier routes (aside from the illegal under-the-counter cash options – emphatically not recommended).

As an international student you are allowed one year of Optional Practical Training or OPT. This is permission, which has to be applied for, to work anywhere in the US for a stated amount of time. You can do anything, from waitressing to investment banking. Many students prefer to save up their OPT year for the end of their studies when they can spend a sizeable amount of time in the States. If you are planning to do this, you should be warned that your OPT year begins immediately after graduation. Others choose to use up a couple of months (the year does not have to be taken all at once) every summer. The great thing about OPT is that you have the flexibility to do what you want, when you want.

The official line is that permission for OPT will come through about a month after applying. Do not assume that the official line is true. The process takes forever. All applications are shipped to service stations in remote parts of the county where they dawdle indefinitely, finally getting to you after you should have already started work. Consult your international advisor on this, but really try to leave three months to get this permission through. The wheels of bureaucracy grind extremely slowly, when they grind at all.

There is another and much quicker option for some individuals. Curricular Practical Training (or CPT) allows you to find paid work anywhere as long as it is related to the subject you are studying. Best for those interested in sciences, medicine or technology where practical internships are plentiful, it is an option worthy of anyone's investigation. For the most part, professors are amenable to this and permission is fairly easy to get. CPT has no time limit and does not detract from your OPT allotment in any way.

Occasionally you can enrol in a class for the summer and get work permission that way. This depends very much on the attitudes of your professors and international office. As deadlines and requirements change on an annual basis, the best idea is to make an early appointment with your international advisor. Inevitably there is always some way to work through the system and get permission for doing paid work. It is just always an arduous process.

Athletic Scholarships – More Money Matters

Every American high school movie worth its salt is guaranteed to have at least one 'jock' in a starring role. These mini-gods of the athletic field are invariably blessed with the best-looking cheerleader as their girlfriend, the adulation of their peers and perfect floppy hair. British athletes may have missed out on this high school experience, but American university offers them a second chance. Those of you with enough sporting talent may still have the opportunity to capture some of this limelight, while also earning sizeable help with the application process and subsequent tuition fees.

Always wanted to be a jock? Here's how...

American universities (even the smaller and more academic ones) consider sport to be one of the most important ingredients in their curriculum. While it is unlikely a Brit is going to land the quarterback position on the U Michigan American football team, there are many sporting areas in which we do excel (or at least rival Americans). Crew (rowing) teams are always on the lookout for international talent and it is not unusual for the top teams to be powered entirely by British, Canadian and Australian students recruited especially for their skills on water. Soccer (football) is developing on American shores and good British players are in demand. Cricketers might find themselves out on something of a limb, but most standard sports (tennis, golf, lacrosse) will be represented on campus and they are all crying out for talent.

It may well be that the recruiters will find you first. If you are the world no. 1 in a particular area, or have consistently played for a British junior team, then you should definitely consider viewing your sporting prowess as a potential admissions passport.

As all admission forms repeat ad nauseam, American colleges are looking for diverse individuals who will allow the school to excel in all fields. Sporting events are huge dates in every school calendar and coaches travel the world to attract the best players.

If you are chasing the ultimate jock dream, you should take note of a few things. Athletes at the top universities are treated royally, but they get away with much less than those in the big public schools. They are expected to maintain high academic levels – and coaches rarely intervene to sort out their schedules. Playing any sport at university level is hard work and juggling this with tough classes can prove difficult. Less rigorous schools place more emphasis on sport and a star football player is treated as a hero all over campus. But elite colleges have their share of sports groupies as well, and both male and female athletes will find that a little bit of lycra or numbered jersey can get them a long way.

And Then There are the Financial Benefits...

The US offers great opportunities for talented athletes, and even a cost-free education. The fount of all knowledge is EducationUSA, part of the Fulbright Commission – run to them for their literature. In summary, what it says is:

Athletic scholarships are awarded for baseball, basketball, crew (rowing), cross-country, fencing, football (American), golf, gymnastics, ice hockey, indoor track, lacrosse, skiing, soccer, softball, swimming and diving, tennis, track and field, volleyball, water polo, women's field hockey and wrestling. Archery, badminton, bowling, equestrian sports and squash have been designated as 'emerging sports', and scholarships in these sports are available to women only in an effort to achieve equality between men's and women's scholarships. Some universities offer martial arts, riflery, rodeo, rugby and sailing, but very few of those will offer these sports on a scholarship basis. Athletic directors and coaches play a central role in award decision-making, so it is important to establish contact with these individuals early in your application process.

Awards vary from a few thousand dollars to over $50,000 per academic year. American football, men's and women's basketball, women's tennis, women's gymnastics and women's volleyball awards almost always cover the full cost.

Scholarships are awarded for a year at a time – so going off the rails once you get there is not recommended. To get one you must have recognisable achievements in your sport – check the websites of the universities you are interested in for results of matches or events to see how your ability compares. Different universities set different levels with those in the National Collegiate Athletic Association (NCAA) being the highest. (See www.ncaa.org and www.naia.org.)

According to long time sports advisor Marva Hall at College Prospects of America, 'Besides being a talented athlete, the NCAA requires all British students to obtain a minimum of five academic GCSE passes with an overall average of E or Standard Grade passes at "6", and they must include English, maths, any science and any social studies such as history, geography, modern studies, sociology or psychology. Unless a student wishes to enrol immediately after completion of GCSE's (something we don't recommend), he/she MUST continue in school with a minimum of two A-levels, and IB or a BTEC Level 3 EXTENDED Diploma.'

Further, 'The NAIA requires an "E" average overall in GCSE/ Standard Grade subjects, or an alternative qualification such as a BTEC or GNVQ, if the student can show that he/she was in the "Top Half" of his/her class.'

Students with an athletic scholarship must 'meet normal university/college entrance requirements and continue to obtain satisfactory grades in order to receive their scholarships'. These academic requirements are generally nothing to worry about and you often get extra time to complete your degree, but just be aware you can't let the academic ball drop altogether.

To search for Athletics scholarships on the internet, use one of the links in the References section at the end of the book and search for the sport you wish to obtain more information on.

Occasionally coaches visit Europe or see non-US students at international events. Even if a coach invites you to play for their team, you must still apply to the university through the regular academic application process. Make sure the college will meet your academic as well as your sporting needs.

Never go by a verbal agreement on a scholarship, or even by a letter from the coach. Details of the scholarship offer must be written into a contract. A coach can offer an award for one year in the first instance, with renewal based on recommendation by the athletics department, which must be approved by the financial aid office. Scholarships are sometimes announced in national and international sporting magazines.

There may be other ways for students (who play at a high level but might not qualify for the any of the above) to play on a US team. Again according to Marva Hall, a student might 'get on the higher education ladder by starting at a junior (or community) college and then transferring to a four year college for the final two years of the degree course'. Although note that junior colleges will now limit international players to 25% of the squad, eg, two for tennis and golf, five for soccer, etc., with or without a scholarship'.

She says gap years are a possibility: 'Students will be allowed one gap year to play their sport competitively before enrolling at university after their last year of study (tennis players will only be allowed one gap semester for Div I)'. Important to be aware however that 'in some cases, the NAIA will penalize a student for each gap year he/she takes after finishing school/college with loss of one year's eligibility per gap year'.

Clearly all of this can be hideously complicated, which is why some students choose to use a placement service instead of going it alone. Do be aware that these services charge a fee, and you will of course want to make sure they have good contacts with US colleges and universities plus do a bit of internet checking for dodgy characters, but there is no doubt there are excellent consultants who keep up with the ever-changing and very strict rules AND know which colleges are looking for students for their teams. UK services are listed in the Reference Section of this book, vetted by us to the best of our ability before each printing.

You can certainly make a direct approach to your sport's coach at individual colleges and universities. You will need to put a sport CV together and the coach may ask for a video demonstrating your abilities.

Visas, Immigration and All That Jazz

On the day the acceptance letter drops through your letterbox you might well be deceived into thinking the hard work, struggle and frustration are over. Think again. The toughest application deadline, the most difficult personal essay and the trickiest SAT paper pale into insignificance beside the hardest and most mind-numbingly boring part of admission to the American college experience. The joys of US bureaucracy and its caring immigration system await you.

If you are one of those fortunate people blessed with an American parent, passport or green card, stop reading now and count your lucky stars. The rest of you must read on and learn how to deal with the constantly changing visa system, the interminable waits at airports and the work restrictions that will dog your next four years.

Note: At time of writing, the situation for international students is in flux due to newly-elected President Trump's unclear policy on immigration. Keep an eye on the *Uni in the USA* website and that of the US State Department (and, of course, the news).

International Student Status

Things became much more difficult for international students after 9/11. Because some of the terrorists involved entered the United States on student visas, there has since been a clampdown on everyone travelling on one.

Of course, things are not as bad as they seem. Almost all the big American universities have an International Office set up specifically to help you with these problems. These offices have people on call 24 hours a day and are used to crises of all kinds.

When you are accepted to the college, they will send you the paperwork (called Form I-20) necessary to apply for a student visa. The visa must then be obtained from the American Embassy in London. Nowadays there is a compulsory interview for all applicants for student visas.

Start to fill out the visa application as soon as your university issues the Form I-20 – and then schedule the embassy interview. The average visa processing time following a successful interview is 5 days, but the wait for the interview can be long, so long that the State Department has helpfully added a constantly updating page giving current wait times. Get used to waiting – this glacial movement by the US bureaucracy is an experience that will change little over your next four years.

As background, the clampdown on student visas coincided with the arrival of the SEVIS (Student and Exchange Visitor Information Service) tracking system, which is intended to ensure people enrolled in a university are actually attending that university. In order for the university to issue you the I–20, they will have to enter you in SEVIS so the authorities can monitor you and ensure you are adhering to the conditions of your student visa. Big surprise: SEVIS (at the very least) allows the American government to have access to personal information about you at all times. Also no surprise: there is a charge for this. However, some universities have offered to refund this charge to encourage international students, so check and see if your prospective college is one of them.

While Brits have traditionally been, for the most part, immune from the hostility of immigration officials, the word among international offices is that recent developments have had a dampening effect on the number of international applicants from areas such as the Middle and Far East. Which means fingerprinting and mug shots have become regulation for anyone travelling into the States on a student visa.

Above all, you should know that these rules continue to change, and some bits of information in this section may be suddenly out of date even by the time this book comes off the press. So for up-to-date information, we repeat: check the US embassy (http://london.usembassy.gov/niv/students.html) and/or the US State Department (http://travel.state.gov)

The Facts of the Matter...

Although it may not be much more difficult than in the past for UK students to obtain a student visa, the process is more intricate and more expensive. However, if you are a genuine student and can provide the information requested, the process should go fairly smoothly. Any student wishing to pursue academic studies in the USA will require a student (F-1) visa, accompanied by a Form I-20.

The student visa application form is available from the US Embassy website. The university that has accepted you will issue a Form I-20 (Certificate of Eligibility for Non-immigrant (F-1) Student Status for Academic and Language Students).

Once you have the I-20 from the university and have completed your visa application, you should contact the Embassy or consulate and book an interview (you can theoretically do this on line, but you already know what we think of their site). You will need to take the I-20 form and the application materials with you to the interview.

PLEASE NOTE: one of the biggest problems, which is easily avoided, occurs when the name on your forms is different from the name in your passport. Make sure that when you begin the application process you use the name that appears in your passport! It is even a good idea to supply a photocopy of your passport with your university application.

REPEAT: the name on your transcript, SAT/ACT registrations, and your primary university applications must ALL match the name on your passport EXACTLY.

When scheduling visa interviews, all US visa-adjudicating posts now give special consideration to students so they will not miss the opening of the school semester. Many embassies and consulates around the world have opened special windows for students, reducing the wait for interview.

The average visa processing time following a successful interview is 5 days but it could be longer so don't leave this as a last minute project. Some visa applicants, fewer than 2% of the total applying, must wait for Washington to complete an interagency security advisory review, which includes checking all appropriate records. More than 90% of those reviews are completed in fewer than three weeks.

As there are often changes in the procedure, do visit the embassy's website for the most current information (http://london.usembassy.gov) before attending the interview.

The State Department Interview

All applicants for an F-1 visa must be interviewed.

Students are subject to the same law as other temporary visitors, and must convince a consular officer that they truly intend to pursue a course of study and will return to their home country when their studies are over. They must also show they can pay for their education, either from family funds, grants or other sources.

In the course of the interview you will have to submit completed forms and materials, pay the application fee (for up-to-date costs, check the US embassy website), present your passport with at least one blank page to attach the visa to, and provide a passport photo – different size from a UK passport photo.

You will need to furnish evidence of sufficient funds to cover all expenses, including fees while in the US, and provide evidence you will be returning to the UK at the end of your studies.

The evidence needed to demonstrate sufficient funds could include bank statements (yours or your parents), scholarship offers, etc. Please note, it does not necessarily mean you have to have a lump sum sitting in the bank.

You simply have to prove, based on account evidence, that you will be able to afford your stay in the US. If your parents are going to assist you, they will have to show statements that demonstrate regular funds will be available. Perhaps most importantly, you will have to demonstrate you will be returning to the UK. You can do this by demonstrating family links, a home in the UK, and other ties and commitments.

Once the F-1 visa is issued, you may travel to the States, but no earlier than 30 days before your course begins. In the subsequent years of working towards your degree, should you leave the US for a holiday, you will not need to wait until 30 days before the term starts to re-enter. The visa will last for the duration of your studies if there is no deviation.

The visa you finally receive will consist of a page in your passport and the accompanying I-20 form. Your name and the most updated version of this form will be registered on all immigration computers. Remember: you must NOT leave your I-20 behind – it is vital for gaining admittance to the country. It is also important you get it authorised at the beginning of your university career by the International Office at your uni and then signed each year thereafter.

You will be permitted to work on campus or off campus (after completion of your first year of study) under limited circumstances. Generally, during term times, you are allowed to work for twenty hours per week and full time during holidays. (See 'Working On and Off Campus' under 'Money, Money, Money' section.)

Finally, when you have completed your studies, you will be

permitted to remain in the US for up to 60 days. However, there is the possibility of extending your stay for up to 12 months following your degree to pursue practical training. For further information regarding working during your degree or training after its completion, please contact your university. (Again, see 'Working On and Off Campus' under 'Money, Money, Money' section.)

Other Options for Getting to Uni in the USA

Work Exchange/Internships

A number of programmes between the US and the UK encourage international understanding through practical work experience (called 'internships' in the US) for up to a maximum of 18 months. The programmes are known as work exchange programmes and vary widely in nature, some allowing participants to do any job available, others more restricted to specific fields. Check and see which programme best suits your situation and needs.

Work exchange programmes can only be administered by organisations authorised to issue the US Government form DS-2019. This allows work exchange programme participants to apply for a J-1 Exchange Visitor Visa at a US Embassy, letting them work legally in the US for a certain period.

Plan your participation in a work exchange programme as early as possible. Some programmes require you to obtain an offer of employment in the US before you apply to them. Programmes may have application deadlines or require you to apply a certain number of months before you intend to leave for the US. Check how long the whole process will take. Allow time for the visa application and, if possible, do not purchase a flight until you know your application has been successful.

Gap Year

For students wanting to take time out before going to university in the UK, it is possible to spend a semester, a year or a summer studying at a US university. You may find there are more possibilities for short-term study in small, private, liberal arts institutions than in larger state-funded colleges and universities.

When you have found universities you are interested in, contact the admissions office for each university, making it clear you will be applying to spend a year in the US before going on to university in the UK. You will be applying for 'special' or 'non-degree' student status. It is possible that you will have to fulfil the same requirements as those applying for full degrees.

Studying in the US even for just a gap year can be expensive. Tuition ranges between $4,000 and $35,000 for nine months. Cost of living can range between $7,000 and $15,000, depending on the region and your lifestyle. And be warned – there are few scholarships available for short-term study.

The academic year generally begins in late August or early September. If you are only interested in a one-semester deal, it is also possible to enrol for the winter/spring semester (normally beginning in January).

Undergraduate Exchange

There are two main ways to study for a short time in the US as part of your UK undergraduate degree: participate in an established study abroad programme through your UK university or apply directly to the US universities themselves. Generally, programmes run for a summer, semester or entire academic year. It is easier to go with an established exchange programme organised by your UK university than to apply to US universities directly. Exchanges are normally run by the International Office or possibly the American Studies department.

If your UK institution does not have any exchange links with any US universities, it is possible to contact US universities directly and apply as a non-degree student. This can, however, be complex and time consuming. You will need to check with your UK institution to see if they will recognise the courses you wish to take at the US institution. If you decide to apply as a non-degree student, then you should read the previous section on gap year study, as many of the criteria will apply to you in the undergraduate situation.

Funding for international students to pursue one year of undergraduate study in the US is very limited, but we do list several resources in the References section of this book. If you find you are not eligible for financial assistance from your UK university or the US university you will be attending, consider approaching multinational companies or local businesses.

Transferring from part-way through a UK university degree is possible – but consider seeking professional advice at Fulbright EducationUSA (free) or contact *Uni in the USA* (www.uniintheusa.com) (not free) because it can be tricky.

On Your Way – Almost! (What to Tell Your Parents)

Sending a child off to university is a big deal for any parent. As soon as the 'Thank God I have the house/car/fridge to myself' mentality has worn off, the 'Why is my little darling so far away?' line of thought steps in. If the little darling in question has decided that the best place to fly from the parental nest to is to America, then all the normal fears, worries and paranoia are multiplied by a factor of ten.

Even if the mother or father in question is in fact American or has experienced the college system first hand, the thought of the Atlantic dividing them from emergency laundry help can cause a fair amount of hysteria. The trick for the child is in learning how to handle this as it arises.

Dealing With Long Distance Family

Probably the first rule of thumb for allaying the anxious parents' fears is to find an international dialling deal or download one of the free online video calling apps (Skype, FaceTime, WhatsApp). Then make sure you remember to call home on a semi-regular basis. Also rest assured that American universities are much better than their English equivalents at managing parents. From the flow of information that will start to stream in before freshman year, to organised weekends specifically designed to allow the parents to actually see what their precious child is getting up to, the college administration really tries to make families feel involved. In doing so, they take much of the pressure off the child.

You should remember that LA is about the same distance from the East Coast as London is from New York and that many of your American classmates will endure similar homesickness and anxious parents. In fact, when your parents are driving you round the bend, you will normally find the same is true for those of your friends whose parents live just down the road. In many ways having family members around 3,000 miles away is good for all concerned (take note of the following points and use them to allay maternal fears). Family relationships are often improved by distance and your parents and siblings will love the fact they now have a built-in American shopper to find them jeans and Reese's peanut butter cups.

You, meanwhile, will find the odd visitor from home is exceedingly welcome. After all, who else can you prevail upon to smuggle in such delicacies as Marmite or McVitties? Furthermore as an 'American orphan' you have the chance to impose yourself on your roommates' families. This makes travel more convenient and allows you to both capitalize on pity for your abandoned status and explore whole new aspects of the States.

One of the things most parents worry about when their child flies across the pond is his or her social life. Will all her friends be American? Will he lose touch with his English peers and prefer to spend his holidays in far-flung corners of the States? In fact, for most English students, the opposite will prove true. American students love to travel and little ol' Europe is number one on their list of destinations. Brits studying in the States are more likely to find themselves operating as a backpacking hostel back home during the holidays than checking into one in the US. Americans love Britain and you will never have any shortage of visitors.

Nor, despite your family's anxiety, should you have any problems maintaining your English friendships. Your school contemporaries may well drift apart as they go to different universities and make new friends, but you should (with minimal effort) be able to become the link between them all. The fact that you will not be making hundreds of new friends in Britain means you are forced to make that little bit more of an effort with the old ones – and normally it pays off.

Now that phone calls and plane tickets are so cheap and social networking ubiquitous, it is easy to stay in contact with all your loved ones, regardless of which side of the Atlantic you happen to be on. And with a little bit of luck, you should be able to emerge from your undergraduate years with solid friendships (who might even, shock horror, have grown to like each other) on both sides of the pond.

Now Hand the Book to Your Parents...

It's time to give your parents something to think about. Show them this:

Your main role as a parent is to be supportive – and support will be needed by the bucketload. Getting in to university in the US is a drawn-out process with a raft of requirements – and all the while your child is bogged down in the middle of a battlefield of A-levels. To venture to another country for university is brave and nerve-wracking for everyone involved, so share the excitement of one of the most significant experiences your child will have – and keep the application show on the road.

How To Choose the Perfect University

There are more than 4,000 universities and colleges in the US, so tracking down the institution best suited to your child can be daunting. You can begin whittling down the selection process by asking him or her the following questions: What do you want to achieve by studying in the US? Would you be happier in an urban, suburban or rural environment? Would you prefer a small college, with only a few hundred students, or a large university with thousands of students? Which climate is more appealing to you outside the UK? What types of activities would you like to see on a campus?

More often than not, the best answers to these questions may not be the usual brand name suspects. Encourage your son or daughter to dig deeper than just the first three or four unis that come to mind; don't let lack of familiarity inhibit the research.

The last and most important question: Ask yourself what kind of budget you have for your child studying in the US.

The Fulbright Commission recommends you take three sheets of paper and head them 'First Choice', 'Second Choice' and 'Safety'. Safety institutions are those to which your child feels sure of entry because their achievements exceed the admission requirements.

These lists will help you to identify what is within your child's reach. Try to be as encouraging as possible about every institution your child zeros in on. Identify the differences between institutions and pin down what makes them interesting. Then match them to the criteria you have generated above.

Application to a US university is technical and time-consuming. Study this book carefully – you will probably see ramifications of the various requirements that your child will not.

To set out these requirements briefly:

Admission to US universities is based on academic merit and standardised tests. Personal recommendations and extra-curricular activities also count. US universities are looking for students who can succeed academically and also contribute to campus life.

The application process takes a long time. For example, if your child wants to begin studying in September 2017, it's vital to get the ball rolling 18 months earlier – i.e spring of 2016.

The first step is to **contact the universities** that your child is actively considering; get on their mailing list.

Complete the **application form** fully. The application form usually consists of a questionnaire about academic and cultural background. It is important to answer all questions honestly and accurately.

Your child will also need an official copy of his/her academic record (or '**transcript**') – not something most UK schools are used to providing, so give them plenty of time and information (copy the section in this book if you like, subtitled "Transcripts" under the "Applications" chapter).

Letters of recommendation – references, but not as we know them – will be needed, too, written by a teacher or employer who knows the applicant's character and work. Check with the institutions to which your child is applying and see if recommendations should be sent separately. Make sure the person writing them understands what is needed. (Copy this information from the "References" section under the "Applications" chapter)

Your child should schedule and take the **SAT** or **ACT**, plus **SAT Subject Tests** (see below).

Entrance Tests

There are no individual university entrance tests, but your child will probably need to take either the SAT exam or the ACT and the SAT subject tests (at least two of the latter are required by the most competitive unis). If the SAT or ACT is required by the uni (and one or the other usually is), the exam has to be taken before you submit an application. Make sure you register for them well in advance, since they fill up quickly.

Talk to your child's current school/college – many of them can advise on the hurdles you face. Register online for the SAT (www.collegeboard.org) or the ACT (www.actstudent.org) and plan to have your child sit these tests and, if necessary, SAT Subject Tests for the first time in the spring of the year he/she plans to apply. The SAT is offered four times a year (October, December, March, May) and can be taken multiple times, so if necessary the test can be retaken in the autumn just before submission of applications. The same policy is true for the ACT, which is offered five times a year (September, October, December, April, June).

Money Matters

The key to financial planning is to start early so you and your child can keep on top of the many challenges. You must be fully aware of the financial commitment involved in studying abroad. Most US students have low-interest government loans. As a UK resident, you are only able to apply for a US loan if you have an American co-signer – and even then it will be a private loan, not a loan from the government. Encourage your child to believe that funding an education abroad is attainable. It's a long and winding road, and parents are definitely needed on the journey.

The non-refundable application fee for each university ranges from $20 to $150 and covers only the processing cost. A visa will be granted only if a student can prove he (or you) has sufficient funds to cover all costs for the first year.

It is difficult to generalise the basic cost of an academic year because institutions set their own tuition fees and the cost of living varies greatly according to location. Tuition, room and board, and fees will run anywhere from $20,000 – $60,000 per academic year (nine months). Students must buy their books, adding as much as $1,000 a year to the cost. For students not living in school accommodation, living expenses are highest in big cities, ranging from $7,000 – $16,000 a year. You will also need to factor in air travel to and from the US, along with health insurance and personal spending money.

The best source of funding for your child's US education is the institution itself. Many of them allocate funds for international students, mostly based on academic merit, although some colleges offer funding based on need. Usually, more funding is available from private rather than state institutions; however, full scholarships are rare. It requires a huge amount of time to research and apply for scholarships.

Funding from independent bodies is less common, but it is available. Some universities give athletic or performing arts scholarships. It is extremely important, if your child wants to apply for a scholarship, to be certain the scholarship is available to international students.

A student visa allows on-campus work for up to 20 hours per week, to help cover living expenses and earn pocket money. But note, none of this income can count towards a visa application. Help your child research and draw up a budget. Is it affordable? How does it compare with the costs of university in the UK? Is the difference in quality really worth it?

Frequent Flyer Tip: Most universities will allow you to pay with a credit card. If you are making a large payment to the university anyway (or perhaps breaking it into several payments, depending on what the bursar allows), it's worth considering making that payment through a credit card that gives air miles; you can still avoid the interest charges by paying the credit card company immediately. And either you or your US student will certainly use the miles.

Health and Safety

One common concern for a parent thinking of sending their child overseas is safety. Rest assured, American colleges (ever wary of lawsuits) take very good care of their students. Most campuses have security staff or police who patrol day and night. Many have an escort service to pick students up and drive or walk them to any destination on or around campus. These services are usually free and operate until late. Most institutions have emergency call boxes located around campus that directly access police emergency lines.

Find out what security services are available and make sure your child will be able to call an escort when needed, or walk with a friend. Occasionally, one institution or another has a tragedy or scandal, often well publicized. If you are concerned about attention to safety and measures taken by the administration to guard against problems occurring again, do not hesitate to call the admissions office and ask to speak to someone about your concerns.

In case of an emergency it is extremely important your child has not left home without as many means of contact as possible. Email addresses, mailing addresses, and phone numbers of family members are just some of the suggested safety contacts. It will be up to you to talk to your child about what means of communication to use and in what order. Most universities have a parent support network, with a designated person to help deal with international students and parents. Before your child makes a definite decision on a university, check the services each institution's International Student Office (ISO) provides.

Don't assume you can call the university yourself with this information if your child somehow doesn't lodge your emergency contact details with them. Because of US privacy laws, some universities insist that all information come from the student and only the student. Some universities can be astonishingly impractical and stubborn about this (in the opinion of the editor), and will not allow you, the check-writing parent, to give or receive information about your own child. Be aware that this might be their policy, and check if you feel your son or daughter might not be a faithful and diligent reporter.

Insurance

International students need to check with the campus health centre to see if their insurance policy will be affordable and suitable. Services vary depending on the size and location of the institution. Some campus health centres offer emergency care, others don't. Contact your centre direct, or the International Student Office, to find out more. Many institutions include a basic health insurance plan in their fees (and this can often be supplemented through the same insurance company if you want more coverage); others require international students to take out all of their own health cover.

Carefully look at the range of insurance plans available from both the UK and the US, to establish which offers the best value for money and the most comprehensive coverage. A perfect health insurance policy covering 100% of the costs for 100% of the time may be too expensive. One that covers the majority of costs may, of course, leave you picking up the tab for the shortfall. There are significant differences between US and UK healthcare policies. You must weigh up the advantages and disadvantages, and plump for the one that's best for you. Principal differences are cost, preventive healthcare, pre-existing conditions and liability insurance. Some student cards offer limited insurance cover. For example, the International Student Identity Card (ISIC) is a globally recognised identification card that carries some insurance benefits.

Communication

Communicating with your child throughout the application process in the UK is crucial. Make time to talk regularly about how it's going. It is a good idea to contact other students who have studied abroad and discuss the realities of living there, including funding, academic life and cultural lifestyle. These people are an incredibly valuable source of information and contacts can be found through the internet or the International Student Office of the institution your child will be attending. The ISO also provides other services for your child once they are in the US, usually including culture- shock therapists and counsellors.

And so to Summarise: Step by Step

What Do I Do and When?

Follow this timeline and you can't go wrong. (And bear in mind this list is for the super-organised. All of these things can be done in less time if you are of the more chaotic variety).

American university years begin, like ours, in September. Start the process at least 18 months before you expect to enrol:

January–June

- Get the preliminaries out of the way. Why do you want to study in the US? Which is the right university for you? Consider your criteria: size, location, selectivity etc. Take your time – applying to a US uni is a challenge enough without applying to the wrong one.
- Will you need financial aid? What are the application/ financial aid deadlines for your chosen universities? Look up application and financial aid deadlines for your possible universities.
- Remember, SAT and ACT tests have to be taken in advance. Check registration dates. Make sure you register for them in time. Register for them several months before you take them – seats fill VERY quickly. Repeat: Obtain test registration and plan to sit the SAT or the ACT and, if necessary, SAT Subject Tests by June (you can take each of these multiple times). See whether the university prefers the SAT or ACT.
- Start practicing for the SAT or ACT (yes, you need to do this!) – 15 hours of prep per week is not unheard of. The format and type of questioning are very different from A levels. Help can be found via books, tutors, classes, and online resources. Your first stop should be collegeboard.org.

July & August

- Go to the university website for applications and financial aid forms. Request catalogues if you want something you can hold in your hands (the photos are usually stunning).
- Better yet, visit the universities that interest you. Before you go, check online to see the campus tour schedule and, if offered, arrange for an on-campus interview with an admissions representative.

- Start to create a list of your accomplishments, activities and work experience. This will help with your applications and essays.
- Keep a college calendar of all admission and financial aid deadlines.
- Register for autumn test dates for the SAT and/or ACT exam and SAT Subject tests.

September

- Register on the Common Application website (www.commonapp.org) and start to create your list of colleges. Read through the whole application form so you know which credentials will be required. Review any supplemental applications for the schools you're interested in.
- Ask your school for an 'official transcript'. Ask your teachers for letters of recommendation. Put their contact details into your Common App form.

October

- Finalise your list of colleges. Consider 'safety' colleges, as well as 'probable' and 'reach' colleges.
- Complete a first draft of your essays – both for the Common App and for any others required in the supplemental applications for individual universities. Think of topics that focus on your experiences and make you stand out from the crowd.
- If you're seeking financial aid, contact the financial aid office at the colleges on your list to see what forms they require.
- If you plan to apply through an Early Decision or Early Action program, be aware that deadlines for early applications tend to be around the 1st of November. Financial aid apps are generally due at the same time. So move all of the aforementioned steps up by at least a month.
- Some of you will have to juggle all of this with UCAS application requirements – get organised early.

November

- If applying Early Decision or Early Action, submit applications on time.
- Otherwise, polish your college essays and proofread them rigorously for mistakes.
- Follow up with referees to ensure that recommendation forms are submitted on time to meet your deadlines.

December

- Submit applications for admission and financial aid. Check that transcripts and references have arrived.
- Decide which of your SAT/ACT scores you want sent to each of your colleges via the respective test websites (www. collegeboard. org or www.actstudent.org).
- Or sit the necessary admissions tests again, if appropriate. (Generally, the last test date that is accepted for regular admission is in December)

January–March

- There may be various application deadlines which must be met (e.g. submitting latest term grades), but mostly you wait for answers from the schools. Look for email confirmations from each university that all necessary application materials have been received.
- Continue to perform well in school; even once you're accepted, colleges want to see strong final term grades.

March–April

- Letters of acceptance or rejection will arrive.
- Pinpoint which university to attend by May 1, notify them of your decision, complete and return any forms/fees they require by May 1 or on date they say. (Don't dally. The most desirable dorms fill up fast, because students in the know will send back their dorm request forms immediately.)
- Send letters of regret to those universities you reject (so your spot can be given to another student).
- If you're on a waiting list, contact the admission office and let them know of your continued interest; update

them on your spring semester grades and activities.

- Still considering a UK school? Check deadlines for decision-making.

June–July

- Apply to the American Embassy for a visa as soon as you get the I-20 form from your chosen university (see Visa section in this book).
- Organise finances (arrange to transfer funds to a US bank; make sure you have funds for travel and expenses on arrival). Finalise arrangements for housing and medical insurance with your university.

July

- Make travel arrangements. Contact the International Student Office at your university with details of your arrival plans.

August–September:

- Start packing! And enjoy yourself.

Glossary for the Transatlantic Traveller

Confused by the jargon? Daunted by having to do all this yourself rather than letting your school gently guide you through UCAS? Read on – all will be explained.

Academics

British	American
First year	Freshman
Second year	Sophomore
Third year	Junior
Fourth year	Senior
Public school	Private school
State school	Public school
Uni	School
Year group	Class (as in "My class is graduating tomorrow")

Food

British	American
Hundreds and thousands	Sprinkles
Aubergine	Eggplant
Chips	French fries
Courgette	Zucchini
Crisps	Chips
Fish fingers	Fish sticks
Jam	Jelly
Jelly	Jello
Porridge	Oatmeal
Pudding	Dessert
Tinned	Canned
Yog/hurt	Yo/ghurt

Relationships

British	American
Bloke	Guy
Fit	Cute/hot
Going out	Dating
Minging	Gross
Pull	Hook-up
Snog	Kiss

Clothes

British	American
Braces	Suspenders (!)
Jumper	Sweater
Pants	Underpants
Trainers	Sneakers
Trousers	Pants
Waistcoat	Vest

In General

British	American
"Sorry"	"Excuse me"
Anti clockwise	Counter-clockwise
Athlete	Jock
Autumn	Fall
Backside/bum	Fanny/tush
Black-tie dance	Formal
Boot (of car)	Trunk
Brilliant	Awesome
Chemist	Drugstore
Clever	Smart
Condom	Rubber

Fags	Cigarettes (watch out here – 'fag' has only a derogatory homosexual connotation in the States)
Film	Movie
Flat	Apartment
Football	Soccer
Fringe	Bangs
Full stop	Period
Gents	Men's room
Lift	Elevator
Queue	Line
Loo	Bathroom/restroom
Maths	Math
Mobile	Cell phone
Nappy	Diaper
Nerd	Geek
Pavement	Sidewalk
Petrol	Gas
Post	Mail
Postcode	Zip code
Pub	Bar
Rubber	Eraser
Rucksack	Backpack
Smart	Well dressed
Sofa	Couch
Tap	Faucet
Tea towel	Dish cloth
Underground/tube	Subway
Very	Quite (saying that something is 'quite good' or looks 'quite nice' is a compliment from an American)
Washing up	Doing the dishes

As in Britain, when an American says, "Hey, what's up?" to you, they do NOT expect a five-minute answer on your cheating boyfriend, overdue paper and aching back. In fact, it is a mere formality – answer with a casual "Not much".

US Holidays

Presidents' Day – winter day off school

Spring Break – drunken student debauchery, usually sometime in March

Thanksgiving – late-November turkey celebration

Veterans Day – Remembrance Day (the only people wearing poppies are Canadians)

Resources, References and Links

Here are some helpful books, organisations and website links to supplement the wisdom we have imparted.

First, you'll Need the Experts: Who are They?

EducationUSA – from the US Department of State

Much more straightforward in our opinion than the tortuous US Department of Education site, but by all means click on ed.gov if you're a glutton for punishment. www.educationusa.info/

US-UK Fulbright Commission

US Educational Advisory Service: www.fulbright.org.uk/study-in-the-usa; tel 020 7498 4010.

The US-UK Fulbright Commission is a not-for-profit organisation, funded by both governments to foster mutual cultural understanding through educational exchange between the US and UK. It achieves this through post-graduate and post-doctoral scholarships, and through its advisory service. The advisory service provides a wide range of information and events to support students, parents and advisors interested in US-UK exchange. As part of the EducationUSA advising network, Fulbright's team is the only official source of information on US study for the UK.

US Embassy – here's where you get your student visa

The US Embassy – http://uk.usembassy.gov/visas/study-exchange/ and http://travel.state.gov/content/visas/en/study-exchange/student.html

The Good Schools Guide University Educational Consultants

One-to-one consulting on the entire uni application process, with selected, renowned consultants who have had years of experience with all kinds of students, and all kinds of colleges and universities. www.goodschoolsguide.co.uk/advice.

Application Essays

Several books on writing college essays are available through the Barron's website, www.barronseduc.com.

Best College Admission Essays, Petersons; www.petersons.com; fifty sample essays plus tips and advice for writing your own.

Help, Need More Money!

Financial Aid Assistance

Broad information on scholarships and loans:

Register on the *Uni in the USA* website and you'll receive a pdf with everything we could find about US uni scholarships for international students – covering how to find financial aid and how to apply. www.uniintheusa.com/how-why/paying-for-us-uni/1525/ scholarships-for-international-students

www.jeffersonscholars.org – a highly competitive University of Virginia scholarship programme; only a few awarded each year

The College Board site: www.collegeboard.com/student/pay/

www.educationusa.info/financial-aid

www.fundingusstudy.org

www.fastweb.com/ib/edupass-21f

www.InternationalStudentLoan.com

www.scholarships.com

www.unigo.com/scholarships#/fromscholarshipexperts

Fulbright Funding Page: www.fulbright.org.uk/study-in-the-usa/undergraduate-study/funding

Athletic Scholarships

College Prospects of America – A sports scholarship placement service and one of the first ones we recommend. Contact Marva Hall, European Co-ordinator (and a former athlete herself): marva@ cpoauk.com, 5 Manland Avenue, Harpenden, Herts AL5 4RE; tel 01582 712364 www.cpoauk.com/contact.htm

Sporting Chance USA – UK contact is Phil Selby: philselby@ sportingchanceusa.com; 3 Forge Cottages, Main Street, South Maskham, Newark, Notts NG23 6EF; tel 01636 918474. www. sportingchanceusa.com.

Pass4Soccer – UK contact is Daniel Gray: daniel@ pass4soccer. com; for over 15 years PASS4Soccer have been securing soccer scholarships in US universities for players from the UK, Europe, and beyond. Tyne Met College, Embleton Ave, Wallsend, Tyne & Wear NE28 9NJ; tel 07763 749028. www.pass4soccer.com

InTuition Scholarships – UK contact is Harry Newton: info@student-scholarships.com; 4 Ravey St, London EC2A 4QP; tel 08456 034054. www.student-scholarships.com.

Sporting Elite: enquiries@sportingeliteusa.com, +44 (0)20 8546 4855; www.sportingeliteusa.com. Talent evaluation service based in the UK; guide student athletes through the US college recruiting process, helping with profile, video footage, US visa process.

Fulbright Educational Advisory Service: www.fulbright.org.uk/about/contact-us

Financial Aid for Student Athletes: www.finaid.org/otheraid/sports.phtml. Not a very jazzy website, but full of lots of useful information.

National Collegiate Athletic Association: www.ncaa.org

National Association of Intercollegiate Athletics: www.naia.org

National Junior College Athletic Association: www.njcaa.org

Further Reading

US University Scholarships for International Students, A Comprehensive Resource for Financial and Funding Opportunities at America's Top-rated Institutions (2015, 2nd edition, by Stephen Fenoglio). Comprehensive guide for students seeking financial assistance for US universities. It outlines the key points and differences regarding available financial aid and scholarships, and details the specific financial offerings of 100 of the top American universities.

Foundation Grants to Individuals (www.foundationcenter.org/products/foundation-grants-to-individuals-online) – An online subscription service with general information about applying for grants to individuals.

Scholarships, Grants and Prizes 2016 (www.petersons.com) provides up-to-date information on a wide range of privately funded awards available to college students – based on ethnic heritage, talent, employment experience, military service, and other categories. Includes information on award amounts, eligibility, the application process.

How to Get Money for College (2017, also from www.petersons.com), offers information on needs-based and non-needs gift aid, loans, work-study, athletic awards and more. The Colleges-at-a-Glance comparison chart lists the full costs that can be expected, aid packages and more, for each of more than 2,100 four-year colleges and universities, organised by state.

2017 Scholarship Handbook (from College Board), available from collegeboard.org and Amazon UK. Covers scholarships, internships and loans.

Choosing a University

Guides and Directories

The College Board – simply the best uni search of any website we've seen. Filter for every possible combination of type, location, course, degree, size college and university in the entire US. www.collegeboard.org

Peterson's: www.petersons.com

Princeton Review: www.princetonreview.com. One of the most tried and true directories of selected colleges and universities, with reviews closest to the ones we do ourselves, plus hilarious but relevant "best" listings (eg Best Party School). Frequently mentioned in *Uni in the USA*. Available in print ('*The Best 367 Colleges*') and online.

Unigo: www.unigo.com. Reviews written for students by students with lots of fun information that other websites and books don't consider.

College Confidential: www.collegeconfidential.com. The internet's largest forum for the college-bound community.

College Times: https://collegetimes.co/reviews. College Times claims it has the largest database of college on the web and is the most honest source of information – coming from the students, uncensored and straight from the source. Includes universities from all over the world.

Barron's Profiles of American Colleges 2017 (Barron's, 31st edition): www.barronseduc.com/school-guides. In-depth profiles of more than 1,650 schools, although not as much fun as the Princeton Review, plus Barron's exclusive rating system, with schools ranked from 'Most Competitive' to 'Non-Competitive', a comprehensive index to college majors, and free access to Barron's website, featuring a college search engine to help students match their academic plans and aptitudes with the admission requirements and programmes of each school.

The College Board College Handbook (2017, The College Board), www.collegeboard.org. Over 3,900 four-year and two-year courses. "The only guide to every accredited college in the US". Indexes colleges by type, special characteristics (eg women only), undergraduate enrolment size, admission selectivity, admission/placement policies, colleges that offer ROTC (Reserve Officer Training Corps), NCAA sports. Colleges are described by state.

The K&W Guide to Colleges for Students with Learning Differences, (2016, 13th Edition), available on Amazon.com. Profiles of 350 Schools with programs or services for students with ADHD or Learning Disabilities.

Colleges for Students with Learning Disabilities or AD/HD (2017, 8th Edition, Peterson's). 700+ colleges offering programs specifically for students with learning disabilities, with detailed information about specific services offered.

Four Year Colleges (2017, 47th edition, Peterson's), www.petersons.com. Latest information on more than 2,500 four-year colleges and universities in the US and Canada, an at-a-glance application checklist to help you get started, tips on surviving standardised tests, scholarships, etc. Newly updated advice for international students and an easy-to-use majors index and entrance difficulty index. Colleges and universities are organised by state/province.

Rankings Compilers

University of Illinois, Champaign-Urbana: College and University Rankings (comprehensive site with links to all rankings compilers; this link goes specifically to those ranking undergraduate institutions): www.library.uiuc.edu/edx/rankings.htm

Princeton Review: www.princetonreview.com/college-rankings/

US News and World Report: www.usnews.com/education

General Information: Helpful websites

www.collegeconfidential.com

www.collegexpress.com

www.commonapp.org

www.iie.org

www.mappingyourfuture.org

www.mycollegeguide.org

www.studyoverseasglobal.com/USA

www.usjournal.com/en/students/info/fairs.html

www.usnews.com/education

www.unigo.com

Sites specifically for Community Colleges

American Association of Community Colleges: www.aacc.nche.edu

National Alliance of Community and Technological Colleges: www.nactc.org

Sites Specifically for Finding Art Schools

www.allartschools.com

www.usnews.com/best-graduate-schools/top-fine-arts-schools

www.artschools.com/programs/

www.incredibleart.org/artroom/colleges/colleges.html

www.accreditedschoolsonline.org/art-schools/

www.findyourartschool.com

Entrance Exams

Taking the Test

ACT Board: www.actstudent.org

SAT Board: www.collegeboard.org

National Center for Fair & Open Testing (FairTest): www.fairtest.org (to find colleges that may exempt from standardized tests)

www.ets.org in Princeton and CITO Group SAT Programme, PO Box 1109,6801 BC Arnhem, Netherlands can also arrange registration

www.fulbright.org.uk/study-in-the-usa in London for information on registration, fees and test centres.

Practising the Test

The Official SAT Study Guide For the New SAT – take practice tests created by the SAT test creator and calculate estimated scores. Includes detailed descriptions of maths, critical reading, and writing sections of the SAT. www.collegeboard.org (and available on AmazonUK)

Cracking the SAT with 4 Practice Tests, 2017 Edition – Princeton Review. There is also a Princeton Review series covering the subject tests. www.princetonreview.com

Cracking the ACT (2017) and *Crash Course for the ACT* (6th Edition) – Both written by the Princeton Review and available through Amazon UK and the Princeton Review online bookstore.

Khan Academy – prepare for the new SAT with free online tutorials, offered in partnership with the test-maker (College Board). Take real, full-length practise tests, watch helpful videos to work through questions, and get personalised SAT practise advice. www.khanacademy.org

The Real SAT II: Subject Tests (The College Board) – Full-length tests for every SAT subject, tips and strategies. www.collegeboard.org

A-List Education – expert support for every aspect of the US university application process, including one-on-one tutoring and bootcamps for SAT, ACT and SAT Subject Tests as well as private counselling for college selection, applications and essays; 167-169 Kensington High Street, 2nd Floor, London W8 6SH, Tel 020 3004 8101, www.alisteducation.co.uk.

CATES Tutoring – From one-to-one tuition to bespoke classes, CATES specializes in American test prep (ACT, SAT, GRE etc), university application and admissions support, education planning. They serve New York, London, and other international markets. We like their style, particularly when coaching an entire class of students. Among other things, CATES are renowned for their work with the Sutton Trust US Programme. www.catestutoring.co.uk.

Kaplan Test Prep – More than 60 years experience and offering a wide range of courses, private tuition and courses, Monday-Sunday; www.kaptest.com/uk. 3-5 Charing Cross Road, London WC2H OHA; tel 020 7930 3130; fax 020 7930 8009; london_center@kaplan.com.

The Studyworks – Courses on ACT and SAT with review of both the maths and verbal sections of each exam. Individual tuition for US entrance exams: ACT/SAT/GMAT/GRE/LSAT/SSAT/ISEE; long time test prep tutor and/or US university advisor for schools including Eton, Marlborough, Harrodian, TASIS and ACS Cobham & Egham, among others. Available at 46 Queens Gardens, London W2 3AA; tel 020 7402 9877. Email sw-mc@hotmail.com

ArborBridge Test Preparation - Online, one-on-one tutoring for all US entrance exams including the SAT, ACT, SAT Subject Tests, and TOEFL. Top tier tutors, a data-driven, adaptive curriculum, and a uniquely personal tutoring experience are available to students around the world. Contact Erica Sin (Director of International Programs) at Erica@arborbridge.com. www.arborbridge.com

English Language Tests

TOEFL: www.toefl.org

International English Language Testing System: www.ielts.org. An alternative accepted by many universities.

Applying as a Transfer Student

Educational Credential Evaluators: www.ece.org

Foundation for International Services: www.fis-web.com

Global Services Associates: www.globaleval.org

International Education Research Foundation Inc: www.ierf.org

Josef Silny and Associates Inc International Education Consultants: www.jsilny.com

National Association of Credential Evaluation Services: www.naces.org

World Education Services Inc: www.wes.org

I UNDERSTAND YOUR HIGHER EDUCATION HERE IS VERY GOOD...

Universities in the USA

In this section of this book we examine in detail some of the many excellent colleges America has to offer. ...

Everyone has a different opinion about his or her university. Where we have found a general consensus on a certain issue, we have reported it as more or less the truth. Where there is a large range of opinions, or views are evenly split on an issue, we have tried to capture these nuances. Obviously, however, we have not spoken to every student at each university. There may be some who would disagree with how we have presented things, and it is certainly possible that your individual taste may clash strongly with that of the students we talked to.

We have not visited every good university in the United States. Readers should not take the universities reviewed here as a definitive list of good ones to consider. Many others are worth looking into. Let us know what you find.

We have not tried to fill our reviews with facts and statistics. All of the technical details – the skeletal outline of a university – are available to anyone on university websites, Wikipedia pages and a range of other online resources.

What is not available online is the real feel of a university: the experiences people have there, the everyday life of its students and the accompanying concerns and commendations they have.

This is what makes our guide unique, and we hope you will find insight into the workings of some of the top institutions in the US and how to find one that's the right fit for you.

American University (Washington DC)

Washington, District of Columbia
www.american.edu
Undergrads: 7,000
Grads: 3,500

How many AU students does it take to change a light bulb?

101 – One hundred to pass the bill through Congress and one to change it.

Don't be confused by the immodest name; just because it calls itself "American" doesn't mean it's going to give you an experience typical of the US. In fact, if there's anything characteristically American about this liberal, multi-national hotbed, it's that it doesn't conform to the stereotypes the name implies – just like the country itself.

One of the big three DC schools (alongside Georgetown and George Washington), American University provides its students with fantastic educational opportunities – not just for the politically minded (although it was ranked the most political by the Princeton Review) but for everyone who wants to participate and take advantage of the super-charged capital of the world's most important country.

The AU Student

Students are happy and engaged at AU. For better or for worse, the college is extremely political, so even if you have no idea how American politics works, you'll soon find yourself captivated by things like primary elections, Iranian diplomacy and Supreme Court nominations. Free-time political conversations are common, and don't be surprised if you go out partying and find the night dominated by an argument over the best way to reform health care. "I didn't care about politics until I got here," said one international affairs major, "but now it's my favourite subject."

Still, students insist that you can have fun here even if your tendencies are more apathetic (or anarchistic). The large range of personalities and backgrounds means that you can always find people on the same wavelength as yourself, while in general everyone is strikingly well-balanced in regards to work and play. A healthy Greek life guarantees that you'll find all the unhealthy activities you could want, while the energised atmosphere means that the student body's active nature is extended to non-political realms, in particular theatre and the arts. "We're busy people, but we're social," said one junior.

More than 1,200 of the students at AU are international, with almost 150 countries represented. The joke is that when someone from another country wants to study in the States, they type "American university" into Google, and pick the first one that comes up.

Whatever the reason, the international atmosphere is a big draw for US citizens and non-citizens alike, and everyone loves it. The international students coming to AU are complemented by the large numbers (more than half) of students who leave to go overseas with the study abroad programme, another big draw. (There are more than 100 AU Abroad programmes.)

Hitting the Books

Though academics are rigorous and challenging, "it's not cutthroat like George Washington, [and] you can probably pass if you just coast your classes." The work ethic is alive and well here, but it doesn't feel forced – people work hard at subjects they enjoy because of genuine interest.

As well as politics, public affairs, and the best international studies department in the world, AU excels in the arts and has famously good business and law schools too. While it has the capacity to offer a top-notch range and quality of courses, the college is still small enough to foster a close relationship between pupils and profs. Students report an excellent out-of-class contact with their accessible teachers, which greatly enhances the learning experience.

The other notable thing about the professors at AU is that they mostly have come to teaching from "the real world". That is to say, they have incredible first-hand experience of what they're teaching. This brings not only an extra depth to classes but some great contacts for graduating seniors who want a leg up in some of the most competitive industries in the country.

In fact, you don't even have wait till you graduate. AU students are famous for securing internships with congressmen or lobbyists, helping run election campaigns, or leading protests – and generally gaining plenty of experience of their own while they're at college.

Social Life

"The great thing about AU is you've got your campus life, plus you've got your DC life," said one contented student. You can feel like you're at college when you're in the relative seclusion of the campus, but the glory of the nation's capital is always there at your feet. It's hard to tell whether the campus or the city life is the more vibrant.

On campus you'll find all the activities – student organisations, student media, student government (particularly strong here, as you might imagine), and student performances. There's almost any group available that you might want, and if doesn't exist, you can always start it. A number of famous speakers (mostly politicians) regularly come to speak. The university is also known for its fantastic community service programme which attracts many students, as does the Peace Corps.

Outside Those Ivory Walls

In town meanwhile, there're even bigger fish to tackle. As one AU student put it: "it's DC, man, it's the most powerful city in the world." And indeed it is, but it's also one of the most fun. Whether you fancy a spin round the incredible Air and Space museum, a gig at the famous 9:30 Club or Black Cat, or just the legendary 'midnight monument tour', it's all there for the taking. DC is full of cool little (and not so little!) bars and clubs of every description, not to mention great restaurants and a budding music scene.

Getting In

AT A GLANCE – Application & Test Options:

– Early Decision, Early Decision II, Regular Decision

- ACT/SAT Test-optional for international students

The admissions process is relatively straight forward, especially if you set up the online "prospective student portal". On average slightly over half of applicants are accepted, but be warned that a fair chunk of the competition will have strong political resumes even by the time they leave high school.

Money Matters

The college is fairly good value for money (certainly a lot cheaper than its DC rivals). AU does not provide any needs-based aid to international students, but it does have some juicy merit scholarships, awarded "based on a combination of outstanding academic achievement, leadership and community service." We know of one British student who recently received a scholarship offer from out of the blue, entirely unsolicited and based only on academic merit. Worth inquiring further with the financial aid department.

Famous Grads

Judith Sheindlin – TV personality ("Judge Judy")

Gary Cohn – Former President of Goldman Sachs, now Chief Economic Advisor to President Donald Trump

Salman bin Hamad bin Isa Al Khalifa – Bahraini Crown Prince

Amherst College

Amherst, Massachusetts
www.amherst.edu
Undergrads: 1,800
Grads: 0

How many students does it take to change a light bulb at Amherst?

Thirteen – one to change the bulb and an a cappella group to immortalize the event in song.

Take every stereotype you can imagine about New England colleges. The Puritan ethic, the white wooden buildings, the preppy students, the snow...

Compile them all and you will have a fairly accurate vision of Amherst. This small college has long been hailed as one of the best of its kind in America, consistently coming at the top of the liberal arts rankings. Small in size and intimate in feel, it offers those addicted to the boarding school experience new avenues of enjoyment and independence with all those old, secure home comforts.

The Campus

Amherst proudly labels itself the 'Fairest College' and it certainly has the charming New England feel that many Brits envision when they imagine an

American university. The campus extends over 1,000 acres and is located on a hill. Old brick buildings jostle with newer and less successful architectural attempts, but the whole is successful and easy to find your way around.

The Amherst student body congregate around a few main buildings. The sporty head for the new and extensive Wolff Fitness Center while the Keefe Campus Center offers dramatic and social service groups a place to go. And everyone meets in the dining hall for meals.

Accommodation

Students live in former fraternity houses or new buildings and living groups can range from the peace-loving loner to the party-favouring ten-man suites. However, wherever you end up, the small size of the student body makes it impossible to leave a room without running into someone you know. All freshmen are assigned housing and the bonds forged in this initial year often define the rest of your college living experience.

The Amherst Student

Preppy is not really a word that has an equivalent in the British educational system. Our nearest counterpart is a combination of rugger buggers, Sloane rangers and Tim-nice-but-dim. Yet even this does not come close to the good old WASPs of New England. Amherst has never quite escaped its reputation as being one of the most preppy of the small American colleges and a large percentage of its undergrad body have been turned out of the country-club attending, Abercrombie and Fitch wearing, jeep driving mould.

This is not to say that Amherst is totally without diversity. In fact it prides itself on its open admission policies and estimates that around 40% of its undergraduate body are minority students. And while its international intake is not as large as at some other schools, it is still substantial (currently around 10%). After all, where Prince Albert of Monaco goes, others are sure to follow...

One of the great advantages of the Amherst experience comes from the small size of each undergraduate class. With only around 450 students in each year it is difficult for social divisions or exclusive cliques to survive. Everyone knows everyone else. When such a limited number are eating, living and working together it is difficult to remain just a face in a crowd.

This small-town environment is great for those who feel comfortable having their every move known. Yet it can be difficult for people who prefer the social whirl and comfortable anonymity of being one among thousands. And once you're established, it becomes ever harder to reinvent yourself.

While it is difficult to generalize, Amherst types tend to be outdoorsy, social and sporty. It is estimated that around 80% of students take part in some form of sport with 30% playing at varsity level. Despite its small size Amherst enjoys a great sporting reputation. The annual football game with Williams is the small college equivalent of the Harvard-Yale game (or the Oxbridge boat race). Crew is also popular – in keeping with the school's clean-cut image.

The fantastic sporting facilities also make this a great place to attend if you are an ardent outdoorsman (or woman). Come winter, the mountains are near enough to make skiing a weekend possibility, and hiking and camping are regular leisure pursuits.

Hitting the Books

Amherst devotees believe that no college can rival their own in the realm of liberal arts. They take pride in the fact that this is a college where complete freedom of choice is encouraged.

Students have only one requirement – the interdisciplinary First-Year Seminar. After that, they are free to design their own curriculum, constrained only by the guidelines of their major or, in the case of many, a double major. This flexibility is great for those individuals who are scared off by the prospect of mandatory core curriculum classes in subjects that they joyfully abandoned after GCSEs.

Students should bear in mind that one of the great things about a liberal arts environment such as Amherst is that it allows you room to experiment – something that most British universities regard with great disapproval. The majority of students at Amherst have a reputation for taking full advantage of this. And despite its easygoing atmosphere, there are a high proportion of ambitious honours students.

Students who aim to get through their university career without ever interacting with a professor should not even contemplate Amherst. This is a college that prides itself on student-faculty relationships and the small size of the campus makes this intimacy almost impossible to avoid. With an average class size of just nineteen, parents will certainly feel that their precious children are getting the attention they deserve.

The children, meanwhile, may wish that they were getting a little less. Professors expect you to talk to them about your aims, problems and queries and they are always available. In fact it is difficult not to run into them on a daily basis. If you are the type of person who needs a certain amount of care and intimacy with those around you (whether this involves knowing your professor's cat's name or hanging out with your dining hall server), Amherst is an ideal college.

This is not to say that Amherst undergraduates can expect a pampered existence. This is a challenging and highly competitive school and the renowned Puritan work ethic is an integral part of campus life. The faint-hearted or easily embarrassed should beware. Professors expect a great deal of verbal interaction from their students and the intimate class sizes mean that a reluctance to participate is swiftly noticed.

The idea of a 'mutual education' is much touted at Amherst. The general idea is that everyone learns from each other, bringing together the future hopes of America in informative and improving debate. While this may be an academic's pipe-dream, this is certainly not a campus where you should expect your views to go unheard or unchallenged.

Considering the smaller size of its faculty and the absence of a grad school, Amherst offers a large number of classes in a wide variety of subjects. However if you have already read the course catalogue a thousand times and still find nothing that interests you, you have the great option of being able to take courses at four other universities.

Amherst is part of the Five College Coalition – which includes Smith, Mount Holyoke, Hampshire College and UMass Amherst (don't get confused). Cross-college enrolment is encouraged and very easy to do, allowing you to pick the best of not just one college but five.

Social Life

The school may be small, the work may be hard, but the party spirit lives on – Amherst's social life closely resembles that of some British colleges. Rather than the Oxford bop, Amherst students enjoy the weekly TAP (which imaginatively stands for The Amherst Party).

These school-wide events feature different themes, music and the ubiquitous keg. Despite its Massachusetts locale, Amherst does not subscribe to prohibition ideas and Brits will be relieved to find that alcohol, most specifically beer, is a key part of student life. If you are teetotal there are many other social options – ranging from coffee shops to campus movies to the numerous clubs and societies.

Dating is not, however, a part of the Amherst student's life. The small size of the campus means that your random 'hook-ups' swiftly come back to haunt you. Thus most people are either in near-marriage relationships or constantly on the look out for fresh blood. Luckily the nearby colleges – most specifically the crowds at UMass – offer much needed social alternatives.

Outside Those Ivory Walls

Upon arrival at Amherst many find it difficult to discern where the college stops and the town begins. The town of Amherst is dominated by its colleges. With five major schools so close, it is a bustling student centre – a relief for those who find the Amherst campus and its students a little too limiting.

Amherst is also a perfect example of a Massachusetts town: pretty, puritanical and with strong literary and historical roots. It was here that the famous American poet, Emily Dickinson, locked herself up in her room for many years, churning out her poems (a situation that many come to relate to in their senior year).

Although Amherst is a relatively small town, its large student population means that most of your needs will be met. Cafés, restaurants and coffee shops abound, although by the end of four years you may feel that you have exhausted all social options. Amherst is situated about two hours' drive from Boston and three hours' from New York City.

But while people talk about taking weekend road-trips to these two cities, it rarely happens, especially once the long, cold, New England winter sets in. Amherst students tend to be of the type that is happiest to stick in one place and do not need the bustle of a big city to entertain themselves on a Saturday night. If you prefer clubs to charm and sun to snow, then this may not the place for you.

Getting In

AT A GLANCE – Application & Test Options:

– Early Decision, Regular Decision

– ACT/SAT required (both with writing recommended but not required)

– Amherst no longer requires the submission of two SAT Subject Tests, but applicants who wish to submit Subject Test results may do so.

Amherst may not be an official member of the Ivy League, but it is one of the "little Ivies" and its admissions process is as competitive as any that you are likely to meet in America. This is partly due to its size.

In recent years, over 8,000 have applied for around 450 places and only 13% are admitted. A strong application is thus vital. Amherst is like other colleges in requiring the SAT or ACT, but the SAT Subject tests are not necessary. A particular emphasis is placed on writing. This is a place where almost all subjects require a constant churning out of words and your application form is a good place to show your mastery of the English language!

Good scores aside, you will need to demonstrate another dazzling side to your character to stand a chance. The Amherst admissions officers are very particular in selecting students whom they think will suit the school. It is thus important to convey in your application why you know that Amherst is the place for you. There is no particular Amherst type, but a life outside academia and an ability to fit into a community are prerequisites. Bear in mind that Amherst does not offer any interviews so the application form is your one opportunity to show them what you are made of.

There is an Early Decision option available but you must be absolutely sure that this is the one place you want to go. Once you hear back from them, if you get in, the decision is legally binding. Also, if you have your heart set on a gap year, be reassured. Amherst is one of the few colleges to actively encourage this.

Money Matters

Amherst is one of the very few US schools to offer need-blind financial aid to international students, with a full ride if proven that it's needed.

Famous Grads

Clarence Birdseye – of Birdseye peas fame

Calvin Coolidge – US President

Albert Grimaldi – Prince of Monaco

Bard College

Annandale-on-Hudson, New York
www.bard.edu
Undergrads: 1,900
Grads: 600

How many Bard students does it take to change a light bulb?

One – but she'll only do it if it's an alternative light bulb.

Bard is perched on the edge of a small town overlooking the Hudson River in upstate New York, and is a college of liberal arts and sciences. Students here are focused on finding their place in the world, not just a career, and they are strongly encouraged to pursue personal as well as academic interests.

The Campus

Students sometimes moan about the claustrophobic size or the distant location of the school, but with the immense beauty of the campus it's difficult to pity them. The park-like grounds include two historic estates, more than 500 acres of fields and forested land, and views of the Hudson River below and the Catskill Mountains to the west.

And if you fancy a big city getaway, the train to NYC takes a little more than an hour and a half from nearby Rhinecliff.

The Bard Student

On the whole Bard is a fairly tight-knit community. Known as one of the most liberal in the country, the student body is famous for tolerance and welcomes a wide continuum of applicants across gender, sexuality, race (even political leaning). Bard students are known to be very involved politically and socially (evident from the number of protests and fundraisers) – they do not let the college bubble keep them from staying fiercely involved with events in the outside world.

Smoking (both tobacco and marijuana) is very prevalent and one of the main sources of complaint from students, and a few have had seriously unpleasant run-ins with substance abuse. The support network is largely respected and able to help in most situations.

Hitting the Books

Like most liberal arts colleges, Bard offers the bachelor of arts degree – with concentrations in more than 40 academic programmes in four divisions (arts, languages and literature; science, mathematics and computing; and social studies). The faculty – student ratio is 1:9, so students have all the advantages and perks of intimate classes and personal relationships with professors.

First years have a mandatory year-long general reading and writing course that covers great works and thinkers through history, studied chronologically, providing students with an invaluable breadth and background to their other studies.

A major Senior Year project forms the "capstone" for all students at Bard; this varies by department but generally provides scope for lengthy research, writing and even performance endeavours, critiqued by the faculty before the student is accepted to graduate.

Overall, academics are extremely rigorous but flexible, aiming to push students to be ambitious in their efforts and especially to develop their critical thinking faculties. Be warned that the traditional focus on arts and social sciences are increasingly being balanced by a new trend towards lab sciences for nonscientists.

Social Life

Although the campus is fairly isolated in terms of location, it's difficult to get claustrophobic – the overwhelming number of on-campus events provide plenty of opportunity to get out and find your passion. The annual Bard SummerScape and Bard Music Festival, both held on campus, are acclaimed arts events attracting top creators from around the world. Strong student music and theatre scenes help keep things buzzing the rest of the year.

There's also a range of great student-run newspapers, journals, zines, and even an all-purpose cafe/library/venue/"Infoshop" called the Root Cellar, home of vegan food, radical politics and egalitarian discussion groups. The healthy life style is rounded off by a range of campus sports (teams are known as the Bard Raptors), of which the most popular is, in fact, rugby (for both men and women).

Over half of Bard students study abroad for at least a semester. There are also great opportunities to spend time at Bard's affiliated (and often very intensive) programs at the Rockefeller University in NYC, or on the Globalization and International Affairs Program, which includes internships in international relations and human rights fields. Also in the Big Apple, the exciting and/or terrifying Bard Prison Initiative gives students the chance to volunteer at jails to tutor inmates.

Getting In

AT A GLANCE – Application & Test Options:

– Early Action, Early Decision, Regular Decision

– SAT/ACT Test-optional

Admission is fairly competitive (30% acceptance rate) but standardised testing (the SAT or ACT) is not one of the admission requirements - so if you're not a great test-taker, this may be a relief.

Money Matters

A large percentage of Bard students are given financial aid, all of which is need based, and many grants are available to international students. What's really great is that you are automatically considered for these when you apply, and they cover all four years of college (assuming you continue to meet the requirements).

Famous Grads

Chevy Chase – Comedian, writer, TV and film actor

Walter Becker – 'Steely Dan' musician

Howard Koch – screenwriter of 'Casablanca'

Chris Claremont – comic book writer, creator of Wolverine and many other great Marvel characters

Christopher Guest – actor (Spinal Tap, Princess Bride and more)

Barnard College

New York, New York
barnard.edu/
Undergrads: 2,390
Grads: 0

How many Barnard students does it take to change a light bulb?

Two – one to fetch it from Columbia University and one to find a way to integrate it into the Nine Ways of Knowing.

Barnard is a beautiful, tiny, girls-only Liberal Arts college. But there's a twist: Barnard is not in a tiny village somewhere in New England. Oh no, Barnard is in New York City itself. It's the Liberal Arts school with a difference, combining the great features of a broad curriculum and great teacher contact with the highly-charged insanity of life in the Big Apple.

Added to this, Barnard is right across the street from Ivy Leaguer Columbia University; the two are affiliated, and share classes and facilities, meaning access to all the juicy goodness of one of the best big universities in the country, as if the best big city in the country weren't enough.

The Campus

Blink and you'll miss it: the jumble of grandiose old buildings that forms Barnard is squashed into a tiny space about the size of one city block. The entrance is immediately opposite Columbia University on the other side of Broadway, and there's a convenient subway stop between the two. Despite being tiny, there is a TARDIS bigger-on-the-inside feeling once you enter, and there are a surprising number of facilities crammed in.

There are adequate sports facilities (including an indoor swimming pool), a smallish library (nice media centre though), and plenty of classrooms and labs, all connected by underground tunnels. Here, as in many parts of Barnard life, students benefit from their partnership with the Ivy League school across the street, where there are huge and high tech facilities of every kind for the taking, including a library system of over 12 million books, which Barnard students are granted access to.

One area where Barnard claims to have the edge over its larger cousin is the cafeteria, and as proof they cite the fact that the Columbia football team eat there (although one doubts that the quality of the food is the only reason for their choice...).

The newest addition to the landscape is the Diana Center, completed in 2010. This striking student center won ArchDaily's 2010 Building of the Year Award in Education and provides 70,000 extra square feet of classrooms, art studios, dining options, space for student organisations and a black box theatre.

Accommodation

The dorms house almost the entire student body – living is pleasantly communal, although study areas are available. Security is an issue for a girls' college in New York and the university takes it seriously, employing plenty of security guards and having all kinds of padlocks, bolts etc. on the doors. Crime isn't much of a problem though, probably because the school is in one of the safest neighbourhoods in the city.

The Barnard Woman

Each of Barnard's year groups consists of around 600 students – their only real similarity being their sex. Barnard prides itself on having a diverse community, incorporating every type of woman and providing them all with a place that allows them to grow in any way they choose.

Strong communities of every type exist on campus and whether you are a party girl or a library fan, you'll be sure to find a home. Furthermore, and definitely due to its gender composition, Barnard is known to be a very tolerant and politically active community. Thus it has been able to accommodate groups as diverse as the strong LGBT community or the many Orthodox Jews who can be found on campus.

This is part of Barnard's charm. Like the city it is situated in, it embraces all ways of thinking and then simply gets on with the affairs in hand. What's more, Barnard has the extra spice of geographical diversity; people come here from all across the country and beyond.

There is a strong community here, typical of Liberal Arts colleges, but living in New York tends to make students more independent-minded and confident – or perhaps it just attracts this type of person. In most pieces of university promotion and literature, they try to brand the students as powerful "leaders"; students claim that they can't be stereotyped, but in general are "focused" and "empowered". That is not to say that they are anywhere close to the typical image of a woman's college student – people are here for the academics and the city, not for the single-sex education.

Hitting the Books

Barnard is extremely committed to ensuring that its students have the best of all worlds – including the academic. Professors are excellent and put a lot of effort into their students. Small class sizes (student:faculty = 7:1!) mean that interaction with professors is straightforward and bonds are easily formed. There are no teaching assistants, at least none teaching entire courses, so no shortage of quality time spent with those who really know what they're talking about. About 50% of the faculty live within a few blocks of the campus anyway, so you often meet your teachers walking nearby.

The general education curriculum, typical of all Liberal Arts schools, is called 'the Nine Ways of Knowing' at Barnard, and officially incorporates the following areas: reason and value, social analysis, cultures in comparison, foreign language, laboratory science", quantitative and deductive reasoning, historical studies, literature and the performing arts. It's enthralling, high-powered stuff, although not necessarily suitable for those who know what they want to do and are keen to focus in on it right away.

Barnard's special relationship with Columbia is extremely beneficial. Barnard students are allowed to take as many classes as they want at Columbia, although they are quick to point out that there are just as many Columbia students who take classes at Barnard. The ability to take classes across the street is seriously advantageous, both because it provides access to the world-class professors and courses of an Ivy League institution, and because it broadens the range of courses on offer. Barnard does not offer any engineering classes, for example, while Columbia has nothing for those who want to do women's studies, but both are available to students from either school.

Academics at Barnard are strengthened by the internships and other positions that students are able to secure in the city. Apparently there are about 2,500 such positions available for Barnard students at various high-flying locations (newscasting, museum curating, political work at City Hall, etc.) and, considering there are only 2,400 students at the school, these seem like favourable odds. No wonder the *Princeton Review* rates the college as having the 10th "Best Career/Job Placement Services" in the US. New York is also often used by professors as an extension of class – trips into the city for a more practical application of knowledge are common.

Social Life

Students like to say that if Barnard is my home, then "Columbia is my front porch, and New York is my front yard". Students take full advantage of all three. The social life at Barnard is adaptable to the individual, depending on how much you opt to stay on campus or go exploring the biggest, most unique city in the world. "You can party every night if you want," said one student, "but you'd miss out on loads of the other things going on."

You can join sororities at Columbia, if that's your thing, although this is not very common. More popular are the range of student organisations, including creative groups of every description, student media and student government. There are some fun events too – most loved is the 'midnight breakfast', an odd tradition that involves a nocturnal feasting on breakfast foods on the night before the first exams.

Sports are surprisingly strong and 15 are offered at varsity level. The college is the only all-female university to have teams in Division One, but there are also plenty of intramurals and social sporting clubs on offer, too. The dance department at Barnard is renowned; there is an excellent (and popular) dance studio that offers several forms of performance dance and boasts several world-famous alumni.

Outside Those Ivory Walls

Once you leave campus, of course, the choices jump to a whole different plane. New York is practically limitless in what it offers to those who seek. As a Barnard student, moreover, you can get free or discounted tickets to hundreds of events. The university is not far from the gargantuan Central Park, and even closer to peaceful Riverside Park, which is always nice for a stroll or an escape from the intensity and traffic.

NYC has the best of everything – shopping, eating, drinking, parks, museums, famous sights, waterfronts, music, theatre, comedy, art – all a big hodgepodge of excitement, diversity and urban bustle among the ridiculously tall buildings on every street. The question is, what's not to do?

Be warned, however, that as great as it is, especially for students, New York is not a place for those who require hand-holding. It can be an anti-social, cut-throat city, and Barnard will not be guiding you through it step by step. Timid or insecure types might want to think twice before plunging in.

Getting In

AT A GLANCE – Application & Test Options:

- Early Decision, Regular Decision
- ACT/SAT required, sees full testing history
- SAT Subjects no longer required

Barnard is tough, admitting 17% of applicants in 2016, and you need a good application. Those who choose to go to Barnard must take the SAT or ACT test, but the university is not just looking at your scores, so try and make yourself seem well-balanced, interesting and generally an asset to the college environment in your personal essay. Interviews are optional, but recommended – check with the college to see if there are any overseas alumni willing to conduct one with you.

Money Matters

There are no merit scholarships awarded at Barnard to help with the high cost of attendance, but there are a small number of needs-based packages reserved for international students.

Famous Grads

Jhumpa Lahiri – hottest writer around

Joan Rivers – American comedienne

Martha Stewart – cooking, insider trading, in home and inmate decorating

Bennington College

Bennington , Vermont
www.bennington.edu
Undergrads: 690
Grads: 140

How many Bennington students does it take to change a light bulb?

Nine. One to screw in the light bulb, and the other eight to have a light bulb theme party around the event.

If you are free-spirited, liberal-minded and don't have an aversion to body hair or clogs then Bennington could be the place for you. It's known not only for its distinctly artsy student body and breathtakingly beautiful Vermont campus but also for the free hand that students have in planning and fulfilling their education. Taking responsibility for your own schooling is not for everyone but for the select 700 students that choose to do so, it is a liberating and deeply engaging experience.

The Campus

Once you visit this 550-acre haven in southern Vermont it's difficult not to fall in love with the place. Seated on a hill-top just above the small town of Bennington, the college campus has outstanding views of the Green Mountains, plenty of space for roaming, and rural touches that give evidence of its beginnings as a farm. Even the main academic building was once a barn and is still referred to as such.

Although there are some wonderful modern facilities such as the Meyer Recreation Barn, the newly-opened Center for the Advancement of Public Action (CAPA), and the Student Center (which houses a café, snack bar, pub, and concert venue), the aspects of the campus which visitors and students are most taken by are its quaint New England-y features.

Accommodation

If someone dropped you down in the midst of Bennington's original dorm buildings, you'd think you were in some cosy little residential neighbourhood during the middle of the last century. These eleven Colonial style cottages look and feel more like homes than college housing to the 30-odd students that reside in each one, lined up and down the "streets" that surround the main green space of the campus, which is referred to as The End of The World.

There are also more modern options available (as well as one off-campus cooperative living house in the nearby hamlet of North Bennington) but no matter what style you choose, your dorm building will have students from all year groups under the same roof, since on-campus housing is provided for all four years and there is no such thing as a "freshman-only" house. This arrangement opens the door to early friendships with upper classmen, who can take you under their wing (or help you to secure the right beverages for your party).

The Bennington Student

Though most students tend to hail from the East Coast or California, the individuals you see roaming the campus are often from a world of their own. Exotic hair colours, face paint, dreadlocks, piercings, homemade clothes, or no clothes at all are fairly common sights – however there is also a fair share of hipsters and Vermont farmer types.

It's been said that Bennington is the place where people who were outcasts or freaks in high school go in order to be in the majority. In any event, it's hard to find many people you would call mainstream. And even though all types of people are able to find their place in this school, you won't find many Republicans (in the American political sense), churchgoers, math-enthusiasts, fraternity bros, or preppy athletes.

A majority of the student body is on financial aid but it is nearly impossible to tell the difference between those paying full-tuition and those paying nothing – wealth is not something that is obvious or even discussed here. Walking through the dining hall, you sense there are distinct social groups – this is hard to avoid in such a small community – however it does not feel cliquey, and because of the small class sizes and housing environments it's easy to weave your way through several different social circles.

There are fewer men than women on this campus, which is a source of frustration, dysfunction, and incestuous dating situations, but Williams is a short drive away and it's not unusual to head south to find men.

Hitting the Books

There are no required courses or 101-classes – instead, highly specific, probing seminars that are created based on the students' needs and the professors' interests. It's unlikely you will ever find yourself in a Bennington classroom where the teacher or any student is not engaged with the topic.

Each term the school publishes a relatively short list of course options (especially compared to the larger universities), but each one sounds more interesting than the next – probably because they are designed around a particular theme by professors who are passionate about their subject. Bennington professors and students alike are given a great deal of intellectual freedom and choice. As a result the classroom debates are marked by enthusiasm, curiosity and multidisciplinary input.

During their four years at the college each student integrates different areas of the curriculum that are of interest to them around a central idea or question – this ultimately results in their Plan, Bennington's equivalent to a major. Once this is declared in the middle of the second year, students must be actively responsible for planning their classes and then developing their final paper that will fulfil this plan.

The intensity and independent nature of the work has been said to produce students that are at times a little self-focused. However, at the end of the day, ample support from the faculty and the close-knit nature of the community reinforces the feeling that everyone is working together. Bennington also emphasises learning through experience – hence the seven week off-campus Field Work Term (FWT) required every January and February. This is not a new idea; FWT has been a central part of Bennington's educational requirements since the College was founded. Through their own contacts or with help from the school, students find work (paid or volunteer) in a variety of fields and in locations around the world, pursuing interests they've developed at Bennington, getting practical experience and making professional connections – and they do this for each of the four years.

Despite strengths in many different academic fields, many students declare, with either great enthusiasm or resentment, that Bennington seems like an art school. It's hard to deny the focus on the arts, especially when you step inside the Visual and Performing Arts Centre (aka VAPA). It's open 24 hours a day and any student, regardless of their academic focus, can use the facilities or take a class in architecture, drawing and painting, printmaking, film and video, photography, and digital design. Performing arts are also strong, partly based on legacy – Martha Graham taught here in the 1930s and made Bennington the center of experimental dance in America at that time.

Bennington may stand out as a highly creative, arts-oriented environment. However, the 'Plans' completed by Bennington students before they graduate address issues across all the traditional academic fields and, if anything, are just more enlightened by the colourful mix of disciplines informing them.

Social Life

Bennington is a bit of a bubble, plain and simple, but you can flourish within this bubble in ways that would be hard to find in the real world. Bennington claims to be the birthplace of "the themed party". If so, they're working hard to keep up the tradition: there are a number of creative soirees hosted every weekend in the dorm common rooms that are generally open to the whole school. Students hold parties with names like Daddy Daughter Dance, Bacchanal, Prom, Dr Seuss, Risky Business, Outer Space Ocean, Mardi Gras, Roll-o-Rama, Ultraviolet Masquerade as well as lots of plays, gigs, and opportunities for contra dance.

The absence of Greek life or competitive sports means that most of the student population are involved in more alternative methods of fun, usually of their own making (how about tea parties, didgeridoo building, or tree-climbing, anyone?). The town of Bennington is a short car ride away, but the amount of social activity on campus begs the question, why would you even want to leave? Although this is certainly not a healthy way to live your life in the long-term, for four years students have a culturally rich, busy, and exciting microcosm on their doorstep.

Outside Those Ivory Walls

Despite the sheer beauty of the college and the number and variety of activities on offer, some students are turned off by the remoteness of the campus. The local town of Bennington has three bars and several mid-price restaurants, but that's about it so many students go to the nearby Williamstown (Massachusetts), Manchester (Vermont), or Albany (NY) for night life. New York City and Boston are both around a three-hour drive for anyone seeking a big city getaway, and NYC is also reachable by train (two hours and 40 minutes from nearby Albany).

On the other hand, if you are fond of the laid-back country lifestyle of southern Vermont, there is no need to go anywhere. There are mountains to climb, lakes to swim, forests to explore, cheese farms to tour, swimming holes to dip in, and quiet cafes where you can escape to for a good cup of coffee, some local maple delicacies, and a comfy seat to do your reading in.

Getting In

AT A GLANCE – Application & Test Options:

– Early Action, Early Decision, Early Decision II, Regular Decision

– ACT/SAT strongly recommended but not required for international students

Bennington is considered a selective school and getting more so, especially considering that the freshman class has fewer than 200 members. But if they feel you can handle the freedom and responsibility of planning your own education as well as contribute something to the community, you will have an advantage regardless of your SAT test scores (which are not required).

Bennington accepts the Common App, but their supplemental application involves several intensive personal essays. An interview is required, but this can be conducted on campus, around the country (sometimes overseas), or over the phone.

Money Matters

Bennington is amongst the most expensive schools in the US but there are a limited number of financial aid packages for international students – typically consisting of a grant and/or loan, and an allocation for campus employment. This funding is awarded based on both a student's financial need and the merit of his or her application.

Famous Grads

Peter Dinklage – aka Tyrion Lannister ("Game of Thrones")

Alan Arkin – actor

Bret Easton Ellis – wunderkind author of "American Psycho"

Boston University

Boston, Massachusetts
www.bu.edu
Undergrads: 18,000
Grads: 14,000

How many Boston Uni students does it take to change a light bulb?

28 – one to buy it from the CVS across the street, one to dedicate it to Martin Luther King, one to throw it spitefully at Harvard, and 25 to have a celebratory party in Allston.

Boston is a city full of universities. On just one short stretch of metro line you can get off at Harvard, MIT and Tufts, to name just three world-class institutions. While Boston University's reputation isn't quite up there with those luminaries, it's only a short way behind – and gaining. And what it lacks in prestige it more than makes up for in the invigorating educational experience you'll receive in one of America's most dazzling (and oldest) cities. It's not surprising that Martin Luther King started the history-changing Civil Rights Movement after finishing his PhD here.

The Campus

Most people think that Boston University doesn't actually have a campus. It's certainly hard to spot it – a lot of people walk through the whole thing thinking that they're just in an interesting part of town. But actually the jumbled stretch of buildings all the way down Commonwealth Avenue from the city down towards the hip-again neighbourhood of Allston is owned by the University and used for the purposes of its students.

Commonwealth Ave runs parallel to the rather lovely Charles River. A ribbon of park land runs between the university and the river, ironically named the BU Beach, and students are known to sunbathe there in summer. Mostly it's used for jogging and contemplating one's hatred of Harvard and MIT, which sit smugly on the opposite bank.

"It really feels like you're in a city, the whole time", say the students, who love its urbanity. It's one of BU's main advantages over some of the big name universities, where you might get better teaching but you won't (or so the BU students claim) have as fulfilling an education, due to being isolated on some too-perfect campus away from the real world.

Having a city campus doesn't mean that BU is poorly equipped, however. The library is great, and the huge gym is loved by one and all.

Accommodation

The dorms are "on the whole, pretty good"; some of the older ones allocated to freshmen can err on the dingy side, while some of the new apartment-style complexes are luxurious. Now home to 76% of the undergraduate population, the accommodation system at BU is the 10th largest in the country, and the university officially guarantees dorm space to everyone for four years. Many upperclassmen, however, move off to cheaper or trendier areas.

The BU Student

With a diverse, urban, and humongous student body (fourth biggest private school in the country), every kind of student thrives here, and they can all do their own thing with other people like them. There is a certain level of cliquiness, and you can point to certain groups that are more noticeable than others – the hipsters, the Asians, the rich kids, the "bros", to name a few – but "you just can't say what a BU student is like". The good news is that there are a large number of international students at BU who fit in well and are a great asset to the college atmosphere.

Unlike similar schools, there is not much of a school spirit at BU, perhaps a result of the more independent natures of the students, but more likely because sports aren't big and it doesn't have a decent (American) football team. Hockey is popular though, and victories are greeted with major celebrations. BU's official mascot is Rhett the Boston Terrier and the school colours are scarlet and white. The mascot is named Rhett as a reference to Gone With the Wind, because "no one loves Scarlet more than Rhett."

As a very city-oriented school, BU students' attitudes are shaped a lot by Boston itself. Ironically, this probably makes them more collegiate and friendly, if anything, because Boston is the mega-college town. An extraordinarily high percentage of the people you see on the street are in their twenties or younger, and so the whole city, of which BU is an active member, feels liberal, switched-on and often artsy and alternative. Students describe themselves as "worldly" and "knowledgeable", and also "charity oriented". They also know how to have a good time...

There are a large number of international students at BU who fit in well and are a great asset to the college atmosphere.

Hitting the Books

Academics are managed through various colleges – the colleges of arts and sciences, general studies, management, engineering, education, communications, and fine arts being the main ones. Arts and sciences obviously covers most of the basic courses, with the college of general studies being a slightly narrower, simpler version for people who aren't sure what they want to study.

Problems can arise when you try to switch college – if you are studying Japanese in the college of arts and sciences but then wish to change to Oriental media studies, which falls under the jurisdiction of the college of communications, be prepared for bureaucratic shenanigans before you are able to do so.

Red tape aside, classes at BU are challenging and "high quality", though students prefer the professors to the curriculum. The former are "helpful", "well-renowned", "have real world experience", and "fantastic", while the latter can be frustrating. Overall, the experience is positive, and most students are intelligent, work hard and enjoy their studies. "You can definitely form bonds with your professors", said one student (no small achievement for a school of BU's size) "and a wide range of well-taught classes means there's always something interesting on offer".

One drawback that gets mentioned is the "narrow minded" curricula that sometimes don't allow for much exploration or wiggle-room, but which professors are good at dealing with. "The things you have to learn are often not that worthwhile", complained a freshman, "but teachers can just circumvent this".

Another problem is competitiveness. BU students agree that they suffer from terrible grade deflation (unlike the kids at Harvard who, they claim, have their grades artificially boosted). This means that people have to struggle harder to get the grades they need, and they know that they do better if their peers do worse. "The academic system turns people against each other", said a science major.

Social Life

As a student in her last year summed it up: "if you are city person, this is definitely the place to be." While there is a campus life at BU, most students get their kicks from what Boston itself has to offer. The combined possibilities are eclectic and include almost anything you could want to do, especially in cultural areas. Be warned though – "there is no coddling" here, so if you need your hand held then you might want to look elsewhere, since some students do slip through the cracks.

On campus, there are hundreds of student organisations, dozens of students newspapers, a small Greek life, a strong music, art and drama scene, MUN conferences, free performances by students and visiting entertainers, and some great events, such as the famous dance marathon, which draw huge turnouts. Also popular are the big name guest speakers, such as Barack Obama, who spoke to 5,000 students at BU during his presidential campaign.

Nightlife is a big part of the social scene. While students deny that BU is a party school, they do say that "people like to go out and unwind after a day of hard work", and there is of course the contingent of folks who get "so wasted, all the time". For the more debaucherous side of things, you should head into Allston, the grimy but vibrant neighbourhood west of campus.

Outside Those Ivory Walls

Boston is one of the oldest and most liberal cities in America. With a fascinating historic old-town, an attractive harbour (just don't ask about Tea Parties...), a big leafy park called Boston Common, and some incredible street performers, it's a lovely place to live.

As a student, it's even better; the number of universities in the city means that the great shopping, eating and performance venues generally cater to students, and all kinds of interesting alternative and not-so-alternative districts and outlets have sprung up all around the city. Health warning: the summers are hot and sticky and the winters Siberian.

The Fenway-Kenmore and Brookline parts of town, known for their great shopping, artsy-intellectual spots and world-class museums, are very close to BU. Across the river is Cambridge, with more museums, shops and galleries (and universities).

Getting In

AT A GLANCE – Application & Test Options:

– Early Decision, Early Decision II, Regular Decision

– ACT/SAT required (both with Writing/essay recommended but not required)

– College of Fine Arts does not require SAT/ACT

The admissions team is looking for interesting students who will help create a diverse and exciting student body. All the normal factors are considered, with perhaps particular emphasis on your secondary school record. But they're not just looking at your test scores, they want to know about all your extra-curriculars: arts, sports, volunteer work are crucial. Getting in is not a breeze; while one third of applicants manage it, much of your competition will have applied to even tougher Boston schools like Harvard and MIT.

Money Matters

Boston University is one of the most expensive schools in the country – total fees topped $65,000 for the 2017-18 academic year (including room and board). International applicants are not eligible for needs-based aid, but there are a good number of scholarships on offer, including a few special ones aimed at engineers, if that's your thing.

Famous Grads

Rev. Dr. Martin Luther King Jr. – the Nobel Peace Prize-winning civil rights activist did his PhD here

Joan Baez – iconic folk singer, worked with Bob Dylan, sang at Woodstock

Yunjin Kim – actress, Lost (TV series), nicknamed "The Korean Julia Roberts"

Brown University

Providence, Rhode Island
www.brown.edu
Undergrads: 2000
Grads:

How many students does it take to change a light bulb at Brown?

Eleven – one to change the light bulb and ten to share the experience.

Do you have a hint of Eurotrash in your character? Or do you prefer hugging trees and making your own clothes? Whether you tend towards the jet set or the hippy, Brown University provides a liberal and all-encompassing campus environment with a prestigious academic reputation. In recent years this combination has attracted an increasing number of Brits to a school that is widely regarded as one of the best, and most fun, on the East Coast.

The Campus

Brown is situated at the top of the steep College Hill, quite a climb from the town of Providence below. Fortunately for the chronically unfit or lazy, regular and cheap trolley buses connect the two. The views down over the city are great but the location means that freezing winds make even the most hardened students wince. In fact, Brown, along with its sister New England colleges, is NOT the place to come if you are a sun lover. For 70% (at least) of the months you spend in school, there will be varieties of snow, ice, rain and wind that make a 'bad winter' in Great Britain seem like springtime in comparison.

Accommodation

Brown follows the New England trend – a beautiful campus, old brick buildings, the occasional bell tower. Founded in its present location in 1770, the campus is centred around the College Green. It is a charming, almost picture-perfect place – the type that producers of the typical East Coast college movie dream about. As a result most students will find themselves living in pretty housing. Some privileged first-years are even situated on 'the Green' in accommodation that rivals that of the most beautiful Oxbridge colleges.

Of course Brown also has its share of notoriously monstrous pieces of architecture where an unfortunate few of you may end up living. The prime example is the concrete, moated Grad Center, designed to contain any student riots (Brown is a politically active place) and definitely the most confusing building on campus.

The Brunonian

When Brown opened its doors to students in the late 1700s, it was the only one of the then seven colleges in the United States to embrace individuals of all religious persuasions. More recently it was the first American college to elect an African-American woman as its President. Diversity and liberalism are the cornerstones of the Brown mentality. As a result there is really no such thing as the average Brown student. Unlike the homogenous, Abercrombie and Fitch clad crowds that throng such campuses as Princeton, Brown genuinely succeeds in attracting students from a multitude of backgrounds.

This is particularly true as regards ethnic and geographical diversity. Brown's campus resembles nothing so much as a huge Benetton ad – with students of all colours, styles and characters. The admissions office makes a special effort to bring in students from across the States and further afield. Almost 30% of each class are minority students and 10% of the student body is international. As a British student you can thus rest assured that you will not be regarded as a creature from outer space but as an essential part of the diversity in which Brown glories.

Once you enter the hallowed gates, the average Brown man (or woman) enjoys the reputation of being extremely tolerant. There are so many different types of people on campus that the eccentric habits and quirks of each are generally accepted by all the others. The Brown system of placing freshmen in units of 40-60 people and always with a roommate quickly accelerates the process of meeting a wide variety of people. And even if individuals do tend to segregate into cliques in their sophomore year, their initial exposure to a diverse group stands them in good stead.

That is not to say that there is not some degree of segregation at Brown. Perhaps because there are so many different types of students, it is always easy for individuals to find like-minded peers. These social groups can become rather insular and some Brown students complain of being solely associated with groups just because they happen to be aspiring thespians or of Asian extraction. The presence of fraternity (Greek) houses on campus also leads to a certain amount of self-segregation within the student body. However, the Brown administration does take steps to promote inclusion and equal access. One example of this effort is that all fraternity parties held at Brown must be open to every student on campus. No door is ever shut in the face of a Brunonian unless he chooses to close it himself.

Brown is known for being one of the most politically active of the East Coast colleges. Students who apply there tend to be liberal and pretty passionate (and vocal) about their beliefs. If you are a die-hard conservative who believes that George Bush was the best thing since sliced bread, then Brown may not be the perfect place for you – unless of course you relish political debate. For the most part, however, political beliefs of all kinds tend to be tolerated and everyone seems to rub along together. Major national and international issues – such as American action in the Middle East – may draw out large groups of protestors but for the most part it is only the hardened activists who stand out on a daily basis.

Hitting the Books

Choice. Freedom. Choice. This would surely be a better motto for the Brown shield than the somewhat clichéd 'In Deo Speramus'. Brown stands out from other universities due to the flexibility, or indeed absence, of its academic requirements. Students are expected to choose their own path, not plod along the one laid out for them some hundred years before. The official line is that each individual is the 'architect' of his or her educational experience. If you are the kind of person in possession of a great deal of personal motivation and initiative, then the Brown system can make you the architect of great things. If, however, you need strong academic guidance and supervision then your own piece of Brunonian architecture could turn out more hut-like than palatial.

Brown has no core requirements. For some British students this can be a great thing. If after your GCSEs, you swore that never again would you look at a chemical equation or critique a sonnet, this flexibility seems the ideal situation. The courses are there if you want to take them but you are never compelled to do so.

Yet this can also be a bad thing. One of the facets of the American educational system that draws Brits across the pond is the fact that it insists on maintaining the breadth of its liberal arts reputation. Unlike the unbending focus of the British universities, American colleges believe that a broad base of knowledge is important to one's education. And, even if you protest, the majority of American schools, with their core requirements, insist on it anyway. The fact that Brown allows you to circumnavigate this part of the liberal arts education is great for those who would prefer to embrace it in their own way. Yet for those who will not, it can erase an important part of the American educational experience.

Brown's only requirements are that a student passes thirty classes and takes at least eight that qualify them for a major. Each major has different requirements so some students will end up taking the vast majority of their courses in a specific area. The lack of initial core requirements allows students to experiment within the different departments before deciding on the direction they wish to pursue. Throughout their college experience they are provided with advisors who help them to formulate plans and make decisions.

Brown students definitely have a lot of personal contact with their professors– the student-faculty ratio is 9:1. Although Brown does have a graduate school it is the undergrad body that attracts the most focus – a far cry from some of the bigger research institutions in the United States. Relationships between professor and student are notably relaxed – often on a first name basis. This interaction is something that many British universities simply do not offer. Brown prides itself on its small class sizes (70% of classes have fewer than 20 students) and in such an environment there is a chance to develop a real relationship with those instructing you. As has been mentioned, Brown is a place that believes in self-vocalization and class discussion and participation is normally an important part of one's grade.

And speaking of grades... one of the unique and, to many, very attractive things about the Brown academic system is the ability to take any class that you want on a pass/fail (or S/NC – Satisfactory/No Credit) basis. The idea behind this is that it gives the students a chance to experiment. Those history of art majors with a sudden interest in biochem can take the course without fearing their letter grade. Some abuse this system – taking classes without doing any of the work – but for the most part it is another good example of the way in which Brown gives its students as much flexibility as possible.

Brown has not escaped the taint of grade inflation that has dragged such schools as Harvard into recent media attacks. Grades on campus seldom fall below a B and are often higher. Anything below a C is a fail – although students can withdraw from classes at the very last moment and it would be a real achievement to actually fail out. The university also never releases these grades to the outside world – another means of encouraging students to experiment and reducing academic pressure.

Brown students are often laughed at by their Ivy League peers for being slackers who never have to fulfil any real requirements. Yet the academic standards, resources and professor accessibility at Brown are as high as at any of its contemporaries. It is the flexibility of the system that leads to this reputation. Those who need a more rigorous academic structure should probably avoid Brown, but for those who like to follow their own paths while always having support behind them, the Brown experience is a great one.

Social Life

Brown is known for being a fun place. It caters to all social preferences whether they involve hard-core socializing or an evening spent in a coffee house with two friends. The campus itself has a number of fraternities – both of the traditional Greek variety and individual co-ed, Jewish or literary equivalents. Around 10% of students on campus are involved with one of these. The parties they throw every weekend are always open to all, but most students prefer to forge their own social lives. There is always something to do at night at Brown – although many students favour smaller gatherings to the keg stands and noise of these larger parties.

The campus itself offers the entertainments of the busy Thayer Street – a social centre for Brown students looking for companionship and caffeine. If this becomes too boring, then there is always the alternative venue of Providence – a city that offers students good restaurants, jazz and fun clubs. Off-campus parties are also extremely popular – fewer people and fewer rules often making them more attractive than the parties held on Brown's campus. Europeans (many of whom are British and Greek) tend to dominate certain parts of the Brown social scene and clubs such as Viva have become an East Coast substitute for the lures of Chinawhite's.

No Brit should expect their American social experience to be akin to their friends drinking their way through the British universities. Even at Brown, a place known for its fun environment, ID checking can be strict – one of the least fun parts of New England life. There is also no real long-term dating scene. You may see many of your friends back home in near-marriage type situations, but Brown students state that those in long-term relationships are in the minority on campus.

Brown students do tend, like all Americans, to get involved in a large number of extra-curricular activities. Perhaps owing to the Brunonian's liberal slant, many of these involve social service of one kind or another. There are also great campus publications, a strong dramatic and musical presence, a well-regarded radio station and, of course, numerous political and social action groups. There are also a large amount of varsity sports available on campus.

While the opportunities available at Brown are plenty, many students moan about the lack of financial resources. Brown is a relatively poor university – nowhere near the British equivalent of poor – but still lacking the endowment of its Ivy League peers. As a result some of the facilities have suffered. There is no concert hall and the sports facilities are badly situated and somewhat run-down. The food also enjoys a below par reputation – although for those of us whose taste buds were annihilated long ago by British school dinners this should not be such a problem. This shortage of cash also affects the size of the financial aid package available to its applicants.

Despite this, however, Brown has become an increasingly popular destination for pond-hopping Brits over the past few years. This is perhaps encouraged by its reputation as one of the most fun of the prestigious Ivy League schools. Whatever the reason, the Brown campus is crowded with wealthy Europeans and Americans, sailing types who want to take advantage of Newport and party types who want to take advantage of the fun night life.

Outside Those Ivory Walls

Providence, Rhode Island is a place on the up and up. Considered one of the least polluted and safest city in the nation, it provides a welcome social alternative for Brown students. Many, in fact, choose to stay there after graduation – true testimony to the charms of the place. Recently there has been a large effort to rebuild downtown Providence – an initiative that has increased its appeal as one of the most attractive New England cities. While it lacks the size and national clout of New York and Boston, Providence is known for having great restaurants (probably due to its large Italian population), fun clubs and a strong musical reputation. Jazz, pop singers and student bands all enjoy large and enthusiastic audiences.

Brown students love Providence because it provides them with a metropolitan alternative to campus life while avoiding the hectic pace of bigger cities. Brown's location just above the town also gives students the chance to have an urban college experience without losing the campus feel. The presence of the prestigious art school RISD (Rhode Island School of Design) just down the hill from Brown also adds to the fun, student atmosphere of the city, and there is a fair amount of communication between the two schools. Should you feel the need to escape, there are easy bus and train services to both Boston (one hour) and New York (four hours).

Getting In

AT A GLANCE – Application & Test Options:

- Early Decision, Regular Decision
- ACT/SAT with Writing/essay required
- Two SAT subject tests recommended but not required

Admittance is tough – and getting tougher. The number of applications has increased dramatically In the past couple of years, such that in 2016 over 30,000 students applied for a place – and just under 2,800 were accepted (9%). The admissions process is a challenging one. Not only are high academic standards expected (the majority of admitted students score at least 1400 on the SAT Test), but the admissions office also seeks out those students with diverse interests or qualities that stand out from the crowd.

Applicants are expected to take the SAT or ACT and two SAT Subject tests are recommended. There is also the opportunity (recommended but not required) to have an interview with Brown alumnae. They will get in contact with you and there are normally a fair amount of them scattered around the UK. These interviews also give you an opportunity to ask about Brown.

Perhaps the most important part of the admissions process is the Brown Supplement, which you are asked to submit prior to filling out the full Common App document. It asks you for bits of information about your background, interests and motivation – via short answers and essays. Every school claims that it is looking beyond academics to the individual and this is certainly true to an extent. At Brown, however, the Supplement really is an essential part of the admissions process and gives you a great chance to promote your own thoughts, ideas and personality. Bear in mind that admissions officials want to see things that distinguish you from the crowd of other eager applicants.

As with most universities, Brown has both an Early Decision option and a Regular Decision plan. Its website offers more information on current deadlines for these.

Money Matters

There is a limited, and definitely not plentiful, amount of financial aid available for international students. It MUST be applied for at the time of admission – all later applications are simply dismissed.

Famous Grads

John D. Rockefeller, Jr – philanthropist extraordinaire

JFK, Jr – journalist – just as cool as his father, and as tragic

Kenneth Starr – you too could prosecute Bill Clinton

Columbia University

New York, New York
www.columbia.edu
Undergrads: 8,000
Grads: 7,000

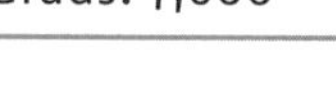

How many students does it take to change a light bulb at Columbia?

Seventy-six – one to change the light bulb, fifty to protest the light bulb's right not to change, and twenty-five to hold a counter-protest.

New York, New York. For those who crave the bright lights of the big city, there is no better place to go to university. And there is no better university than Columbia, the urbanite darling of the Ivy League. Columbia not only offers you immediate access to every metropolitan resource you can imagine, it manages to combine this with a campus that makes you part of a college community.

And, when you're not out exploring Soho or jogging in Central Park, you are busy struggling with the homework that makes this one of the top educational institutions in America. With strong academics, great school spirit and one of the most exhilarating environments in the world, this is a school where Saturday nights will never be dull.

The Campus

Columbia was founded in 1754, making it the fifth oldest college in the US. It was initially named King's College, but after the Yankees decided they were better off without the Brits, its name was changed to reflect the roots of America.

When it began, New York was far from the bustling city it is today and Columbia was situated in what would now pass for the countryside. This may be the reason for the spacious campus environment, an unusual quality in a college surrounded by the big city. Students who crave the American-college feel will not lack quads, old brick buildings and beautiful architecture – Columbia has managed to embark on the new without getting rid of the old.

Brits should, however, be warned that if they are searching for an old world East Coast campus feel, Columbia may prove a disappointment. The university is a huge institution which encompasses fifteen different undergrad and grad schools on its extensive Morningside Heights campus.

As a result, it feels like a little oasis of student life amid the stresses and strains of an adult city. Most of the faces in your immediate environment will be young ones and the area is shaped by the students who live in it. Columbia College – the undergraduate school of Columbia University – is small enough to have a real sense of community, but its existence inside a vast university means there are always new people to meet. And, for those men who get sick of Columbia girls, the close affiliation with the all-female Barnard College offers whole new avenues of exploration!

Accommodation

Students enjoy life on the Columbia campus so much that 90% of them choose to live there for their entire college career. Columbia has great housing and 60% of students are guaranteed a single room. It may seem strange by British standards but in America it is not unheard of to live in doubles for most of your college career.

Most freshmen at Columbia choose to live in either Carman Hall or John Jay – buildings that inevitably turn into social centres for that class. On-campus accommodation is definitely the way to go – after all, who wants to pay the extortionate housing prices of NYC?

The Columbian

It takes a certain type of person to thrive at Columbia. New Yorkers are known for being as tough as they come and life at New York's top university follows this trend. Many quiet country mice will be turned off by the overwhelming nature of the big city, the constant noise, and the proximity of Harlem – historically one of the least affluent and most crime-ridden areas of Manhattan. Now, however, the neighbourhood around Columbia is expensive, trendy and firmly part of the Upper West side. To such an extent that it's felt the campus no longer feels so much like an "island of safety", resulting in the loss of some of its cultural identity.

Nor is this a school where the administration is prepared to baby you along. Columbia students (like thousands of their contemporaries) moan about the amount of work they are expected to do, the number of courses they have to take and the fact that the faculty expects a constant and high-level of commitment from them. Yet when questioned, they fiercely defend their school. It seems that those who survive that initial 'sink or swim' feeling, grow to love and appreciate both Columbia and New York for the independence their 'tough-love' approach inspires.

Although Columbia produces a class of highly independent and determined individuals with degrees in street smarts as well as academics, it does offer them a certain amount of help along the way. Columbia is well-known for the superiority of its advising system. This extends from the faculty to the in-dorm assistants, ensuring that you always have a place to go to with any questions. Columbia also has a nationally famous website 'Go Ask Alice' that answers any questions about sex, drugs, alcohol and general student debauchery that you could possibly think of posing.

Columbia students like to work hard but they also like to play hard. Luckily this is a university that offers them the opportunity to do both. Columbia has great resources, great teaching and about a million and one extra-curricular pursuits that you can get involved in. Whether you are playing in orchestras, ripping up the sports pitches or taking part in the huge social action programmes that work with New Yorkers, chances are your schedule will fill up within days of arriving on campus.

The Columbia atmosphere is not for the laid-back. The bustle of the busiest city in the world is right outside your doorstep and even the laziest students are energized by it. Furthermore, Columbia actively expects you to do more in life than academics (something that some of the more uptight East Coast universities could learn from). It is thus perfectly possible to take five classes, belong to two clubs and one sports team and still enjoy an active social life. Be warned though – your eight hours' sleep a night might suffer slightly!

One of the nicest things about Columbia is the amount of school spirit its students have. While students at colleges that bask at the top of the Ivy Leagues routinely bitch about their academic institutions, students at Columbia, a school that is normally ranked slightly lower, rave about their university. School events such as Homecoming (another of those bizarre American occasions involving sports teams and beer) help to increase this sense of belonging to the community.

After all, how difficult is it to sport what has to be one of the nicest university colours (a perfect baby blue) and gather around one of the coolest university football symbols (the lion)? Columbia students even managed to remain enthusiastic when their football team hit the infamous 'Streak' of failure back in the 1980s – forty-five losses in a row! And in a sense this sums up the

Columbian student – enthusiastic, optimistic and determined to succeed in a high-pressure and demanding environment.

Hitting the Books

Columbia College enjoys the unique position of maintaining an intimate academic community within a major and wealthy university. As such its undergraduates have access to all the resources they could possibly want – including strings of research labs and an impressive college library.

Yet, at the same time, they work in small classroom settings – around 70% of the classes have under twenty students – and thus benefit from actually getting the attention of the professor. Sometimes this attention may seem a little much, especially for those British students who prefer to hide in the back of a large lecture hall. With a student-faculty ratio of 7:1, there is little escape – a disadvantage for those students hoping to breeze their way through college but, ultimately, one of Columbia's biggest strengths.

For while NYC offers Columbia students the chance to play hard, the faculty also expect them to work hard. This is a competitive environment and requires a certain amount of dedication. For one thing, Columbia students take five classes a semester, one more than the average number, and a significant juggling feat for those Brits who are used to specialising.

But while the moans may go up around campus, this curriculum actually allows Columbian students a huge degree of flexibility in choosing their courses. The most popular majors include English, History and Politics but many students choose to double major. The ultra-talented, and ultra-efficient, may even find time to do joint degrees with either the fantastic Juilliard school of music or the school of engineering.

Some Columbia students complain about the bureaucracy of their academic system and state that the individual student has to be both assertive and energetic in finding out what they want to do. Columbia does not baby its students but, clichéd as it sounds, the more you put in, the more you get out.

And, of course, you get to do it all in a centre that could not be more conducive to academic learning. Whether you're taking a history course, studying Egyptian art or struggling with the finer points of physics, New York is guaranteed to have a library, organization or exhibition just for you.

Core curricula are the dread of many British students headed across the Atlantic. After all who wants to take more maths after finishing GCSEs? Columbia, however, is renowned for core classes which pride themselves on stimulating their students in intellectual discussion about the matters that are truly important to the world. This may all seem a bit pretentious, but students rave about the small seminars and the chance they get to pick apart the world's great philosophers, writers, artists and politicians on a weekly basis.

This core curriculum spreads over the first two years and consists of an initial course in Literature Humanities (affectionately known as Lit. Hum.), and a sophomore course in Contemporary Civilization (CC). These courses are backed up with foreign language, science, music and writing classes.

One of the great things about an American education is that it takes you in knowing nothing and spits you out knowing at least a little bit of everything. Columbia is the master at this and many would argue there is no better or more comprehensive core education available. And, to top it all off, you even get to do a year of mandatory PE – just when you thought you had left aerobics behind you for good!

Social Life

Columbia College offers a diverse community within a diverse city. Thus, whether your ideal Saturday night is spent at off-beat poetry readings fuelled by small black espressos, or at the most fashionable nightclubs fuelled by something even stronger, you are sure to find both the people and the place.

New York City offers Columbia students a plethora of opportunities and, more importantly, the chance to kick off the campus dust from their heels and explore the wider world whenever they choose. And when they prefer to stay at home, Morningside Heights offers the typical student run of coffee shops, pizza parlours and cheap bars. These provide those crucial meeting points for the weekday nights when you are just dying to escape your dorm room. Luckily the close community in the Columbia dorms means you are guaranteed other people to procrastinate with.

Columbia does have a Greek scene – not as strong as that of the Southern schools – but still an important part of the university experience. This is nice in so much as it provides you with a social forum that is open only to undergraduate students – giving you a chance to bond with your classmates.

There are twenty-two Greek organizations at Columbia, and the College estimates that about 10% of its students are affiliated with them. Aside from the parties, keg stands and eternal brother/sisterhood, these frats and sororities also often offer an alternative place to base your social life. Many of them own pretty NY brownstone houses in the immediate area – allowing you to stumble out of the party and be home in five minutes.

Outside Those Ivory Walls

There is no better selling point for Columbia than New York City. This is truly a town that never sleeps and Columbia students have it all on their doorstep. Whether you want to go to an art gallery, cheer on the Yankees, or hit the newest club, it's all just a cab ride away. And while living in New York is expensive, Columbia students quickly learn the best ways to negotiate the city.

Anxious parents might worry about the dangers of sending their kiddies off to the big bad city. Certainly New York has its fair share of crimes but, owing to the lock-'em-up attitude of Mayor Giuliani in the late 1990s, the city became and has stayed a much safer place. Columbia dorms all have great security and provided you use your common sense, New York is as safe as anywhere else.

And for those stay-at-homes who can't be bothered to get on the subway, Morningside Heights is filled with student hangouts – from diners to coffee houses to laundromats. Columbia students do not even have to leave their campus to have access to everything they could desire. And when they do leave, the whole of New York is waiting for them.

One small note: Although NYC provides nearly everything your heart can desire, it is not big on nature. If you feel the need to breathe fresh air and see the sky, your best bet is to get a bus or train and head for the greater world. The East Coast offers some great areas to hike, ski or sunbathe. Just remember, it is permissible to leave the island of Manhattan!

Getting In

AT A GLANCE – Application & Test Options:

- Early Decision, Regular Decision

- ACT/SAT, Writing/essay not required

- SAT subject tests not required

Columbia continues to be one of the most popular universities in the United States. It has always been selective (after all, it is an Ivy) but in the past ten years the % of admits has gone from 12% down to 7%. And 90% of these fortunate students were in the top 10% of their high school class.

Applicants should bear in mind that Columbia also offers some awesome combined programmes. If you are poised to become the next Jacqueline du Pré you should remember that a joint programme with Juilliard is a possibility. And if you tend more towards engineering or science, it is possible to do combined degree courses.

All of these options require excellent grades. Columbia requires that everyone take the SAT or ACT, but the SAT Subject tests are no longer needed (they'll accept them but you're not at a disadvantage if you don't submit these test scores). More important than the exams, however, is the extent to which you show yourself to be a well-rounded and dedicated individual.

Columbia is known for being a school that focuses as much on the person as on the grade and will count your school magazine/prefect/tutoring/generally being an all-round superstar as being just as valuable as a string of straight As. It is possible to interview with the Columbia graduates who are scattered around the world but if you can't set it up, it is not considered essential.

Columbia offers the option of Early Decision applications but make sure that you're committed before you submit the form. It's legally binding, and if you're accepted you have to go. For those who plan on taking the traditional British gap year, Columbia is very relaxed about deferment – provided you can prove you are actually doing something with the twelve months.

Money Matters

Finally, although there is a certain amount of financial aid available, Columbia is not need-blind for its international students.

Famous Grads

Allen Ginsberg and Jack Kerouac – Columbia defined the beat generation

Art Garfunkel – Paul Simon's 'other half'

Alfred Knopf – Publishing magnate

Cornell University

Ithaca, New York
www.cornell.edu
Undergrads: 14,000
Grads: 7,000

How many students does it take to change a light bulb at Cornell?

Two – one to change the light bulb and one to crack under the pressure.

When Ezra Cornell founded his Ivy League school in 1865, he gave it the motto – 'I would found an institution where any person can find instruction in any study.' His non-sectarian college was aimed at all people and catered for all interests. Cornell has taken this legacy and made it into one of the most thriving universities on the East Coast. Cornell, aka 'The Big Red', is the largest of the Ivy Leagues and allows you to study anything from agriculture to hotel management to the more conventional arts and sciences.

This diverse academic experience takes place in one of the most naturally beautiful campuses in America. Cornell has none of the quaint and well-planned elements that define most New England campuses. Instead its buildings are situated on a huge expanse of rural land, complete with rivers, waterfalls and acres and acres of parkland. For those looking for a fun campus life, great academics and the chance to go swimming in your very own gorge, Cornell is a very appealing option.

The Campus

If you are a country bumpkin you will feel right at home at Cornell University. The site was literally founded on Ezra Cornell's farm in 1865 and there is still a highly rated College of Agriculture for those who want to get back to their rural roots. Even if you choose not to study the finer points of turnips, you will be surrounded by a natural beauty that you are simply not going to find at many universities in the US.

The campus is situated on a hill overlooking Cayuga Lake and contains three gorges and many hiking paths. The hill means that in the winters (which are invariably long and cold), every student gets to try out their sledding skills on dining hall trays. And in the summers, the gorges (complete with waterfalls) provide an excellent place to cool off.

The whole place was laid out by Frederick Law Olmsted – the same man who designed Central Park – and it has the same spacious, yet organized, feel. Despite its somewhat random position in what other schools like to label 'Middle of Nowhere, NY State', Cornell has some architectural masterpieces that students are rightly proud of. Most famous of these is the McGraw clock tower which stands at the heart of campus. Three times a day, teams of student chime-masters ascend the stairs and play the alma mater theme tune as well as a variety of other songs, including a selection of Beatles favourites.

Other focal points on campus include Ho Square(!), where students petition, protest and generally hang out; the footbridge on Beebe Lake which is meant to ensure marriage if you and your other half cross it holding hands; and the beautiful Uris Library, which houses one of the world's largest collections on witchcraft. Cornell also embraced the modern with the I. M. Pei-designed Johnson Museum of Art, one of the most interesting buildings on campus. Not only does it host art shows, concerts and other exhibitions, it also acts as a giant outdoor movie screen in the summer.

Accommodation

The campus for the College of Arts and Sciences, which you are most likely to be a part of, is divided into two parts. The North Campus houses all the freshmen, creating a first-year bonding experience essential in such a large university, and the West Campus houses all the sophomores (except for those who choose to live with their fraternities). There are a total of thirty-three residential halls on campus ranging from traditional Gothic styles to the less attractive modernist concrete.

Juniors and seniors have additional housing options, dorms centred around a particular theme (international house, anyone?), university apartments in Collegetown, or their own choice of off-campus housing. The housing system provides pastoral care but also encourages independence – something that many students say is essential when they finally get into the real world.

The Cornellian

As Ezra Cornell so proudly boasted, Cornell is a university where 'any person' can do pretty much anything. As a result it attracts a diverse student body. Cornell is the only Ivy League to be both a public and a private institution. While most of you will be heading for the private College of Arts and Science, the university has six other undergraduate schools. These are the College of Agriculture and LIfe Sciences, College of Human Ecology, School of Industrial and Labour Relations, College of Engineering, College of Architecture, Art and Planning and the world famous School of Hotel Administration (which supplies managers for hotels around the globe and oversees Cornell's own prestigious hotel).

This mix of academic experiences, and the fact that several of the colleges are state-funded with lower tuition fees, ensures that Cornell draws a veritable mish-mash of people from every corner of America. It's reach goes far beyond as well – almost 20% of undergraduates hail from outside the USA.

If there is one thing linking the Cornell community together, it's school spirit. Regardless of the season there are always thousands of students thronging the campus, of every conceivable background, ethnicity and religion. And, nearly all of them will stop and extol its virtues. This love for the alma mater may be encouraged by the fact that, if you are stuck in the middle of nowhere for four years, you pretty much have to love your campus.

Cornell undergrads feel passionately about 'The Big Red' and fiercely defend any insults levelled against the 'Bear' (their mascot) institution. There is a healthy sense of fun on the Cornell campus; something that is testified to by the large number of pranks that take place – most of them involving the hijacking of McGraw tower in some capacity.

When Cornell was initially founded, it was intended to be a university open to people of all religious persuasions. This legacy of tolerance and non-discrimination continues today. Cornell was the first American university to open a black fraternity and it continues to have a strong and well-integrated minority population (estimated at around 45%). It also has a lot of privileged, privately educated white kids, many of whose parents attended Cornell back in their day.

Although, as at all universities, students complain that certain groups like to self-segregate, it is generally agreed that Cornell students are both easy-going and accommodating. This is good news for crazy Brits who will benefit from slotting right into a diverse environment that is rarely found in England.

You will also have to adjust to the American impulse to take part in pretty much everything that is going on, all the time. The extra-curriculars at Cornell are exhaustive and exhausting. A typical day might begin with a volunteer programme in Ithaca, followed by some IM sport, then an article written at the Cornell Daily Sun (a higher-class publication than its name might suggest), followed by an evening tech rehearsal for the annual student production of the Rocky Horror Show.

Somewhere in there you also have to fit three or four hours of class, a little studying, some food, a couple of hours of sleep, a bustling social life and, given that this is Cornell, a jog along the gorge. This may seem exhausting, but soon it becomes second nature and you can't imagine what you once did with all that free time.

Cornell is not for everyone. It is a huge school and as such it is easy to get lost in the crowd. Cornell students need to have a certain amount of resilience and the courage to promote themselves both academically and socially. It is Ivy League folklore that Cornell has the highest suicide rate of any of the colleges, something which is traditionally blamed on the gorges. This unfortunate hearsay may no longer be true, but Cornell does have a full advising system in place for those who feel lost.

However, for Brits, it may also be the university that feels most like a home from home. The fact that many of the older years live off-campus, coupled with the pub-like mentality of fraternity life, provides those longing for a little bit of British 'uni' life with a somewhat similar experience in America. And for those to whom this very mentality is anathema, the school spirit and diversity of Cornell ensures that almost all will find their own niche.

Hitting the Books

It is a standing joke among Ivy League students that Cornell undergrads get away with having to do absolutely no work. This is certainly not true and there are many far more serious contenders to this claim (for example, the 'we have no mandatory courses' Brown). Cornell students vociferously advertise the amount of work they do have, citing the three to four classes they attend each day as well as the dreaded prelim (aka mid-term) exams that take place two or three times each semester – in contrast to once a semester at other universities.

Cornell students are fortunate enough to have a huge range of courses (over 4,000). Students can take subjects offered outside their own school and design their major to suit their own personal interest. As a rule, members of the Cornell faculty are thought to be approachable and helpful to undergrads.

One caveat: Cornell has a huge graduate school and this often becomes the centre of attention. Many undergrads complain about the fact it is the graduate students who get the best housing, professors and resources while they are left out in the cold. One of the reasons behind this frustration may be resentment of the bureaucracy that defines Cornell. Your professors could be the nicest in the world, but it doesn't help you with the endless red tape that is involved in changing class, registration or navigating the advising system.

And while the size of Cornell provides a wide range of possible class options, it also means you are unlikely to get the professor-student intimacy that characterizes smaller institutions. This, of course, depends on you. If you are brave, go to your professor's office and ask for their advice and help, you will benefit. If you are sensible, look out for the smaller seminars, and try to take classes that number around fifty students, you will feel connected. If you are neither brave nor sensible, you may end up as one in a sea of bored faces in a class of over four hundred.

Of course, sometimes it is fun to be one in a huge class; Cornell's Psych 101 is famous for enrolling over 2,000 students and most of them love it. When you are in a large class, professors will try to ensure that you meet with either them or one of their TAs (normally grad students) to discuss issues in much smaller groups. But you should be prepared for the fact that this is not a university that is going to offer you much in the way of one-on-one tutorial time, unless you figure out how to make that happen for yourself.

Cornell does not require much from its students in the way of core classes. Freshmen have to take two writing seminars, which are available on a huge variety of topics and are designed to set you up for the rest of your college career.

There is also a two-semester physical education requirement – following the American mindset that fitness is key to every happy life. However, if you are exercise phobic, fear not. These requirements can be filled by yoga or fly fishing! And, as a final piece of eccentricity, all students must pass a swim test before they are allowed to graduate – three laps of a pool swimming any stroke that takes your fancy.

This relaxed attitude to academic requirements pretty much sums up the Cornell attitude. If you want rigour, it's there but the onus is on you to go and get it. If you don't want it, the hope is that you'll still manage to pick up a lot just by following the crowd.

Social Life

The Cornell College of Arts and Sciences is the largest in the Ivy League. When you combine it with the six other undergraduate schools on campus and the huge number of graduate students, you get a vast community of young adults living pretty much on their own in the middle of nowhere. It would be a sad testament to the Cornell student if this environment resulted in a boring social life. Fortunately, it has not – and Cornell is a fun place to attend college.

The huge size of the student body undeniably contributes to this social atmosphere. In such a large group of people virtually every taste has to be catered for. Therefore, whether you are interested in celebrating the Hindu festival of Diwali, a large event on campus, or in throwing fish at the Harvard ice hockey team during the annual match, you are sure to find a group of people who want to join in. Saturday nights on campus can involve anything from catching the latest screening at Cornell's very own cinema (anything from classic movies to foreign films to recent releases), to hitting a couple of bars in Collegetown before dancing the night away in one of the local clubs.

Cornell University is another institution that embraces that curious American custom – the fraternity. It is estimated that around a third of the campus are involved in the Greek societies with many of the sophomores actually living in their buildings. The college administration, fearful of drunken students and potential lawsuits, tries to maintain some control over the alcohol situation by insisting on university catering services, but most parties are still very much influenced by the heavy-drinking culture.

This means that Cornell feels more like a big football school (despite the unconvincing status of its football team) than many of its East Coast contemporaries. In many ways your social experience here will be more like the average British pub culture than that at many of the more rarified American colleges. However if you are not into keg stands and beer pong, you should rest assured that there are plenty of less hardcore options available to you and the many who share your reticence.

Outside Those Ivory Walls

Cornell, along with Dartmouth, has become the butt of many jokes for its less-than-perfect location. Harvard has Boston, Columbia has New York, Penn has Philadelphia... and when compared to these great cities, poor old Ithaca doesn't really have much of a look in. However, before you too succumb to the idea that Cornell is severely crippled by its geographical status, it is worth taking a closer look at the situation. While Ithaca may not be the biggest town in the world, it is a substantial one and it offers pretty much every facility students may need.

Unfortunately, if you are one of these people who does want to hit the metropolis on a regular basis, you are doomed to disappointment. New York City, while in the same state, is five hours away by car. Even getting to the university can be a problem for the international traveller – involving a flight into one of the New York City airports and then a local flight into Syracuse airport.

However, students looking for a little bit of excitement should not despair. The local and aptly named Collegetown, situated right next to the Cornell campus, provides a great place to hang out. Cornell is a huge university and thus there is a large student demand for all traditional amenities – entertainment, bars, clubs and coffee houses. Collegetown supplies all of these and is continually thronged by students who want a break from the on-campus frat scene.

Cornell has a great social life and it really doesn't suffer from its location. In fact, visiting students who have to make do with the dubious delights of places such as Harvard Square are frequently envious of the bars, dance clubs and arcades that make up Collegetown. Furthermore, many juniors and seniors live off-campus and entertain in a way (dinner and drinks parties) that hints at what real-world socialising may eventually be like.

In addition to these more social pursuits, Cornell also offers its students some of the most extensive outdoor benefits in the Ivy League. Surrounded by National Parks, it provides some great trails for the enthusiastic hiker, one of which actually starts at the door of an on-campus dorm. In the winter, skiing is readily available as well as sledging and skating; in the summer, long walks through the Cornell Plantations and swims in the gorges are popular choices. Even the most urbanite student will miss the natural beauty of the place at the end of his four years.

Getting In

AT A GLANCE – Application & Test Options:

- Early Decision, Regular Decision

- ACT/SAT, but Writing/essay not required

- Subject tests are required for Arts and Sciences (two subjects of your choice) and Engineering (Mathematics 1 or 2 and a science of your choice) but not for the following: Agriculture and Life Sciences; Architecture, Art, and Planning; Business–Applied Economics and Management; Business–Hotel Administration; Human Ecology; Industrial and Labor Relations

Cornell currently receives over 40,000 applications for 3,500 spots in its incoming freshman class. This is pretty tough going, but you should not be disheartened. The rate of acceptance (around 17%) is higher than that of most Ivy League schools (which is usually under 10%). What's more, Cornell is the biggest Ivy League college (bigger = more spots). It also does not place as much weight on SAT scores as some of the others do, and goes out of its way to offer international students a little leeway on their scores.

Cornell requires that you take the SAT or ACT and two SAT Subject tests. It also offers you the possibility of an alumni interview – something definitely recommended since it will give you an additional perspective on a place that you may only have visited briefly, if at all.

Cornell also requires the normal application essay – in the format of a long essay. Questions follow the traditional American pattern of trying to get to the bottom of your personal belief system – some current examples include: 'What quotation or motto describes your values? What event has occurred in your life that was influenced by other perspectives? What question would you have liked us to have asked? Answer it.'

It is this essay that really forms the heart of your application and it is important to put some serious consideration into how you answer it. Your application can be submitted either online or on paper (but don't forget to take into consideration the inevitable delays in the international postal service).

Cornell does now offer the Early Decision option to its applicants. Only do this if you are committed to attending 'The Big Red', because if you are accepted, you must withdraw all applications to other schools.

Money Matters

There is a small amount of financial aid available to international students, but it does not come in the guaranteed-to-all-who-really-need-it package of some of the other Ivy League schools. Therefore, if you are eager to pursue this route, you need to look into it as soon as possible.

Famous Grads

Christopher Reeve – what's good enough for Superman, should be good enough for you

E. B. White – hooray for Charlotte's Web!

Adolph Coors – if Coors beer isn't your favourite drink now, it soon will be

Dartmouth College

Hanover, New Hampshire
www.dartmouth.edu
Undergrads: 4,200
Grads: 2,100

How many students does it take to change a light bulb at Dartmouth?

None – Hanover doesn't have electricity.

Ever read The Cat in the Hat? The creator of green eggs and ham hailed from Dartmouth, smallest of the eight Ivy League schools. Tucked away in a remote corner of New Hampshire, Dartmouth is not for those who seek the bright lights of the big cities. Yet for those seeking a university experience that allows them to travel, ski on their own slopes, and assemble a wardrobe based around the colour green, while simultaneously exposing themselves to some of the best teaching around, Dartmouth is a top choice. After all, if it was good enough for Dr Seuss, what's stopping you?

The Campus

Dartmouth was founded in 1769 by the Rev. Eleazar Wheelock, and was designed to educate Indian tribe children and the sons of the British. His mission was to spread Christian morals and beliefs from one to the other in an attempt to civilize the area. Hence the school motto remains 'Vox Clamantis in Deserto' – a voice crying out in the wilderness. While New Hampshire is no longer the wilderness it once was, it is still not the most cosmopolitan place.

However what it lacks in urbanity, it makes up for in breathtaking beauty. Situated between the Vermont and New Hampshire mountains, Dartmouth students have the option of hiking on their own trails, skiing on their own slopes and skating on their own pond. Certainly not something that England can offer.

The Dartmouth campus is situated around the Green, initially an area used for herding cattle and now populated by sprawling students in the summer and snowballing students in the winter. The Green is also the site for some of the more pagan of the school's festivities – bonfires for fall Homecoming, ice sculptures (yes, it is that cold) for the Winter Carnival, and all manner of celebrations for the spring Green Key. Dotted around the Green are the main residential buildings and classrooms of the campus. Many of them are in classic New England fashion (think red brick, white spires) – most notably the beautiful Baker Library. There are, however, some more modern additions, including the 'Hop' or Hopkins Center for the Arts – the performance centre on campus.

Accommodation

About 90% of students choose to live on campus in the attractive buildings situated near the Green. Some of these are themed houses (international, substance-free, etc.), but most combine all majors and ethnicities for a diverse living experience. The dorms house a mixture of year groups, excluding freshmen, who have their own dorms. (Bonding with your 'freshman floor' is a great part of the Dartmouth experience.) And most students eat together in the nationally renowned dining halls – forget the usual cafeteria experience, this food is really good.

The Dartmouth Student

Dartmouth has been labelled the 'country club' of the Ivy Leagues and despite the original vision of a Native American/English school – catering to all nationalities and cultures – diversity was a serious problem at Dartmouth. But the student population now seems to come from a great range of states, countries, and socio-economic backgrounds, and the university would appear to have shrugged off its legacy of white privilege – about 1/3 of undergrads are of an ethnic minority and 8% are international.

Although Dartmouth is the smallest of the Ivy League schools, the student body is large enough to encompass all friendship groups and Dartmouth prides itself on a sense of community. As long as you are open with everyone, everyone will be open with you. In many senses the Dartmouth atmosphere bears much resemblance to that of a British uni. If you are feeling homesick, tea is quietly served in the library every day at four (faculty and students welcome). Even more importantly for those used to non-Draconian drinking laws, there are the Greek houses – where most of the drinking goes on in private – and Fuel, a gig venue that offers free beer on tap for students 21 and over.

In fact, Dartmouth as a whole is an extremely friendly place. Although there are graduate schools, grad students are outnumbered by the undergrads at a ratio of two to one. The number of young people and the isolated position of the school ensure a close-knit campus community that bonds over the cold and the colour green.

The life of the average Dartmouth student is very much defined by the unique D-Plan or semester schedule. Any Brit who comes to the US is bound to be perplexed by the term system that universities have. While most colleges divide the year in two, cutting out Easter holiday and focusing instead on the summer, Dartmouth offers an entirely different solution. They split each year up into seasons (yes, there are actually seasons in New Hampshire). The student then has a choice as to where to spend the four ten-week terms. It is obligatory to be on campus for the first three of both freshman and senior year and for the summer term of your sophomore year. But you can then also choose to study off-campus – either abroad or in some form of internship – for as many as three other terms. Confused? The Dartmouth website explains all this brilliantly – even allowing you to plot your own academic schedule for the next four years.

This D-Plan system means that Dartmouth students are constantly on the move. While this can be disruptive, it also means that you are continually being exposed to new people and new ideas. Even the potentially off-putting notion of a summer spent at school is actually much loved by the student body who devote most of it to sunbathing and lazing around with friends. Dartmouth students pride themselves on their sense of community. From the first days on campus when everyone is hooked up to the much famed Blitz email network, to the regular alumni events and large turnout at sports events, the Dartmouth student body moves as a pack and is proud to do so.

Despite its isolated position and relatively small endowment, Dartmouth has pretty much every resource you can think of. And students don't hesitate to use them. There are a plethora of clubs and societies on campus and everyone gets involved with something. Whether you are writing for The Dartmouth (one of many papers that claims to be the oldest college publication), or doing research at the hospital of the prestigious Dartmouth Med School, your days will be busy. And if you have a free moment, you can always go watch the fruits of someone else's labour – performances of every variety abound.

Hitting the Books

Dartmouth is known for having one of the most dedicated faculties in the country and students cannot sing their praises loudly enough. Perhaps it is because the community is fairly small, or perhaps it is because New Hampshire just attracts a better brand of professor. Whatever the reasons, undergrads never feel neglected. They are the primary focus on campus and they feel the benefits. The class sizes are very small (student:faculty ratio is 8:1), professors are required to teach undergrads, and the relationships formed in an academic setting often extend well beyond the classroom. As a result students seldom feel alienated or lost regarding their academic well-being and, if they do, advisors who actually care are always on hand. It is hardly surprising that Dartmouth continually ranks top for teaching in a variety of nation-wide league tables.

Dartmouth offers over 2,000 courses in twenty-nine departments – a huge amount of flexibility complemented by the fact that no one has to choose a major until the end of sophomore year. You have the freedom to structure your college experience around one subject area (and meet the distributive requirements within your preferred departments) or tap into the vast array of subjects and courses to explore your own personal interests.

The closest thing at Dartmouth to a core curriculum is their liberal arts programme for undergraduates, which encompasses ten courses taken across eight different intellectual fields and requires that students immerse themselves in three different cultures (Western, non-Western and Cultural Identity).

Dartmouth also prides itself on the cosmopolitan atmosphere on campus. Over 50% of its students study abroad and everyone is required to pass a language requirement. In fact a French professor, Prof. Rassas, developed a new system of teaching languages that is now widely followed – in addition to normal classes, students are required to meet three times a week (often at 7.30am) to be drilled in grammar and vocabulary. This drill is usually led by a fellow student and, believe it or not, is actually considered fun.

While Dartmouth may be isolated, it has every academic resource that the overeager undergraduate could desire. From the oldest research library in the country (the spired Baker Library) to the labs at the famous med school, Dartmouth students have it all at their fingertips. And they are continually encouraged to use it. The D-Plan means that students are encouraged to seek out what appeals to them – whether it involves archaeological digs or an internship at Goldman Sachs. Academics are important, but only in so far as they serve the overall picture; flexibility and personal interest are prized above all else.

Social Life

It's Saturday night. It's cold. You're surrounded by mountains. The nearest city is two and half hours away. What do you do with yourself? Surprisingly, many Dartmouth students have been able to come up with fun and satisfying answers to this question. Despite its location, Dartmouth students enjoy a social life that others at better-connected schools might well envy. While there may not be the number of venues that big cities offer, Hanover has enough restaurants to keep the students happy and there is always a large amount going on (and Hanover and the Dartmouth campus are all pretty much one).

Dartmouth is known for having a stronger drinking culture than many American universities – although it still pales into insignificance besides places such as Newcastle! This may well be due to the fact that fraternities and sororities still play a large part in on-campus social life. (Of course, it may also be due to the fact that there isn't that much else to do but saying this goes down less well with the average Dartmouth man). More than half of students choose to be affiliated with one of the fourteen fraternities and eight sororities (as well as three co-ed ones) that exist on campus. Although this may all seem a little bit too like a scary American movie to you, these organizations really do serve to spice up student social life and offer an alternative group of friends.

In an effort to ensure that the campus is not totally dominated by these Greek groups, 'rush' (the process of selecting or being selected) does not take place until the sophomore year. This may seem a little unfair to overeager first years, but it does ensure that everyone has a chance to get to know each other in a situation that is not dependent on which Greek initials you sport on your jumper.

One caveat about social life: Students at most Ivy League schools complain that romance is dead, dating a thing of the past and true love something that is only found when taking a class on Romeo and Juliet. While a lot of this is mere griping, it is true that the whirl of an American student's daily life leaves little time for relationships. At Dartmouth this is complicated by the D-Plan. Students are constantly moving around and it can be difficult to develop a short-term hook-up into a long-term romance when one or both partners are jetting off to pastures new for the next semester. Something for the relationship junkies to bear in mind.

Outside Those Ivory Walls

If you enjoyed The Sound of Music as a child, then you will feel right at home at Dartmouth. While the mountains of Vermont and New Hampshire may not be quite as impressive as the Alps, they still form a pretty imposing backdrop to your daily life. Unfortunately for those who prefer shopping to sledding and clubbing to climbing, Dartmouth does not have as much to offer. While the town of Hanover is pretty and enjoys an extremely close relationship with the university, it is also small and can really only offer students a momentary escape from campus life.

However, those students who choose to go to Dartmouth firmly believe that the limited options available to them help form a close community. While Hanover has sufficient restaurants, coffee houses and entertainment to suit those who crave a world off the Green, the campus society itself provides plenty of entertainment. Dartmouth students make their own fun and the combination of frats, obscure school traditions and community atmosphere means that there is rarely a dull moment.

And for those who need an urban fix once in a while, Lebanon airport offers daily flights to both New York City and Boston (which, if you are one of the few who has a car, is only a three-hour drive). Montreal is also a weekend destination of choice.

What Dartmouth lacks in urban entertainment, it makes up for in rural pursuits. This is not the sort of place where a hatred of the outdoors will get you very far. Almost all incoming freshmen participate in an introductory and wildly popular outdoor trips programme, designed to accelerate the bonding experience so favoured in America. While not everyone would choose to meet their friends for the next four years in an atmosphere defined by hiking, tents (or cabins, for the lucky ones) and tinned food, many find it a good way to break down initial social barriers.

And everyone is in agreement that the surrounding countryside is gorgeous. Hiking continues to play an integral role in the lives of many students and for those who prefer more glamorous pursuits, the long winter provides ample opportunity for hitting the fourteen-trail Dartmouth ski mountain!

Getting In

AT A GLANCE – Application & Test Options:

– Early Decision, Regular Decision

– ACT/SAT required, with Writing/essay

– SAT Subject tests not required, but recommended

Dartmouth is not the kind of place that people put on their application list as a fall back. The students who decide to apply there are determined and ever increasing in number. In recent years, only 9-10% of applications have been accepted (roughly 2,300 out of the 23,000 or so who applied). And the majority of these students have SAT scores above 1400. While Dartmouth does not place emphasis on academics alone, a strong background is needed if you are to succeed.

Dartmouth requires the customary SAT or ACT test but no longer asks for the SAT Subjects – and it does go out of its way to state that it understands that international students may be at a disadvantage. It also offers the possibility of an alumni interview – a forum that allows the school to question you, and more importantly, you to question the school. Many Dartmouth graduates are based in the UK and it is normally possible to locate one relatively close to you. If you cannot, it will in no way count against you.

As well as official academic reports and the more revealing interview information, Dartmouth also asks for letters that champion your cause. In addition to the guidance counsellor/school principal and teacher reports commonly required, Dartmouth also places importance on a 'Peer Evaluation' letter – written about you by one of your friends. So it may pay off to start being really nice to people NOW!

Lastly, you can apply to Dartmouth on an Early or a Regular Decision basis. Remember, Early Decision is binding so it is important to be sure before you send in that envelope.

Money Matters

Dartmouth is an expensive university but there is good news: it is one of the few schools that offers need-blind admission to international students. This means that they will admit a student without considering the applicant's financial situation – and will back the policy with an ample source of funding.

Famous Grads

Robert Frost – great American poet

Dr Seuss (Theodore Geisel) – Cat in the Hat, Green Eggs and Ham...

Nelson Rockefeller – VP and millionaire

Duke University

Durham, North Carolina
www.duke.edu
Undergrads: 6,700
Grads: 8,000

How many students does it take to change a light bulb at Duke?

A whole frat – but only one of them is sober enough to get the bulb out of the socket.

Duke University's rise to great heights in the rankings game is well deserved. Once dismissed as a mere prep school continuation for the Southern elite, this beautiful college, set in the heart of the South, has now established itself as an academic and sporting success drawing students from all over the nation.

If you are a basketball fanatic, a lover of the South, longing to join a fraternity, dying for some warm weather or merely in search of a top tier US education that avoids the

East Coast stereotypes, then Duke is well worth your consideration. Duke offers a highly social campus set a mere fifteen minutes away from other top Southern schools (UNC Chapel Hill among them) as well as great academics and a thriving school spirit. After all, who wouldn't want to be known as a Blue Devil?

The Campus

The Duke campuses are famed for their beautiful architecture, lovely grounds and wonderful climate. They are also famed for the fact that there are two of them. Students love to moan about the division that this sets up – although they are, in fact, connected by bus or a short walk. Indeed, for many, the combination acts as an advantage. Not only aesthetically – East Campus is the older of the two, complete with Georgian architecture while West Campus epitomizes the Gothic style, topped off by the soaring Duke Chapel – but also socially.

Accommodation

Freshmen all live on the East Campus, allowing for a mass bonding experience. Upperclassmen live on the West Campus – a transition that lets them leave the frenetic pack socializing of freshman year behind and settle down in their own fraternities or smaller residential halls. The fact that 90% of Duke students choose to live on campus suggests that the groans about the division of the two sites are really just because there isn't much else to moan about.

The Duke Student

The Blue Devils are known for being a friendly lot and, while the university has expanded far beyond its Southern roots, a great deal of the Southern charm remains. This emphasis on manners (which British students will find not dissimilar to that back home) used to come with other qualities that were more daunting.

Girls on the Duke campus could expect their peers to be impeccably turned out while boys largely fell into the frat house scene and the drunken revelry of the blue-blooded and conservative elites. Many thought that Duke was a superficial place which, despite its attempts at diversity, hadn't really shaken its 'little rich boy' image.

Now, however, Duke seems to have moved beyond those stereotypes; students say "more people are curious/driven to learn". Noticeably more students are from overseas, and that bastion of the cocktail party and little black dress, the sorority and fraternity scene, is actually shrinking.

Hitting the Books

Students also take pride in their academics, and many believe that it is their will to work that has pushed Duke to its high place in the college rankings. Certainly the faculty is excellent and more than willing to put in the man-hours to accommodate personal interaction with their students.

While it may be difficult at first to find your intellectual calling, the sheer number of courses coupled with an inquisitive spirit will ensure that you discover your place. Students find themselves facing a rigorous core curriculum, ensuring they graduate as well-rounded individuals who are fluent in basic maths as well as Shakespearean sonnets. But they also have two years to decide what major to pursue and the option of pursuing more than one if they simply can't make up their minds.

Duke students like to boast that Harvard is the 'Duke of the North' and certainly their academic strength is helping them to build a premier reputation. Despite the large number of grad students, Duke maintains a healthy focus on the undergraduate. Its freshmen seminars and focus groups ensure that even the babies of the college feel they are getting enough attention.

And after the halcyon days of college are left behind, students go on to hugely successful careers across the board. Duke boasts of a 99% acceptance rating for those of its students heading to law school and an 80% for those looking at medicine. Certainly the enthusiasm and confidence of the average Devil gives them a boost in the job market. Lately, it seems that everyone who goes to Duke ends up in either San Francisco or NYC. The tech sphere has become a big draw for grads and NYC has always had a huge alumni network.

Social Life

One thing that brings together the entire student body is the craze for the Duke basketball team. Even if you have no conception of this game beyond a hazy association with netball, you will soon find yourself joining the ranks of Blue Devils who stalk members of the top national team around campus and live in tents for weeks in order to get game tickets. Nor does this enthusiasm for their campus stop on the sports fields. Duke students are keen to join everything – among the many groups on campus are the top improv troupe in the country, a strong student newspaper and a good arts programme.

Duke likes to be known as a party school and the frat scene ensures there is seldom a dull Saturday night.

Outside Those Ivory Walls

Durham is a classic college town with the requisite watering holes, but with a very definite distinction: terrific food in great restaurants, many of them farm-to-table with locally grown ingredients. It's often referred to as "The Foodiest Town in the South" and most students think that's an accurate assessment. From trendy to whole hog barbeque, you can expect to eat really well while you're here.

Getting In

AT A GLANCE – Application & Test Options:

- Early Decision, Regular Decision
- ACT/SAT required, with Writing/essay
- SAT Subject tests not required, but strongly recommended

If all this sounds like a good option for you, then head to North Carolina (itself an experience) to take a look around. Take time to chat with a Blue Devil Advocate – these student tour leaders are renowned for being both honest and highly persuasive! Sign yourself up for your SAT or ACT now, plan to sit two SAT Subject tests (strongly recommended though not required) and be prepared for a very competitive admissions process.

Not only will you be up against plenty of other people who all have the required excellent grades, test scores, and extracurriculars, the application numbers are swelled by all those people who have dreamed of going to Duke their entire lives (thanks to following the Blue Devils from their cradles).

Money Matters

At Duke, financial aid is awarded based solely on need (just make sure that you check the "financial aid interest" box on the admissions application). However, all applicants for admission are automatically considered for the few merit scholarships – you don't need to fill out a separate application (except for the Robertson Scholars Leadership Program).

Famous Grads

Richard Nixon – President of the USA

Melinda Gates – husband Bill is a more than generous donor

Anne Tyler – writer

Emory University

Atlanta, Georgia
www.emory.edu
Undergrads: 7,600
Grads: 6,600

How many Emory students does it take to change a light bulb?
That depends.

Talk to folks at Emory for more than a few minutes, and you'll find a recurring theme in everything they say. Emory is a place of variety. No two students have the same experience here.

What is remarkable is that, while providing a huge range of educational experiences, which each individual can tailor to his own taste, Emory manages to bring all the diverging strands together and create one of the most rewarding and close communities of any college in the country.

On top of this, students enjoy superb academic instruction, a pulsatingly vibrant social life and a university that sits in the top 20 rankings of US universities.

The Campus

Emory's main campus is a gorgeous marble-based affair occupying sizeable grounds in an affluent, peaceful region of eastern Atlanta. The centre of campus is dominated by a gargantuan hulking hospital, where med school students gain experience.

The surrounding buildings, however, are exquisite structures of gleaming white stone and terracotta roofs, spaced perfectly among delightful green lawns and wooded areas. Constant construction and renovation, much bemoaned by students, has produced ultra-high tech facilities in most buildings. The library is superb, rated one of the finest in the States.

Accommodation

Dorms range from new to "in need of repair", and from really top-notch to mediocre. All freshmen are required to live on campus, as part of the administration's attempt to foster a close-knit community. Sophomores must also live on campus, but are given the option of moving off to the "Clairmont Campus", a few minutes' walk away, where there are funky apartments to rent. Juniors and seniors can also find room at Clairmont, though some choose to live off-campus.

The Emory Student

The people studying at Emory have arrived from every conceivable location and background. The college is among the most ethnically diverse of any of the top twenty; minorities make up almost 1/2 of the student body. The two main groups of students, though, are local Southerners and a surprising Jewish contingent (mostly from the Northeast). Unaccountably, for what was originally a Methodist College, Emory has a larger percentage of Jews than any other school in the South: about a third of the undergraduate population. There is also a considerable range of wealth disparity, with the preppier students at one end, and the 'financial aid kids' at the other.

The school is small enough for seeing familiar faces to be commonplace, and this helps to create a great sense of community, as does the isolated feel of the campus. Cliques are not eliminated entirely, but everyone feels so much a part of the same system that interactions in classes, organisations or residence halls are always smooth. The large numbers of international students have no problem feeling at home, even if certain nationalities (eg the large number of Koreans) tend to keep to themselves.

Hitting the Books

Excellent academic reputations aren't achieved without effort, and indeed the work ethic exhibits a sturdy vitality among the students at Emory. Most students are very hard working, though there are also those who remain a little more laid back: the business school in particular has a reputation for laxity (they only have classes four days a week, for example).

The classes tend to be rigorous, though like everything else they can "vary a lot", both in quality and difficulty. Nevertheless, the experience is almost invariably "intense". The emphasis here is on the sciences and business, and some students claim that "Liberal Arts take a back seat." Others say they're "very challenging" – you just can't make a rule for anything here.

Profs are generally "decent", while unfortunately the considerable numbers of outstanding teachers are frequently rotated off to other institutions. Students are frequently surveyed and asked to contribute their opinions on their professors to public forums, allowing a good level of evaluation and improvement of the faculty. Professors by-and-large maintain a high level of out of class contact with their pupils, and are always "free and willing to talk", even if you "sometimes have to take the initiative."

Classes at Emory are generally as small and focused as you'd expect at such a reputable university, and indeed two-thirds of them have twenty students or less, while only 7% have more than 50. Less popular majors in particular benefit from small class sizes and teachers who certainly aren't any lower quality than those instructing the big subjects.

Undergraduates benefit from contact with big name speakers – Jimmy Carter, Salman Rushdie, and the Dalai Lama are all official members of the faculty, for example, though don't expect to see them around on a daily basis! Students report that they have been able to speak directly with some of the most famous practitioners and researchers in their fields.

It is worth noting that Emory has a reputation as a good place to study for pre-professionals, due to the great post-graduation employment opportunities provided by the school's ties to various big companies in Atlanta. Many students, though probably not the majority, view their education here as a step on the ladder to a job, rather than an education for its own sake.

Social Life

Emory's campus life positively hums. Emory students are ultra-engaged, and "no one is apathetic", according to one senior. Everyone appreciates the resulting atmosphere, which is conducive to an awesome creativity and what students call a "dialogue of ideas".

As a rule Emory parties as hard as it works, with students famously "punishing their brains during the week and their livers on the weekends". There are great local clubs, and older students also like to head downtown or possibly to the Georgia Tech campus to join in the festivities on offer in Atlanta. "Experience shuttles" take students to various interesting or shopping-rich neighbourhoods of the city.

On campus, students can partake in hundreds of organisations, most active on "wonderful Wednesdays". There's the usual array of performance and other creative groups, student media and government, and loads of community service opportunities. There are subject-specific groups ("chemory" science club is popular), there are sessions organised by the university itself to help students, such as the "stress and meditation" group. A lot of great stuff is organised as part of the administration's community-obsessed drive, including "songfest" (for freshmen), tons of "icebreakers", random workshops, tea tasting, ice cream socials etc.

Sports are not huge, but there are great athletic facilities and fun intramural opportunities, and the tennis and swimming teams are extremely competitive. Greek life is active at Emory, with its usual lion's share of the good parties.

Outside Those Ivory Walls

As mentioned in the Georgia Tech write-up, Atlanta is the state capital of Georgia, largest city in the South, and not the greatest model of a well-planned modern city (its own fault, since most of it has been purpose-built and rebuilt since its historical Civil War days).

However, Atlanta is now a modern metropolis of sky-scrapers and big-name companies. There is as much to do as in any big American city, and Emory students, especially older ones, take full advantage. Although the traffic can be unbearable and the roads are a muddle, there are plenty of venues, events and vitality (even for such a hot and sultry locale).

Atlanta is also a famously international city, at least by the standards of the South, with lots of consulates, including a British one.

Emory itself is located in the very American "Druid Hills" area of the city, a peaceful, well-off region full of trees and large family homes, away from anything resembling the somewhat polluted, concrete image Atlanta has built for itself. Students report a strong "bubble feel" on campus and in the surrounding neighbourhood, and will often approach trips into downtown Atlanta almost as tourists.

Emory has another campus out in the Georgia countryside, a little ways east of Atlanta, in a small college town called Oxford. This smaller campus is actually where the university was originally founded by Methodists in the 1830s, until it was relocated to the more luxurious Druid Hills with money donated by Asa Candler (the founder and owner of the Coca Cola Company). The Oxford campus is said to be harder working and even more isolated than the main campus, not to mention a lot smaller.

Getting In

AT A GLANCE – Application & Test Options:

– Early Decision, Early Decision II, Regular Decision, Emory University Scholar Programs

– ACT/SAT required, Writing/essay is optional

– SAT Subject tests not required, but recommended

Right around 25% of applications to Emory are successful – the university is rigorous in its approach and will inspect all the details of your application. Emory is especially looking for how interested you are in the school itself; it expects you to be able to demonstrate why you think it is a good match for you and preferably to have shown some interest, if not by visiting the campus itself then by talking to a local rep or requesting one of their "video visits".

Money Matters

Fees are high (total costs can be over $60,000 per year) and, unfortunately, next to no aid or scholarships are available to international students.

Famous Grads

Newt Gingrich — Former US Congressman and Speaker of the House of Representatives

Peter Buck – lead guitarist, R.E.M.

Alben Barkley – Vice President of the USA (1949-53)

Florida State University

Tallahassee, Florida
www.fsu.edu
Undergrads: 32,600
Grads: 9,000

How many FSU students does it take to change a light bulb?
2 – one to find a bigger, better light bulb than The University of Florida, and one to change it.

A flagship university for the state, Florida State is a popular choice for locals and out-of-state students alike. The experience may not be typically Floridian – you won't find any Cuban cafe con leche or stunning beaches here in the famous Panhandle (unless you drive an hour or so to the snow white sand beaches of the Gulf of Mexico) – but it is quintessentially American, complete with varsity sports, fraternities and a gorgeous brick campus. The international program here is fantastic – and the large numbers of students that study abroad nicely compliment the students that study here from abroad. British students here inevitably have a great experience.

The Campus

FSU has a beautiful and spacious 400 acre campus, full of great facilities, impressive buildings and old oak trees hanging with moss. At peak times, the lawns and paths can be so crammed with students that it's hard to push your way through the crowds, although students think the university has done a really good job of utilizing space and beautiful wide brick sidewalks make the tightly packed older parts of the campus seem bigger.

Buildings are constantly being renovated, leaving them in various states of repair. The older ones can feel a bit outdated (or at least did last time we looked) but are changing fast, while the newer (or recently-improved) ones are impressively modernised with all kinds of cool technology. The library (Strozier) was renovated not long ago to make more space for students (and the oh-so-important proximity to caffeine with one of only two 24/7 Starbucks in the US – the other is in Las Vegas!); it has a system for borrowing books from nearby libraries so their long tentacles can have any book sent over in a matter of days.

Students speak well of their environs, modestly proclaiming them superior to any other university in the state, and praising the campus shuttle-bus system and the general ease of getting around the campus along the tree-lined paths. Many students do without cars, which is a good thing since parking is a nightmare.

Note: FSU has four overseas study centres – in London, Florence, Valencia, and Panama City – and some 60 programmes in 20 more cities around the globe. Students can study abroad at just about any point during the course of their four years at FSU, or can apply to complete their first year of studying entirely overseas through a great scholarship programme called First Year Abroad (FYA)(see below under Getting In).

The FSU London Study Centre – containing all classrooms, 26 self-contained flats, library and labs – is located in a row of 17th century houses in Bloomsbury, near the British Museum. Amazingly for buildings in the middle of central London, the effect of the whole place is bright, airy and roomy. And of course, you can't beat the location. Not just because it's in the heart of the tube system....half the university population of London is in the immediate vicinity.

The FSU Florence Study Centre is located in the 15th-century Alessandri Palace, close to the Duomo, the Ponte Vecchio, and the Uffizi Gallery.

The Valencia campus is near the old town, with features dating back to the 10th century; the Panama programme is in the City of Knowledge not far from the Panama Canal and the Camino de Cruces National Park.

Accommodation

Back in Tallahassee, dorms are a mixed bag and filled mostly with freshmen and sophomores (1st and 2nd year students). The oldest (and most charming) dorms built in an L shape on one side of campus (Gilchrist, Broward, Landis, Bryan, Jennie, Reynolds – near the Suwannee dining hall next to Landis Green) have been renovated and are generally thought of as newer and better kept: they're suite-style, meaning two rooms share a shower and toilet. The other community style dorms (other side of Landis Green or far side of student union area) have one bathroom for the whole hall...but are being demolished or renovated campus wide. It's mostly just luck which ones you get (though an early application helps), but new students should be spoilt for choice with so much construction under way. Older students live in the array of alternative student housing and apartments available around the town.

The FSU Student

FSU students are warm and friendly, representing a good cross-section of American demographics. Fraternities and sororities are popular, but members tend not to hang out with the many alternative scenes on campus (everything from hippies to punks).

Almost all students are united by the strong college spirit (the 'Noles, or Seminoles, named for a tribe of Florida native-Americans who wore their feathers down as a sign of their pacifism...at odds with the FSU's warlike teams!), and by their distaste for the big rival, the University of Florida 'Gators. The school pride comes to a climax every home football game, when the whole city is overwhelmed by FSU celebratory craziness and enthusiasm and the football stadium – recently expanded to be a few microns bigger than rival University of Florida's – fills to its 78,000 seat capacity.

Students report a good diversity. "You see everything here" said one, "from straight-up partiers to people who never leave their books, and everything in between." Geographic diversity is good too, and the school is "great for international students", as people are very accepting and integration is easy. The "Global Pathways" pairing program helps with this, enabling interested locals to become friends with students from around the world.

Hitting the Books

Teachers here "really know what they're doing", and students really feel like "they are there to help you". In later years, especially, the "amazing", Nobel and Pulitzer-winning professors are very personal with students, though this is made somewhat difficult in the huge classes for introductory courses, which are often 200-300 people strong, and have squeezed as many as 1,500 students in one lecture. Generally though, class sizes are not an issue and average around 20-30.

Work load is not unbearable here – "overall it's pretty easy", said one student, though he noted that this is far from true in some classes, especially math and the sciences.

FSU has one of the best film schools in the country. Only admitting 20-odd students per year, the film program is ultra-selective. Also worthy of note is the famous "Mag Lab", a state of the art high magnetic field laboratory that requires over 300 staff to run and provides unparalleled research opportunities for the science departments. The lab is the only one of its kind in the country, and the largest of its kind in the world. Scientists gravitate to FSU just to be near it.

Social Life

FSU has a great range of extra-curriculars and social events to get your teeth into. As one of the biggest party schools in the country (usually in the top 10 or 20, according to the *Princeton Review*, with many students working around the clock to maintain that exalted ranking), there's always a house party or a bar to get to, especially for those involved in the exuberant Greek scene. There's even a popular on-campus club venue that has hosted numerous big-name bands and comedians.

The artsy community is big and exciting, offering great free concerts with all types of music (check out the opera school!), impressive modern-art displays, independent theatre groups and advance film premiers organised by the high-flying film school. And now for something completely different: official university credit can be earned taking the introductory class for FSU's student-run Flying High Circus (the circus programme has been proudly offered at FSU since 1947).

Political life is also energetic, with the university located a short drive from the State Capitol, where students frequently intern. The Republican and Democrat student groups are popular (with the latter outnumbering the former these days), as are traditional student protests, and the student government is a big deal (but generally monopolised by frat kids). Owing to the school's roots as an all-female college until 1949 (the boys went to the University of Florida in Gainesville, with a well-worn road between the two), women's groups are influential and popular.

International and humanitarian programs abound. The study-abroad program is among the top five in the country, sending thousands of students across the world every year to study, intern and volunteer.

FSU sports are huge and famous: the football (American) team recently won the National Championship (again) and is regularly amongst the top teams in the nation, and so is the baseball team. Great athletic facilities mean that anyone can practice the sport of their choice to a reasonably high level. There's also a wonderful beach sauna by the gym.

The 700+ student organisations cover almost anything you could want – from horse riding, dance troupes and cricket to debating and media. Outdoorsy activities are popular and numerous, and the university provides loads of equipment to explore the various lakes, bike trails and "The Rez" (reservation) on a nearby lake...think swimming, kayaking, canoeing almost year round, thank you sub-tropical weather (except for a few incredibly freezing days a year when even the large fountain at the front gates freezes in mid-stream).

Outside Those Ivory Walls

Populated mainly with students and politicians, Tallahassee is an odd location for a state capital, located way up in the northwestern Florida Panhandle just south of Georgia and Alabama. With three universities within its smallish city limits, the town has been called, perhaps unfairly, "a college town with a drinking problem", but all those students and politicians make for a fairly buzzy place. Expect to see a mix of scenery: many run-down areas blend in with the cool alternative culture warehouses and music venues, with lots of hills, leafy suburbs and masses of shady oaks and palm trees.

Getting In

AT A GLANCE – Application & Test Options:

– Early Decision, Regular Decision

– ACT/SAT required, Writing/essay is optional

The application process is not as rigorous as at some similar-standard schools, but due to the ever-growing population of the state, popularity of the school, and its rise in the rankings FSU is now more competitive and getting harder every year. Fewer than half of applicants are now offered a place, and the autumn 2017 class was one of the most competitive in the history of the university.

But if you can make the cut, one exotic option now open to British students is the First Year Abroad Program (FYA), where they can spend their first year of studying at one of the international FSU campuses in London, Valencia, Florence, or Panama.

The two deadlines to apply to FSU are in early November and early February, with applications based on GCSEs (including at least one foreign language GCSE), predicted A Levels, and SAT or ACT (FSU accepts either exam, but does not require the essay).

Students who are accepted can then apply for the FYA programme, where they can spend their first year of studying at one of the international campuses in London, Valencia, Florence, or Panama.

Money Matters

Fees are very reasonable by American standards, and students who are doing well with their studies can apply for financial aid on a semester-by-semester basis, and there are some scholarships on offer.

The FYA program offers a pretty incredible cash savings, as well: if the student maintains a B average whilst abroad, he/she automatically qualifies for an out-of-state tuition scholarship (70% of tuition costs waived) for the next three years on the main campus in Tallahassee.

Famous Grads

Jim Morrison – lead singer of iconic 60s psychedelic rock outfit, The Doors

Hunter S. Thompson –author and journalist (Fear and Loathing in Las Vegas)

Scott Stapp – lead singer of 2000's rock band Creed

George Washington University (Washington DC)

Washington , District of Columbia
www.gwu.edu
Undergrads: 10,000
Grads: 14,000

How many students does it take to change a light bulb at George Washington?

21 – One to change the light bulb and 20 to start a light bulb-saving campaign to petition Congress

George Washington University is often not mentioned among America's greatest schools, but whatever you do, don't dismiss this hidden gem. A buzzing, urban community near the centre of the most powerful city on earth, this university offers an international atmosphere in a politically charged environment. Fourteen elected representatives in the current Congress are GWU grads, and many more have gone on to high-flying positions across a range of (mostly political) occupations. With a hugely diverse student body, excellent quality of teaching, the best financial aid in the country and a glorious location in the capital, it's not hard to see why students come here from around the world.

The Campus

The origins of GWU do indeed lie with its namesake, the first president of America. But although it was George Washington's vision to create a national centre for learning in the fledgling country's capital, it wasn't until the presidency of James Monroe that the Reverend Luther Rice, following Washington's wishes, established the 'Columbian College' in 1821, and it wasn't until 1904 that the university took on the name of the nation's first liberator. Only in 1912 did the campus shift to Foggy Bottom, the part of the District closest to Washington's home state of Virginia, where he had originally intended his educational establishment to be.

GWU's campus may not be visually striking or particularly nice to look at – the buildings are mostly an unappealing urban mix of modern brick and concrete – but it makes up in location and cosmopolitanism what it lacks in architecture. Indeed, students generally commend the fact that you could walk through the university without knowing it was one of the capital's most highly sought colleges. The city-centre atmosphere means that you can feel part of the bustle of everyday life whilst relishing the relative shelter of being a student. And if you do want a relaxing respite from the city, GWU features at its centre (and in all the prospectuses) a delightful red-brick courtyard, complete with fountain, where Washingtonians can go to breathe freely now and again.

Besides, if you want to see amazing and beautiful architecture, it takes just a few minutes to walk to the White House, and not much longer to get to the Lincoln Memorial and the other world-famous sites of Washington DC. The area is generally well served by metro, and the campus is set out in blocks within DC's renowned grid-system, where the streets are named after letters (east to west) and numbers (north to south), so it's impossible to get lost. GWU is also very compact, which makes getting to classes easier and adds to the city feel.

For anyone who really hates concrete, GWU has a second campus called Mt. Vernon, three miles away in the less metropolitan northwest area of the city. Named after the original country residence of George Washington himself, the 23-acre Mt. Vernon campus was acquired in 1999 from Mount Vernon College for Women. Now happily coed, 'The Vern' still gives a nod to its female legacy with the Elizabeth Somers Women's Leadership Program, an academic course available only to first-year female students.

The second campus provides a more spacious and aesthetically appealing alternative for GWU, with leafy boulevards and playing fields, not to mention more hi-tech facilities for science, art and dance. The campus is served by the 'Vern Express', a shuttle bus which operates 24-hours and connects students to the city centre.

Accommodation

First-year students at GW are normally divided into 'Thematic Housing' so theoretically your residence will be filled with people that have similar interests to you. The eight 'themes' range from a 'science village' to a 'culture and arts house'. This system makes it very easy to integrate into the community and make friends quickly, but it often means that there is little interaction between houses; thankfully, this is not a big problem in a university as compact as GWU, where sociability is almost impossible to escape. Accommodation at George Washington overall is top notch, though notoriously pricy: the university often finishes in the top ten for colleges with 'dorms like palaces' according to the *Princeton Review*.

The Washingtonian

Although the university suffers from many of the same stereotypes as its more famous neighbour Georgetown ('preppy', upper-class), GWU is distinctly not a Jesuit school and is just a bit edgier. It was created by an Act of Congress that specified its secular status, so students need not fear any religious tension. Even if GWU takes its name from the man who led the charge to rid the country of evil British control, the diversity and cultural mix mean that Brits will be able to fit in with the student body much more easily than many other colleges in America. Students flock here from over 130 different countries and all 50 states of America, and there is a massive range of ethnic and social backgrounds represented.

Perhaps the most accurate stereotype for George Washington students (and indeed for any students in the District) is the political one. Students are frequently able to secure internships on 'The Hill' (ie the Houses of Congress) and participate politically in activities ranging from campaign management to think-tank work and demonstrations. The District of Columbia is known as one of the most liberal places in the country, and though this isn't true of the entire student body, politics at George Washington is about as progressive as it gets outside of the Bay Area in California.

Hitting the Books

GWU offers more than political studies; it's divided into nine 'schools' covering areas such as law, engineering and business – and expert instruction is provided across a spectrum of academic subjects, from media to medicine.

There is also an excellent Study Abroad Program, which annually sends about 900 students to 50 countries around the world.

The most famous school at GWU is the excellent Elliott School of International Relations, where future diplomats, ambassadors and politicians find training. Any kind of political study is superbly taught here. Students have unique opportunities to interact with incredibly important people, and lectures have been given by the likes of Mikhail Gorbachev (final Soviet Premier), Abba Eban (Israeli Foreign Secretary), and both Bill and Hillary Clinton. However, the number of august or even interesting speakers may be shrinking fast, since students and administration have recently been quick to ban or uninvite speakers as soon as there's a squeak from potential offendees....even banning a recent speaker invited to demonstrate that free speech and academic freedom are alive and kicking on the GWU campus.

With a student-faculty ratio of 13:1, individual attention is higher than average, but there is room for improvement. Another potential drawback is the number of 'adjunct' professors. These part-time tutors can be wonderful to work with because they normally are involved with DC-based projects and careers that give them first hand experience they can pass on to their students (as well as priceless contacts in powerful spheres). However, not being fully integrated into the university, they often find themselves pulled away to other pastures, leaving students without any real continuity of teaching. The turnover rate is worrying, but most students feel it is made up for by the scintillating expertise that comes with it.

Even if your reaction to politics is a yawn, don't discount George Washington out of hand. The business program is also excellent (and comes with almost as many internship opportunities as lectures), and the computer science program is world famous and one of a select group accredited by the National Security Agency. The medical school was responsible for saving the life of Ronald Reagan in 1981 after he was almost assassinated, and Vice President Dick Cheney also received emergency treatment there. There are 87 available majors, of which 76 have less than 100 students. This selection makes the university more expensive, but it also means there is a wide variety of courses in which you will have a bit more personal attention.

Social Life

As might be expected, the politically charged atmosphere gives rise to a particularly dynamic student body. With more than 300 student-run organisations to choose from, a freshman might feel overwhelmed, though most quickly adapt to the snappy pace of life and the abundance of opportunities it provides.

Events and activities are chalked onto the pavements in creative ways, advertising everything from Dodgeball to Bhangra. There's a range of sports (basketball is big), academics and media (a daily online magazine, a bi-weekly paper over 100 years old, and at least one radio station), and opportunities to volunteer with social groups working in the famously impoverished areas of Washington DC (not to mention the abundance of NGOs in Washington) and of course massive amounts of political activism to get your teeth into.

The Student Association (SA), which controls all student activities, is a typically Washingtonian affair – modelled on the US government and divided into a legislature, executive and judiciary. The SA runs some of the most famous student associations in the country, from a world-renowned Model United

Nations to one of the most illustrious chapters of the Students Global Aids Campaign. Partly as a way to get your mind round all these activities, all GW freshmen on arrival are given a comprehensive student-led orientation by a group which calls itself the Colonial Cabinet, one of the biggest such orientations in the US.

There is plenty of opportunity here for those who like to party, and not just parties organised by the university. One area where GWU definitely has the edge on Georgetown is the Greek community, which generates events and activities for those who want to fraternise and, er, sororitise. Those who prefer a more chilled approach to socialising will feel at home too; students extol the lack of peer pressure and their ability to enjoy themselves in whatever way they choose. The diversity of the student body is helpful here – students can be who they want to be and will always find like-minded souls to share the experience.

Outside Those Ivory Walls

Washingtonians insist that their campus is the best situated in DC. Whether you fancy a spin round the incredible Air and Space museum, a gig at the famous 9:30 Club or Black Cat, or just the legendary 'midnight monument tour', it's all there for the taking. DC is full of cool little (and not so little!) bars and clubs, not to mention great restaurants and a budding music scene.

Getting In

AT A GLANCE – Application & Test Options:

– Early Decision, Early Decision II, Regular Decision

– Test-optional, but if you are part of one of the following groups, you are still required to submit ACT/SAT scores:

- Applicants to the accelerated seven-year B.A./M.D. program
- Applicants who are home-schooled
- Applicants who attended secondary schools that provide only narrative evaluations rather than some form of grading scale
- Recruited NCAA Division I athletes

Although GWU has a great reputation, in most people's minds it sits in the second tier of universities. This means that entrance here is a little easier than at rivals such as Georgetown, though it is by no means a safe bet. The university accepts around 1 in 3 applicants, as opposed to the 1 in 6 at Georgetown, or 1 in 15 at Harvard, making it an appealing choice for those who feel they might not be judged well by the terrifying standards of the Ivy League and other big-shot unis.

But GWU doesn't turn out successful statesmen by accepting just anyone, and applications must be strong to secure a place. A rigorous academic program at your secondary school is important, so British students could be at an advantage. Interviews and SAT Subject tests are often not required. It is recommended, as usual, that you visit the university or talk to a representative in the UK (they can sometimes be found at school fairs) before applying, just to get a feel of what the university can give you, and what it wants from you.

GWU operates an early decision system, which is highly recommended if you know this is the place for you. You must submit your application a couple of months earlier than normal, and if accepted, the decision is binding. Applying for an early decision demonstrates enthusiasm for the college, and may give you a slightly greater chance of success.

Money Matters

Fees at GWU are not pretty. Tuition costs are nudging the highest in the country, and are rising at astronomical rates up over 60% in the past decade. Fortunately, a couple of factors make the pain more bearable:

- Firstly, all fees are quoted under a fixed rate scheme which means that the price of your whole four years is known from day one, and the university guarantees that this won't change.
- Secondly, if you're lucky enough to have permanent US residency or citizenship, GWU provides the most needs-based financial aid of any university in the country. Roughly 60% of undergraduates receive some kind of aid. Sadly, international students are not eligible for this assistance.

Famous Grads

Harry Reid – Senate Majority Leader

Colin Powell – Bush's first Secretary of State

Courtney Cox – Actress: Monica on Friends (contrary to her perfectionism on the TV, she dropped out after a year!)

Georgetown University (Washington DC)

Georgetown, Washington, District of Columbia
www.georgetown.edu
Undergrads: 7,600
Grads: 5,400

How many students does it to take to change a light bulb at Georgetown?

Four – one to change it, one to call Congress about their progress, and two to throw the old bulb at the American U. students.

This Jesuit college was founded in 1789 in Washington DC and has remained a thriving institution for the last three hundred years. Located a stone's throw away from the centre of American government, it has an informed and politicized scholastic environment.

It is also one of the few universities in America where international students blend right in; it has an acclaimed Foreign Service school which surprisingly, given America's frequently insular attitude to the rest of the world, actually advocates the merits of being able to locate Europe on a map. As a result of this internationalist atmosphere, foreign students head to Georgetown in droves. And why not? After all, what's good enough for Bill Clinton should be good enough for you.

The Campus

The founders of Georgetown did a pretty good job picking out their site – situated on a hill, overlooking the Potomac River, in the middle of the nation's capital, the campus' location could not be better. The buildings, on the other hand, are a mixed bag – some pretty architecture and a great deal of modern work that leaves a little to be desired.

However, while it may lack the quaint, dreaming spires feel of the New England campus, Georgetown has the bustling feel of a university in a big city and a surprising amount of space. (As a side-note to any anxious parents, it is also situated in one of the safest parts of DC.)

The surrounding area is also one of the prettiest and most historic in town – old brick housing on streets that are conveniently named after letters of the alphabet. Although the metro system is a little unreliable in this part of DC, it is an easy bus ride into the centre of a city that (as befits a capital) always has something going on.

DC, unlike New York, has a fairly relaxed atmosphere and a much nicer climate (except for in those humid summer months when you remember it is a city built on a bog). And for those students who want to escape the big city, there are plenty of open parkland spaces designed to make the Londoner feel at home.

Accommodation

All of the freshmen on campus live together in dorms and by the time people move onto their next three years of housing, many of initial barriers have been broken down and bonds formed across every divide, religious and otherwise.

The Georgetown Student

Perhaps because of its political connections and prime real estate position in one of the more exclusive parts of Washington, Georgetown has always had a reputation for drawing in rich, white, prep-school kids – the inevitable step between Philips Exeter and a seat in Congress.

Georgetown appeals to educationally minded Europeans who flock to the excellent School of Foreign Service. Yet, despite these crowds of international students all over campus, students have traditionally complained about the lack of any real ethnic or religious diversity. In recent years diversity has increased, but WASPy cliques with a strong elitist attitude are still very much a presence on campus – and tend to look fondly on the class-conscious Brit.

Georgetown remains a Jesuit university and a strong Catholic presence still thrives on campus. It is estimated that approximately 50% of the students are Catholic. While religious tension is seldom part of the everyday environment, some non-Catholic students have complained that, at least in the initial months, they feel very much in the minority. Religious traditions, such as the refusal of the campus medical system to provide the birth control pill, are subjects of strong debate.

Most students, however, agree that the campus is both large and diverse enough to accommodate any belief system or political opinion. The Hoyas (as Georgetown students like to refer to themselves) are a pretty friendly bunch and the fact they frequently aspire to future political office means they are only too happy to practise both their people skills and their international diplomacy!

The student body at Georgetown is, as one might expect from a politically savvy group of young adults, extremely active. Many of these kids are in training for a campaign trail or podium speech (successfully, it would seem: the list of ambassadors, heads of state, elected officials, military leaders amongst the famous alums has to be seen to be believed) and there are always a hundred and one things going on.

Whether you choose to get involved in social programmes (parts of DC are among the poorest in America), political organizations or the omnipresent sports teams, you can expect to have a good part of each day taken up by those extra-curricular activities that many Brits are too busy lazing in the pub to ever get around to doing. Students here also tend to be from fairly prosperous families – and there are a lot of rich and ambitious individuals around. Be warned – people here take their position in life, and their future advancement, extremely seriously.

Hitting the Books

The Georgetown campus is made up of four undergraduate schools – the School of Foreign Service (SFS) and the School of Arts and Sciences (where most students would be headed) and then the School of Business, and the School of Nursing. As a prospective student, you apply to and are accepted by a particular school.

Once on campus, however, undergraduates can take classes at any of the colleges. Each school also imposes a liberal arts core curriculum upon its students – ensuring that its nurses can quote Shakespeare as well as sew up wounds and its diplomats can balance their chequebooks at the end of the year. The SFS cannot be recommended highly enough – with a wonderful curriculum, great travel options and a premier academic reputation – it is the place to start if you are looking for an ambassadorship someday!

Despite their curricula requirements Georgetown students are more than enthusiastic about both their class loads and their professors. Although class sizes are sometimes a little bigger than the ideal, smaller sections, office hours and informal meetings ensure that students get more than enough time with their teachers.

Political students are particularly turned on by the Georgetown environment – many of their professors are also involved with the political administration and classes often feature surprise appearances by congressmen or senators. Internships on the Hill are also a possibility for the very lucky – or politically savvy.

If your interests fall more towards saving humanity than accumulating power, the local NGOs (mostly situated in Dupont Circle) also offer internships aplenty, while internationalists can take refuge at the lines of embassies that pop up all over DC.

Social Life

If you are the type of student who looks forward to spending four years doing keg stands and joining fraternities with names like Kappa Kappa Delta Phi, then Georgetown is not the place for you. But, despite not having a Greek scene, there are more than enough parties and events for everybody else. The campus itself has certain annual rituals – where else in the country could you attend an undergraduate Diplomats' Ball? – that are always packed with people.

Outside Those Ivory Walls

When on-campus casino nights get too much for you, DC offers a plethora of other options. The Georgetown area itself is home to some very cool bars, nice (although expensive) restaurants and fun clubs. And for those seeking a bustling but more studenty nightlife, the Adams Morgan area (famous for being the place where underage presidential twins came to grief) offers streets of great Saturday night options.

Getting In

AT A GLANCE – Application & Test Options:

- Early Action, Regular Decision
- ACT/SAT required, Writing/essay is optional
- Three SAT Subject tests "highly recommended" (essentially required)

Unsurprisingly, the nationally renowned standards of Georgetown make this an increasingly competitive place for admission. In recent years, approximately 16% of applicants have been offered a spot, which is more than a little daunting. Although you might have a slight edge as an international student, a strong application is essential. (And Georgetown uses its own application, not the Common App.)

They 'highly recommend' that you have three SAT Subject tests (versus the normal two) and require a pre-entrance interview. The interview is mandatory but there are alumni situated in London and other places in the UK who are only too happy to make sure you are the right kind of person to do honour to their alma mater. Sell yourself to them, but also make sure they sell the place to you – getting the inside scoop is all important in choosing the right place for you to spend the next four years of your life. Georgetown does not offer Early Decision but they have something called Early Action, which gives you a chance to apply early and get notification in December, but it offers no advantage in getting in and is not binding.

Money Matters

Be warned, while Georgetown does have a few financial aids packages for international students, you have to ask for them and need-blind admission (tho offered to US students) is not an option.

Famous Grads

Bill Clinton – statesman extraordinaire, need we say more?

Felipe de Borbon – Crown Prince of Spain

George Tenet – former CIA chief

Georgia Institute of Technology

Atlanta, Georgia
www.gatech.edu
Undergrads: 14,000
Grads: 6,400

How many Georgia Tech students does it take to change a light bulb?

About 230 – ten to conceive new light bulb technology, one to sell it to NASA, 175 to build a new research facility with the money, 35 to install the new lighting technology to power the lights for the football game against UGA, and at least a dozen undergraduates to complain about the work load.

The MIT of the South, the Georgia Institute of Technology is one of the most formidable powerhouse of scientific research available to undergraduates who really want to push themselves. The experience will not be easy and for some not even enjoyable, but it will let you be part of the one of the most cutting edge research institutions in the country.

Georgia Tech also provides a classic, if work-oriented, college education, with opportunities in sports, the arts and campus life. If you want an easy ride then forget it, but if you want top class academic rigour, combined with an intense work hard/play hard attitude, then this is the place for you.

The Campus

Georgia Tech dominates the western portion of midtown Atlanta, with a sizeable campus achieving the perfect collegiate mix of seclusion within a big city. Like Atlanta itself, the Georgia Tech campus has been undergoing loads of construction work in recent years, and now boasts all the high-tech facilities and state of the art buildings that you would expect of a technology-based institution, with further upgrades on the way.

The university recently acquired "Tech Square," an assortment of fancy buildings with restaurants, book shops and a hotel. The Square is located across a big highway from the university, connected by an aesthetically superb new bridge, and was one of the sparks which helped to regenerate the previously run-down midtown area.

Although it had the highest crime rate in the country during the 80s, Atlanta's security has improved massively, especially around the Georgia Tech area; these days, the university police force has only a few petty crimes to deal with.

Accommodation

Students report mainly good things about their surroundings, praising the walkability and great buildings. Most freshmen and a good number of sophomores and juniors live in the dorms on campus, which get mixed reviews but seem generally not too shabby. The characteristically impressive fraternity and sorority houses (of which about a third of students are members) are also on campus.

The Yellow Jacket

The Georgia Tech stereotype is exceptionally intelligent, computer literate, shy and probably a little nerdy. Like all stereotypes, there's some truth to this perception... but not much. Like other large public schools, Georgia Tech has a broad-based student body.

Georgia Tech students, called 'Yellow Jackets' after the official mascot Buzz (a bee or wasp of some kind), are generally outgoing and friendly, love to party and enjoy the same things as college kids across the country. Students are active in on-campus organisations, off-campus parties, and plenty of varsity and intramural sports (see Social Life section below). True, most of them do work fiendishly hard (especially the engineers), and there probably isn't anyone on campus who can't distinguish a bit from a byte, but otherwise the Jackets are diverse and interesting – with nary a shirt-front pocket protector to be seen. About 50% of students are from Georgia, the rest from the other 49 states and many countries overseas.

Hitting the Books

The university is dominated by the engineering department, which enrols 50-60% of the student body– it's where you'll find the real psychos who work all day every day. Outside of engineering, and even in some cases within it, the work load is manageable, if challenging. "Work is hard, but not necessarily plentiful," said one junior.

Georgia Tech only offers Bachelor of Science degrees – even in the Liberal Arts school. This doesn't mean that there are only science courses available. Plenty of non-scientific courses are popular and well taught (especially in areas like business and international relations), but they generally have a technological bent. You're not going to find any "easy" fringe courses here – so if you were looking for basket weaving then look away now.

Ultimately, the people working ridiculously hard at Georgia Tech are doing so because they love their subject and are interested in their work, and they have a lot to be interested in – this school is responsible for mindblowingly exciting projects and some of the most innovative work in the world.

Research opportunities here are unparalleled, and they're not confined to the graduate students. Undergraduates, especially if they're persistent (and if they're engineers), can often get involved with top-quality stuff, and everyone loves the way "all the science components aren't just repeating old experiments – everything here is creative and extremely cutting-edge."

Research programs can be a problem too. Professors are under huge pressure to focus on their research at the expense of undergraduate teaching; many classes are taught by bored post-grads or junior profs who are clearly more interested in their tenure than their students. Contracts with major companies and service-providers, guaranteed on the strength of Georgia Tech's research reputation, are fundamental to the university's budget (and the funding behind all those big new building developments on campus), so there are financial pressures to maintain the research side of the college at all costs. There is no spoon-feeding here, but luckily teachers are required to hold office hours which you should use as much as you can.

Still, professors tend to get better and more helpful the older you get and the higher the level of your course. There is the usual contingent of mega-faculty, including some world-renowned speakers like NASA directors and ex-senators.

Although admissions for Tech are not as rigorous as you might expect, the university operates a ruthless and more than slightly daunting drop-out policy, whereby it is content to force under-achieving students to leave at the end of the first year, ensuring that only the best remain to earn their degree. This happens to a massive one in three students! You can normally return just once, but will be gone for good if you don't live up to standards a second time.

Despite this, students don't seem too concerned with their situation, saying that the experience is "a test of self-discipline; if you stay on top of your work, everything will go fine". Almost everyone here was top of his class at high-school and has to readjust to being little more than mediocre at college. Many of them are summarily out-performed by ultra-dedicated international students.

One of the biggest positives here is that everyone loves "being around people who have come to learn". What's more, they know their degree will be one of the most respected by employers in the country (and they will have some amazing networking opportunities) – but they don't expect this to come without a price.

Social Life

Academics at Georgia Tech are legendary for the stress levels they elicit. The *Princeton Review* ranked the school the 10th toughest college, with some of the unhappiest students in the country. That was in 2001. The rankings caused outrage among the administration, provoking a backlash against the Review. They criticized its methods and highlighted the enjoyable features of a Tech education. GT appears on neither ranking now, and even though students still call graduation "getting out", it's difficult not to agree with the administration that there's more to Georgia Tech than just non-stop work.

There is as much on offer here as any high-flying state school – tons of student organisations, plenty of sports and all the big parties, not to mention the incredible range of things to do in Atlanta. The party scene at GT revolves around the Greek life, especially for men, who outnumber females here two to one. Students like to party hard in the little time they have away from their books, so there's plenty of drinking and so on, but most students are responsible enough to keep things from getting out of hand.

For a science-based college, arts are surprisingly ubiquitous. There are always top-notch theatrical performances, concerts and art exhibitions (both student and outside performances), normally sponsored by the student centre. A cappella groups are very popular, as is the famous marching band that plays at all the sports games. The aptly named "Glee Club" is a nationally-renowned choral group. Improv comedy and dance troupes are going strong, and student newspaper and radio is up to scratch.

Scientific groups are also, as you might expect, very popular. For example, car building (off-road/F1/solar-powered vehicles alike) is funded by GM (or at least it has been up to now.... watch this space!) in an attempt to court GT engineers for future recruitment, and it attracts lots of excited car fanatics.

Sports are almost as big a deal here as they are at the more typical big state universities. In particular, the ancient rivalry with the University of Georgia (known as "Clean, Old-Fashioned Hate") gets the Yellow Jackets extremely fired up. The football and basketball teams are not national champions, but they do exceptionally well considering that all athletes are required to be as academically accountable as everyone else. Since Georgia Tech is small for a state school, tickets to games at the big stadium (free) are easier to come by.

For more ordinary sportsmen, there are great facilities of every description, including the huge Recreation Centre which houses the swimming pool used in the 1996 Olympics, and plenty of intramural options.

Outside Those Ivory Walls

Atlanta, state capital of Georgia and largest city in the South, is a sprawling urban mess – a classic case study in how not to build a city. Rich in history, as a major railway centre (first called Marthasville) and the last bastion of Southern forces against the North in the civil war, Atlanta is the home town of Martin Luther King Jr, who was born and raised in the Sweet Auburn district; his home and grave (nearby) are still open to visitors.

Atlanta has been rebuilt several times and is now a modern metropolis of skyscrapers and big-name companies. There is as much to do as can be imagined in any big American city, and Tech students, especially older ones, take full advantage. Although the traffic can be unbearable and the roads are the worst, the centre of town is pleasant and full of fun places to hang out or visit, not to mention an awesome night life, first-class shopping and museums. Check out the world's biggest aquarium, CNN, the Coca-Cola Company's headquarters, and the beautiful Piedmont Park.

Atlanta is also a famously international city, at least by the standards of the South, with various consulates (including a British one) trade or chamber of commerce offices. The busy Hartsfield-Jackson Atlanta International Airport is a major hub, and can whip you off to just about anywhere.

Getting In

AT A GLANCE – Application & Test Options:

- Early Action, Regular Decision
- ACT/SAT required, Writing/essay is optional (but recommended)
- SAT Subject tests optional

Georgia Tech tends to attract interest only from the brightest and best – and fewer than 1/3 of these talented applicants are currently accepted. Strong credentials are required if you want outdistance the competition and convince the admissions team that you're not going to be a drop-out after year one.

Money Matters

The college is well endowed (CocaCola money) and provides generous financial aid, with about 80% of incoming freshmen receiving help. Unfortunately, the system is harsh for international students. GT's website dedicates only a short paragraph to financial aid for international applicants, which puts it bluntly: "International students are not eligible for federal or state financial aid programs. Institutional scholarships administered by our office are not awarded to international students."

However, a glimmer of hope may be available through the merit-based Stamps President's Scholarship Program, which is open to both US and UK eligible applicants. The competition for this grant is ferocious...but not insurmountable. Definitely worth checking into.

Famous Grads

Jimmy Carter – President of the United States, 1977-1981, and Nobel Peace Prize winner

John Young – NASA astronaut and first commander of the Space Shuttle. (Georgia Tech has at least 15 astronauts among its alumni.)

Michael Arad – Architect of the World Trade Centre Memorial (selected from over 5,000 applicants)

Hampshire College

Amherst, Massachusetts
www.hampshire.edu
Undergrads: 1,500
Grads: 0

How many Hampshire students does it take to change a light bulb?

Dude, if you needed a light, you just had to ask.

Hampshire is a member of the prestigious Five Colleges consortium (meaning students are able to take classes and use the facilities of any of the other four Amherst, MA, schools) but is an entirely unique college experience unto itself. This is because of the passion students and teachers alike have for alternative, experimental education – the main source of the love-hate relationship that so many have with this school. Hampshire is "home to serious academics turned off by the ivory tower's strict disciplinary boundaries".

The Campus

Even though the campus is not the most aesthetically pleasing of places (the style is described as "Brutalist" and prison-like) and lacks many of the most basic college staples (a convenience store, post office, etc.), students are easily able to take excursions to the very cool college towns of Amherst, Northampton and Springfield.

Accommodation

Room parties and intoxication are a staple. Three quarters of students live in college-owned accommodation.

The Hampshire Student

There is a school-wide off-kilter quality that allows those who have never been able to fit in before to find their place. Dreadlock-sporting vegans will feel that they are no longer in a minority. The college was the first to boycott apartheid South Africa in 1979, setting a nationwide trend.

However, there is constant concern on campus that Hampshire is increasingly become a more normal kind of institution. Student groups have frequently called for action to keep things radical and alternative, and generally the college has been able to (intentionally or not) continue attracting applicants that chime with this ethos of experimentation and anti-normal protest.

Hitting the Books

Despite its best efforts to avoid classification, Hampshire is essentially a liberal arts college – but with several unique twists that stress education over letter grades, and a DIY academic environment. Creative subjects such as film, theatre, art and music are especially well-taught.

Professors are known to encourage students to go against the mould, get outside their comfort zones and bend disciplines to fit their interests. (interdisciplinary work is the rule rather than the exception). Often, new and intriguing subjects are taught really well, but they're equally likely to be "unbacked, subjective nonsense that students take to be 100% true", according to one sophomore.

The non-traditional and ever-changing curriculum is designed to be responsive to student interests and flexible enough for you to be able to design your own path. A big premium is placed on the student's own motivation and organisation in this regard: those who are apathetic about learning should stay away.

Other Hampshire buzzwords include "narrative evaluation" (written reports that replace letter grades) and "portfolios" (with a greater focus on project work than other colleges) – instead of the more typical GPAs and distribution requirements.

In the last year, students do not take any courses but rather complete one "advanced project" (not necessarily a written thesis – could be a creative collage, practical engineering, social organisation and more), and two "advanced learning activities" which could mean anything from internships to independent studies.

Social Life

Although ultimate Frisbee is more or less the only sport on campus, and social life can get claustrophobic or "incestuous", there are a huge number of ways to get involved with the community outside of class.

Be warned though: there's is very little "school spirit", and "many community institutions are brittle or simply non-existent", according to one student. There's not even a yearbook, let alone Greek life. Yet the studious-cum-laid back atmosphere and lack of school pride is also praised by students for keeping things unpretentious.

Getting In

AT A GLANCE – Application & Test Options:

- Early Action, Early Decision, Early Decision II, Regular Decision

- Test-blind policy (does not consider ACT/SAT, even if perfect score)

Admission difficulty is said to be average (accepting around 70%).

Money Matters

Costs are high, in line with other private liberal arts schools, but Hampshire offers several merit-based scholarships as well as needs-based financial aid (of which over 60% of students are recipients). International students are eligible for needs-based aid up to the cost of tuition (but not other costs).

Famous Grads

Ken Burns – documentary film-maker

Charlie Clouser – musician (former member of 'Nine Inch Nails')

Chuck Collins – political activist

Barry Sonnenfeld – Film director (the Addams Family and Men in Black films)

Jon Krakauer – Mountain climber and author of Into Thin Air, Into the Wild and more

Liev Schreiber – actor (Scream trilogy, Salt, X-Men Origins) and director (Everything is Illuminated)

Harvard University

Cambridge (Boston), Massachusetts
www.harvard.edu
Undergrads: 6,700
Grads: 14,000

How many students does it take to change a light bulb at Harvard?

One – he holds the bulb and the world revolves around him.

You can always spot the British people who get into Harvard. Ask them where they're going to university and they'll somewhat shiftily reply, 'America'. Ask them where in America and they'll say, 'Somewhere in Boston'. Pry further and you'll eventually be rewarded by a combination of pride, humility and general embarrassment as they mumble, 'Harvard'.This false modesty is rewarded in England, because Harvard is one of the few American universities that anyone over here has heard of.

The oldest university in America, it also (rightly) prides itself on being one of the greatest. From its early beginnings to the latest league rankings, Harvard has stayed at the head of the field – a name that carries worldwide recognition. With faculty that dominate international academia, a mere 37 billion dollar endowment to play with and alumni who sing its praises across the globe, Harvard is definitely one option that you want to leave on your list.

The Campus

Harvard's campus is akin to that of so many of the other big New England universities – a mix of charming old and fairly revolting new. Of course, Harvard, founded in 1636, revels in the fact that its old is older than anyone else's and its new, while almost universally disliked, was designed by architects such as Le Corbusier.

The campus centres around the 'Yard'. This attractive expanse of green, enclosed by red brick buildings, plays host to the oldest dorm rooms (once used to house troops fighting the British), the magnificent Widener Library, the striking memorial church and throngs of students tossing Frisbees, sunbathing, snowballing or participating in 'Primal Scream', the biannual naked run! Freshmen enjoy all the advantages of living in this heart of the college campus, placed in smaller houses with more supervision and more exposure to their year group than the older classes.

The extended Harvard campus consists of a collection of houses (modelled on Oxbridge colleges) where the upper-class students live. Some of these bear the good old New England names of their Puritan founders (Eliot, Winthrop, Kirkland and Lowell) and have changed little since the eighteenth century. However, the housing lottery can be cruel and other students find themselves relegated to the old Radcliffe quad with its modern monstrosities and long walk from the central campus. At Harvard, however, divine recompense ensures that those houses that are modern and isolated generally offer better accommodation than those that are attractive and central.

Inevitably each house develops its own sense of camaraderie and people grow to love even the ugliest dorms. In addition, the advantage of en masse freshman housing means that initial bonds often last entire university careers. Thus the disadvantages of being housed for some period nearer to Canada than the Yard are softened by the fact that friendship groups are dispersed all over.

Accommodation

Many students gripe about the Harvard campus and its accommodation. The noisy Mass Avenue cuts straight past the Yard and ruins the tranquil feel that John Harvard initially aimed for, while Harvard Square has sacrificed much of its eclectic intellectual charm and succumbed to big brand name shops.

Students also consistently moan about being crammed into rooms with little space or privacy. (In American colleges it is not unusual to find yourself with a roommate for some of your four years, something that rarely occurs on our side of the pond.) Yet, moan as they may, most students would probably agree that your room serves as little more than a base from which to conduct the rest of your frenetic life. Similarly, although Harvard has, like all modern universities, had to lose some of its olde worlde charm, it remains a vibrant and attractive place that the vast majority of students are proud to live in.

The Crimson Man/Woman

Whatever else you can say to insult them, Harvard students are never ones to be left behind. Most of them are used to being the best in their high schools and the combination of all of these IQs (and egos) in a high-pressure, academic environment often leads to some explosive results. It is said that every year Harvard would be able to fill its freshman class with people who have achieved 100% on every SAT exam they took.

It speaks highly of Harvard Admissions that they try to look beyond academic achievement and gather together a group of people whose talents are broader.

And they get what they want. Harvard has, and always has had, the highest yield rate among its applicants, a statistic that suggests it is near impossible to turn down. After all, author bias aside, Harvard is Harvard.

Arriving at Harvard can be a rather daunting experience. You may well find yourself sharing a room with a concert pianist or eating with someone who has already won two Olympic medals. This is one of the most valuable parts of the Harvard experience. Every individual there is interesting and talented – you just have to take a deep breath and remind yourself that the admissions committee can't have screwed up that badly picking you. (Harvard lore has it that most students spend their freshman year asking, 'How did I get here?' and their sophomore year wondering, 'How did you get here?' – so don't be too nervous those first few days.) Just remember, everyone is there for a reason – and that reason doesn't have to be an ability to make straight As.

Inevitably, all these brain cells and talent can lead to a competitive and ultra-focused environment. People at Harvard are always stressed out and (like every other elite school in the country) enjoy nothing more than moaning about how much more work they have than anyone else in the entire world. While the problems of adjusting to the strains of a bigger workload and new social environment mean that some freshmen can have a tricky time, most people quickly settle down.

And by their second year, students have easily learnt how to juggle the bare minimum of work with the maximum amount of free time. After that, the moans simply become another status symbol!

Harvard students always like to be protesting about something. If they're not bemoaning the latest curricular changes, they're launching a living wage campaign against the university administration. Grumbling about grades is only one minor indication of a valuable desire to get involved and change things.

Harvard students love participation and no day is complete without a mind-boggling range of extra-curricular activities. Whether they are organizing marches on University Hall, writing a weekly column for the renowned daily Crimson or involved in a social-service scheme that benefits half of Boston, there are few Harvard students who spend all their free time in bed. With well-respected orchestras, choirs and drama troupes, not to mention the numerous sports teams, Harvard offers something for almost everyone and most people are only too keen to pursue an extra hobby (or seven!)

Harvard students like to revel in their tradition and history, but are also keen to point out that the university has come a long way from the rich, white man ethos that defined it for hundreds of years. This is not to say that Lowells, Winthrops, Cabots and a handful of other Mayfloweresque names do not still haunt the campus. The traditions of these East Coast elite continue to thrive, but an influx of international and minority students have diluted them.

The problem for the future lies in integrating these groups. Many Harvard students complain that self-segregation means that the student body (while apparently diverse) is still fairly socially homogeneous. But the average British student will encounter more varied ethnic, religious, and political backgrounds in one day at this university than in their entire high school career.

Almost everyone eventually discovers that Harvard students are friendly, enthusiastic and easy to get to know. The fact that the university boasts the largest endowment of any in America points to the commitment and affection of its alumni. It is also vital in ensuring that Harvard students are spoilt rotten. Money can be wheedled out of the university for just about any purpose, whether your desire is to set up a tiddlywinks club or to get a grant to go and study the beers of Bratislava. And once you have your grant, you'll almost certainly discover a student who has done the very same thing before and a top-notch faculty member who is keen to support you.

Hitting the Books

Words cannot describe the calibre of some of the Harvard faculty. This is an institution that regularly recruits the best brains in the world, seduces them to Cambridge with promises of tenure and academic glory and then plonks them down in front of a class of undergrads. While the best brains in the world might resent such treatment, the undergrads benefit hugely and the teaching resources at Harvard are truly the thing that make it one of the world's best universities.

Harvard has first-class academic resources – from the vast Widener Library (beware, it is so huge you can lose mobile reception and be gone forever) to the incredible science labs and all of them are available to the eager undergrad.

One of the more amazing things about Harvard (and there are many) is the fact that you are continually brushing shoulders with the gods of academia. Students really do see famous poets drinking in the local bar or world-class philosophers running late for class. Meanwhile the pull of the H-bomb (or Harvard name) brings in speakers that range from Bill Clinton to Ali G.

Professor-student interaction and contact with these big names is much encouraged, and faculty members could not be friendlier. All students need to do is screw up the courage to have a conversation with them and select their classes carefully. If you pick wisely and listen to people around you, you could end up in a seminar with someone as illustrious as President Faust herself.

Harvard students quickly learn the importance of never taking no for an answer. There is a renowned story about a professor who rejected all 200 of the applicants for a fifteen-place seminar and then accepted everyone who complained. American university has no place in it for British manners and reserved modesty.

There are numerous services and tutors who are more than willing to look out for you, but you have to ask them to do so. Go to office hours, talk to your professors (after all how scary can a Nobel Prize winner or poet laureate be?), think about your courses and you will come out as the educated graduate your parents always hoped you would be.

Unlike many universities where the core liberal arts requirements are fulfilled by a prescriptive list of classes, Harvard's curriculum includes courses that address public issues and practical decision–making in hopes of making salient connections between the classroom and real–life topics.

Despite this, Harvard's course load is still fairly structured and can be extremely hard work. Those individuals who wish to spend four years in a pub, and believe that Widener Library is merely a place with great tobogganing opportunities when it snows, should think about whether Harvard is really the right place for them.

Sophomores must declare a major (or concentration, in Harvard-speak) in the spring of their second year. Some of the departments do allow you an easier ride of it but others have masses of requirements that can overburden even the most dedicated geek.

Luckily there are plenty of people (including your subject tutor) who can help you find the right balance. And once you've found your interest, you can be secure in the knowledge that almost nowhere else in the country will be able to offer you quite the same level of research facilities, labs and general guidance (thanks to those 37 billion dollars).

Social Life

While Harvard tries its hardest, it has never really been able to shake off its 'put forty geeks in a room and you get a really bad party' image. Students still look back to its brief heyday in the swinging sixties, while Yalies mock from their more social campus. But while students may have to work a lot harder than their British peers to discover what's going on come Saturday night, there are plenty of social opportunities out there for those who want them.

Freshmen may find themselves caught in an eternal cycle of dorm room cruising and the inevitable ID problem (Puritan Massachusetts has no mercy), but by the second year most students have established a social niche. Sports teams can normally be relied on for the infamous keg parties, while the slightly more civilized head for the plethora of restaurants and bars that Cambridge has to offer. The even more adventurous also have the option of the Boston club scene – Lansdowne Street offers a million club venues – where the whole university decamps for college parties on a fairly regular basis.

Harvard also hosts that strange institution – the "final club". These male-only buildings, scattered around the Harvard campus, offer another refuge to the socially intrepid on a weekend night. Boys should, however, beware: as freshmen they stand as much chance of getting into one as a snowball does in hell (unless of course you have a contact on the inside). 'Punch' (or recruiting) process takes place over sophomore year and allows each club to self-select its members for the next three years. Each club has a distinctive character – the Porcellian (or Porc) is the iconic finals club, often bracketed with Cambridge's Pitt Club and Oxford's Gridiron Club – and they offer a great place to go and party outside university jurisdiction.

Girls, however, are frequently heard to complain that the atmosphere can be more like a meat market than socially enjoyable, and in recent years have formed their own single-sex organisations (in addition to branches of national sororities). Much debate is ongoing as to whether these undeniably elitist clubs are beneficial or detrimental to Harvard's image, and whether they will continue to exist in their current form. But Brits seem to love them and no one can deny they throw some great parties!

Outside Those Ivory Walls

Cambridge itself is merely a suburb of Boston but to hear most Harvard students talk, you would think it was a self-contained town in the middle of nowhere. Although eager freshmen come to Harvard keen to experience life in a big city, many find that they rarely venture beyond the boundaries of Harvard Square.

For those who do – and it is strongly recommended that you at least try – a whole new world opens up. Boston is a wonderful city (commonly believed to have the greatest number of affluent young singles in America) and packed with students. Whether you like clubbing, marathons, Italian pastries or ducklings, Boston is the place for you. A mere ten minutes by the famous T (underground) or a slightly longer and much more expensive cab ride, Boston is one of Harvard's best and most underused resources.

If your tastes lean more towards nature than Newbury Street (Boston's equivalent of Oxford Street), then Harvard also allows for a certain amount of travelling. In the winter, if you are dedicated enough to battle through the inevitable snow, there are ski resorts close enough for weekend trips if you are lucky enough to have a friend with a car. In the warmer months, the wonderful Cape and Martha's Vineyard are reachable by bus. Meanwhile opportunities for hiking, sailing and all those other outdoorsy things abound.

Finally for those who find Boston too limited (which is pretty hard given its size and diversity), New York is near enough for a weekend visit. About four hours by car or one hour on the wonderful air shuttle, it offers a great alternative for those who crave the amusements of the biggest city of them all.

Getting In

AT A GLANCE – Application & Test Options:

- Early Action, Regular Decision
- ACT/SAT required, with Writing/essay
- Two SAT Subject tests required

Harvard takes a certain amount of pride in boasting about the number of immensely talented and academically superior students it rejects each year (94% did not make the cut in 2016). This can be somewhat disheartening to the already nervous applicant. But while there can be no doubt that Harvard demands your highest grades and maximum academic effort, it also values those other random things that make up such a diversely amazing student body.

So speak out to them about your record for the 100m or your early years in outer Mongolia. If they went for grades alone, they would have a pretty boring freshman class and it's your job to show the other side to your character. The big chance to do this is in your admissions essay. The more random the subject and the more passionate you are about it, the better you will do.

On a more factual level, Harvard demands the standard SAT or ACT test and two SAT Subject tests. It also pays attention to international exams, so make sure you speak up about your A levels (they can also come in useful if you want to get out of required classes later on).

There is also the option of an alumni interview – something that you should definitely take up (and remember it is as much for their benefit as it is for yours). Harvard grads love to talk about the best days of their lives in their dear old alma mater – and you can learn a lot about its good points (and its bad) by simply listening. So make the effort to jump through all the hoops Harvard puts in your path – in the long run they're beneficial.

They have a particularly helpful website: the Application Tips section (www.admissions.college.harvard.edu/apply/tips/index.html) has been created in an effort to take as much mystery out of the process as possible.

Money Matters

Admission to Harvard is need-blind (financial need is not considered during the admission process) and it is one of the very few universities in which international students have the same access to financial aid as United States citizens. What's more, the Harvard Financial Aid Initiative provides aid to not only low income but also moderate income students; families with annual income of up to $65,000 (an unusually high threshold) are not expected to contribute anything to college costs, and expected contribution is between 0 and 10% if family income is between $65,000 and $150,000. This is a wonderful resource and one that not enough people know about. Your education here could, conceivably, cost you less than your tuition fees would in England.

So definitely bear this in mind and don't be ashamed or reluctant to enquire. American colleges are well aware of the huge financial burden they place upon their students and they are extremely clued in to how to lighten it.

Famous Grads

John Adams, John Quincy Adams, FDR, Teddy Roosevelt and JFK – all presidents of this great nation

T. S. Eliot – biggest star in the Harvard poetic galaxy

Tommy Lee Jones – just to show we have our lighter side as well! (Roommate of Al Gore!)

Hunter College

Upper East Side, New York City, New York
www.hunter.cuny.edu
Undergrads: 15,000
Grads: 6,000

How many Hunter students does it take to change a light bulb?
One, but he can do it on the subway on the way there.

Do you want to wake up in a city that never sleeps? Do you want to make those little town (little island?) blues just melt away? Come "be a part of it" at Hunter, NYC's cool commuter college.

A public "city" university in both the official and urban sense, Hunter has a long history of educating the residents of America's greatest metropolis, no matter what background they come from. Nowadays, it continues to give folks from all walks of life a chance to engage in one of the most exciting college experiences on offer – study in the heart of New York.

The Campus

If you wanted to study in America because of the beautiful, open, tree-filled campuses, then Hunter is not the place for you. The college revolves essentially around the junction of 68th St and Lexington Ave in uptown Manhattan.

The college buildings on all four corners of this intersection are regular New York fare – tall and oldish, and two of them are connected by a neat glass tunnel suspended above the road below.

The non-stop traffic and general urban buzz means that Hunter provides no collegiate seclusion from the city, a positive for most students (though a few say they would prefer a more traditional campus).

Inside the main buildings, however, things are much more pleasant, and a friendly, university atmosphere pervades. Students gather in the corridors or "the bridge" to talk over a coffee, or grab a lunch at the third-floor café with its outdoor terrace.

Apart from a seven-storey library (housing a lot more than seven stories!) facilities are never much better than adequate on the Hunter campus itself, and often in dire need of renovation.

But in some ways Hunter students profit from the best facilities in the world – all of New York City. The subway stop at Hunter's doorstep whisks students off to all corners of this vast city every day, though some attractions, such as Central Park and a few awesome bars and restaurants, can be comfortably walked to.

Don't be surprised if many of your classes are in world-famous museums (Hunter is not far from "the Met" – one of the most prestigious art and history museums in the world), but also don't complain if you have to commute to find a decent gymnasium.

Accommodation

There's only space for about 600 students (about 3% of the total) in the university's sole residence hall, and most of it is reserved for honour students. That means you'll probably have to find accommodation somewhere in the big scary metropolis – potentially a daunting prospect for a young Brit just out of school.

But once the necessary adjustments to New York life are made, it's easy to warm to the thrill of the experience. Be warned though – the city is not cheap. Of course, if you're used to London you won't be too shocked.

The Hunter Student

Hunter is as diverse as New York itself ("it's the city condensed into a little space," as one student put it), with people from every conceivable economic and racial background, as you can tell from the various national student organisations (Polish, Colombian, you name it). Some rank it as high as 3rd most diverse in the country.

People here are use to every form of individualism and craziness, not necessarily from the student body itself but from the people they see on the streets every day. "Nothing fazes you after you've been at Hunter for a while", said one junior.

The college certainly doesn't feel typical of America; it's more of a multi-cultural mish-mash which conforms to no set values or stereotypes, again like the city itself.

Even traditional student demographics like age go out the window here – you'll be sharing classes with 35 year olds with one career already behind them, as often as you will with wet-behind-the-ears 18 year-olds. The resulting environment precludes all possibility of cliquiness; people are very accepting of each other, and integration of even the most socially awkward (or, of course, international students) can be wonderfully smooth.

Unfortunately, however, the nature of the school is such that it's difficult to create a close community, since the majority of students leave campus every day after class to far flung homes around the city.

This can make it hard to forge relationships, and some students barely interact with each other at all outside of classes, because they already have plenty of friends in the Lower East Side or Williamsburg or wherever they live.

This is not to say students are unfriendly or antisocial – far from it. Students frequently mention the welcoming, friendly nature of their peers as one of their favourite things about the school, and you just have to hang out around the cafeteria at lunch time to feel the warm-hearted vibe that the worldly, confident students exude. You can also make friends easily at one of the student or college run organisations, and of course during classes.

Hitting the Books

Academics are the selling point at Hunter; the small, intense classes are "challenging and motivating", and occasionally stressful, especially the competitive ones. The "helpful" professors are usually of a high quality (with one or two outliers), good at motivating students and generally approachable outside of class.

Work ethic is strong, owing to the large numbers of students who are studying for professional reasons and are dedicated to their work (the highest proportion of such students can be found in the night classes), but there are also those who expect easy grades and will slack if given the opportunity (and suffer with a much duller experience).

As already mentioned, the city provides lots of exciting bonuses for classes – field trips are common and it's easy to get real experience of what you're learning about. If you're doing a film course for example, you can interact with the media hub in midtown, while scientists can use Central Park or the Hudson River as their very own laboratory.

Coupled with this are the enormous range of easy-to-secure internships at whatever job you want to get started in. Hunter students have positions at CNN, the Natural History Museum and many other internationally prominent places.

The college is academically well-rounded, though stand-out courses are in media studies and performing arts, as well as nursing, languages (including classics), and public service.

Social Life

There may not be a huge campus life at Hunter, but with New York City effectively serving as the greater campus, get ready for a social life to end all social lives. What there is on campus can be pretty fun, though: a good number of interesting groups (150), college-organised parties about once a week, one or two sports (try the fencing), an excellent Model United Nations team, student media and government and a small Greek life.

Outside Those Ivory Walls

Once you get out of the college (not hard to do!), the options become so plentiful and impressive that it can be hard to choose. NYC has the best of everything – shopping, eating, drinking, parks, museums, famous sights, waterfronts, music, theatre, comedy, art – all a big hodge-podge of excitement, diversity and urban bustle among the ridiculously tall buildings on every street. The question is, what's not to do?

Be warned, however, that as great as it is, especially for youthful students, New York is not a place for those who require hand holding. It can be an anti-social, cutthroat city, and Hunter is not going to be guiding you through it step by step. The whole experience at the university allows for a lot of personal autonomy, and is very open to individuals' creativity, which makes the city life all the more heady and exhilarating. But shrinking violets might want to think twice before plunging into the Big Apple.

Getting In

AT A GLANCE – Application & Test Options:

– Rolling basis admissions for Autumn and Spring programs

– ACT/SAT required

Hunter is a CUNY college (City University of New York), meaning that local NY residents are massively subsidised. This in turn means huge numbers of impoverished folk apply here to avoid the big price tags of NYU or Columbia, and consequently competition for places is very high, with only about one in four applicants earning a place. Strong applications are in order.

Money Matters

As for fees, Hunter is one of the best value-for-money schools in the country, with basic tuition and fees (but not room and board) for out-of-state residents at around $17,000. You may want to factor in living expenses before selecting Hunter because of its price, however, as they are a lot higher than at colleges in other cities. There is some merit-based aid, but no needs-based aid for international students.

Be warned that Hunter has a reputation for having an application system full of red-tape. Some bureaucratic problems may have to be endured.

Famous Grads

Nick Valensi – guitarist for indie rock band The Strokes

Gertrude Elion and Rosalyn Yalow – Nobel Laureates in medicine

Marjorie Morningstar – eponymous heroine of the classic Herman Wouk novel

Johns Hopkins

Baltimore, Maryland
www.jhu.edu
Undergrads: 5,300
Grads: 1,800 (excluding professional schools)

How many students does it take to change a light bulb at JHU?

None – no one changes it. The less competition, the better.

For those students who like the idea of a small college with big research opportunities, Johns Hopkins is an option that should not be left off the list. This relatively small institution was founded in 1876 as the country's first research university and has gone from strength to strength since then. Situated in Baltimore, a city with dubious charms but only 45 minutes away from the nation's capital, Johns Hopkins has established a reputation for itself as a school based on hard work and success.

The Campus

Johns Hopkins is most famous for its world-class medical school and hypochondriacs should rest assured that any ailments contracted in this area will receive some of the best treatment in the States. While rivalry for the two undergraduate schools (one catering for the Arts and Sciences and the other for engineering) is less overwhelming than that at the med school, both are considered to be excellent institutions.

Situated on the Homewood campus in downtown Baltimore, these two relatively small colleges offer great facilities and unparalleled research opportunities. English, science and (unsurprisingly) pre-med courses have a reputation for excellence as does the International Relations programme – a great option for Brits hoping to refine their diplomatic skills.

Accommodation

Although the students love to complain, many actually admit they enjoy the small and friendly atmosphere of the campus. A fairly active Greek scene, numerous sporting events and such anticipated occasions as the Spring Fair keep everyone busy.

And the fact that the freshmen and sophomores all live and eat on campus ensures a constantly vibrant environment. Juniors and seniors meanwhile benefit from having the option of living in off-campus apartments – something that is common in England but often impractical in America.

Hitting the Books

Each year group at JHU is relatively small (around 1,500 kids) and fairly competitive, holding its students to a high standard. No matter what department you find yourself in (and there is a great degree of flexibility), you will have to learn to argue logically and always be able to answer the many 'whys' thrown your way. This is not a school for fluffy thinking.

Most of the professors are top researchers (a fact that, and you have been warned, can play havoc with their teaching skills) and expect their students to pay as much attention to fact as they do. The scientific spirit pervades the campus – even humanities majors have been known to moan about it!

Perhaps because of this close connection between the sciences and the humanities, Johns Hopkins offers no core curriculum. As a result many of the students double major or take minors between the two schools. No one here is afraid to work hard – and the university is more than happy to go on throwing degree options (including masters and doctoral programmes) at you!

Social Life

JHU is a campus that is proud of its sporting prowess, affiliated with one of the top music schools (the Peabody Conservatory) and supports numerous extra-curricular activities. For those who like to be kept busy while enjoying a diverse and focused environment, this is a good place to keep as a 'potential' on that all-important short-list.

Outside Those Ivory Walls

One of the grumbles about Johns Hopkins is its location. While Baltimore is a big city, many of its entertainments lie quite some way away from the suburbs of campus. The Homewood neighbourhood offers the usual run of student attractions, but many JHUers feel the need for something more.

And central Baltimore is, for those without a car, just that little bit too far. Luckily downtown Baltimore and the Inner Harbour area have plentiful charms of their own and are closely connected by regular shuttle buses. Most students are quite happy with a social life based on campus parties, these nearby attractions and the occasional trip to Washington DC.

Getting In

AT A GLANCE – Application & Test Options:

– Early Decision, Regular Decision

– ACT/SAT required, Writing/essay is optional

– SAT Subject tests encouraged but not required

– However, Engineering students are strongly encouraged to submit Math 2 and a science SAT Subject test

Johns Hopkins requires standardised test scores (eg SAT or ACT) but these "should not be viewed as a predictor of admissibility." This is a tough school to get in to – barely one in ten applicants get an invitation.

Money Matters

Johns Hopkins offers both need- and merit-based financial assistance to international applicants, but it's limited and - be careful - it's need-aware, so a request for aid can affect the chances of being admitted.

Famous Grads

Michael Bloomberg – financial whiz and New York mayor

Madeleine Albright – political strongwoman!

Andre Watts – pianist

Kenyon College

Gambier, Ohio
www.kenyon.edu
Undergrads: 1,600
Grads: 0

How many Kenyon students does it take to screw in a light bulb?

Six. One to screw in the light bulb, and five to form a search party to find him in the nowhere that is Gambier.

Kenyon was founded in 1824 in the very small town of Gambier, Ohio as a place to escape from the 'vice and dissipation' of city life. Even today, there is no sign of any kind of city life here. The town does not even have a traffic light, but this beautiful remote hilltop is home to one of the nation's best liberal arts colleges and it attracts students from all over the country (and, increasingly, the world). Kenyon's English department is a big draw. However Kenyon students get excited about their classes across a variety of fields, are passionate about their education as a whole, and are undeniably in love with their school.

The Campus

Thank goodness Kenyon has a beautiful campus with lots to do because you won't find much more than corn fields and Amish country outside the school for miles around. The campus may be small but it's a gem and makes you think 'this is what a college should feel like'.

The tone is set by Old Kenyon Hall, a grey stone Gothic revival building, but the surrounding buildings are, almost without exception, equally stunning. They line up and down the green, criss-crossed with paths, that is the centrepiece of the campus. On any given day, this is where you'll find students chatting, throwing a Frisbee or doing their reading under a tree.

That is, unless winter hits – central Ohio gets real winters – and then you're far more likely to find people in Gund Commons or in Middle Ground, a popular college coffeehouse where you can often enjoy live music along with your cup of coffee or homemade soup. The new athletic centre (the KAC) draws in students looking to break a sweat but also those who want to use the study lounge or visit the sushi/smoothie bar.

On the other hand, if you want to get back to nature, Kenyon is home to a 380-acre nature preserve, just adjacent to the campus.

The Kenyon Student

Everyone at Kenyon is there for the simple reason that they want to be. In such a remote location students have no choice but to reach out to each other and as a result this is a tight-knit community.

The college is definitely diverse in terms of personality types, but less so in terms of racial or socioeconomic measures. Many Kenyon students complain about the homogeneity of the student body, but others disagree, pointing to the strong LGBT community, increasing number of international students, and various religious denominations.

The stereotypical Kenyon student is thought to be intelligent but quirky, rich but modest, studious but big drinkers. The student body is liberal but not as much as at comparable schools like Oberlin or Bennington – and there is certainly a strong community of conservative students and professors who are not afraid to speak their mind.

Hitting the Books

Kenyon academics are top-notch and demanding but the professors are friendly, generous, and open. They will always know your name and are readily available to help you or just chat.

Academic life here rests on relationships between dedicated teachers who are top scholars and talented students who welcome the challenge of ideas, and there is a great sense of mutual respect.

There are 31 majors to choose from; however English continues to be the most popular and most respected. So much so that it can often be very challenging to get a place on a course. The overall atmosphere is competitive but definitely collaborative, and students are supportive of one another. The Kenyon education tends to be focused on 'learning for the sake of learning' rather than being a career-oriented one.

Social Life

Let's not beat around the bush – Gambier, Ohio does not immediately come to mind when you're looking for a lively social life. And there is really nowhere else to go in the area (unless you are up for partying in corn fields – which, we might add, is worth considering). However, because the college understands this predicament, it makes a big effort to keep things happening on campus.

Kenyon has dozens of student organisations and a long menu of activities – plays, sporting events, concerts, and social board activities such as laser tag or a trip to the cinema – and it's extremely easy to get involved (especially when you consider the close proximity of everything).

If you spend the weekend lying in bed watching old reruns of Gilmore Girls and dreaming of life at a bigger school, this comes down to your own laziness (or love of satirical mother-daughter dialogue) – not a lack of things to do on campus.

Although this is not always true at small liberal arts schools, Kenyon also has an active Greek life that spices up the campus nightlife. And, as a rule, it is not essential to be a member of a frat or sorority in order to attend the parties.

Outside Those Ivory Walls

Cornfields. Need we say more?

Getting In

AT A GLANCE – Application & Test Options:

- Early Decision, Early Decision II, Regular Decision
- ACT/SAT required
- SAT Subject tests optional

Kenyon is considered a selective school with its acceptance rate of just under 25%. And, like most small liberal arts colleges, tuition is high.

Money Matters

Kenyon works hard to be accessible to students of all backgrounds. Almost half of their students receive financial help based on need, often in a combination of grants, scholarships, loans and campus employment. There are also merit-based scholarships for you high achievers out there.

Famous Grads

Rutherford B. Hayes – U.S. president

Paul Newman – actor and entrepreneur

Saskia Hamilton – poet

Lewis And Clark College

Portland, Oregon
www.lclark.edu
Undergrads: 2,100
Grads: 1,600

How many LC students does it take to change a light bulb?

Eight – two to organise a cake-bake fundraiser, five to write a song about it, and one to change it.

Lewis and Clark is a hidden gem of a Liberal Arts College. With a beautiful campus and small but friendly and diverse student body, this is an option seriously worth considering for those who like their education broad and on their own terms. This school welcomes and understands international students, which helps to ensure your experience there is a happy and fulfilling one.

The Campus

The campus at LC is small and green (in both senses of the word), thirty minutes south of the centre of Portland on the "Pioneer Shuttle" that runs every hour. The buildings are pleasantly spaced across the 130-odd acres, with neatly defined areas for classes, residence and sports. The architecture and setting are vaguely reminiscent of a leafy French chateau, set on a wooded hill above the city with views over the sweeping landscape of Oregon and the spectacular volcanoes Mt. St. Helens and Mt. Hood. The gardens and trees are delightful, with a beautiful terraced garden for strolling and pensive moments on the east side of campus.

The campus does not feel squashed, but it is small enough for everything to be on hand and easily navigable. It's size, together with the university's requirement that students spend at least their first two years living on site (unless they are already residents of Portland), foster an unusual degree of community and cohesion among the students.

Students complain about the food options available, but there are a number of collegiate cafes on campus, as well as the dining hall in the main student building, with a good range of meals available. Sports facilities are not bad for a small college, with a gym, swimming pool and tennis courts all available.

Accommodation

Dorms are arranged in themed blocks, including a fantastic international house, and are allocated according to questionnaires completed before starting at the college, meaning that in theory you share with people with similar lifestyles – a system that apparently works very well.

The Lewis and Clark Student

LC has a west-coast hippy reputation, but with its own flavour, different from the student demonstrations of Berkeley or the modern counter-culture of Seattle. Students at LC like to do cake-bakes in aid of Darfur, rather than shout their demands for human rights from the roofs of police cars. What is typical of the LC student body is a warm friendliness and a willingness to open themselves to new experiences and people.

The large chunk of international students (including more than 120 "Third Culture Kids") influences the general mood of the college. Among the Americans, a large proportion hail from California and the North West, most of them straight from high school. When asked what their favourite aspect of the school is, LC students frequently say things like "the international atmosphere" or – touchingly – "that everyone is so friendly".

Even so, some students grumble that LC can be a bit "cliquey". This is not a reflection of elitism or overly-wealthy students (it is more common for rich kids at LC to fake poverty than vice versa), but more an indication of the tight social groups that form in most universities. Athletes keep to themselves for example, and though students are what can be called individualistic, they are often so in groups – as seen most famously in "the gang that decided it was never going to shower". Of course, in their case a lack of social interaction was no shocker.

Hitting the Books

LC is often stereotyped as the laid-back younger-brother to nearby Reed College's (over)work ethic, but students at LC still do plenty of work. The work load varies by subject, but you give as good as you get – students who are naturally hard-working will not find it difficult to work to their potential, but those who favour a less rigorous approach to their studies may not be pushed to do more than the minimum. "Standards of academic exertion," said a relaxed LC student we spoke to, are "in general kind of low".

Students extol the helpfulness of the teaching faculty, saying that professors are "high quality, friendly and always available". Class sizes are small (average 19) and the student:faculty ratio is 12:1, meaning lots of individual attention for those who seek it.

LC is an excellent place to study certain subjects; its programs in International Affairs, Environmental Studies, Psychology and Biology have won national accolades, and Political Scientists are increasingly high-flying, with several winning impressive awards. Foreign Languages are also popular and well taught, enriched by the high number of international students.

Important symposia are held at LC in fields including Gender Studies, Environmental Studies and International Affairs, attended by some of the highest-ranking practitioners of those fields. Study-abroad opportunities are a big draw, with about half the students taking semesters in countries across the world. LC has one of the top debating teams in the country.

As might be expected, creative arts are big here, with several professional writers and poets on the staff, a famous classical music department and two prestigious art galleries on site. The college has held two worldwide symphonic festivals in the past five years and professional-level performances in Dublin and the Greek islands.

Social Life

Students here mention a "bubble" when talking about LC's social life. Although there are ample opportunities for hitting the pretty funky town, social activities are generally contained within the campus, which doesn't feel part of Portland at all. If you hate the idea of being adrift in a big city, or being a small fish in a big pond, the LC "bubble" – with its friendly parties, communal music-making and hippy-flavoured activities – may provide the perfect security blanket.

Sports do not dominate (or even factor in) the average LC student's free time, and Greek Life is non-existent (students don't miss it!).

Outside Those Ivory Walls

Portland blends the modern west-coast metropolis with rough-and-tumble pioneering attitudes. So there is liberal politics, but no sales tax. Like its northwestern neighbours, Seattle and San Francisco, Portland is accomplished in the arts, and brims with alternative culture outlets and micro-breweries. It is not far from several natural gems (to which LC organises regular excursions) and enjoys a temperate West Coast climate.

Getting In

AT A GLANCE – Application & Test Options:

– Early Action, Early Decision, Regular Decision

– ACT/SAT highly recommended, but not required for international students

– SAT Subject tests not required for all students

Getting into LC is not hard, but it's getting tougher, with the application success rate around 60%. Interviews are optional.

Money Matters

LC is not cheap, but happily (and very unusually) financial aid is available to international students as well as locals as part of the effort to maintain diversity in the student body. About 15% receive aid on a needs-based basis, with the average aid package covering about half the tuition costs. Scholarships are also available for the brightest and best.

Famous Grads

Becca Bernstein – artist

Earl Blumenauer – successful politician and congressman

Monica Lewinsky – notorious White House intern and intimate associate of Bill Clinton

Massachusetts Institute of Technology

Cambridge (Boston), Massachusetts
www.mit.edu
Undergrads: 4,500
Grads: 6,500

How many students does it take to change a light bulb at MIT?

Five – one to design a nuclear-powered bulb that never needs changing, one to figure out how to power the rest of Boston using that nuked light bulb, two to install it, and one to write the computer program that controls the wall switch.

Three little letters: MIT. So short and yet, along the same lines as those three little words – 'I love you', SO powerful. The Massachusetts Institute of Technology has a reputation and an influence in this world that cannot be underestimated. Some might think of Matt Damon frantically scrawling incomprehensible algebraic formulas in Good Will Hunting.

Others may prefer to dwell on the fifty-six Nobel Prizes this college has raked in and the employment opportunities it affords. Whatever your association, for those of you interested in science (whether of the rocket or nuclear variety) this college, situated in the heart of New England, remains the best of the best.

The Campus

MIT prides itself in opening up to its students the mysterious beauty of the mind. It might have been in its better interests to simultaneously focus on the beauty of the campus. If your number one priority in picking a university is an aesthetically charming location, then MIT will sorely disappoint. As befits a college that focuses so much attention on the future, its architecture is modernistic and, for the most part, concrete.

While it is not totally bereft of attractive buildings, it suffers badly by comparison with such 'quaint' neighbours as Brown, Harvard and Amherst. This is particularly true in the seemingly eternal winter months where endless slush and snow enhance the general impression of overwhelming greyness.

The ugliness of the MIT campus is fortunately relieved by the beauty of the surrounding area. While the campus is seemingly stripped of all vegetation, those in need of a landscape fix can find it on the banks of the Charles River. Cambridge, situated just across the river from Boston, is a bustling place that prides itself on being the most opinionated zip code in America.

This is perhaps unsurprising given that the bustle is largely composed of throngs of students and academics from the illustrious, and ever so slightly pretentious, Harvard and MIT. Despite the opinions, all these whizzing brain cells make it a fun and lively town to hang out in.

Accommodation

All freshmen live on campus and, owing to the real estate prices in Cambridge, many upper-classmen opt to do the same. Campus housing is guaranteed for all four years. The eleven residential colleges and various fraternities and sororities provide the loci for student life and tend to be more charismatic and slightly more attractive than the rest of campus. Academia may take place in sterile classrooms off a succession of neon-lit corridors, but at least students return to a pseudo-home they have selected and made their own.

The MIT Student

MIT is a campus obsessed by brains. If you do not relish the odd academic challenge and the daily competition that springs from being surrounded by America's brightest – this is not the place for you. MIT students are hard-working, ambitious and personally motivated. Walking through the corridors you get the feeling that not only does everyone know where they are going, they all plan to get there as soon as possible.

Yet the fact that everyone on campus is extremely intelligent does not lead to excessive rivalry. Perhaps because many of these students were regarded as 'nerds' in high school, or because they all exist under the same stifling academic pressure, the majority of individuals are very tolerant of each other, resulting in a great sense of community.

As far as the ethnic composition of this community goes, MIT has one of the most diverse campuses of the great American colleges. There is a particularly strong Asian-American community, making up about 30% of the campus – almost the same proportion as Caucasians. There is also a sizeable international student presence, but mostly due to the 40% representation among graduate students. (Those who do not salute the Stars and Stripes make up around 8-10% of each undergraduate class.)

MIT has had some problems in straightening out the gender balance – science still being a testosterone-dominated playground. But MIT has none of the reactionary views of some British counterparts and women can be assured of fair and enthusiastic treatment. Single women can get excited about the 54:46 ratio – although all applicants should bear in mind that a large percentage of students of both sexes rarely emerge from the classroom or library. MIT students frequently moan about the lack of attractive dating options on their campus – a half-fit girl or guy will swiftly become a hot commodity, but those of you who view university as the time of the fling may be disappointed.

Rest assured, though – the average MIT student is not without a sense of fun. Quite the opposite in fact. MIT is known for its brilliant pranks – they now have an entire museum devoted to their favourite 'hacks'. Students love to channel their brains into the absurd as well as the serious and, given the size of their brains, the results are normally stupendous! One of the most renowned jokes involved rerouting an entire building's electrical system so the lights could be used to play a giant game of TETRIS. Other beauties have emerged from the long-standing feud with Harvard and include the disruption of several Harvard-Yale football games with various incendiary devices!

Hitting the Books

Obviously the concepts involved in splitting the atom and powering the world require a certain amount of brain and elbow work and this is reflected in the MIT students' constant complaining about the vast quantities of work they are expected to do. This is not a place where you can expect to have the odd slack week (or even day).

Still, the pressure is not as high as it has been in the past. Freshmen are all expected to follow a programme that covers certain basic requirements, but first year classes are now graded only on a 'pass/no record' basis. This means if a student does work at the A, B, or C level, a "pass" is recorded on his or her external transcript; if a student should happen to do work at the D or F level, the external transcript will show no record of the student ever having taken the class.

MIT launched this system for freshman year in order to help students adapt to doing MIT-quality work, give them flexibility to explore academic, research, and social opportunities, and emphasise learning for its own sake – without the added pressure of grades. Students can now relax a little as they strive to get their bearings.

MIT students may be perpetually busy but at least they know they are getting the best possible instruction. As both a research and teaching institute, MIT is almost unparalleled. Both the professors and the teaching assistants who trawl through the guts of each class are extremely well-reputed. MIT students quickly come to appreciate that science's greatest discoveries come about through team work and their subsequent relationships with both their peers and the faculty are extremely strong. There is a huge amount of back-up available.

MIT consists of five separate schools (Architecture and Planning, Engineering, Science, Management, Humanities, Arts and Social Sciences). Yet it is impossible to apply to a single one of them. All students at MIT must build on a similar academic base and by the end of their first year in college, the freshmen class is well-grounded in the basic theories of a number of scientific fields. These initial classes are famed for introducing students to the fundamentals, often involving hands-on experience.

Having learnt to crawl, students are then free to run wherever they choose. Nor does MIT restrict all its students to staring at a test tube. Majoring in the humanities is a possibility and the fact that students can cross-register in an unlimited number of Harvard classes, makes this a great opportunity.

Flexibility is the name of the game at MIT. Leaving aside the SCIENCE, SCIENCE, SCIENCE mentality there is a great deal of choice. No major is declared until the end of freshman year and for the indecisive, further chopping and changing remains an option. Cross-registration between different departments is not only allowed but encouraged.

Whether you are building roofs or investigating the neutrino, you will find a wide array of courses with class sizes varying from the large foundation courses to the most intimate seminars. Freshman year may see you confined to certain subjects but after that the university (graduate courses included) is your oyster. And the bureaucracy tries its hardest to make all the pearls as easily accessible as possible.

Those who believe that admission to MIT ensures they never have to write an essay, study a painting or learn a language again swiftly find they are mistaken. MIT undergrads face the same core requirements as other liberal arts colleges. Study abroad is popular for many (although perhaps not so applicable to the Brits who come from abroad).

There is also the option of combining the best of both worlds – namely the academic giants of Harvard and MIT. Despite the disdain in which these two giants hold each other, cross-registration between the two schools works wonders for both MIT poets and Harvard scientists.

No one denies that MIT academics are among the hardest in the world and the faculty gives its students plenty of chances to let off steam. One opportunity comes with the much anticipated, although still optional, IAP (Independent Activities Project) that takes place for four weeks each January. This stress-relieving period gives MIT students a chance to pursue whatever really interests them, whether social service, environmental research or further splitting of the atom, without worrying too much about grades. And all of this takes place with the full resources and faculty support of the university.

The intensity and rigour of the MIT academic system is renowned. If you are not prepared to work hard, you should not bother to apply (unless, of course, you are the reincarnation of Einstein in which case you shouldn't have too much trouble). Yet those of you who are reading this and cowering in fear should bear in mind that while MIT expects a great deal from its students, it is fully prepared to offer them just as much in return.

The excellence of MIT grads could not be attained without the excellence of their resources. This is a rich university, supported by both alumni and government funding, and almost all of its students benefit. Whether through financial aid or the efficient and up-to-the-minute campus resources, the dollars that keep flowing into MIT help to make many a struggling student's time more comfortable.

The fantastic computer system is, perhaps unsurprisingly, almost beyond compare, and the administration seeks to match its human efficiency to its mechanical one. Many MIT students, therefore, find that while the academic pressure is on, the complexities of day-to-day living are much reduced.

Social Life

When one thinks MIT, one does not think party school. Images of working late by the glare of the library lamp are far more prevalent than visions of keg stands, sorority girls and police break-ups. While it is true that MIT is not going to break any records for its social status, it is unfair to suggest that people who go there do not know how to have fun. There may be large contingents who choose not to go out, but there are enough people who do to ensure all but the most hardened party animal a thriving social life.

For those who are prepared to leave the lab, MIT offers a great deal of extracurricular activities. While there are no nationally ranked sports teams, all students seeking a bit of fresh air can get their athletic fix through an intramural sports team (although PE also fills a part of the compulsory core requirements). Particularly popular, due to the proximity of the Charles, are the delights of the crew team.

Excess energy is also burnt off through music (very strong on campus), arts and social service groups. The dedication MIT students show to their test tubes is mirrored in other areas of their lives, and those anxious about whether activities exist outside the laboratory can breathe easy. The ethnic diversity of the campus also leads to a number of cultural activities. While most of these involve samosas or saris, there is a definite market for the Union Jack and tea at five!

The secret to social success seems to lie with the refusal to allow the work pressure to get to you. A couple of hours off will not, after all, kill you. Cambridge provides a multitude of escape options – bars, coffee shops and restaurants. And if it lacks anything, it is a safe bet that Boston will have it in duplicate.

If you choose to go to MIT it is important to make the effort to get out there and meet people. While the importance of the first few weeks has been slightly relieved by the recent decision to stop allotting housing after a roommate selection period, it is still vital to look outside the mountains of work and embrace the people who will help you get through it.

One way of finding a ready-made group of friends is by joining a fraternity or sorority. Unusually, for a New England school, these societies play a large part in the MIT social life, owning some of the nicer houses on campus and throwing some of the wilder parties. They are certainly an appealing option for many.

Even Harvard students, who like to pride themselves on having a better social life than the 'scientists', have been known to turn up at and even enjoy the odd MIT party. This combination of frats, local options, extra-curricular activities and the diversity of the student body ensures that there is a social life out there for every kind of MIT student.

Outside Those Ivory Walls

MIT may not be the most beautiful place in the world and it may not always be the most sociable. Yet for those in need of an aesthetic or party fix, there is one great advantage – the town across the river. Boston is THE student city – thronged with undergraduates from Harvard, BU, Tufts, BC, and of course MIT.

This bustling and fun student presence is only one part of the vibrant city. In architectural and historical terms this place is as near to London as you are likely to find on the US side of the Atlantic and there is almost as much to do. And, for those on the marriage market, it supposedly boasts the greatest number of affluent singles in America!

From the clubs that throng Lansdowne Street (hired out regularly for student parties) to the Italian pastries that make the North End the place to eat, Boston offers something for everyone. Whether you want to ice-skate on Boston Common, do a spot of shopping on Newbury Street or just laze on the banks of the Charles, Boston can provide it. And its all just ten minutes away on the T – a subway system that would make Boris Johnson weep with envy.

Boston is SO close that almost everyone ventures into town on a fairly regular basis. For those homebodies who are reluctant to step off campus there are other options. Cambridge is a suburb defined by two of the greatest universities in America – Harvard and MIT. As such, it offers a plethora of restaurants, bars and coffee shops.

The best idea is to head for somewhere with 'Square' in the title – whether Harvard, Davis or Porter. For those whose wanderlust extends beyond good ole

Massachusetts, there are also many travel opportunities. In the winter good skiing is only a car drive away – the more adventurous can make it to Canada (with its lower drinking age) for the weekend.

Another popular draw is New York, only a couple of hours away by train or the infamous 'Chinatown bus' – an inexpensive but bone-shattering ride!

Getting In

AT A GLANCE – Application & Test Options:

– Early Action, Regular Decision

– ACT/SAT required, Writing/essay optional

– Two SAT Subject tests required (Math 1 or 2 plus a science)

Difficult does not even come close to the application requirements needed for MIT. Impossible would perhaps be closer to the mark. There is a reason that this school has produced so many Nobel Prize winners – it takes only those students that it perceives to be, if not perfect, then as close as possible. Out of the roughly 18,000 applicants for each freshman class, only 8% (or fewer) are accepted. When you consider that over a third of those eager seniors scored a perfect 800 on at least one of their SATs, you begin to realize what you are up against!

It is a given at MIT that you will be academically superior to 99% of the world. The ability to pull As out of nowhere will impress no one. Instead the MIT admissions office likes to concentrate on signs that you know how to channel your immense brainpower. You need to show originality, initiative and an ability to stand out from the crowd.

Wowing them with the fact you got top marks in your A level physics module is simply not enough. Prove that you have been noticed as well! America is full of science fairs and national academic competitions for its most prestigious students. If you came first in a British equivalent, tell them about it. If you have spent six months of your gap year doing a rocket science internship, don't leave it off that application. Once you have hit upon these indications of your drive and brilliance, you only need the glowing recommendations and brilliant grades and you're all set!

Remember also something that most important of the ten commandments of application forms – show them you're a person. This is especially vital at a place like MIT, which many (especially those at liberal arts colleges!) actually believe is inhabited by mad scientists intent on producing robotic genii students. In fact the MIT admissions board want to accept people who are not only notable for their scientific ability. If you play an instrument, speak umpteen languages or have a social conscience, you should make sure they know about it.

One of the best ways of doing this is through the interview. This part of the process is optional but highly recommended, and is a great way to find out more about the university. It is conducted by a member of the MIT Educational Council – a highly formalized name for the many grads of the university!

Several of these alumni are scattered throughout the UK and it is easy to set up a meeting. These interviews, while intimidating, should not be scary and do not possess the power to decide on your admission chances, although they can certainly sway them. As long as you have spent a little time in preparing some serious (and light-hearted) questions and answers you should be fine.

Money Matters

MIT is one of the few schools with a great financial aid programme for international students. If you need fiscal support to deal with the astronomical American fees this is definitely a good place to apply. Consider this early though – financial aid applications need to be submitted in plenty of time.

Famous Grads

Kofi Annan – managing the UN is a breeze after rocket science

I. M. Pei – the architect of recent years

Buzz Aldrin – the second man to walk on the moon!

Middlebury College

Middlebury, Vermont
www.middlebury.edu
Undergrads: 2,500
Grads: 0

How many Middlebury students does it take to change a light bulb?

Five – One to change the light bulb and four to find the perfect J. Crew outfit to wear for the occasion.

It's hard to find anything wrong with Middlebury. Located in a small but quintessential college town in western Vermont (itself the quintessential New England state), it is one of the happiest and most highly regarded liberal arts colleges in the country. Known for being very rigorous and academic, Middlebury also has a native Vermont crunchy attitude – and granola is served at every meal.

The Campus

The campus and surrounding area are exquisitely beautiful, and there's a lively social scene, although many students will complain they don't get to enjoy it as much as they'd like because of the intense work load. The *Princeton Review* rated Middlebury 6th in country for the categories of both "students work the hardest" and "best quality of life". This tells you something about the attitude on campus, which is jovially nicknamed "Club Midd".

Dorms, food and sports facilities are all excellent. The microbrewery in town is a big draw. The college even has its own ski slope on huge and glorious Bread Loaf Mountain, and it also owns Robert Frost Farm (once home to America's best loved poet), the jewel in the crown of what is often considered the most beautiful state in the Union.

The Middlebury Student

The student body has everything from the 'uptight preppy white kids' to the 'environmental hippies' but the majority largely fall somewhere in the middle. The common thread is that students here are bright, passionate and outdoorsy. On top of this, the college organises as series of projects, courses, spaces, activities and other opportunities that aim to foster "creativity and entrepreneurship".

As might be expected, the ethos is liberal; Middlebury was the first all male college to accept women in 1883, and the first to graduate an African American in 1823. The major international climate change campaign 350.org was started in the college by a group of students and their professor Bill McKibben, a world-famous environmentalist. The college made it a goal to be carbon neutral by 2016 and, sure enough, announced last December that it had reached this major sustainability milestone, many years in the making. Political and environmental courses remain very popular.

Hitting the Books

Other well-regarded majors include economics, English and international studies, and the language programs are internationally renowned (for the summer sessions, you have to sign a pledge to speak only your target language for the duration of the course). Study abroad is also popular.

Professors get high marks and the student:faculty ratio is 9:1, meaning small class sizes. As evidence of the breadth of their interests, 60% of those who graduate do so with either a double major or in an interdisciplinary program; only 40% pursue a normal major in one subject.

Social Life

Winters can be harsh so close to Canada, and can cause severe loneliness and isolation with such a small student body, especially for those used to big cities. But Middlebury does its best to salvage them with a yearly Winter Carnival, featuring bonfires, ski races and a Winter Ball among other snowy other delights.

The college is big on outdoorsy activities – so much so that the freshman campus orientation at the start of the year includes such informative activities such as hiking, canoeing and organic farming (don't panic, it's only voluntary).

For the sporty, the Middlebury Panthers field many competent teams in regional and national leagues, but they're best known for their broomstick prowess: Middlebury is the birthplace of Muggle Quidditch, which is a bona fide student organization (its members play each other and other schools' teams). Rugby, football (soccer, not American) and winter sports are also big.

Getting In

AT A GLANCE – Application & Test Options:

– Early Decision, Early Decision II, Regular Decision

– Testing required: either ACT, SAT, or three SAT Subject tests in different academic disciplines

With a 2016 admission rate around 17%, Middlebury is one of the most selective liberal arts colleges there is – almost as tough as the Ivies.

However, your chances of getting in might be slightly better if you opt to enrol in February – Middlebury is unusual in that, in addition to the typical September intake, they admit students in February. These "Febs" are selected from the entire applicant pool and are notified of admission at the same time as students admitted for September. You can also graduate mid-year; in fact you might prefer to, since the tradition is for all February graduates to ski down a mountain at the College's own alpine ski area, the Snow Bowl, to receive their degrees.

Money Matters

Although you will see them on the very short list (8) of "need-blind" colleges/ unis, at Middlebury that's only really true for domestic students; they're "need-aware" for international students (meaning they do take your ability to pay into account).

However, once you're admitted, they'll meet 100% of the demonstrated financial need of any student, US or international. So if you're outstanding enough, and they want you, they'll find a way to make it affordable for you. But the decision to accept you will go into a complicated algorithm, depending on how much they have available to fund their very top students who need it. Obviously all very competitive.

Be super aware: as an international student you must apply for financial aid at the time of applying for admission to Middlebury (deadlines are on their website).

Famous Grads

Alexander Twilight – Middlebury made him the first black man to earn a Bachelor's degree in 1823

Ari Fleischer – White House press secretary

Eve Ensler – creator of 'The Vagina Monologues'

Roger L. Easton – Principal inventor of the GPS

Mount Holyoke College

South Hadley, Massachusetts
www.mtholyoke.edu
Undergrads: 2,300
Grads: 0

How many Holyoke students does it take to change a light bulb?

...Oh, Daddy had a man for that!

A small, old, prestigious, all-female liberal arts college in rural Massachusetts (one of the so called "Seven Sisters", traditionally the women's Ivy League colleges where the smart girls went when Harvard etc were male only), Mount Holyoke remains firmly among the Massachusetts academic elite and one of the best of its kind in the country.

The Campus

The gorgeous rural campus is set in the splendour of the beautiful Pioneer Valley, with free buses provided to the collegiate towns of Amherst and Northampton, and the awesome cities of Boston and New York not too far away.

Many, however, feel they don't even need to leave campus to have a great time – there's lots of involvement in clubs, sports, student groups, artistic endeavours, etc, as well as the excellent study-abroad program.

The 800 acre grounds contain various treasures such as a famous 18-hole golf-course, a botanic garden, horse-riding tracks, waterfalls and a well-respected Art Museum. Sports are not a huge part of college life, and largely involve horses, rackets or golf clubs – unless you want to go off-site, in which case it involves bikes, skis or hiking boots.

Accommodation

Almost all students live on campus for all four years (it's mandatory for most), and some of the residence halls are essentially vast Victorian mansions. In a quaint tradition, the halls provide students with milk and cookies ("M&Cs") every night. Sophomores also anonymously donate a week's worth of gifts to unsuspecting freshmen in a practice known as Elfing.

The Mt Holyoke Student

The student body is open-minded, diverse, and academically motivated (and it has a large number of international students – 25%). It also has a sense of humour and a soft gooey centre.

There's a strong sense of community – many would say "family" is the better choice of word – and more school pride than at comparable liberal arts colleges, especially pride in the legacy, strength and success of its students and alumni. This lasts after you graduate, as the alumni act as an amazingly powerful support network for each other.

Hitting the Books

Like other liberal arts colleges, the Holyoke experience is rigorous and rewarding. There is a strong focus on academics here, which is more than justified considering the incredible calibre of the professors, their accessibility, and the tiny size of classes.

As a member of the "Five College Coalition", which includes high-flyers like Amherst and Smith, students can enrol in the programs at the other four schools – theoretically providing access to more than 5000 courses. And besides the wide ranging offerings from the Five College arrangement, Holyoke also allows you to design your own major if none of the regular subjects take your fancy.

The academic program is further enhanced by the four boringly-named "centres" on campus, eg for leadership, the environment, global initiatives and so on, which organise special guest lectures, workshops, conferences, internships and hands-on learning opportunities.

As if there weren't enough number-based alliances for you, the university is also part of the Twelve College Exchange Program, which lets students take semesters at other top institutions like Vassar and Dartmouth.

Social Life

Holyoke has the usual array of clubs, sports, student groups, artistic endeavours, etc, as well as a excellent study-abroad program. However, what makes this college special is its traditions, such as the annual shows by students and faculty that parody college life, and the secretly-chosen beautiful autumn day when classes are cancelled, the campus bells toll and the students hike up Mount Holyoke itself.

Before commencement, graduating seniors paddle down a river in canoes with lanterns singing college songs, and then carry laurel garlands to the grave of Mary Lyon, the college founder.

Getting In

AT A GLANCE – Application & Test Options:

– Early Decision, Early Decision II, Regular Decision

– Test-optional (except for home-schooled applicants)

Holyoke is not for the faint of heart or light of wallet. It's selective (50% of applicants were given the nod in 2016), but not nearly as hard to get into as its neighbour Amherst. Also, it's one of those few unis where you don't have to show them your SATs.

Money Matters

Even though over 25% of Holyoke students are international, the school provides limited need-based assistance. Applying for aid is competitive and based on both your academic achievements and financial eligibility. You also might want to know that any financial aid will not cover full educational costs; you will have to pay some of your own way. There are other ways to score, though: Mt Holyoke offers several special merit scholarships for high achieving first year students. For instance, Trustee Scholars each receive a full tuition scholarship renewable for eight semesters.

Famous Grads

Emily Dickinson – Famous 19th century poet

Jean Picker Firstenberg – Past director and CEO of the American Film Institute

Susan Kare – Designer of many of the interface elements for the original Apple Macintosh

New York University

New York, New York
www.nyu.edu
Undergrads: 19,400
Grads: 19,000

How many students does it take to change a light bulb at NYU?

Two – one to get the light bulb, and one to go to the departmental advisor and see what the advisor thinks is best.

If you are the type of budding intellectual who believes that dressing in black, sipping espresso and reading Kafka in the corner of a dark coffee house is the way to go, NYU should be near the top of your potential US college list. Situated in the artsy Greenwich Village, near the ever-cool Washington Square, NYU draws in a diverse and talented bunch of students from across the nation (and, increasingly, the globe) and gives them a first-rate education in one of the most exciting cities in the world.

The Campus

Founded in 1831 for the purpose of ensuring that leadership and talent were fostered among all classes of society, NYU grew so fast for the next century, adding students, professors and buildings, that until recently, the campus had no real coherence and students had to travel all over Manhattan to get to class. Now, however, the school has colonised the entire area around Washington Square, providing a solid geographical location for students to both live and work in, and the school spirit of the Violets(!) is growing stronger than ever.

The NYU Student

Students who attend NYU tend to hold strong opinions and have specific interests. The University consists of several different undergraduate schools, many of which are world-renowned for their strength in a particular field. Among these are both the Tisch Institute of the Arts and the Lawrence N Stern School of Business.

If you do not have your heart set on Broadway or Wall St, you can also find a place for yourself at the College of Arts and Sciences. The NYU community brings all of these disparate talents together and allows students to take classes between the schools. This flexibility enhances both your academic experience – you can be a history major and take sculpting – and, more importantly, your friendship groups, allowing thespians to mingle with economists.

NYU is noted for its tolerant and accepting attitude towards people of every kind of geographical, racial and ideological background. Some complain there is a liberal bias, but while student debates are vigorous and frequent, they tend to take place in a good-humoured atmosphere.

Certainly no one seems to be bad-mouthing the institution. NYU applications have grown substantially over the past few years, including among international students (who now make up 25% of the undergraduates).

Hitting the Books

NYU students take their studies seriously. Approximately 60% of NYU students go on to further studies and intellectual discussion is very much the ethos that binds the community together.

While the academic programmes at NYU are fairly flexible, all undergraduates in the College of Arts and Sciences face the rigours of the Morse Academic Plan (the core curriculum devised by Samuel Morse of Morse code fame). This plan ensures that freshmen and sophomores have grounding in a foreign language, the arts, the social and natural sciences, and other cultures.

This rigorous programme prepares students for the intensive studies of their junior and senior years. NYU is academically excellent but can be very tough and the emphasis put on the interests of the individual mean that the individual has to do an awful lot of work.

Outside Those Ivory Walls

For many students the most attractive part of NYU is its location. Few university students have thousands of restaurants to choose from, world-class art galleries to peruse, Central Park to go jogging in and the shops of Fifth Avenue just a few blocks away.

Some complain that being in the city means that students find less time to bond with each other, and it is true that the campus and its inhabitants tend to merge with the surrounding city. But most students love this sense of being a part of the real world and getting to know people who live outside the bubble of academia.

NYU may not be the best college for you if you are the kind of person who likes to slack off or if you want a bona fide American campus experience. New York can be a lonely and scary place for those who are not gregarious or determined enough to go out there and make something of it. But if you have a city-loving side, a genuine interest in knowledge and an appreciation of faculty and students who feel the same way, then NYU is a good place to consider.

Getting In

AT A GLANCE – Application & Test Options:

– Early Decision, Early Decision II, Regular Decision

– Testing required – only one of the following:

- SAT (essay optional)
- ACT (writing optional)
- 3 SAT subject tests
- 3 AP exams
- IB diploma or high-level exam results
- Nationally accredited exam to show student has completed secondary school education, eg A-levels, Bac, Abitur etc.

Even though NYU is not part of the Ivy League like its neighbour Columbia, it is the dream choice for many a big-Apple loving Brit. Make no mistake – even though it's a big school, it's not easy to get in; slightly fewer than a third of the applicant pool is successful. Like most US schools, they use the Common App and look for impressive test results. But their approach to standardised testing is quite different (and flexible) – there are a variety of ways to satisfy this requirement, from sitting the traditional SAT/ACT to submitting A-level or IB results.

Money Matters

NYU encourages all incoming freshman to apply for financial aid, regardless of your financial situation and even if you think you probably don't qualify. They offer support in the form of loans, scholarships, grants, student employment, as well as financial support for their Study Away program. 100% of NYU applicants are considered for merit-based aid; however, only 1-2% of undergraduate scholarships are based on merit alone. Instead, the majority of these scholarships are based on a combination of need and merit combined.

Famous Grads

Alan Greenspan – former Federal Reserve Chairman

Clive Davis – music industry executive

John Woodruff – Olympic Gold Medalist (1936)

Northwestern University (Chicago)

Evanston (suburb of Chicago), Illinois
www.northwestern.edu
Undergrads: 8,000
Grads: 8,000

How many students does it take to change a light bulb at Northwestern?

Two – One to screw it in and one to tell him how to do it according to the manual.

From Old England to New England... For many Brits this leap across the Atlantic is quite far enough. Yet for those adventurous souls seeking to leave the familial nest yet further behind, there are a multitude of university options available beyond the pilgrim fathers' East Coast. One of the best of these is Northwestern University, a first rate university college situated right next to Chicago.

Best for those amongst you who wish to write, sing, doctor or act your way through university, it combines a strong academic reputation with a vibrant student body. Offering a chance to rediscover the secrets of the Midwest, Northwestern has plenty to give to those with that old pioneering spirit.

The Campus

Northwestern does not do things by halves. It has not one campus, but two. Not one undergraduate school, but six. This array of opportunities might seem daunting to some, but in reality all of its facilities are very closely linked. The main campus, inhabited by the six undergraduate schools and the grad school, is situated in Evanston, the suburb just north of Chicago.

Founded in 1851, Northwestern is a pretty place. While it lacks the picture-perfect quaintness of some of the East Coast schools and the fierce modernity of other newer colleges, it succeeds in combining the old and the new in a pleasing mixture – most important for any place in which you plan to spend four years of your life.

But the stunning thing about the Northwestern campus is not its architecture. Nor is it even the view, on fine days, of the imposing Chicago skyline. Instead it is the great Lake Michigan which the campus is, well, in...or all but. This huge sea-like body of water, complete with beaches, is an integral part of

Northwestern's charm. Whether you are of the ardent jogger variety or the more relaxed (aka lazy) BBQer, the lake will play a vital role in your college experience and offers the perfect place to go and vent your frustrations or homesickness.

Water, pretty buildings, lots of greenery and beautiful views, combine with the proximity of Chicago, easily accessible by the 'el' train, to give you pretty much everything you could desire in a campus. But be warned. In any movie or TV show set in Chicago, you will have seen the bitter wind and snows that pile up around miserably hunched over, bundled up actors. This is not just a special effect. Winter in the Midwest is a killer and the winds coming straight from the lake do not exactly improve the temperature. Sun worshippers, look away now.

Accommodation

Residential life at Northwestern is all-important in securing a good group of friends. This is partly due to the large size of both campus and college – factors that can make forging relationships difficult. Two-thirds of the students live on campus, with the remaining 1/3 either commuting from home (all those Chicago residents) or living off-campus.

As a freshman you are guaranteed on-campus housing as long as you remember to request it in your application. Do REMEMBER or you could well find yourself left out in the cold!

There are also eleven residential colleges at Northwestern, grouped around specific interests or skills. Some people choose to live in these and there is an international one available. But as we keep repeating: choosing to distance yourself from Americans is not the swiftest way to make friends. It is much better to throw yourself into the crowd from the beginning.

The Northwesterner

The Midwest is a strange, strange place and for the average Brit; the first weeks at Northwestern may well be a cultural muddle. A large majority of Northwestern attendees hail from the Midwest – and will be AMERICAN, AMERICAN, AMERICAN in a way never dreamed of back in London. Their national identity will be far more pronounced than that of students at the reserved East Coast or hippy West Coast schools. In fact, in many ways those who attend Northwestern will gain a perspective on the society of the United States that the majority of Brits either never reach or simply fly over.

This is not to say that all Northwestern students are country 'hicks' or Mafia-esque Chicago transplants. In fact the majority of them are upper-middle-class conservatives. There is some racial diversity, with a large number of Asian students, but it is not as heterogeneous an institution as it might be. Nor does Northwestern have a particularly large international community – fewer than 10% of undergraduates hail from outside the States – so if your goal is to surround yourself with a buffer zone of similarly confused Europeans, you may have a hard time.

Northwestern students are known for being dedicated to a host of extra-curricular activities. Due to the presence of the journalism, music and communications schools, the standard of publications and performances on campus is extremely high. The radio station is the largest student-run one of the nation and the Waa-Mu theatrical show is nationally acclaimed. In this flurry of activity it pays to be an individual who likes to get involved.

Of course, there is always the option of lying back by the lake and watching the world go by, but if this is your entire life then the frantic bustling of the average Northwesterner might eventually lead you to throw yourself in. Motivation, motivation, motivation – an essential quality of most Northwestern students and something you will need yourself if you plan to attend.

This is not to say that students here don't know how to relax or to have a good time. It's just that everything they do, they like to do well. For instance, take a look at their football team, the Wildcats, a name you will be chanting in your sleep by the time you graduate. The Wildcats are not just a football team. They are also proud members of the prestigious Big Ten group. Football fever runs high on campus – one more example of an area in which Northwestern succeeds.

Northwestern is lucky in having a graduate school, research institutes and alumni that keep its finances fairly healthy. As a result it has great resources, very modern sporting facilities and constantly renovated buildings. The general idea is that the sizeable endowment goes into making life easier for its students – something that is accomplished by an efficient and motivated college administration.

Hitting the Books (or Newspaper, or Spark plug or Cello)

Northwestern is both made and crippled by the fact that it is not one undergrad university, but six. All six of these schools enjoy a good reputation and their location on the same campus means that, as far as social and collegiate interaction goes, they are as one. The largest of them all, enrolling over half of each class, is the Weinburg College of Arts and Sciences (WCAS) – the typical American educational experience.

Then there are the satellite schools, the School of Communication, the School of Education and Social Policy and the McCormick School of Engineering and Applied Science. Finally there are two extremely good and prestigious colleges for those who have already found their vocations – the Medill School of Journalism and the School of Music.

On the surface, the presence of so diverse a collection of faculties seems great. Students can cross-register for courses in all the colleges (although this can be a difficult process) and there are also opportunities for joint degrees. If you are the next Brunel or Bach and you want to study in a specialized environment that also contains students with many different interests, then Northwestern may well be the perfect place for you. However, if you remain unsure as to your vocation, you may find it both frustrating and difficult to bridge the gap between all these institutions.

Whichever college you end up at, and WCAS is an ideal choice for many of the great undecided, the words 'liberal arts education' are guaranteed to haunt your academic career. All six of the schools require that you take a series of core classes to round out your education. This in part soothes the frustration of those who want to combine classes from all the colleges. The engineers still end up speaking French and the musicians practising physics – in short the great 'diversity' of subjects that all American universities pride themselves on is present in full force.

The average Northwestern student will also find himself working pretty hard. This is a competitive college and the majority of classmates were at the top of their high schools. Professors push their classes to the limit but are normally available to those students who need a helping hand. The size of classes varies but the larger classes (as at most of these schools) are broken up for more in-depth discussion groups. Students' lives are also made easier by the fact that it is now possible to do absolutely everything online – from registering for classes to checking in with all professors.

One of the reasons academic pressure is felt more at Northwestern is the tri-mester system. Actually for the average British student who has spent his or her life in a ritual of Michaelmas, Easter and Summer terms this is not a new thing. Yet it does mean the extra chore of having to take exams three times a year (as opposed to twice).

This causes its own problems – terms are shorter and you have little time to get your teeth into one subject before you are handed an exam paper and told to go and register for another. For those who feel the pressure of exams, Northwestern, with twelve sets in four years, might not be the ideal location.

One of the great advantages of a Northwestern education is the importance that it places on exposing its students to the rough and tumble of the real work place. Perhaps because of its close ties to specialized areas (engineering, journalism, music), there are an abundance of internships and work experience options available. Students at the Medill School of Journalism actually have to be interns as part of their academic requirements. This commitment on the part of Northwestern to set you up for life beyond college is exemplary and an extremely important part of your college experience there.

Social Life

Northwestern is a fun university – a quality helped by its great campus and closeness to Chicago. The campus itself provides a wide variety of events, parties and entertainments for its students. The fact that so many are involved in theatrical productions, musical concerts, and other artistic ventures means there is always something to do or see. Yet the housing system, the fairly large student body and the size of the campus can initially make it difficult to meet people and forge friendships.

The option of the fraternity or sorority is one method of meeting many people instantaneously and it has become huge on campus. This uniquely American concept is automatically the first association that 90% of Brits have with American schools. Not helped by films such as *Animal House*, *Legally Blonde* and the *Skulls*, most British students now believe that all Americans feel a compelling need to be part of something with an inexplicable Greek name, a bunch of really weird traditions and an eternal brother/sisterhood of similar freaks. In fact, this is not true. As Greek life at Northwestern shows, many simply see these societies as a way of expanding their friendship groups.

Greek life at Northwestern is very important. It is estimated that around 40% of the student body belong to a sorority or fraternity and 'rush' (the system of recruitment) takes place every fall. Many students choose to live in these societies, which are key in organizing many of the events and parties on campus. A recent attempt has been made to clean up their big-drinking, hard-living reputations, but alcohol still plays a large part in their lives.

Some of the fraternities and sororities are socially based, but others centre more on ethnicities or interests. While those not involved often complain that Greek life is too dominant on campus, even they admit that there is not the fierce segregation between the initiated and the non-initiated that plagues other Greek-based colleges.

Outside Those Ivory Walls

'My kind of town, Chicago is' warbled Frank Sinatra. After four years at Northwestern you may well feel the same way. Chicago, the third biggest city in the United States is quite unlike anything you will experience in the United Kingdom and offers a cultural awakening all of its own. Northwestern is ideally situated just north of the metropolis and only a short ride away by the famous 'el' train. Even when confined on campus, Chicago's skyline still dominates the view and, as soon as students have exhausted the good but few restaurants of Evanston, they can hit the town for a varied and fun night out.

It seems a waste of time to list everything that Chicago can provide in the way of amusement. Just as with London or New York, it is a veritable mixture of everything the student heart could desire. Plays, films, concerts and exhibitions appeal to the more artistically minded, while the sports teams, restaurants and clubs draw the red-blooded student crowd. And all of this takes place among some of the most magnificent modern architecture in the world.

Many Northwestern students only make the trip into Chicago on the weekends. Still others find that the campus provides sufficient amusements to prevent them from going in at all. Whatever your own opinion, it is a great place to have close at hand. The only possible disadvantage (aside from the weather!) is that Chicago does rather stand alone, isolated from both East and West Coast and is that little bit further (culturally and geographically) from the motherland. Still for a city that has everything you could possibly need, this factor soon ceases to be so important.

Getting In

AT A GLANCE – Application & Test Options:

– Early Decision, Regular Decision

– ACT/SAT required

– Two SAT Subject tests recommended (three required for home-schooled students)

Northwestern is on the up. As a result, so is the competition involved in getting in. A strong application and good grades are essential if you are to stand a chance. Out of the 37,000 applicants for 2016, only around 3,400 (9%) were admitted – a yield not much higher than the Ivy League schools. Although a similar standard is expected across all six undergraduate schools, students should be aware that you apply to the one that catches your interest individually.

The university requires all applicants to take the SAT or the ACT test. They also recommend you take two SAT Subject tests. While 'recommend' sounds encouragingly as though they are actually providing you with the option, it is in fact HIGHLY advisable that you do take the exams.

Rest assured though, Northwestern does understand, and take into account, the concept of A levels. It advises anyone with predictions below a C to think twice before applying. Remember to put down your predictions, AS and GCSE results on your application form – they are a very important (and well-respected) guide to just how clever you are! Also bear in mind that if you are a young Mozart and aiming for the extremely competitive and excellent music school, an audition will be required.

Northwestern is known for its extremely tricky and abstract essay questions. Rather than the clichéd contemplation of 'my most moving moment' or 'my hero', required by most universities, these personal essays stretch the creative and imaginative powers of each candidate to the limit. Think before you write.

There is an Early Decision programme at Northwestern. Yet you should beware. Unlike most other colleges, this university does not tend to forward applicants to the Regular Decision pile. If you plan to jump in early, you should really have your heart set on this being the only lace for you.

As with all these universities, it is important that your application gives a picture of you the person, as well as you the brain. After all, a sense of humour is one of the requirements listed on the application website!

Money Matters

There is no financial aid of any kind available for international students unless they are also registered as permanent residents of the United States.

Famous Grads

Cindy Crawford –if only all the girls looked like her

Warren Beatty – if only all the guys looked like him!

Charlton Heston – this place is heavy on future Hollywood stars

Oberlin College

Oberlin, Ohio
www.oberlin.edu
Undergrads: 2,900
Grads: 20

How many students does it take to change a light bulb at Oberlin?

Three – one to change it and two to figure out how to get high off the old one.

Oberlin is the sort of college that either represents your idea of seventh heaven or hell on earth. Situated in small-town Ohio, about 45 minutes away from Cleveland, it draws an eclectic collection of students from all over America. The Oberlin student body is known for being progressively liberal, extremely politically correct and just that little bit wacky. Students tend to be experimental, eccentric and decidedly left-of-centre and the faculty members aren't much different.

Proponents of the traditional Oxbridge or New England system will regard Oberlin as a radical's joke, but few would deny the strength of its academic reputation or the prominent position of many of its alums.

The Campus

Although Cleveland is only a short drive away, there is always something going on in Oberlin itself – a town that really functions as an extension of the eccentric student-body and offers just about everything they could want.

The majority of students at Oberlin are extremely happy with their situation and love the outspoken and politicized atmosphere on campus. This is truly a place where rock musicians mix with classical violinists (again the Conservatory is a focal point of campus life), poets with politicians and radicals with even more radicals.

Accommodation

Students at Oberlin have a number of accommodation options that reflect the tolerant attitude of the school. In addition to the more standard dorms, there are also nine programme houses where students can pursue a particular interest or belief, plus the famous co-op system, where students live together and take on the responsibility of feeding and cleaning for themselves (something that sounds standard for us Brits, but is much less usual over here). The flexibility of the living system means that students can find out which of the many groups on campus makes them most comfortable without committing four years to any one of them.

The Oberlin Student

Since its foundation in 1833 Oberlin has led the pack in liberal mentality. Kept together by abolitionist money in the early years, it was the first college to allow women and one of the primary educators of African-Americans. Oberlin students are, almost without exception, idealistic and campus dialogue is defined by conversations about just how each and every individual can make the world that little bit better.

Even deciding what type of milk you want to put on your cereal (organic? soy? goat?) can turn into a philosophical debate; an earnest protest against steamed vs fried chicken in General Tso chicken as cultural appropriation caught the national zeitgeist and made news across the US. Some might find this enthusiasm (which undoubtedly has a particularly American flavour) irritating, but most would agree that it is never boring.

While Oberlin prides itself on its diversity, it does attract a lot of well-off, white kids (often rebelling against parental authority), and a group of extremely talented musicians (studying at the world-famous Oberlin Conservatory). It also has a sizeable number of international students – around 13% of the fairly small class. Despite the disparate ideological convictions of most of the students, everyone tends to get along well – in part because of the confining nature of the attractive campus.

Hitting the Books

Academics are embarked on with enthusiasm and liberal-mindedness and student-faculty bonds are extremely strong. This is a university that positively encourages interdisciplinary learning and courses are taken in a huge variety of subjects.

Students are also actively involved in the educational process, whether they are giving their views to the administration or teaching a class in the Experimental College. Classes are small and challenging and known for being academically excellent. The well-reputed faculty caters to people who love to learn but who also love to discuss and dispute as they do it.

Social Life

With a student body this ideological, there are any number of clubs, protests, papers and bands to get involved in and it is a rare Oberlin student who does not seize every chance to participate.

If you are a reactionary who loves George Bush and disapproves of sex, drugs and rock and roll (all integral parts of the Oberlin education), then this is not the place for you. But if you like to think outside the box and want a strong academic environment that permits you to learn with hundreds of like-minded people, then this may be one of the best options out there.

Getting In

AT A GLANCE – Application & Test Options:

– Early Action, Early Decision, Early Decision II, Regular Decision

– ACT/SAT required, Writing/essay optional

– SAT Subject tests not required

Oberlin is a highly selective liberal arts college – just under 30% of applicants were given the go-ahead in 2016, and only 15% of all international applicants were accepted. That's because – and this is worth quoting directly from their website – "More than 80 percent of our international students receive institutional financial aid, with the average aid package covering about three-quarters of the cost of attendance". If you are a close student of this book, you will realise this is a HUGE amount of financial aid for international students.

But because the international financial aid budget does have limits (albeit stratospheric), the international admission process is extremely competitive—particularly for students with high financial need. That's taken into account as they consider applications. Not surprising given the nontraditional nature of the student body, a holistic view is taken of each applicant to get a sense of not only their academic qualifications, but also of what they are like as a person and what they will contribute to the Oberlin community. They want you to submit SAT or ACT test results (the best scores from each sitting) but do not require the SAT Subject tests.

Money Matters

Oberlin awards financial aid to meet 100 percent of the demonstrated financial need of students. In 2016, 80% of their international students demonstrated some sort of need and succeeded in receiving aid, resulting in the school doling out a whopping $59 million. It tends to be awarded in a three-part package that includes grants, low-interest student loans, and money earned through student employment. They sponsor a limited number of merit-based scholarships as well, which you can receive in addition to your need-based aid if awarded.

Famous Grads

James Burrows – Emmy award-winning producer and director of several long-running TV shows

George Walker – composer, first African-American to win the Pulitzer Prize for Music

Christopher Browning – historian of the Holocaust

Pepperdine College

Malibu, California
www.pepperdine.edu
Undergrads: 3500
Grads: 3000

How many Pepperdine students does it take to change a light bulb?

Two – one to change it and one to give the sermon.

Pepperdine is a Christian college and has clearly been blessed by God for it. Perched on a prime stretch of the Malibu hills overlooking awe-inspiring beaches and ocean with a near-perfect climate, it would be hard not to be a believer at this school. Academics are top-notch, and the students are friendly and happy. Even Richard Dawkins would be reluctant to say no.

The Campus

Rated in consecutive years as having the most beautiful campus in the country (no easy feat when you consider the competition), Pepperdine really is something special. A sharp climb into the hills off the world-famous Pacific Coast Highway, where people come from miles simply to drive and admire the landscape, Pepperdine provides searing views over the Pacific Ocean and the spectacular beaches below. This really is California at its best and most stereotypical, with excellent surfing opportunities and well-tanned, healthy students sunbathing or taking exercise à la Baywatch.

The campus is not too big and there are great facilities, both sporting and academic, including one of the most exquisite baseball diamonds in the world where you can hit your home-runs into the ocean.

Accommodation

The dorms, where 95% of freshmen and a large chunk of the rest have accommodation, would be considered well above average in normal circumstances, but with the view and the location they are transformed into priceless real estate, which students can use at bargain rates.

The Pepperdine Student

The stereotypes are manifold. Mostly it's the rich preppy crowd, complete with the "Barbie girls", jocks, frat-boys, Texans and typical Southern Californians. These folk are complemented by clever kids who attend the school on a scholarship or heavy financial aid. The attitudes at the school are shaped by the Christian aspect – meaning that students say they are "excited by life", have happy, outgoing personalities and are generally optimistic.

Unfortunately the wealth of most students means things can lean towards the superficial, with importance attached to designer labels and make of car, for example. Politics are conservative here, and experimental or radically-minded students are the exception rather than the norm.

Despite being in the minority, unconventional personalities can have a great time at Pepperdine. There are a fair number of non-Christians, LGBT and international students, all of who seem to rub along happily enough within the student body. Do be prepared for mandatory chapel every week.

Hitting the Books

Academics are excellent at Pepperdine. The university follows a liberal arts program with the traditional focus on the Core Curriculum (which includes courses on religion) in the early years. Professors are high quality, challenging and personally involved with the students in small class sizes and one-to-one meetings out of class. Professors are also conservative in the main, staying true to the Christian aspect, and every now and again you may come across one that "needs to be fired", as one student put it. The post graduate business and law schools are the most famous departments, with nation-wide reputations.

Students describe the work-load as "not too grueling", "heavy, but not more than you'd expect for university," and "more than at a state school", and the commitment to study among the students is strong.

A major positive aspect of the school is the study abroad program. Over half the students spend at least a semester in a foreign country, the second highest proportion of any university in the US. Students almost always return from these experiences reinvigorated and, dare we say it, more open-minded in their attitudes.

Social Life

On campus, the zero-tolerance regulations against drugs and alcohol mean a quiet social life, and the nearby town of Malibu is small. Social gatherings are "not in your face", as one student put it, "...you have to go look for them". Nevertheless, opportunities for beach- and hill-type activities abound, and it is popular for students to drive into Los Angeles or Santa Monica to get the desired injection of clubs and party scene.

There are lots of extra-curricular choices. Sports are not big, but there are nationally-acclaimed teams in volleyball, water-polo and baseball. Wilderness activities are popular, including hiking or mountain-biking in the beautiful surrounding hills. Pepperdine also has a great Peace-Corps team, and lots of opportunities to get involved in community service schemes

Getting In

AT A GLANCE – Application & Test Options:

- Regular Decision
- ACT/SAT required, Writing/essay optional
- SAT Subject tests not required

Pepperdine is reasonably selective – just under 40% of applicants were admitted in 2016 – but nothing like, say, the uber-cutthroat University of Southern California (17%).

Money Matters

This is a relatively small private school and fees are high and aimed at the wealthy. Although there is no needs-based financial aid for international applicants, Pepperdine maintains its academic calibre by providing plenty of aid for the less-well-off but intelligent in the form of scholarships and loans (but, like most US schools they require an American co-signer for loans). Here's some good news – all admitted students, including international, are automatically considered for the Regents Scholars' Awards, which are handed out to approximately the top 10% of all admitted applicants. So you definitely have a chance at one of those.

Famous Grads

Chace Crawford – Actor, 'Gossip Girl' (TV Series)

Adam Housley – National Correspondent Fox News, Emmy Winner

Rod Blagojevich – Former Governor of Illinois (2003 – 2009)

Princeton University

Princeton, New Jersey
www.princeton.edu
Undergrads: 5,000
Grads: 2,500

How many students does it take to change a light bulb at Princeton?

Two – one to mix the martinis and one to call the electrician.

Think of every Ivy League stereotype your fevered mind can come up with. The beautiful buildings, the beautiful weather, the beautiful people strolling around in beautiful clothes and making beautiful conversation. Now take away the weather and you have a pretty good picture of how Princeton is generally perceived.

The Campus

Princeton University was founded in the then small settlement of Princeton in rural New Jersey. The initial charter was given in 1746, making it the fourth oldest college in America. Despite its original moniker, 'the Garden State', New Jersey is now more frequently associated with petrol stations and strip malls, and the town of Princeton has embraced suburbia, numbering 30,000 inhabitants. However, the Princeton campus has remained relatively unchanged, despite new additions both architectural and demographic (think, not just rich white men).

Princeton occupies a 500-acre spot in the middle of the surrounding town. This large area is filled with the traditional smattering of Gothic libraries, modern architecture and red brick houses. However, Princeton has succeeded where other colleges have failed and all the buildings blend into one pleasant whole.

Whether students are lounging on Cannon Green, rushing frantically into the famous Firestone Library or crowding out onto Prospect Avenue (aka the Street), they are almost always surrounded by beautiful architecture and a pleasant open space. Many of the buildings have played a historically important role in American history. The famous Nassau Hall (which also figures in the rousing Princeton song) housed British soldiers during the American Revolution and (after our somewhat ignominious defeat) served as the temporary capital of America under George Washington.

Accommodation

Small wonder that many students are only too happy to live in such a historical setting. It is expected at Princeton that all first and second years will live on campus in one of the six residential colleges. This division of these two classes into blocks of around 400 makes for a great community and a fun living experience in which you can very much make your own way while still having people around you who know the ropes.

And these colleges have their own dining halls – delaying the pressure of choosing an eating club until your junior year. Juniors and seniors live in other on-campus dormitories (or off-campus). They have the option of eating in the clubs on the Street or in the other facilities that the university provides for those who balk at the idea of having to join a club to eat.

The Princetonian

For years Princeton gloried in the fact that the confines of its campus housed the offspring of the richest and most blue-blooded American families. It was truly the place where the WASPs (White Anglo-Saxon Protestants) went en route from Philips Andover and before they took their place in daddy's firm.

However, although hints of this privileged past linger on here and there, the Princeton campus no longer swarms with similarly khaki-clad, polo-shirted individuals. And although it is still true that the undergraduates are among some of the wealthiest per capita in America, the WASPy, conservative image is unquestionably on the way out – which students say is not adequately pointed out.

You are as likely to find someone in a hoodie as you are to find someone in a polo shirt, the LGBT and women's centres are massive on campus, and "from my first semester I was exposed to political protest, buddhist talks, and ultimate frisbee." Students think the administration makes a real effort to make the campus inclusive, in no small measure because generous financial aid means that just about anyone who clears the high fence to get in will be able to attend, and once on campus, no one really needs to spend any money if they don't want to.

Freshman Summer Initiative allows promising students from the poorest schools in the country to get a head start on their studies – additional evidence that Princeton has moved to a much more liberal place than its reputation used to suggest.

Even in the old WASPy days, it would be wrong to say that Princetonians were intolerant of those who differed from the stereotype. As a whole, it was and is an accepting and friendly community with a strong school spirit ('Go Tigers'). The huge amount of money that pours in from alumni testifies to this very real devotion to the Princeton establishment (as well as to the consoling fact that Princeton grads do actually make money and you will not be a struggling student forever!).

There is one thing that links all Princeton students, regardless of race or finances: their brainpower. You will be amazed by the diversity of the people you meet, but you will be still more amazed by the things they have done and the things they say. This intelligence is coupled with a serious desire to achieve everything possible in a four year space.

America is a nation of overachievers and Princeton is no exception. Whether playing in the orchestra, directing and producing your own musical, writing for The Daily Princetonian or joining the oldest debating society in America, you will find that your schedule quickly contains more hours for extra-curriculars than it does for sleep. And slackers among you should be warned, the University really encourages students to get involved with whatever interests them outside the library.

There is always something going on at Princeton and students never get the chance to complain that they're bored. Despite its Ivy League (for which read 'all brains, no brawn') status, Princeton has a number of successful sports team. And if you're not out there playing, you're expected to be on the sidelines cheering and, if the mood takes you, painted like a tiger.

It is impossible to graduate from Princeton without gaining a certain amount of the all-pervasive school spirit. Whether they are celebrating the beginning of their student lives with Opening Exercises or the conclusion with Class Day festivities, Princetonians do it with pride and a certain amount of rowdy singing. And after all, what's not to be proud of?

Hitting the Books

There are only a handful of things you can criticize Princeton for – its paltry off-campus options and WASPy cliques – being two of the most obvious. But there is one thing that only the very brave or very stupid dare to critique – its academics. It is undeniable that Princeton offers one of the best educations in America.

The undergraduate experience is all the better because the university has a small graduate population and thus focuses its attention on the academics and well-being of the undergraduate above all else (in fact, there are no graduate programmes without an undergrad counterpart). This means that during your four years of education, you will be spoiled for choice and continually under the attention of some of the best professors in both the nation and the world.

The commitment of the faculty is one of the nicest traits about Princeton. In recent years the university has gathered the best minds in America to teach its undergraduates (often luring them away from other top universities with substantial pay packages and tenure track offers). Today the faculty-student ratio stands at about 7:1 and all teachers are required to perform teaching duties as well as their own work.

This means that students will actually end up being taught by the expert in a particular field as opposed to a struggling graduate student who speaks very little English. This access to such superb academic instruction can be one of the most challenging things about Princeton, but it is also one of the most rewarding.

Princeton definitely expects commitment from its students and the magnificent Firestone Library, which has more than 70 miles of shelving, is continually filled with undergrads exhausted by the pursuit of knowledge. Traditionally, students take four courses each semester until their senior year when they reduce their course load to three in order to focus on their thesis. However, many ambitious Princeton minds choose to take on even more. Princetonians are required to choose their major by the end of their sophomore year. There is a wide range of options, but some of the favourites include History, Economics, English and Politics.

Princeton also puts its undergrads through their paces in a core curriculum that, as at other universities, requires a certain breadth of knowledge. Some of this is instilled in the tradition of preceptorials. Established by Woodrow Wilson and loosely based on the tutorial systems of Oxbridge, they are an integral part of the academic experience. These preceptorials place small groups of undergrads in weekly contact with their professors, providing them with a valuable opportunity to rub shoulders with the greats. Princeton rightly places a great deal of emphasis on this professorial-student bond and likes to talk about the importance and trust of this relationship.

This is exemplified in the Princeton honour system. Once they sign a pledge of honesty, students are allowed to take exams without the presence of a proctor. This is symptomatic of the Princetonian attitude. They treat you like an honourable academic contemporary and you are expected to behave like one.

This emphasis on intellectual integrity is also put to the test by the hoops that Princeton requires you to jump through in your junior and senior year. Unlike most universities, Princeton insists that all of its undergraduates write both a Junior Paper (the JP) and a senior thesis.

Although this is a significant amount of work, Princeton believes that it helps you to organize yourself for the real world as well as, after you recover from the numerous sleepless nights and caffeine fixes, giving you a real sense of achievement. Throughout the process you are under the guidance of a member of the faculty, another example of the care that the Princetonian administration takes of that most lowly academic individual – the undergraduate.

Be warned, however. Many students complain that the care Princeton takes of its undergraduate can, at times, be overwhelming. The core curriculum is extremely rigid and students often feel their academic flexibility is limited. Study abroad is also not really encouraged by the administration – although many justly feel that the calibre of academics on campus means that they have everything they want right there.

Social Life

It is easy to imagine the social life of the average Princetonian fifty years ago – lots of white men sitting around in their eating clubs, sipping port, smoking cigars and talking about the next crew race against Harvard. Times have changed since then and the increased diversity in the student body has shaken up the stuffy traditions of previous generations.

Princeton students now find every weekend on campus offers a vast variety of plays, musical performances and cultural occasions, not to mention the odd celebration of a football triumph or two. Whether your taste is for drunken keg stands or a quiet espresso while you listen to Brahms, you will find like-minded individuals on the Princeton campus.

One thing has, however, remained relatively unchanged despite the passing of the years. The process of selecting and then participating in an eating club is still a unique part of the Princeton experience. The eleven eating clubs situated on the Street provide the nutritional and social haven for juniors and seniors. The clubs cater for around 150 people and, until fairly recently, if you wanted to eat you had to join. Nowadays the clubs are optional but many students still view them as an integral part of student life. Some of them are open to all through a lottery process while others maintain the old exclusivity, selecting their lucky members in the 'bicker' held at the end of sophomore year.

These clubs are far more than just a munching-ground. Given Princeton's lamentable lack of off-campus options, they also serve as party centres for the university and frequently provide anyone who wants it with a drunken Saturday night. (It is also widely rumoured that one of them has a cache of A grade papers available for its members to use when writers block strikes!)

It should be noted that while Princeton has a great on-campus social life (helped by the genuine efforts of the faculty to build a student centre that actually has fun stuff going on), it remains exactly that, on campus. Some students are fine with staying in the same square mile every weekend of their college career, but others find it quickly becomes insular. Luckily for these people, NYC is only a short trip away.

Outside Those Ivory Walls

Princeton has many things going for it, but the local town is really not one of them. Princeton, New Jersey is an old and established place, and has notably failed to embrace the twenty-first century. As a result, students frequently complain they have very little to do once they step off campus grounds.

The area is charming, with small restaurants and pretty houses, but – with none of the bustling bars, clubs and shopping districts that usually characterise a university town – the choices are flatly described by at least one student as "paltry". Even student eateries are limited in number, most of the restaurants falling into either the expensive-bring-the-parents or gross-who-would-eat-that categories...an exception being the famous Bent Spoon ice cream shop.

Luckily, however, most Princeton students are satisfied by the active social life on campus supplemented by the basic fare of cinema, meals and coffee in local Princeton. And when they feel the need to kick up their heels and have some metropolitan fun, New York and Philadelphia are only an hour away by frequent train and bus services. This is short enough to make a day trip feasible and a weekend trip extremely enjoyable. However, most students simply cannot be bothered to make the effort.

Finally if you go to Princeton you should also not forget about the natural world outside the campus walls. Although 'beautiful' New Jersey is sadly no longer beautiful, it does have areas that are extremely special, and it is definitely worth while devoting at least one weekend of your undergraduate experience to exploring this bit of America (strip malls optional).

Getting In

AT A GLANCE – Application & Test Options:

- Single-Choice Early Action, Regular Decision

- ACT/SAT, with Writing/essay required

- Two SAT Subject tests recommended, especially for Engineering (Math 1 or 2, plus either Physics or Chemistry), but not required

Nobody ever said it was easy. Princeton is almost always near the top of any ranking lists you choose to look at, competing normally with Harvard (and often beating it!) for that valuable first place. And since the university made an effort to open up their doors to people other than Mr My-great-great-great-grandparents-sailed-on-the-Mayflower, admissions have become even more competitive. For the class of 2020, the university accepted 6.4% of those who applied (of which, 12% were international). Given that there were more than 29,000 applications, this makes for an awful lot of disappointed people.

Princeton requires that all applicants take the SAT or the ACT by the December of the year in which they apply. These results are then submitted with the Common App and Princeton supplement.

The Princeton form is one of the longer of the college supplements, consisting of questions as varied as 'What's your favourite word?' (you have to wonder if they are running psychological assessments on your answers), as well as the more typical 'What has changed your life? How do you deal with X?' questions.

Interviews with alumni are also available and should be taken up if possible as they provide you with a good opportunity to discover more about the place you are considering devoting four years of your life to. Princeton expresses a particular interest in special talents and your life outside your books. So if you have built an orphanage in Afghanistan or sung in Westminster Abbey, shout out about it. America is not a modest nation and British reticence, especially on application forms, will do you little good.

Princeton actually encourages the British idea of a gap year (something that is not true of all US colleges). If you want to do this, you must apply, be accepted and then defer.

Money Matters

Princeton's application process is need-blind for international students as well as US applicants, which means they "meet the full demonstrated financial need of accepted students with a no-loan aid package".

Famous Grads

Woodrow Wilson – President of the United States

Ralph Nader – a once much-hated politico

David Duchovny – smart in real life as well

Reed College

Portland, Oregon
www.reed.edu
Undergrads: 1,400
Grads: 30

How many students does it take to change a light bulb at Reed?
Just one, and he powers it on his own brain's energy-output.

Intensely eccentric, ferociously hard-working and one of the most unique educational experiences on offer, you'll either love or hate Reed College. Definitely not for the weak of heart, nor for those seeking the classic American college – but you will feel the vibes the minute you open their brochure if this place is for you. Others, beware.

The Campus

If you attended an old-fashioned British Public School, you may experience a sense of déjà vu when you first arrive at Reed. Victorian-style mansions dominate spacious lawns, with residence halls, classroom blocks, a large library and sports facilities strewn across 100 pleasant acres. The spectacular centrepiece is the famous Reed Canyon, the college's very own river-gorge, complete with beautiful lake and woodland wildlife, which splits the campus neatly into north and south.

Accommodation

The residence halls, in which 70% of the students find accommodation, are widely praised, with most students enjoying large single rooms. Some have interesting themes (dorms for cat-owners anyone?) including five language blocks for exclusive Spanish, French, German, Russian and Chinese practice.

The Reedie

Reedies are an evolving species, much stereotyped, unquestionably unique. Often contrasted with their Portland-based neighbours at Lewis and Clark College, Reedies are said to "work harder, party harder and do harder drugs". Although the majority are Caucasian west-coasters, the student body is nevertheless healthily diverse, with a solid 7-8% international students. The admissions team prides itself on aiming to pick interesting and creative individuals, and this means there is a nice range of personalities that keeps the unavoidable cliquiness to a minimum.

Studying is a big part of any Reedie's life, and Reed has developed a reputation for endless toil, which is not undeserved. Some students complain that it is "difficult to escape" the work culture which dominates free time and conversation. Reed has been described (by non-Reedies) as a place where people who don't fit in go to university to be with others who are similarly socially awkward. As one student put it, "we're geeky kids, but we're all geeks together". The term reedie has come to mean pretentious or work-obsessed in American slang, with connotations of people who care more about academic pedantry than real-life concerns. This is undeserved.

Reed has had a traditionally "edgy" or hippy student body, though nowadays the culture tends more towards the mainstream. This doesn't stop the quirky nature of the college being expressed to the full in the bizarre student organisations and wacky parties, nor has it blunted the edge of the strong political leftism that is prevalent. In truth, the bohemian reputation was and is mostly a product of the university's drug policy, which openly tolerates use of illicit substances.

Consumption of such substances, however, is on the decrease, and students are emphatic that drugs are not a problem for those who don't want them to be. Plenty of help is available for those who take habits too far, and education about the problems caused by drug abuse is spread by students and the administration.

Hitting the Books

If you're looking for an academic powerhouse to attend in the US, Reed has to be on your shortlist. The beauty of the Reed education is that it combines some of the best and most intense teaching in the country with a fully-rounded Liberal Arts curriculum, meaning that graduates leave with in depth knowledge in an impressive range of subjects. It is a tribute to the college that they manage to produce a proportionately huge number of award winners (including the second-most Rhodes Scholars of any Liberal Arts college), as well as the third-highest percentage of students – from any university in the USA – who go on to earn PhDs.

The professors at Reed are superb – praised by the students as "what makes Reed Reed". Teachers are always helpful and generous with the time and dedication they lavish on students, and show a real interest in teaching. "All you have to do is show you're interested too," beamed one student, evidently implying that this was a given at Reed. The faculty:student ratio is an enviable 1:10, meaning much attention for students and great "conference" style classes that promote quality discussion and learning.

The curriculum at Reed is laced with typically innovative and unusual requirements. All students must take a course in Humanities, giving them knowledge of the classics and ancient history. In order to graduate, students must complete a thesis in their final year which they spend two semesters writing under the guidance of a tutor. In another brilliant twist, Reed operates largely without letter-grades, preferring to emphasise the quality of work over the result achieved. Grades are awarded, but are only available if they are explicitly requested or looked up. Instead, students find their work returned with extensive comments that help them learn from what they are doing right and wrong. Reedies joke that this is an excellent system because it spares them from seeing the discouraging results that they would earn under the rigorous standards of the college.

Budding physicists who want to get their hands on the real thing should check out Reed's kick-ass nuclear reactor, which is the only one in the world operated exclusively by undergraduates. Rumour has it that the reactor, used for bragging as much as research, was built without the knowledge of the US government (which will presumably be calling in UN weapons inspectors to take action before Reedies get out of hand).

Social Life

Reed works more than it plays, but when Reedies aren't working, they certainly know how to have fun. In social life, as in everything else, the student body displays an ingenious and quirky imagination, and this gives rise to an uncanny knack for finding great ways to spend free time.

Reedies benefit hugely from a generous super-wealthy alumnus, Betty Gray, who provided for the construction of the Gray student-centre, and the Gray fund. Also known as "the opportunity to go somewhere cool for free just about every weekend," the Gray Fund is exclusively for recreation. One presumes that Betty took pity on future generations of Reedies after suffering a particularly gruelling college experience. Her funds continue to finance all kinds of activities, including excursions, free concert tickets and the like.

This, coupled with a proliferation of amusing, intriguing, and often downright crazy student organisations (Guerilla Theatre of the Absurd, Defenders of the Universe, Zombies vs Humans, Cookies for All...) make for as vibrant a social community as one could wish for. Also worth mentioning is the student radio station, KRRC, which is one of the finest in the country.

Founded with the specific goal of not replicating east-coast Ivy League-style education, Reed has no fraternities, nor any varsity sports teams. Nevertheless, there are plenty of parties, some resembling traditional Greek life, though students insist they are less elitist and that "at Reed kids actually look after each other".

While good facilities are available for conventional sports, Reedies once again display their eccentricities by excelling at ultimate frisbee, fencing and – a particular boon to Brits – rugby. All students must take PE, which involves a sport of the student's choice, ranging from archery and kayaking to juggling and everything in between.

Reed has a politically radical reputation (unofficial motto: "communism, atheism, free love"), established during the McCarthy era when the firing of a Marxist professor provoked mass protests from the students. Since then, the students have jealously guarded a certain level of autonomy from the administration.

Dialogue and relations between the two have reached a happy equilibrium, and the school now runs itself according to the "Honour Principle", which essentially relies on trust. The administration does not make or enforce any rules, and the students agree to behave like adults and sort problems out sensibly by themselves. What sounds incredible for most undergraduate schools Reed pulls off rather well, with few complaints from the students.

The "student senate" runs most of the extracurricular activities, including the student union, newspaper, and ski cabin on nearby Mt. Hood. It is also responsible for allocating funds to student organisations, which it collects and distributes according to referendum votes.

Two major events in the Reed calendar are Paideia and the Renn Fayre. The former is a week-long "festival of learning", when anyone can give classes on anything they choose. The resulting mish-mash of wacky lectures and brilliant new ideas is a scintillating experience.

The Renn Fayre is equally chaotic – a three-day explosion of fun and nonsense that precedes the last week and exams and is seen as a release from the intensity of hard work pent up during the year. The activities are too bizarre to be believed, and the general free-for-all is kept safe by the student 'karma patrol' which stays sober and provides bagels and water for exhausted participants.

Outside Those Ivory Walls

Portland, with much on offer for every taste, is nearby, though students visit town less frequently than might be expected, and in some extreme cases will barely leave campus for a whole semester. But it should be noted that Portland is often considered to be one of the nicest cities in the US...trendy, fun, walkable with endless and wonderful food trucks, and one of the world's largest, beloved and most eccentric bookstores.

Getting In

AT A GLANCE – Application & Test Options:

– Early Decision, Early Decision II, Regular Decision

– ACT/SAT required

– SAT Subject tests optional

Applications to Reed have multiplied in recent years, and the standards of entry have risen accordingly; the acceptance rate is now about 1 in 3. Applications must be strong, but the admissions team is also looking for individual flair and dynamic personalities, so don't trick yourself into thinking it's just about the SAT/ACT scores.

Money Matters

Reed is expensive (as are most private colleges in the US), but financial aid can be generous, allocated according to need and strength of application, and about 10% of international students who apply for aid are awarded grants, loans, or work opportunities. This means that there are no academic scholarships available.

Famous Grads

Steve Jobs – co-founder of Apple

Larry Sanger – co-founder of Wikipedia

James Russell – invented the CD, and by extension was the father of the digital revolution

Rice University

Houston, Texas
www.rice.edu
Undergrads: 3,900
Grads: 2,700

How many Rice students does it take to change a light bulb?

Four – one to change it, one to take it out again and claim it for his own college, one to take it out yet again and throw it at the administration, and one to point out that it was all done just as expertly as at any Ivy League school.

With brilliant, quirky students, an unmatched faculty and a fantastic range of sports and social events, Rice has much to offer every type of student. The university is changing rapidly though, so beware – many warn that it is losing its charm and its most attractive qualities, while others are happy to see the change of style push the school ever-upwards, at least in the rankings.

The Campus

It is debatable whether the old saying "there are more trees than people at Rice" is still true. What is for sure is that Rice's delightful 300 acre campus is pleasant and functional, and the facilities far surpass what might be expected of a college of its size. While the lawns and gardens are beautiful, the buildings are also striking (perhaps due to the world-famous architecture department), with a mix of Spanish tiles and East Coast brick.

Some are more ambitious, such as the Chemistry block designed to look like the school's mascot, the owl, the Politics department with strange staircases (allegedly built to confuse any terrorists that might want to disrupt the big-name speakers who give speeches there) or the enigmatic "Dr. Seuss building" (so named for the bizarre design).

Rice has good academic facilities, but is known more for its sporting ones, which include a new athletic complex and an enormous football stadium where President Kennedy famously gave a speech about his determination to send men to the moon, not too long before he was assassinated in another Texas city.

In fact, Rice has a strong connection with astronautics, since nearby Houston Space Centre is built on land donated by the university and several alumni and faculty have been professional astronauts. When we visited, a mechanical engineering professor had just returned from repairing the Hubble Space Telescope, which he apparently accomplished whilst wearing a T-Shirt signed by the whole department.

When David Leebron became the President of Rice (in 2004), having previously worked as the Dean at Columbia University in New York, he immediately setting out to "Ivy Leaguify" the college. Leebron was at first controversial – there were concerns about crushing the unique spirit and best foibles of the school – but his bold moves in attracting bigger donors and professors have raised the reputation of the school from excellent to among the very best.

Accommodation

Most freshmen and an awful lot of the other students live on campus. Unlike many colleges, students often try to linger on campus as long as they can, because they love the living arrangements. The dorms are divided into "colleges", in a system very similar to the British public school "houses" or Oxbridge's colleges. Students are assigned to colleges arbitrarily when they arrive ("like the Sorting Hat", as one put it), and each college has a traditional and unique spirit or area of excellence (again like Harry Potter). Some colleges are known for their athletes, others for their academics, others for their parties, but everyone loves the system, which is often named as the single best thing about Rice.

The Owl

The student body has traditionally been one of the most attractive aspects of a Rice education. The *Princeton Review* rates the school among the top 15 in the "Happiest Students" section, and indeed the enthusiasm and joi de vivre here are palpable. Students have a lot of pride in what they are, but it is an entirely unselfish, modest kind of pride – one that springs from real fulfillment.

They are proud of their academic record, proud of their ability to work hard and party hard, proud of their sporting prowess and proud of their general knack for making interesting and fully-rounded personalities out of themselves. "Everyone's on the same page in that respect," said one senior, adding modestly "and we're all just dorks at the end of the day."

Rice has traditionally attracted a slightly off-beat crowd from a wide range of backgrounds, most of whom are looking for a top-notch education without the elitism and other drawbacks of the big East Coasters, but also without the out-and-out hippies of the really small liberal arts schools. There is a fair number of international students (13%), and also a good diversity of socio-economic and racial profiles, and students assure us that "no one has a problem fitting in".

However, the tides have been turning. Some blame it on the arrival of President Leebron, and some think it started when a popular teen magazine, Seventeen, named Rice the "coolest school in the country" way back in 2002, much to the amusement (and bewilderment) of the students. Either way, the demographic has been veering ever-closer towards the mainstream and fees have risen, along with applications from wealthier students.

Still, Rice is a long way from the elitism associated with schools like Princeton, and the positive distinguishing characteristics of the student body (enthusiasm, interesting personalities, etc) are far from dead. Rice students share a strong communal spirit with their peers, and the sense of everyone being "in it together" is very prominent. You see it in the crazy traditions, the powerful honour code and in the intense academic stamina, not to mention the fierce support of school sports teams at big events.

Hitting the Books

Rice is frequently ranked in the top twenty best undergraduate programs – regardless of the criteria. With an unbeatable student:faculty ratio of 6:1, the university combines the wonderful small-class, intimate student-teacher relationships of smalls schools with the big-hitting academic machinery of an Ivy.

Programs in areas as diverse as engineering and performance music are among the best in the country, while the small architecture department is world famous. The politics department was first established by former Secretary of State James Baker and has continued to attract big-name speakers (including Presidents) ever since. Rice is a pioneer in nanotechnology, and holds a Guinness World Record for creating the smallest car (out of atoms).

The work load is large and challenging, the students are hard working and competitive, and everyone feeds off each other's work ethic. In work, as in everything at Rice, there is a strong communal spirit among the students, which is fostered and honed by the "caring" and "available" professors. This manifests itself in the honour code, which allows teachers to set take-home tests without fear of cheating, and encourages both student and teacher to get to know each other outside the classroom.

Rice is much better known for its sciences and engineering than its arts or humanities, and non-scientists generally have slightly less enthusiastic views about the teaching. It is ironic, therefore, that there is no medical school at Rice. However, for those pre-med students who are reluctant to leave Houston, the neighbouring Baylor Med School is one of the best in the country.

Social Life

Do not underrate the "party" bit of Rice's "work hard, party hard" culture. Rice is a famously "wet" campus, and there is an unstated consensus between administration and students that students are permitted wild parties and as much alcohol as they want, but in return they behave responsibly and seldom overstep reasonable limits. You're not going to find the classic TV frat parties here (and not just because Rice has no Greek life). In the words of one student: "the social scene can be a little weird at times." But that doesn't stop everyone loving it!

The spectacular range of social events is planned by the students and paid for by the university. Famous examples of these include NOD (Night of Decadence...), Baker 13 (running in the nude), and of course the "Beer Bike" (bicycles, alcohol, and lots of water-balloons), which is so popular that alumni often return just to take part. Before students are even matriculated at the start of their Rice years, pre-freshmen can attend "Owl Days", an introductory couple of days of parties, drinks and performances that is unanimously loved.

Colleges are the main source of parties, with each one organising its own events that everyone can attend. "There is always something to do on the weekend," said one happy student. There are jazz concerts, themed parties, poetry slams or just hanging out on the lawns or in the great coffeehouses and pubs on campus. Rice is also home to a number of excellent media groups, including student-run newspapers, a radio station and a TV channel.

Sports are huge at Rice, which is one of the smallest schools in the country to have teams in the top Division One basketball and football, as well as one of the best college baseball teams around. Other sports such as swimming and volleyball are also played to a high standard.

Outside Those Ivory Walls

Students don't live life in a bubble at Rice, they live "between the hedges" (a reference to the shrubbery along the campus' entire perimeter). There is so much fun to be had on campus that few feel the need to leave, especially in the early years. Yet Rice is located perfectly in America's fourth largest metropolis, Houston, and those who want to experience the city that lies beyond campus will find a treasure trove of delights. Houston is aglow with cool venues, funky old restaurants and bars and oil-rich mansion-filled districts.

The university is next to a metro stop and a major motorway that takes you rapidly to all parts of the city, though perhaps the best attractions are no further than the nearby Rice Village. Houston is pretty close to beautiful beach town Galveston, a popular destination for sea lovers

Getting In

AT A GLANCE – Application & Test Options:

– Early Decision, Regular Decision

– Testing required: Either SAT with two Subject tests, or the ACT

Rice is tough to get into, almost on a par with the most competitive schools in America. In recent years, there were 19 applicants for each place in the freshman class – with about 1 in 6 accepted. One unique part of an application to Rice is "the box", a little area reserved for applicants to simply do something interesting and eye-catching. Students advise you to be creative with this, but don't draw yourself outside of the box in a thinking pose – it's been done before.

Money Matters

Rice started life as a free college, and until recently it was still extremely good value for money. The last decade, however, has seen the total yearly cost rise to $60,000, in line with other pricey schools. Lots of financial aid is available, however.

Famous Grads

Candace Bushnell – author, Sex and the City

Larry McMurtry – Pulitzer and Oscar winning author (Brokeback Mountain screenplay)

Alberto Gonzales – notorious Bush administration Attorney General

Sarah Lawrence College

Bronxville, New York
www.slc.edu
Undergrads: 1,300
Grads: 340

Located in Westchester County, New York, Sarah Lawrence is considered a top-tier liberal arts college, known for its superb writing programme. Their very different learning environment means that students don't have to deal with grades, requirements, tests, or majors and have the luxury of classes with roundtable discussions and fewer than twenty students.

This is a school for students who, above all else, want to be well-educated; the world of careers, salary, and business takes more of a back seat.

The Campus

Only thirty minutes away from New York City, the campus feels surprisingly quaint in its forty wooded acres. The first thing that strikes you is how pretty and compact it is, mostly centred around one main grassy green. Naturally, this makes it very easy to get around – and only about five to ten minutes to get anywhere on campus.

There are the usual college gathering spaces – art performance venues, lounges, cafes, discussion spaces, publication offices, a radio station, a space to practice spirituality in peace – but there is no main student centre so people often spread out around the campus or go to their dorms to hang out.

Accommodation

Sarah Lawrence was designed with the belief that there should be little separation between life and work, so dorms, classrooms, and offices are mostly housed in the same ivy-covered Tudor buildings.

These include everything from a mishmash of former private houses and apartment buildings shared with non-students to traditional suite-style dorms, and even a converted section of the President's house – and each one of these has a personality of its own.

With the exception of the New Dorms, most of the buildings are quite old and beautiful and form a picturesque backdrop for the changing seasons.

Autumn is especially gorgeous, when this heavily wooded campus is covered with the stunning red, yellow and orange leaves that New England is so famous for.

The Sarah Lawrence Student

This school is not for those who prefer the straight-forward structure of a 'normal' college; instead it attracts very individualistic and motivated students. As a general stereotype, think Hipster. Vintage, urban, bohemian, cultured, arty, independent, liberal, original – anything but mainstream.

Students tend to be non-conformist; they enjoy going against the grain. You would be hard pressed to find a typical jock or prep type that many associate with the average college student.

What you will find is an independent, creative, articulate person (more than likely a woman, given the 70/30 ratio) who has an opinion on just about everything.

While SLC students come from all over the US (and about 15% overseas) a high proportion come from the East Coast (primarily New York) and California. As a community, Sarah Lawrence is not incredibly diverse, but they are very accepting of all different groups. There is a sizeable LGBT community.

Given that 70% of the student body are women and many of the men are gay (or 'metro-sexual', thus confusing everyone), the available guy population is severely lacking. But, to be honest, most find it very relaxing and actually like it this way. Yes, it gets frustrating occasionally, but it's not as bad as everybody thinks.

Life in such a bee hive of high-flyers and strong opinions makes for great conversations and debates everywhere and anytime...and by no means just in the classrooms.

The habits of high-achievers rub off on you and you find yourself working much harder than you had ever thought you would. Of course, there are slackers, but it's tough to pull that off in such small school when you are surrounded by a strong work ethic and such lively subject material.

Hitting the Books

Sarah Lawrence's distinctive academic program is not for everyone, but if it suits you it is almost guaranteed to be life changing.

Curricular requirements are extremely flexible – students are simply required to take 10 courses in at least three out of four areas of study: Creative & Performing Arts, History and Social Sciences, Humanities, and Natural Sciences & Mathematics.

Because the academics are so self-directed, students actually care about their work; and because there are no grades, people are motivated solely by their curiosity and interests. Instead of majors there are concentrations and instead of exams students are required to develop their own research-based 'conference' project, typically a 20-30 page paper submitted at the end of term.

Classes tend to be small seminars – think 13-15 students in a class – creating an environment that thrives on open discussion and exploration. Even lectures (which are a requirement) only have around 40 people, which is nothing compared to the 200 odd that you might get in an British uni. In addition, you have fortnightly half hour conferences with your teachers to discuss topics from class and work on your conference project.

A major part of SLC education is your 'don', who is there to help with everything. You meet once every week, and talk about everything from your classes and teachers to your living situation with roommates to what you did over the weekend. Your don is your guide and helping hand throughout the whole process of college and, provided you get along well, your friend.

SLC students rave about their teachers – who are described as incredible people; not only are they bright and approachable, they also have amazing CVs and great connections.

Social Life

Anyone looking for a vibrant on-campus party scene should take Sarah Lawrence off their list. The nightlife stays pretty chilled. Most parties consist of small groups of people gathering in a dorm room – listening to music, playing beer pong – or loud music and dancing at the Blue Room, which is basically a campus club.

The exceptions to this routine are the 'formals', which happen once every semester and are universally loved. A huge tent is set up on the lawn with a dance floor, DJ, speakers and lights, and just about everyone turns up, from freshmen to seniors. On these occasions, you're amazed to see how many people actually go to SLC.

Apart from the formal nights which are pretty awesome, it can get a little boring after a while. As mentioned, the gender imbalance makes for a less than marvellous dating scene, so mass exodus on the weekends leaves the campus pretty much like a ghost town. Bronxville has a few restaurants nearby but by far the best place to party is New York City – see below.

Outside Those Ivory Walls

Though SLC is located in the affluent suburb of Bronxville, the college is also close to the larger community of Yonkers. Sarah Lawrence historically had tense relations with the neighbouring areas, but this friction has subsided and students regularly walk into town – Bronxville is a ten minute stroll from campus – for the coffee shops and some relatively inexpensive restaurants.

It also has a few bars but, because of the so-called 'Republican feel', students tend to steer clear. Students go into Yonkers for eateries, groceries, social work and 'Sarah Lawrence nights' at a nearby pub.

When Sarah Lawrence students are really in the mood to go out, they tend to go to New York City, which is a 30-minute train ride from the nearby station.

Obviously, there are a million things to do – shopping on 5th Ave, a gallery in Soho, dinner in Chinatown, a Broadway show, Central Park, the list goes on. If, on any given Saturday night, SLC feels like a commuter school then the attractions of Manhattan are partly to blame.

Getting In

AT A GLANCE – Application & Test Options:

– Early Decision, Early Decision II, Regular Decision

– Test-optional

Sarah Lawrence values strong writing skills and the clear expression of interests, perspectives, and goals – so think carefully about your application's essay and short-answer questions (and check meticulously for grammar and usage errors!).

On the other hand, they don't care about your SAT scores, so if you are not great at multiple choice testing this may be your dream school. Admission difficulty is average and the acceptance rate is just around 50%.

Money Matters

Once you get in, it's just a matter of finding the tuition fees, which are high but in line with most US small private liberal arts colleges. Importantly, Sarah Lawrence does award a limited amount of need-based financial aid to international students, so don't be afraid to ask about this.

Famous Grads

Rahm Emanuel – former Chief of Staff to President Obama, now mayor of Chicago

Vera Wang – fashion designer

J.J. Adams – film and television screenwriter, director, executive producer

Savannah College of Art and Design

Savannah , Georgia
www.scad.edu
Undergrads: 9,800+
Grads: 2,100+

How many SCAD students does it take to change a light bulb?

At least ten. One to sketch the floor plan, one to design the light fixture, one to ensure its sustainable, one to 3-D print it, one to design the room's interiors, one to design the process, another to capture it all on film, one to edit the footage, another to photograph from start to finish and another to design what everyone is wearing.

SCAD is simply one of the best art and design colleges in the whole of the USA. Just ask its students. To study here gives you great opportunities regardless of what major you choose, from graphic designers working with Amazon and Google to fashion majors working with Coach and Gucci. Going to SCAD is possibly the best decision this reviewer has ever made and the doors it opens makes the hard work totally worth it.

The Campus

Savannah College of Art and Design is set in buildings scattered throughout the beautiful historic district in Savannah, Georgia. SCAD has done a lot for this city, including renovation of most of the buildings that students work in. The school thought it better to revamp and fix buildings with historic significance rather than tear them down, so most of the classrooms and studios are in renovated buildings located throughout the city.

This does mean that the campus is spread out, but all within walking distance -– or as most students do, you can make use of the SCAD bus service. The service will pick you up at the dorms and take you wherever you need to be, on time and as reliable as clock work.

You can bike or long board most places as it is convenient and the city itself is beautiful, especially on a sunny day. Most of Savannah is on a grid plan which has a large park in the centre called Forsyth. This has a large grass area great for chilling with friends or studying.

It's also worth mentioning that there are amazing SCAD programmes and campuses outside the rarified atmosphere of Savannah, namely in Atlanta, Hong Kong, and Lacoste, France.

Accommodation

Freshmen live in a few dorm options – O-House, Spring House, Turner House or Turner Annex – usually with a SCAD-assigned roommate. Living in Turner, in particular, you really get a sense of what SCAD is all about. The people you meet all have high aspirations like yourself, ranging across all types of majors – from game design to fashion marketing.

As you go through your college career, you can continue to live in SCAD accommodation or you can find a house to rent with friends. There are many properties that rent out, so finding a place within your budget is never very difficult.

University Man/Woman

Not everyone here is a peppy, fun-loving hippie, although they are around. At the end of the day, most of the student body have one thing in common: they're focused on achieving the highest standard they can. They tend to be pretty collaborative, which often leads to more creativity and better work all round.

Around finals, the school totally changes and everyone becomes a little more intense and on edge. Best to avoid the coffee drinkers.

Hitting the Books

Academics at SCAD are why you want to be here. It is ridiculous, the facilities and courses offered. They're all broken down into subsections so you get a much more direct approach to what you want to learn. For instance, at a larger state uni, graphic design and illustration might be offered as classes. At SCAD there are full degree programmes in industrial design, graphic design, production design, interior design, illustration, as well as specific coursework in, for example, comic book storyboarding.

This list goes on and it's not like one of these is less popular or the facilities are inferior to the others: everything in SCAD is constantly being updated and replaced with better tech to allow students to create whatever they can come up with...3D printers, film cameras, editing equipment. Whatever your project needs, it's there.

That's where collaboration comes in: you make friends, and they can help you out if you need access to the industrial design workshops or a fashion major can help out on maybe a photo-shoot. The possibilities are only limited by what you make of them or as limitless as your time frames allow.

Classes are tough and, as SCAD operates in the quarter system, not semesters (so, 10 week blocks), you are always pushing against what you would like to make and what you have time to achieve. This is stressful at times, but in the real world you have deadlines to make that aren't going to be pushed back. This system teaches you how to manage your time effectively.

The learning curve is tough at first but after your first quarter or two, you work out the kinks and settle into the workload and how you work best.Teachers are brilliant and unbelievably supportive; they sit with you and analyse your designs and give constant feedback. You can email them at any time and they'll respond ASAP. They are all experts in their respective fields and will challenge you to break away from common trends and get out of your comfort zone.

Your perception of what good design is will probably change over and over. Instead of just looking at what's commonly accepted now and regurgitating it, SCAD students are encouraged to create their own style and keep pushing to find that next level to achieve in their work.

Finals week is intense. As your career advances, your work becomes more intricate and SCAD pretty much becomes a ghost town student-wise. People lock themselves in their rooms working for the perfectionist vision they have in their head. Finals week is crazy busy at print shops or dead silent from concentration. It's only a week; time management is the easiest way to avoid being stressed and up all night.

Outside Those Ivory Walls

On your down time, you have to check out the city; Savannah is beautiful and mostly a historic area. The campus is not like the ones in movies – it's not built around one hub. Because it is spread throughout the city, this allows you as a student to see more of Savannah and take in the culture, which you will be immersed in and either love or hate.

The great thing about it is that it is steeped in history, yet because of the SCAD students, it has the feel of an urban city centre. It is always bustling with students going from A to B talking about new tech and ideas they have for their respective classes.

With everyone being so individualistic, the streets are awash with different colours, styles and languages. Coffee is the lifeline of SCAD students...coffee shops are always packed with students working and chilling together. There are several areas around Savannah that are considered hubs for students, mostly coffee shops or restaurants.

On a sunny day, Forsyth is the place to be, with people playing football (British), Frisbee, hula hooping, you name it. This writer has spent more than a few days there working on his laptop, enjoying the sun, and chilling with friends. Or you can head for the beach, which is actually warm and sunny for much of the year and only a few miles away.

Possibly because Savannah is so historic, there isn't really the big club scene you might be used to back home. However, because it was a serious port of trade back in the day, there're many good bars and restaurants. The bars are great, often with live music and loads of different drink options. As they frequently have to serve us Brits, they come prepared. This reviewer favours a local pub run by a great couple who immigrated from Manchester 30 years ago. Live football, great atmosphere and chips done right.

The clubs are not the largest, but people know how to get rid of the week's stress by dancing their nights away. After homework of course.

Getting In

AT A GLANCE – Application & Test Options:

- Rolling basis admissions
- ACT/SAT required

Getting into SCAD isn't like most schools. Although, as an international applicant, you may have to take the SAT or ACT, SCAD focuses more on the art right off the bat. Depending on the programme, you may have to submit a portfolio of your work – which you should probably tweak or edit beforehand.

It is competitive to get in. However, it's totally worth the application, since most people who leave here actually get a job, thanks to the real-world experience part of their degrees.

Money Matters

Scholarships are available to students for academics and possibly sports if you qualify for one of the teams. SCAD offers swimming, football (British), lacrosse, tennis, equestrian, fishing teams etc (and if you don't want to fully commit to these programmes, then quarterly team events are organized so you can play if you just love the game).

International students can get any funding an American student can, except for grants from the US or Georgia governments. SCAD offers scholarships based on need, academics or achievement, for all levels of students (freshman, transfer or graduate) and some of them are "stackable" (meaning you can get several at once).

Even better, once you've been there for a year and earned a certain number of credits, there can be yet more funding available. If needed, the admissions staff can help guide you through funding questions and forms.

Scripps College

Claremont, California
www.scrippscollege.edu
Undergrads: 950
Grads: 10

How many Scipps students does it take to change a light bulb?

16 – ten to set up an artistic team to select the most beautiful light bulb to match the campus, five to publicise the fact that girls can change bulbs just as well as boys, and one to screw it in.

Scripps sits relatively undiscovered in sunny California, like a hidden pearl waiting for the diver who is willing to take the plunge. An all-female liberal arts college founded on the highest principles of independent thinking and educational fulfillment, this is a tiny school with some of the luckiest students in the country. As part of the renowned Claremont Consortium, Scripps offer an open invitation to sample classes at four other great schools located minutes away. The educational experience is truly matchless.

The Campus

Rated by the *Princeton Review* as one of the top ten most beautiful campuses (in a country full of beautiful campuses), Scripps is small and dazzling. Located in the distant Los Angeles suburb of Claremont, it is at the centre of the seven Claremont Colleges, with the other undergraduate colleges of Harvey-Mudd to the north, Pitzer to the east, and McKenna and Pomona to the south.

The whole "consortium" is a unique structure of university, designed in such a way as to permit a small-college liberal arts education, as well as access to all the facilities and benefits of the famous educational behemoths.

The campus somehow manages to feel simultaneously laid-back and electrified, with airy lawns and handsome buildings filled with bustling and stimulated students. Everything is close together, even with the big leafy spaces between them.

Facilities at Scripps itself are not out-of-the-ordinary. They include a few decent libraries, a superb new gym, and a cool little student-run coffeehouse ("The Motley"). But with its proximity to the other four colleges as well as the shared facilities, Scripps has easy access to everything it could need.

Accommodation

The on-campus dorms, in which all the students live, are spectacular. Students gush about the paradise they enjoy, describing their sublime surrounding as "just ridiculous" or "like a resort". "We know we won't live anywhere as nice as here again," said several girls just before graduating. As another put it, "I live in the dorms with the worst reputation, and I still have a fireplace and a piano and a fountain outside my window."

The Scripps Woman

Sophisticated, easy-going, pleasant and with a lot to say, the girls at Scripps wear the mark of their education in every gesture and every perfectly articulated syllable. Taught to cultivate their interests and ideas, and challenge what they learn, students rapidly develop well-rounded personalities and a fierce intelligence. Mostly from wealthy West Coast backgrounds, there is not much socio-economic, racial or even geographical diversity at Scripps, nor any real international community to speak of.

Despite this, the college invests a lot of effort in making sure everyone is well looked-after and fully integrated into the often-cliquey Scripps society. At such a small school, it is relatively easy to prevent anyone from "slipping through the cracks" and there are whole teams of students charged with helping those who may be suffering culture shock or are finding it difficult to get involved. Some may find the caring Scripps blanket over-protective, but generally students are grateful for it, with some mentioning the "nurturing community" as their favourite aspect of the school.

The classic Scripps stereotypes are essentially the same as those for any woman's college – the raging feminists, the wealthy country girls and perhaps a handful of hippies. Though students admit that Scripps girls are "more gender-conscious than the average person", they deny being as feminist as some might make out, describing themselves instead as open-minded.

Attending such a small college means a certain lack of anonymity, which carries both advantages and disadvantages. On the one hand, you can get to know almost everyone in your school and thus live in a tighter, friendlier community, but on the other hand, well, you have to know almost everyone in your school. This can be indusive to unhelpful gossip and cliques (some have called it "suffocatingly small"), though the negative effects are somewhat dissipated by the ease of socialising with the other neighbouring colleges.

Hitting the Books

Without doubt, the most common answer to "what's your favourite thing about Scripps" is the teaching faculty. Professors here are challenging, helpful and always available. With a teacher:student ratio of 1:11, students feel very much "not a number" among faceless lectures. Close personal relationships are formed with the professors, who encourage students to visit them in their free time, both for work and often just socialising.

The work ethic among students is described as a "decent mix" between hard work and relaxing time. The small classes mean that you can't skip the lessons or the reading assignments without the teacher knowing, and this fosters a responsible learning system. Students take work very seriously, and some complain that people can get fanatical about it. The solid, sensible work ethic means that free time is appreciated and used well.

Humanities is normally noted as the college's top department, but sciences are also strong, and there is no particularly weak area. The beauty of the consortium education is that students can take up to two-thirds of their classes at other colleges, massively expanding the range of subjects and quality of courses available.

Social Life

Scripps itself has harsher drinking rules than its sister schools and tries to keep itself quiet and clean, but it does organise a massive number of activities and events for the students. This is much needed to make up for the lack of anything to do in the nearby district – Claremont Village is pleasant and peaceful, with a few nice restaurants but not much more in the way of social venues, and Los Angeles proper is too far away to make frequent visits worthwhile, especially for the carless majority.

Still, Scripps has a fun social scene. Even though students are perhaps more of the "hanging out with friends" variety instead of extreme party-goers, most people regularly go to some great parties (expect plenty of free drinks!), generally on the weekend, and usually on the campus of one of the other colleges.

The bubble effect is rarely a cause for complaint among students, who are mostly divided into those who choose to do very little and those who do everything they possibly can. With a "ridiculous range" of student organisations (but no Greek life), and a great mix of extra-curriculars based both in Scripps and the other colleges, the options are huge, encompassing exciting artistic groups, competitive sports teams and quirky clubs.

Getting In

AT A GLANCE – Application & Test Options:

– Early Decision, Regular Decision

– ACT/SAT required

Scripps admits only a few hundred applicants each year. Being one of these lucky individuals requires an excellent application, and normally an interview either in person or by phone. Those who are successful are normally of a high enough caliber to have received places at other excellent institutions, so for those who request it the college can put you in contact with Scripps students who are more than willing to explain the school's pros and cons in enough detail to make your decision easier.

Money Matters

Scripps is expensive and poorly endowed, but some merit scholarships are available. Everyone who applies is automatically considered, including international students, and about 34% of those admitted receive merit scholarships (ranging from $10,000 to $22,000).

Famous Grads

Anne Hopkins Aitken – one of the modern mothers of Zen Buddhism in the western world

Elizabeth Turk – sculptor and MacArthur Fellow

Hon. Judith N. Keep – first female Chief Judge of the United States

Skidmore College

Saratoga Springs, New York
www.skidmore.edu
Undergrads: 2,700
Grads: 0

How many Skidmore College students does it take to screw in a light bulb?

One–and his maid, butler, cook, poolman, and gardener.

Ask just about any student at Skidmore to describe what makes their school tick, and you're bound to hear the words "creative" – and probably in more than one context. Skidmore is on a short list of liberal arts schools (including Bennington and Oberlin) where the fine arts have a very important place alongside traditional academics. And that can't be a bad thing: Newsweek *recently named Skidmore one of America's "25 New Ivies". But rest assured, it does not have the ego of an Ivy League.*

The Campus

Skidmore is somewhat off the beaten track in upstate New York, in a small wooded campus that, for some, is reminiscent of a summer camp. Even though the college has 850 acres, the buildings are all in a fairly compact area in the middle and nothing on campus is more than a few minutes away. The approach is through a park-like setting and the campus buildings (which are for the most part relatively new) were built to blend with the surroundings.

The Tang Art Museum is Skidmore's renowned arts facility and contains more than 4,500 works by artists that include Goya and Lichtenstein. However, works of art are not restricted to this building; many student and professional sculptures are scattered around the campus. There are also multiple theatre spaces, the Lucy Scribner Library (which contains half a million volumes), a beautifully renovated student centre, and an impressive array of student art studios.

The Skidmore Student

Students at Skidmore are described in various – and vastly different – ways. Some say the community is mostly rich, liberal, and Jewish whilst others say the school is full of artistic, tree-hugging stoners. Regardless of what students claim to be the majority, you'll find all types of people here. (Even a few jocks! – a rarity for a small liberal arts college.)

One of the biggest campus controversies is homogeneity – the student body is not very racially or socioeconomically diverse – but most students don't mind it that way. It's safe to say that students at Skidmore are creative and smart, however they are just as likely to proclaim that they're well-rounded.

Hitting the Books

Skidmore students rave about the small class sizes, the close collaborative relationships with professors and generally lenient requirements for their majors.

This is a liberal arts school, but they're big on professional tracks as well—business, nursing, education etc. Skidmore has a fantastic 3+2 engineering programme with Dartmouth: you can major in anything, say, business, but also go to Dartmouth and get an engineering degree— ending up with two bachelor degrees! Go to Skidmore for 2 years, then 1 year at Dartmouth, return to Skidmore for 1 year and then a final year at Dartmouth – fab!

There is a sense that learning itself is a creative process here, and professors encourage you to take classes outside of your major or minor in order to become more well-rounded and open-minded. What's more, professors are dedicated to helping you succeed and make themselves readily available to chat or offer assistance on their own time.

Classes are a good mixture of lecture and discussion; however, as they advance, they tend to become more discussion-based. Most professors require class participation so don't expect to show up to class hung-over or half asleep.

Skidmore students' study habits range from very intense to pretty lax. Though the library is frequently crowded, the workload depends on how much students choose to challenge themselves.

Social Life

Skidmore is small and can be a bit cliquey, but it's easy enough to escape the bubble and head into Saratoga Springs at a moment's notice. You don't really need to leave in order to have a new experience or change of scenery, though – there are a vast number of social opportunities on campus. This is a liberal arts college with a creative bent, so naturally on any given weekend there is some form of live music, art, film, theatre and/or dance – in a public space or possibly just in someone's dorm room.

Skidmore has no Greek life so most parties take place in dorms and off-campus apartments and drinking tends to be a popular way to pass the frigid winter months. The Outing Club is also hugely popular; it's one of Skidmore's oldest student organizations and makes regular excursions in the winter for alpine and cross-country skiing, snowshoeing, and ice climbing.

Outside Those Ivory Walls

Saratoga Springs is larger than your average college town but maintains a very quaint 'early-Americana' feel. The main street in town is lined with several 19th century buildings including some of the hotels originally built to cater to visitors of the area's restorative mineral springs. If you happen to visit during the summer when the Saratoga Race Course is in operation, you may think you've stepped back in time – this thoroughbred track is the oldest continuously-operating sporting event in America and at first glance doesn't look as though it's changed much since the 1860s.

At any other time of the year, Saratoga Springs offers a standard array of stores and restaurants and an admirable bar scene – and, only a mile away from campus, it's all within reach (on foot, bike, or campus shuttle bus).

Getting In

AT A GLANCE – Application & Test Options:

– Early Decision, Early Decision II, Regular Decision

– Test-optional

Admission difficulty has traditionally been average but in recent years, with numbers of applications climbing, the acceptance rate has gone down to about 1 in 3.

Money Matters

Skidmore is able to offer both merit and need-based financial aid to a limited number of students who are not US citizens or permanent residents.

Famous Grads

Ben Cohen – Ben and Jerry's co-founder

Nancy Evans – Founder of iVillage

Grace Mirabella – Author and magazine editor

St John's College

Annapolis, Maryland
www.stjohnscollege.edu
Undergrads: 500
Grads: <100

How many Johnnies does it take to change a light bulb?

16 – one to read Descartes' famous masterpiece On the Changing of Light Bulbs, and fifteen to form a discussion group and argue about the existential implications of light bulb changing.

Whatever else you might say about St. John's, there's nothing else quite like it available to undergraduates in America. With a unique four-year curriculum, based on the "Great Books" reading list, in-depth discussion style classes, and a tiny number of intelligent, passionate students, this bizarre university will either change your life or leave you begging to escape.

[NB: St. John's has two campuses – at Annapolis and at Santa Fe. This article is about the Annapolis campus; while the Santa Fe campus is very similar in its methods we understand that there are significant differences that should be properly researched if you wish to study in New Mexico instead of Maryland.]

The Campus

St John's has some of the most handsome buildings in an exceedingly handsome town, down near Annapolis' quaint, touristy waterfront. The third oldest university in the country, the place is bursting with history and, combined with the brick architecture and expansive lawns, feels reminiscent of a big country dwelling for a British aristocrat in the Shires, with a 18th century colonial twist perhaps.

Accommodation

Facilities are adequate for the modest needs of the college, with some of the older buildings requiring frequent renovations to remain useable. Most students live in the dorms on campus, which are perfectly pleasant if a tad expensive.

The Johnny

St John's students ("Johnnies") are cast with two stereotypes – neither of which gives you a full or accurate picture. Outsiders think of them as "grungy, procrastinating theorists" – in other words as pretentious bookworms who care far too much about obscure academics. But, as one student put it, "we, on the other hand, stereotype ourselves as simply wanting to learn."

Johnnies are also known as mostly wealthy, white and 60-70% male, though increasing abundance of financial aid and an admissions team that is actively seeking to diversify the student body are helping to roll back the boundaries on this front. Rather than their socio-economic homogeneity, it is actually the aforementioned desire to learn and improve themselves that unites the large range of personalities that are attracted to St. John's.

Johnnies tend to be individuals – you can say good-bye to peer pressure. You'll definitely meet lots of quirky or unusual people, some of them downright strange. "If it seems like they're acting weird, they're actually just learning to be themselves," explained one senior.

Still, the bonds you can form with the interesting people you meet will far outweigh the potential problems caused by weirdness. Because people are so interested in what they are learning and so willing to explore new ideas, almost everyone learns very quickly how to develop their thoughts most effectively and (more importantly) how to express them. Due to the discussion style of classes, students get a lot of public speaking practice and tend to become very articulate.

Hitting the Books

Study is what it's all about at St. John's, and they've developed a unique time-tested method that helps students attain pinnacles of academic perfection. Students leave incredibly well-read, well-developed and well-prepared to face life with as large a cerebral head-start as can be imagined.

For all four of the years they spend at St. John's, students follow the "Great Books" curriculum, which means that they have to read a considerable list of the greatest works by the greatest minds from around the world and across history. Freshman year is dominated by the very earliest, mainly Greek, authors (Plato, Sophocles etc) and the list works more-or-less chronologically from there.

Having read some of the most important ideas and literature from the last 3,000 years or so, students go to classes which are presided over by expert professors, but they don't sit and listen for hours while the teacher explains what they've just read; on the contrary, it is the students who have to work out the significance of their reading through group discussion. Different professors contribute different amounts, with some staying virtually silent and other participating vigorously, but they make sure never to leave their role as moderator.

Clearly, this method of learning is not for everyone. At the end of the sophomore year, the whole year-group goes through the notorious "Disablement", when the faculty discusses each student individually to evaluate whether the college is the right learning environment for them.

Those who aren't suited to St. Johns normally get the hint and leave, if they haven't left of their own accord already. In the junior and senior years, the work gets a lot harder, so if there are any doubts it's normally better to move back to a more standard style of education. Disablement comes in addition to the semesterly "Don Rag", an eccentric process in which tutors discuss a student's progress in the third person despite the student being in the room.

The pros and cons to the methods practiced at St. John's are manifold. "The key," according to one student, "is that you have to see how everything's related." The things you learn from Aristotle can be applied to your understanding of Hobbes. Newton gives you the basics for Einstein.

Students soon learn to appreciate that life isn't as easily divided into convenient "subjects" as normal schooling would have you believe, and that actually the whole body of human knowledge has to be taken as a whole if it is to be fully appreciated. This means that all the classes feed off each other, so that college is essentially one big lesson.

This style of schooling fosters an enviable ability to think well and an incredible depth of world understanding. Tutors "encourage wrongness," in a "quest to find what's real and true": all questioning is good, especially when the questions are answerless, and being wrong can only lead to greater ultimate knowledge. Students enjoy not having "to worry about someone's red pen".

On the other hand, when classes aren't taught by teachers, their quality depends on how good your classmates are at group discussion. In the first months, especially, when students haven't yet honed their technique, you might find a lot of classes ruined by people who speak too much or too little, people who think they know more than they do, or people who've simply had a bad day. "Sometimes, you just want the teacher to tell you the answer," admitted one student.

Similarly, you have to bear in mind that the set curriculum gives you very little choice in what you study, with only a tiny bit of wiggle room here and there. For some, this is so frustrating that they quickly leave, but most like the simple organisation, and the feeling that "I'm really gaining something...I have a lot of faith in the program." It is true that the reading list has been edited and improved consistently over the decades since it was developed by the University of Chicago in the 30s, and it's designed to give you as solid an education as you can imagine.

One aspect that students invariably praise is the "openness" of learning here. Everyone loves being part of such an intense learning community, and it's not uncommon for discussions of Hegelian ethics (or whatever) to continue outside of the classroom. "I know I won't have conversations like I have here ever again", sighed one senior, ruefully. The openness also extends to the faculty, who are accessible and very connected with the students. There are only eight students for every member of the faculty, and the largest class in the school has only 20 people.

In the end, an education at St. John's definitely has the capacity to "change your life", "leave you a completely different person" or whatever other cliché you care to pick. Just speak to the students and alumni to see for yourself what an impact it can have.

Social Life

While it's probably fair to say that social life takes a back seat at St. John's, it certainly isn't fair to say that you can't have a good time outside of class or when you're not reading the latest Jean-Paul Sartre.

The main extra-curricular activity is sport, which is played at various competitive (but not ultra-serious) levels and includes some local variations (have a go at "Johnny football"). The only sport played against another school is croquet, in which St. John's has proudly vanquished their opposition (the nearby Naval Academy) on a regular basis.

St. John's has many more student organisations than you would expect of such a small school, and even a mini student government and a newspaper (NOT called the Don Rag). There are several theatrical and musical performances put on each year, and lots of dance lessons available to prepare people for "waltz parties" where you can dance in old fashioned clothes and have strawberries and Champagne.

You're not going to find any really crazy parties here, but there are plenty of fun events, and the somewhat quixotic (but aptly named) "reality" group is responsible for organising parties which are always successful and well attended.

Outside Those Ivory Walls

Although St. John's is an extreme bubble environment, and students are very much removed from the real world, cities like Baltimore and Washington DC are nearby. Plus, you can always hit Annapolis for decent shopping and dining opportunities, as well as charming streets and buildings and a famous waterfront. You might want to do this often, as the St. John's cafeteria is apparently pretty terrible.

Getting In

AT A GLANCE – Application & Test Options:

– Early Action, Early Action II, Regular Decision

– Officially test-optional; however, ACT/SAT required for international students

St. John's has a surprisingly low level of competition, considering its academic prowess, so you have a much better chance of getting in here than at more conventional universities (in 2016, around 3/4 of applicants were offered a spot). And the admissions team is currently on a diversification drive, so international applications will definitely get attention. The key thing is to make it clear how interested and excited you are about the St. John's "educational experience".

Money Matters

There are no merit scholarships available, but there is a limited amount of needs-based aid available to international students to help with the cost of attendance, which is high but not unreasonable.

Famous Grads

John Bremer-British born educator, philosopher, author

Francis Scott Key– lyricist of US national anthem, "The Star Spangled Banner" (written when the flag was seen still flying through the smoke of British guns – just before America lost the War of 1812)

Charles van Doren– infamous for involvement in rigged game show, "Twenty-One"

Stanford University

Stanford , California
www.stanford.edu
Undergrads: 7,000
Grads: 8,800

How many students does it take to change a light bulb at Stanford?

One, dude.

There are many contenders for the crown of best Californian university. The dazzlingly smart CalTech puts in one bid that cannot be lightly dismissed and both UCLA and UC Berkeley are strong runners. But time and time again the victory goes to a school that is widely judged to be one of the best universities in America – Stanford. Situated in Silicon Valley, 30 miles from San Francisco and commanding views of the Golden Gate Bridge, Stanford is an institution that calls out to students and academics all over the world.

The college was founded in 1891 with the death of millionaire Leland Stanford's teenage son. Devastated by the loss of his only child, he and his wife decided to build a university that would enable them to treat the children of California as their own. Over a century later, their legacy has developed into one of the greatest of the American colleges – a highly selective and incredibly successful academic institution that (provided you can deal with the trek to California) should be at the top of any prospective student's list.

The Campus

This 'Ivy of the West Coast' does not only rest on the laurels of academic success, it also enjoys one of the prettiest campuses around. As with all the Californian schools, the year-round sunshine and blue skies do much to increase the atmosphere, but even in the event of a freak Ice Age, Stanford would remain a beautiful place. Initially the Stanfords used the land as a horse farm and the old Red Barn still stands today. Now, however, a spacious and well-planned campus surrounds it. While planning their college, the Stanfords consulted with the deans of several prestigious universities and their efforts more than paid off. The famous Frederick Law Olmstead (the driving force behind New York's Central Park) was placed in charge of the design and the campus remains an architectural and aesthetic success 100 years on.

Stanford is connected to the nearby town of Palo Alto (smack in Silicon Valley) by a mile-long drive lined with palm trees. As you walk down it, the attractive sandstone buildings of the main campus open out before you. The Main Quad, with its Californian-style architecture is the heart of the university – the home of the beautiful Memorial Church (complete with mosaic front) and also the site of the infamous Stanford 'Full Moon on the Quad'. In one of the more fun college traditions, incoming Stanford freshmen experience a rite of passage when they are kissed by outgoing seniors on the Quad under the first full moon of their first year. (Definitely a custom that many a desperate senior across America wishes their college would adopt.)

Other notable parts of the campus include the Herbert Hoover observation tower (named after Stanford grad and US president) which offers fantastic views of the local area, the bustling White Plaza and the amazing Rodin collection (the biggest anywhere in the world except his museum in Paris). Stanford campus, despite the somewhat frightening threat of the next big earthquake, is one of the most beautiful on offer and any student who gets to spend four years lounging around on the sun-soaked quads gazing out at the rolling foothills (Stanford-owned, of course) will hardly be able to believe their luck. Rainy old England will seem a long way away.

Accommodation

With such a beautiful location on offer it is hardly surprising that around 94% of students choose to live on campus for all their time at university (especially when one considers the cost of off-campus living). Stanford has really solved the issue of options in housing, and students have the choice as to with whom and how they want to live. Students can live in dorms that span across the four years or within their year group – most specifically in the freshman houses that give nervous first-years a chance to find their feet among their peers. Others can choose to live in dorms that are themed to their liking – some explore a particular ethnic aspect of the States (such as the Native American culture) – while others focus on a particular interest.

Whatever your choice, chances are that you will find living on 'The Farm' (the cognoscenti's name for the campus) to be an incredible experience. Affection for Leland and Jane Stanford's contribution remains strong – their family crypt becomes the site for the annual Halloween celebration where students show their thanks by literally dancing on the graves of the founders.

The Stanford Student

The Stanford motto, chosen by Mr Stanford himself, is 'Let the wind of freedom blow'. As far as freedom of personal choice among the student body of Stanford goes, the wind seems to be blowing pretty hard. Although this is a much smaller (and thus much more personal) body of students than its UC neighbours, the diversity among each class is still extremely high. Stanford has always had a reputation for catering to a particular type of student – in one sense the Californian equivalent of the WASP – in other words the privileged legacy child in a West Coast setting. Yet while such individuals play out their fathers' lives on the Stanford campus, the admissions board ensures that classmates from a variety of ethnic, religious and socio-economic backgrounds dilute them.

Despite this diversity, many feel that the campus is dominated by Asians and Californians. Europeans may find they are less well-represented here than at

East Coast universities – Stanford seems to attract many of the Asian international contingent (it is after all closer to home!). Other students complain this uneven balance makes the university cliquey and that friendships are forged on the grounds of race or bank balance rather than values and interests. However, this is a grumble that holds true for many universities and Stanford does no worse than anywhere else at dealing with problems that continue to plague a polycultural America.

Most Stanford students quickly find their place in the community and are constantly amazed by the wealth of experiences that their classmates bring with them. School spirit runs high and the laid-back attitude of Californian life permeates the campus.

Many state that while things seem quiet on the surface, students are working incredibly hard in order to stay afloat. Yet, while it is undeniable that Stanford students face a large amount of work, the sunshine and the beautiful campus add to an atmosphere of relaxation that snowed-in and built-up New England schools can never achieve. Whether they are cheering on their home football team (the Cardinals) in the Big Game against Berkeley, or releasing their exam tension in the cathartic Primal Scream (which ripples across campus in the build up to finals), Stanford students tend to be a united and high-spirited bunch.

The Stanford sports teams are internationally renowned and regularly dominate the West Coast rankings. The importance of athletics on campus does mean that there is a strong jock culture – something that can be off-putting for the average, lazy Brit (who may find that going to the gym swiftly becomes part of his or her day).

There are masses of other activities to get involved in at Stanford, and many are willing to sacrifice valuable relaxation time for a higher cause. A large percentage of students are involved in outreach programmes in the surrounding area, while others hone their journalistic skills at the Stanford Daily.

If you prefer to spend your spare time in a more relaxed setting (and provided you have some musical talent), you can always join the university band whose spirit-raising pranks and much-loved mascot (The Tree) add extra cheer during football matches and other school events. Cheerleading is big as well – now may well be the time to achieve that Bring It On moment (and boys, don't worry, there are spots for you!). Whatever your interests, you will find that someone else shares them, the only thing that may be hard to find are the hours in the day to pursue them.

Hitting the Books

The reputation that Stanford has upheld for so long does not come easily. No matter how relaxed their attitude, every student will tell you that being enrolled at Stanford means that hard work is expected and that slacking off now only means longer hours at a later date. Leland Jr (the teenage son in whose memory the college was conceived) was an extremely precocious child – speaking languages fluently and amassing a large collection of art by the time of his death aged fifteen.

Stanford students live up to his illustrious memory, by putting in long hours and asking a lot of questions. Many even take co-terminal degrees – a special Stanford programme that allows you to earn your bachelors and your masters in one fell swoop.

Stanford students are, however, helped in their pursuit of knowledge by a brilliant faculty. Getting an offer of tenure at Stanford is a mark of distinction in the professorial field and many academics flock there for the scholarship and the sunshine. As a result, Stanford has one of the strongest faculties around and an enviable student-teacher ratio of 5:1. Professors are very approachable but this is not a cosy hand-holding institution.

While the relatively small size of the campus means that teachers are much more available, the level of academic competition means that no one is going to be standing over you and watching your every move. Getting that reading done is up to you, but you can be assured that if you do work your way through War and Peace, or the finer elements of molecular science, some of the world authorities will be on site and more than willing to discuss it with you

The easy relationship that exists between pupil and teacher at Stanford is aided by the trust that has been built up over the years. Stanford students adhere to an Honor Code, requested by the students and indicative of their serious approach towards their studies. These studies encompass a core curriculum which requires courses in writing, language, the humanities, natural sciences and foreign cultures. This firm liberal arts foundation is intended to act as a springboard for the more intensive work required once you have finally selected a major. And, owing to the three quarter (rather than semester) system, under which Stanford operates, students are able to sample more classes in less time before they devote themselves to a particular major/concentration. Again, the faculty are on hand to help you every step of the way, and the flexibility (no major has to be declared for the first two years) means that you have a huge amount of time to make up your mind. And, if you need to take time off, and go abroad, the university is behind that too – in fact Brits can take advantage of an exchange programme with Oxford.

Stanford has always been a progressive school, offering co-education from the time of its founding and demanding that its students be not only cultured but also useful. Today it continues to advise students on how they can best serve the world while furthering their own knowledge.

Many students go on to public service careers or join the Peace Corps, although an equal number succumb to the lures of Silicon Valley (almost everyone at Stanford finds themselves in a computer science class at some point), and the somewhat more fiscally rewarding task of serving technology. In a sense this is simply giving back to the university – much of Stanford's wealth stems from Microsoft and Hewlett Packard.

Social Life

Stanford students tend to be an outgoing bunch and their relaxed attitude to life makes this a fun school to attend. Even for those students who come from out-of-state, the California approach becomes contagious and the weekends are a time for lying back and enjoying oneself (however many deadlines one has). California's clean living is also catching and this is not a campus that has a big interest in drugs, hard partying and the seedier parts of a rock and roll lifestyle. It is, on the other hand, a campus that (in a nice liberal Californian way) takes a fairly lenient approach to alcohol. For those Brits who fade away without a local pub as a gathering ground, this is one of the few American universities that might not cause too many withdrawal symptoms. Having said that, drinking to excess (very unhealthy) is not a regular feature of campus life, except for at the Big Game against UC Berkeley when, frankly, anything goes.

Much of the social life at Stanford revolves around the dorms or on campus; people spend a lot of time simply hanging out, visiting the 24hr pizzeria or catching the weekly flicks put on by the university. For those who fancy a more rowdy party, the fraternities and sororities (to which around 20% of the campus belong) tend to spring into life at the weekend when they often open up their doors to the whole campus. If you are the type of individual who needs more than a few keg stands, some guitars and a lot of chatting, then San Francisco offers a wealth of opportunities – although getting there and back takes a large chunk out of your Saturday night.

Rival schools like to say that '99% of Californians are hot, 1% go to Stanford'. This assessment is more than a little cruel and Stanford attracts its fair share of beautiful people. Few people actually complain that Stanford itself does not offer sufficient social life. Whether they are attending Homecoming, fighting over tickets for the annual Viennese Ball or kissing as many people as possible in moonlit Quad, Stanford students know how to have a good time (and those who don't swiftly learn how to take advantage of the local area).

Outside Those Ivory Walls

A Stanford student is never short of things to do, places to go or people to see. While the actual town of Stanford is not much used by students, there are hundreds of weekend options available in the wider area. The nearby Palo Alto, famed for its amazing, amazing shopping, is often dismissed by students as too expensive and not particularly nice but San Francisco, the city of the Golden Gate Bridge and every cosmopolitan excitement imaginable, is less than an hour away by the much-used Cal Train.

SFO is a wonderfully diverse and cultural city with mind-blowing views, great shops and delicious restaurants for those who get bored of the already numerous collection situated closer to campus. Once a year a huge scavenger hunt in the big city is organized in an attempt to familiarize freshmen with the local area – and many find themselves going back on a much more regular basis. The trip to the big city winds its way through Silicon Valley – the technological heartland of America, a place populated by Stanford grads and one of the most prosperous regions of the States.

For those who would rather leave big cities and industrial genius behind them, Stanford is also near to a wide array of more rural pursuits. The Sierra Nevada mountains, with their numerous hiking options are only four hours way, the Pacific is a relatively short drive (45 mins) and the ever-popular Death Valley experience can also be done in a weekend. The famous Yosemite National Park is also easy to get to, and many students choose to camp there when life at home is simply getting too much for them. Californians are obsessed with healthy living and environmental awareness. Stanford is unusual in managing to combine the two with a location that offers every technological and big-city benefit. Whether you are into raving, windsurfing or just lying around in the quad chatting to friends, you can be sure that Stanford will cater for your every taste.

Getting In

AT A GLANCE – Application & Test Options:

- Restrictive (single school) Early Action, Regular Decision
- ACT/SAT, with Writing/essay required
- SAT Subject tests are optional, but welcome

Unsurprisingly a university as good as Stanford is highly selective in its admissions process and extremely competitive to get into. In 2016, only 5% of applicants were admitted – and these are the ones with the strongest grades and highest recommendations. As around half of the students hail from California (thus honouring Leland and Jane Stanford's original intention), there is an additional pressure on international students and those from the forty-nine other American states. Stanford, however, has always been proud to educate those from across the world and international applications are very much encouraged.

Stanford (like almost all other US schools) likes to say that it places a huge amount of importance on the personal achievements of each prospective student. While a large part of this may just be college-speak, it is still important to emphasize on your application all you have achieved outside the classroom. The Stanford student body is a diverse and dynamic group of people and you need to prove yourself worthy of entry into this elite club.

Stanford does not offer interviews – believing that they are entirely subjective and offer no real insight into a person's character. It is thus important that you make your personality appeal on paper – as there is no chance of selling yourself in person. A Restrictive Early Action application option is available – but it must be only to Stanford (no additional schools). As far as tests go, Stanford requires only the SAT or the ACT. SAT Subjects are not required but Stanford strongly recommends two for international students.

Money Matters

International students are eligible for financial aid, but it's limited and is not need-blind, so a request for financial help is taken into consideration in the admissions evaluation and may well jeopardize your chances. On the plus side, if you do apply for aid during the application process and are then admitted, they are committed to making sure that you're covered, no matter where you're from.

Famous Grads

William Hewlett and David Packard – Stanford did a good job admitting these guys

John Steinbeck – one of the stars of a long literary tradition

Sigourney Weaver – an educated actress(!)

Swarthmore College

Swarthmore, Pennsylvania
www.swarthmore.edu
Undergrads: 1500
Grads: 0

How many Swarthmore students does it take to change a light bulb?

Eight–It's not that one isn't smart enough to do it, it's just that they're all violently twitching from too much stress.

One of the very finest liberal arts colleges in the country, Swarthmore is often up there at the tops of all the rankings lists, sometimes even above rival schools like Amherst and Williams. There's good reason for this fantastic reputation. Swarthmore's alumni read like a Who's Who of 20th century innovation.

The academic program is incredibly rigorous, but despite the ultra-challenging and hard-working nature of the university, especially for those who are engaged in the tons of extracurricular activities and attempt to have a social life, Swarthmore is very flexible and extremely supportive. Students are friendly, interesting and engaged, and the campus is simply stunning.

The Campus

Swarthmore is frequently described or ranked as one of the most beautiful campuses in the US, and that is not an exaggeration. Situated about 11 miles outside of Philadelphia, its rural beauty feels as if it could be 100 miles from urban life. The whole campus is one great arboretum, with thousands of different trees, flowers and plants.

The architecture is mostly a sort of mix of traditional 19th C stone buildings, except for a few of the newer academic buildings, such as the quite modern Science Center. However, one legitimate complaint many freshmen have is the irrational labelling policy of the college. Every tree, bush, plant, shrub, daisy... has a label! Yet some (most) of the buildings do not have labels, baffling many a red-faced freshman trying to find their first classes on time.

But the campus is small, only 399 acres, so it doesn't take long to learn your way around it. Yet there is enough space for Swarthmore to have its own "wildlife" area called the Crum Woods, site of the iconic outdoor amphitheatre ,where the annual opening ceremony and graduation take place.

Accommodation

All freshmen live on campus in dorms and most students will live on campus for their whole time at Swarthmore – as do about 93% of the student population. For the first two years you can expect to have a roommate unless you are lucky.

There is a very efficient (and complicated!) "lottery" system used to allocate rooms. However, it is very fair and gets the job done well. The school is helpful enough in finding roommates and rooms for students so finding a room for the new academic year is not a particularly stressful experience.

A note on the quality of housing: in general the accommodation is perfectly acceptable, but a few of the dorms are markedly better than others. The newer, modern dorms such as Alice Paul dorm are much, much nicer than the older dorms, such as Willets.

There are, of course, benefits to a slightly more run-down dorm, since the college mantra to dorm maintenance must be "leave it how you found it." Worse dorms usually mean more fun.

The 'Swattie'

Well, like any group of 1500 people, the students at Swarthmore (called "Swatties") do not conform to one or even two simple descriptions. However, as a quirky liberal arts college with an ethos promoting social justice and campaigning, there is one type of student that Swarthmore certainly attracts, or perhaps creates. That is the socially conscious, "wanting to make a difference" type of person.

This obviously varies, but every student will engage to some degree with politics and other topics surrounding social justice during their time at Swarthmore. Active student campaigning on campus has, at times, even made the national news. Whether you agree or disagree with other students' opinions, you will be expected to take a stand, so you had best start formulating some opinions early.

Most student think this is a wonderful aspect of the college, although some mutter darkly that it can create students who may be a bit too righteous and not enough fun.

On the other hand Swarthmore has a very diverse student body and students comment there are very few who aren't genuinely friendly and nice.

As a British student, you will be one of only a handful. Swarthmore is hardly known in the "Old World" and as a result, there are only one or two British students in each year group. This can be bad, because as a new student you won't be have anyone from home to talk to about football (not "soccer") or complain with about the ridiculous drinking laws.

However, there is a good side to this: it immediately makes you a unique student in the eyes of your colleagues. This British male has lost count of the number of times that other students have got a bit over-excited about the fact that some people really do talk with an British accent.

Albeit with few British representatives, there is a well-functioning international club that includes all international students. Called I20, this is a great club that will immediately link you up with the rest of the international community at Swarthmore, which is nice if you are struggling to adapt to the US.

Hitting the Books

The academic program is incredibly strong (possibly too strong, for those who aren't up to the challenge), and students have access to courses and facilities at two other nearby liberal arts schools (Haverford and Bryn Mawr – both excellent) and at the University of Pennsylvania (UPenn) in Philadelphia.

One thing that any British student must adjust to immediately when attending a US university, perhaps especially Swarthmore, is the grading system. The grading is cumulative rather than exam-based (ie you cannot just breeze through term and ace the exam; your grades on every piece of work count towards your final grade) and the grade boundaries are extremely high (+93% for an A).

However, there is a plus side to this grading system; the professors make it crystal clear what you need to do to get a good grade. Top grades are achievable (and expected) and can be coupled with a busy extra-curricular life.

Swarthmore also has a very open curriculum: students don't declare majors until the end of their sophomore year and there are not that many requirements. (In order to graduate, a Swat student must have 3 credits in each of the humanities, social sciences and natural sciences, including 2 credits in a language of their choice. They must also have completed 3 writing courses.)

Swarthmore provides superb individual treatment to each student. Rather than being treated as a "name and number" as a member of a lecture hall of 200+ people, at Swarthmore you can expect to be taught by professors (rather than graduate students) in every class.

You can expect professors to know your name, and you can expect to be able to meet your professor at least once a week if you need help. This sort of access to faculty is quite special. Of course, considering how much you (or your parents) will be paying for you to go to Swarthmore it's only what you might expect.

Social Life

Swarthmore is one of the only top liberal arts colleges to still have Greek life. Most of the social scene revolves around the two fraternities and single sorority on campus. However, these fraternities aren't like your big state school fraternities. They are fully inclusive, and by college rules they cannot turn away anyone from their parties without good reason (ie the only way to get kicked out is by making an idiot of yourself).

They are also the last bastion of "bro" behaviour (the frats, not the sorority) at Swarthmore, so if you are the type of person who needs that there is a place for you. The rest of the student body is pretty much "bro" free.

Swatties certainly do not party very hard; if you're looking for all-nighters every night of the week, you will not find any of that at Swarthmore. However, Swatties definitely know how to have fun and the college helps fund a lot of the parties that are thrown. Although, obtaining and drinking alcohol doesn't appear to be an overwhelming problem (to this reporter) at Swarthmore, there are ongoing efforts to balance sensible containment so that more extreme drinking games and consumption aren't pushed underground.

Outside Those Ivory Walls

There is not much of a town to speak of at Swarthmore; the "Ville" is more like a small village than a town (in fact, is officially the Borough of Swarthmore). However, there are the essential shops that students might need: hairdresser, pizza place, grocery store, Chinese restaurant. The ville is effectively part of the college, and students spend most of their time in or around the campus.

There is a train station on campus, and it is only about half an hour to the centre of Philadelphia from Swarthmore. The journey to New York takes at least 2 hours, so students don't tend to head all the way up to the Big Apple. Some students make it out into the city every weekend; some students (such as myself) just aren't as ambitious and hardly ever leave campus.

Some of the other essential shops you might require – post office, bank and bookshop – are, conveniently, right on campus. Also, the campus is about a mile from the Baltimore Pike, which has a Target and shopping mall along it, where students can get just about anything else they might need.

Getting In

AT A GLANCE – Application & Test Options:

– Early Decision, Early Decision II, Regular Decision

– ACT/SAT required, but not the Writing/essay component

– SAT Subject tests not required (but if you're interested in the Engineering programme, you're encouraged to send results for the Math 2 Subject test)

One of the most competitive schools in the country, Swarthmore only accepts about 12% of applicants, so you need a seriously strong application here. However, once in, you can expect to be able to go as far as you would like in the intellectual community. Swarthmore has one of the highest graduate school acceptance rates in the world, and every year sends students off to all the best graduate courses you can think of.

Money Matters

About averagely priced for a good liberal arts college (ie expensive), Swarthmore reserves enough financial aid for about 50% of accepted international students, though this is needs-based only.

The general perception is that international students at Swarthmore have to be relatively wealthy to attend. Although there is an element of truth to this, it's not completely accurate and there are many different scholarship opportunities.

Famous Grads

Alice Paul – Suffragist and National Women's Party founder (class of 1905)

Nancy Roman – NASA's first Chief of Astronomy in the Office of Space Science (and 'mother of the Hubble Telescope')

Edward Prescott – 2004 Nobel Laureate in Economics

Note: Swarthmore has the second highest number of Nobel Prize winners per graduate in the US.

Tufts University

Medford, Massachusetts
www.tufts.edu
Undergrads: 5,200
Grads: 5,600

How many students does it take to change a light bulb at Tufts?

Two – one to change the bulb and one to explain how they did it every bit as well as any Ivy Leaguer.

Ask anyone to expand on Tufts' reputation and they will probably mention two things – elephants and international relations. This small but prominent university, located on a hill next to Boston, is dominated by its college mascot (who appears in statues all over the campus) and its excellent international relations programme (most famously at the graduate Fletcher School of Law and Diplomacy).

Tufts has long been known as the school that steals from the waitlists of the Ivy Leagues, and recent action on the part of the past two presidents has seen it progress in leaps and bounds. Particularly welcoming to international students (probably because we give the Americans a chance to practise their diplomacy skills outside the classroom), it is a good option for those looking at small and reputable New England colleges.

The Campus

Tufts is situated just outside Boston (easily reachable on the fabulous T). Students like to say that they get the best of both worlds – the benefits of the nearby thriving city, and the aesthetic and spatial advantages of being slightly apart from it. The campus is located on a hill and is divided into new buildings and older, more classical architecture.

Certainly, it is both spacious and pretty and the hill provides you with plenty of sledging opportunities (and a constant work out). Some of the college buildings are more than a little shabby (the administration has recently started to pour money into renovating them), but the whole is both attractive and easy to get around. Approximately 70% of students live on campus – freshmen and sophomores are required to do so.

Accommodation

Approximately 70% of students live on campus and freshmen and sophomores are required to do so. After that students can choose from on-campus options, fraternities and sororities or local off-campus housing.

The Tufts Student

The student body at Tufts hails mainly from the northeast and tends to fall into the preppy, New England, middle-to-upper-income tier bracket. While its international relations programme does attract students from across America, this is not the type of school that will introduce you to a huge variety of students. Reputed (a little unfairly) as a second-tier Ivy, Tufts brings together ambitious and hard-working students who are eager to get involved in everything.

Despite the notably hard freshmen requirements, Tufts students pursue multiple extra-curriculars from day one.

The college daily and weekly newspapers (unusual in a school of this size) are particularly well thought of and the campus is strong in both communications and media. And if you're the singing type, you'll be happy to find there are a number of a cappella groups.

Hitting the Books

Tufts is recognised for its strong academics. Despite its relatively small size, it has a great research programme and offers a huge number of courses. What's more, students can cross-register in classes at many other Boston schools (if they can't find something in the extensive Tufts course catalogue) and the more culturally minded ones can also pursue joint degrees at the New England Conservatory and the MFA. Academic exploration is encouraged; out of the 34 credits you must fulfil, only ten of them need be in your major.

Students have a great deal of flexibility in choosing their interests and more than a quarter of them pursue a double major. This does not mean they are exempted from all requirements. Tufts ensures that its students get a well-rounded education and its freshmen can frequently be heard moaning about all the courses they have to take.

However, throughout this process, the heavy involvement of the professors enables undergrads to get the best possible advice whenever they need it – the thing that has really earned Tufts the reputation it enjoys today.

Social Life

Tufts has also managed to maintain a strong school spirit outside the classroom. If you are an ardent fan of football (known as soccer in the US), this is the place for you. Both soccer and baseball dominate the campus and pull out many a cheering fan to their respective fields. And if sports aren't your thing, the university also regularly invites world-renowned speakers to address its students.

As far as your social life goes, the local area (Medford/Somerville) has some great restaurants and Boston offers pretty much everything you could need. Freshmen on campus tend to be very involved in the Greek system (of which around 15% of undergrads are members), but the older years prefer to look elsewhere for weekend amusement.

And would-be dating addicts should beware. Many students complain that Tufts lacks any romantic scene – most of your classmates will either end up in long-term relationships with each other or stick to those partners from out of town.

Getting In

AT A GLANCE – Application & Test Options:

– Early Decision, Early Decision II, Regular Decision

– Testing requirements: either SAT with two Subjects tests or the ACT (but the SMFA at Tufts' BFA program simply requires the SAT or ACT)

Currently, about 14% of applications to Tufts are successful – these odds are a bit better than at its neighbours down the road in Cambridge, Mass. If you are interested in applying to Tufts, you must submit a Common Application, the Tufts supplement (which includes two short answer essays), SAT or ACT test scores and two SAT Subject tests. But if you opt for the ACT instead, you don't need to provide Subject tests.

And good news! – you don't need the extra essay for the SAT or the Writing section for the ACT. Alumni interviews are available and a good idea.

Money Matters

Financial aid is unlikely to be an option – Tufts has only limited funds available for its international students.

Famous Grads

Pierre Omidyar – founder of eBay

Kostas Karamanlis – former Prime Minister of Greece

Michelle Kwan – Olympic medalist and World Champion figure skater

Tulane University

New Orleans, Louisiana
www.tulane.edu
Undergrads: 8,400
Grads: 5,000

How many Tulane students does it take to change a light bulb?

1000s – Think of all the relief workers and money from charitable donations! But certainly no help from the Bush administration.

Tulane has everything going for it – excellent academics, fun students and awesome social life, all set on a beautiful campus in one of the coolest towns in the country. Interested? You should be. Tulane is considered a Southern Ivy, complete with top-fifty rankings and nation-wide recognition.

If this all sounds too good to be true, then you should take a trip to New Orleans and see for yourself – even if you don't like the university you'll be guaranteed a great time in America's most fun-lovin', trumpet-totin', seafood-eatin' and hurricane-fearin' city.

The Campus

Set in the St. Charles Street mansion district of New Orleans, the impressive colonial architecture of Tulane looks as if it was barely scathed by Hurricane Katrina. It remains resplendent in its particular bend of the Mississippi, adjacent to the famous Audubon Park (great for jogging) and Loyola University, and 30 minutes by streetcar from the notorious French Quarter (15 minutes by normal car).

In fact, Katrina had a major impact on the university, forcing students to leave the city for at least a whole semester and ripping big holes in the budget. The school's recovery efforts were substantial and widely praised. Even now, 11 years later, many students continue to help out in some of the worst-hit parts of the city.

The grounds are spacious and filled with lawns and trees, but the university is small enough for everything to be pleasantly walkable. Although most buildings are modern, there are very few eye-sores and the main old-fashioned French-style mansions at the front attract tourists who aren't even thinking about what goes on in them. During term-time, the lawns throng with dense crowds of students bustling about on their way to whatever activity that awaits them, or simply sunbathing on the grass.

Students speak well of the campus, with one or two mentioning a lack of decent work-space as the only drawback. Facilities are otherwise top-notch, with the incredibly large omni-functional sports centre being particularly impressive (and probably the only ugly building on campus). There is always new construction underway, as the current President feels it is important to prevent the campus from stagnating.

Accommodation

All freshman and almost all sophomores live on campus, in generally praiseworthy dorms, while the older kids tend to move out into the nearby student-dominated neighbourhood, where the housing is "more fun" and barely more expensive.

The Tulane Student

Tulane is famously full of students from the affluent Northeast, many of whom are looking for the high quality education of that region of the country, but without the climate or the attitude. Unfortunately, their overwhelming influx into the university means that Tulane is often seen as little more than a Northern school that happens to be in the South, and indeed the student body as a whole is generally mainstream.

Although they are perfectly friendly, you're not going to find much "Southern courtesy" among the students here, and the small number of Louisiana locals complain of a certain "pushy" feel. Having said that, the prevailing atmosphere on campus tends more towards the laid-back end of the spectrum rather than the stressful urgency more typical of the North. Preppy trends among the largely Caucasian student body are mostly dissipated by the large number of students on financial aid.

Tulane enjoys a "cohesive campus culture", which seems to be a polite way of saying that most people are conformist and there is not a massive variety of personalities. It is interesting to compare the student body of Tulane to that of next-door Loyola, which is said to be more "artsy", while Tulane is "smarter, richer and smaller." The two universities get on very well, and there is a reasonable amount of cross-campus interaction.

It should be noted that the tight cohesion of the student body masks an unexpected diversity, geographically at least: 75-80% hail from 500 miles away or more. Although the international community is not huge, students tell us that overseas undergrads would find very little obstacle to smooth integration, and Brits especially will be loved for their accent. "Everyone will have a chance to shine here", enthused one student.

Hitting the Books

Though they may not be as intense as some colleges, students generally love the academics at Tulane. Professors are high-flying (two Nobel Laureates on faculty), but also "accommodating, passionate and not outrageous in their demands." Students praise the way that all the courses, no matter how good, are "taught in a way that you'll really enjoy." Class sizes vary, but are generally a comfortable 20-30 pupils per class.

The work ethic at Tulane is hard to pin down. Students talk about a "spectrum" of attitudes, though they usually are quick to point out that it's "more good than bad". What's great is that, as one student put it, "if you want to work hard, you really will excel". Nevertheless "on the whole, people do what they have to do" and not too much more. As always, certain departments tend to foster a harder-working attitude than others.

Psychology is the most popular major and Tulane, in general, is sciences top-heavy, with a new bio-environmental research facility recently added to its campus. Still, the finance and business schools are excellent, as are the departments for Latin-American studies and foreign languages (especially Spanish and French). Architecture and medical schools are famously good as well.

Social Life

Tulane is ranked among the top party schools in the country; these students certainly know how to have fun. Greek life, which includes about 40% of the women and 1/3 of the men on campus, is disproportionately influential over Tulane's social affairs; frats host hundreds of crazy parties, especially in the autumn, and are much more inclusive than those at other schools. In addition to fraternity events, students spend a large portion of their free time in the bars near the campus, and at occasional house parties.

On campus, there are even more social events (though perhaps not as frenzied), as well as huge numbers of student organisations of every kind. Water-based activities such as sailing and fishing are popular, and there is top-level baseball played in the spring, but otherwise sports are mostly of an informal nature. For the more creative students, the music and art scenes are flourishing and provide plenty of opportunities. Students note that it is perfectly possible not to get involved with any of the many things to do, but such cases are rare.

Many students complain about the "disorganised" and joy-killing administration, which they believe has targeted some of the social life, especially the fraternities, in a negative way. Interaction with the administration can be strained and painfully slow, we hear.

Outside Those Ivory Walls

Tulane students "don't go downtown as much as you might think," but they have a good relationship with New Orleans, and who doesn't? When asked to name their favourite aspect of the school, they frequently say that the opportunity to study in such an incredible city is unsurpassable.

Rich in history and culture, New Orleans was the capital of both French and Spanish colonies, leaving it with a distinctly exotic flavor that gives it the unofficial title of "northernmost Caribbean city". Although it was devastated by Hurricane Katrina in 2005, and some parts are still recovering, the essential flavour of the city was left intact, and most of the famous parts, including the whole French Quarter, are as thriving and energetic as they always were.

With a reputation spanning centuries for debauchery and merriment, New Orleans is home to many of the oldest and best festivals and parties in the country. Couple this with a funky music scene and art galleries, great shopping, museums, and sublime Cajun seafood cuisine, and it's hard to think of a more exciting place to live in America.

The one complaint that students occasionally raise is that in its efforts to preserve its awesome traditions and history, New Orleans is not a very modernised town. The public transport system, for example, is geared totally towards tourists, and is terrible for practical use.

Getting In

AT A GLANCE – Application & Test Options:

– Early Action, Early Decision, Early Decision II, Regular Decision

– ACT/SAT required

– SAT Subject tests optional

Tulane University was named by Kaplan/Newsweek's college guide as one of the 25 "Hot Schools" in the nation in 2008 and nothing much has changed since then. Unsurprisingly, competition for places is getting considerably tougher, as the university selects ever-more capable students. In recent years, the application success rate has been around 30%. Importantly, Tulane uses the Universal College Application (www.universalcollegeapp.com/) instead of the Common App.

Money Matters

Tulane is well-endowed and even provides needs-based aid for international students, though not as much as for US citizens, apparently awarding up to $20,000 for the most needy, and more for merit (academic or athletic) scholarships.

Famous Grads

Newt Gingrich – former right-wing US Congressman, former Speaker of the House and leader of the "Republican Revolution"

Jerry Springer – former Mayor of Cincinnati (Ohio) and world-famous TV personality

David Filo – co-founder of Yahoo!

University of California – Berkeley

Berkeley, California
www.berkeley.edu
Undergrads: 26,000
Grads: 10,000

How many students does it take to change a light bulb at UC Berkeley?

2,001 – one to demand his right not to change the bulb and 2,000 to organize the strike in support of him.

UCLA may be the giant of the University of California schools but its sister school, Berkeley, situated in the Bay Area outside San Francisco, is the older sibling. As the first of the Californian universities, Berkeley has earned the right to call itself simply 'Cal' and for the 22,000 undergraduates enrolled there is no question that this precedence is academic as well as chronological.

National rankings consistently place Berkeley ahead of UCLA and it draws crowds of ferociously intelligent and even more outspoken students from across the Golden State and beyond. The lure of being a mere ten miles away from San Francisco and yet completely ensconced in one of the most dynamic campuses in America is hard to resist.

The Berkeley Student

Berkeley has always been the American university most known for its liberal attitude and democratic principles. The spirit that led to mass protests and riots in the sixties continues to thrive today and students are proud of the outspoken nature of their classmates and professors.

If you are a shy and retiring flower with no opinion on politics and a preference for a cliquey environment, then Berkeley is definitely not the place for you. If however, you enjoy making friends across diverse groups, wrangling with your professors and mounting your own soapbox in Sproul Plaza (the centre of campus debate and always home to at least eight different protests), then Berkeley is right up your street. Students adore the fact that this is a school that is proud to encourage independent thought and you can rest assured that, no matter what your British eccentricities, you will find yourself valued and included.

Hitting the Books

Berkeley's democratic principles also overflow into the classroom and the admissions policies. Students are actually able to teach their own classes if they are unable to find a faculty member already offering what they want. These are known as DECal classes (or Democratic Education at Cal) and they fall completely under a student's jurisdiction.

In other respects, however, there are many similarities between an education at Berkeley and one at UCLA. Both schools are enormous and prospective students need to be prepared to make much more effort to find an academic (and social) footing. Professors, often brilliant, are not at all keen to hold your hand, and while the resources are there, the onus is on you to discover and use them. Competition is also rife, despite the laid-back appearance every student aims for, and independent thought is crucial if you are to succeed.

Social Life

School spirit runs high at UC Berkeley – probably helped by the fact that their mascot, the Californian Golden Bear (nicknamed Oski) is one of the cutest around. But Berkeley students do not limit their excitement about their community to chants at the huge football games, or mass attendance at such quirky traditions as the Daffodil Festival.

Instead students tend to be massively involved in any number of outreach groups, social programmes, mass activities and, most beloved of all, protests. It is virtually impossible to get through college at Berkeley without getting roped into one of these, and most students find they are the most valuable part of their entire experience. Indeed, the movement of UC Berkeley students after graduation reflects their dedication to college and the community – 'Cal' sends more students to the Peace Corps than any other school, while a huge proportion of others go on to do PhDs.

Getting In

AT A GLANCE – Application & Test Options:

- University of California application deadlines
- ACT/SAT, with Writing/essay required
- SAT Subject tests can be used to showcase academic mastery

Admission into Berkeley is a bit harder for a Brit than admission into UCLA. Both universities fall under the same California quotas, but as Berkeley has the (marginally) smaller campus, your chance of acceptance is even lower. Currently, one in 5 applicants is admitted, but this includes California state residents so the % of out-of-state acceptance is much lower, and only about 9% of all international first year applicants are accepted. Berkeley does, however, place great importance on personal characteristics and estimates that while 50% of its choice is necessarily affected by grades, the other 50% depends on the leadership skills and individual strengths of each class of applicants.

The SAT or ACT test is required but, unusually, Berkeley does not request teacher recommendations or offer interviews to prospective students. This means that a huge amount depends on the strength of your personal statement. This focus on the individual, their views and their objectives nicely sums up the attitude of Berkeley throughout a student's university career.

Money Matters

Just like its sister school UCLA (and other state universities in America), Berkeley can't offer any financial aid to international students – it's only available to US citizens. So this is a situation where you really need to look into private organizations that offer scholarships (check out some leads on the Resources, References & Links chapter).

Famous Grads

Steve Wozniak – Co-founder of Apple Computer

Zulfikar Ali Bhutto – both President and Prime Minister of Pakistan (of course, at different times)

Gregory Peck – Academy Award winning actor

University of California, Los Angeles (UCLA)

Los Angeles, California
www.ucla.edu
Undergrads: 30,000
Grads: 13,000

How many students does it take to change a light bulb at UCLA?

One. He just holds the bulb and lets the world revolve around him.

For those Brits who have always longed for the bright lights and laid-back lifestyle of the West Coast, UCLA is an option that should definitely be taken into consideration. The fortunes of UCLA and the surrounding city of Los Angeles have always been linked. Over the past century, both have grown beyond their founders' wildest dreams and both now enjoy prosperity and a certain superstar status.

Certainly UCLA is one of America's top universities; a veritable metropolis, it boasts superb facilities, beautiful weather, top academic ratings and varsity teams that regularly fill up Olympic spots. As part of the California state system, however, around 90% of places are filled by California students. Aside from heightening the competition for international students, this requirement also means that any Brits applying must be able to embrace the California lifestyle.

Still, with the Pacific Ocean just five minutes away, star-studded Beverley Hills just down the road and access to some of the brightest (and most laid-back) American academics, many would agree that the cultural adjustment required is not that much of a burden!

The Campus

UCLA is HUGE! With 43,000 full time students and a hefty number of faculty and staff members, it is closer to a city than a normal campus school. Indeed it even has its own hospital on site.

Founded in the 1880s, UCLA moved to its present location in 1929 and since then has grown (like the city that surrounds it) at an exponential rate. The four original buildings survive and the campus, while lacking the quaintness of the New England schools, has an architectural charm of its own.

The beautiful weather, palm trees and proximity of both mountains and ocean undoubtedly help, but the dormitories and classrooms are an aesthetic success in their own right. From the great Powell library to the more modern quarters (all in the middle of being corrected for any seismic calamities), the buildings serve to unite the vast campus into a pleasing whole and give students a break from the pulsating city that surrounds them.

Be warned however – despite its overall attractiveness, the grounds are not easy to get around and not all the accommodation on offer may reach the expectations of your California dreaming.

While UCLA consists of a number of different undergraduate and graduate schools, the majority of undergrads will find themselves in the College of Letters and Sciences. This academic institution has traditionally divided itself (both geographically and socially) into two halves. This split is made along the line of intellectual preference (or, as the Bruins would have it, each individual is categorized by their level of geekiness).

The North Campus is the home of the humanities – attracting those interested in the liberal arts, media or social studies. This is also the spiritual home of the many 'beautiful people' (for which one can often read wealthy West Coast kids with daddy's credit card).

Meanwhile the South Campus calls out to the scientists, the engineers and those who choose to spend their days staring at test tubes – in other words, the brains of the operation. While such sweeping generalizations are obviously mostly inaccurate, a certain amount of rivalry continues to exist between the halves and various disparaging comments about brainpower and beauty are constantly fired across the boundary.

Accommodation

UCLA is fortunate enough to enjoy a great setting within the heart of a bustling city and a large amount of space for its students to play, work and live in. Given their prime location, and presumably the expense of nearby real estate (Beverley Hills is just down the road), most students choose to live in campus dormitories during their first year.

The university offers a number of different housing options, including various themed floors – for those who want to bond with fellow artists or mountain climbers.

These dorms form the basis of most students' friendship groups and, while in later years it is common to move out into the university apartments situated on the south-west side of the campus, it is extremely sensible to stay on campus for your freshmen year. After all, in a university with this many people, good bands of friends are important to come by.

The Bruin

How can one possibly define a UCLA student? Given the sheer numbers of them, it is safest to say that they defy generalization – except perhaps for a hearty love of their alma mater and a propensity for wearing the colours blue and gold. It is also a given that the vast majority will be Californians.

Many myths about the West Coaster have reached British ears; they're all hippies, health freaks, obsessed with the environment, into technology, and bent on fame and fortune in entertainment. While some of these rumours are true (health is very big – it comes from being able to run outside in fetching bikinis while getting a tan), California encompasses a huge variety of individuals. From its ranches and its beaches, its mountains and its deserts, its cities and its hamlets, California teenagers set out en masse and head for UCLA.

So while your British accent is bound to make you stick out like a sore thumb, you should be aware that not everyone around you came from the same high school. And you carry the trump card – as an alien from out-of-state, everyone is going to want to visit you!

The sunshine in California has a great effect on the population and the majority of the students pride themselves on their laid-back attitude to life. Certainly everyone on the West Coast seems friendly and happy. However, UCLA is a very competitive school and everyone is aware that a certain amount of work is necessary to maintain the right grades.

Thus, although some sunbathing goes on, it is accompanied by a degree of hard work. Students often report that, owing to the curve on which UCLA grading operates, there can be a degree of rivalry over academic placings. So if you get stuck on that biochem homework, don't expect your classmates to be bending over backwards to help you work it out.

Yet, while academics may raise the odd hackle, the Bruins tend to be more united than divided. UCLA is a university possessed by a huge amount of school spirit and events such as Homecoming, the famous Beat SC Week and even Engineering Week (OK, so it's not all cool) attract huge numbers of people. UCLA is one of the top sporting teams of the nation – in fact its athletes have won an extraordinary 195 Olympic medals since 1920.

Whether you are a fan of (American) football, which reaches its climax with the huge annual match against USC, or of basketball, in which case you may well be camping out during March Madness, you are sure to find a stadium full of fellow hooligans with which to celebrate or commiserate. And you can take pride in the fact that, unlike those sad excuses that pass for East Coast teams, your school is unrivalled throughout the US of A.

For the large proportion of UCLA students who are not preparing to be drafted into the NBA, there are many other options available. Despite the laid-back attitude that Californians pride themselves on, almost every Bruin is involved with at least one extra-curricular activity.

From writing for the Daily Bruin, which is one of the largest daily newspapers in LA, to community service in one of the less privileged parts, of the city, there are literally hundreds of activities available. And while the lazy may shrink from these energetic pursuits, all of these extra-curricular options are instrumental in helping you form a social group, meet new people, cement old friendships and appreciate the amazing setting in which you are spending four years of your life.

California is one of the most diverse states in the country and you should be prepared for a similar variety of ethnic, religious and financial backgrounds among your classmates. Although UCLA is known to have more than its fair share of rich Cali kids, they are diluted somewhat by many students from less privileged backgrounds.

Colourwise, the number of whites is equalled by the number of Hispanics and Asians – nicely completing the Benetton ad effect.

Yet while ethnic diversity certainly exists in numbers, many students complain that social groups tend to divide themselves upon ethnic or financial lines.

You, as the weird foreigner that defies all American categories, have the perfect excuse to plough into each and every group and establish friendships as you go. But make sure you do this from the beginning – in such a sea of faces it is easy to become just one of an extremely large crowd.

Hitting the Books

There can be no denying the fact that UCLA provides its students with a sound education. The majority of Americans will argue that you will receive a stronger academic experience among a more diverse group of people down the road at Stanford or even at the sister-school of UC Berkeley but few will find too much to complain about at UCLA.

The real problem lies in the fact that on such a huge campus, a much larger effort is required if you are to make your mark – both academically and socially. While your accent will at least help your professors to distinguish you from all of those Californians, the transition from even the largest of secondary schools will be immense. The old granny maxim of 'from big fish in small pond to little lost tadpole' seems very appropriate.

This sense of isolation is not helped by the fact that classes at UCLA are, by necessity, rather larger than those at smaller schools. This means that even if you are being taught by a leader in his or her academic field (and UCLA has many of these), you may still be unable to spend any time interacting with them on a personal basis.

Many at UCLA complain that professors, while fascinating individuals and renowned researchers, are not very good at actually communicating with the lowly students who sit before them three times a week. Bridging this gap is important if you are to make the most of your academic experience at UCLA, but you may have to fight your way through the crowds of other overachievers bent on the same mission.

This is not to say that the academic system at UCLA does not have its advantages. For one thing, the university has some of the best resources around and the library and research opportunities are wonderful. UCLA is also one of the few universities that chooses not to follow the semester system.

Instead it works on a three quarter system. Many enjoy this as it means that they get to experience more classes during their time at university. This is particularly beneficial if you find that you seriously misjudged quite how interesting Geology 101 was going to be. However it also means that you have less time per class and face exams on a more regular basis.

For those who fear that continual assessment will be one of the more stressful parts of the American experience, UCLA could turn out to be a nightmare. But for those who are good at exams and want to have a chance to experience every possible course, it might be a dream come true.

For the first two years, most students will find they are taking lower-division courses. These consist of broad and often introductory classes that help you to decide what direction you want to head in when you finally choose your major at the beginning of your third year (giving you lots of time to decide and then change your mind).

After that you embark on upper-division classes that focus on specific departments and are smaller in size. Certain departments are particularly strong – the film programme is one of the most famous in the country.

Whatever your major, students also face a type of core curriculum in the form of a GE (or general education) class. Also known as 'cluster courses', these span a year and allow you to experience academic disciplines that range across a variety of departments – in effect operating as a whistle-stop tour of all the options that await your final academic decisions.

Because they last for a year, they also provide you with an opportunity to cement both social and academic relationships at an early point in your student career.

Social Life

On your first day at UCLA you are more than likely to be overwhelmed. The thousands of people, all sporting cute Californian tans and laid-back attitudes may send you into unexpected pangs of homesickness for the grey skies and grotty pubs of good old England.

But by day two you will undoubtedly have discovered that, not only does everyone else feel just as lost as you do, but there are so many people here and so many things to do that it is nearly impossible to be left out in the cold.

Your social life at UCLA is something you can really choose to mould for yourself. At smaller colleges like Williams or Bennington, you may have no choice but to befriend everyone in your class, but a school as large as UCLA seems to offer an unlimited number and array of people.

Much of the social scene here is influenced by which of the many groups you identify yourself with. People tend to peel off according to their interests – but it is perfectly possible to avoid being typecast. If you are an avid scientist who enjoys surfing, chances are you'll find people who feel the same way.

The patterns of the social scene may be a little more difficult for the average Brit to work out. For one thing, all that sunshine and beach living takes a certain amount of adjustment. Parties on the UCLA campus take place in a variety of guises and after a Bruin victory there are parties like you've never seen before. Whether you are heading for one of the glitzier LA bars, partying in one of the frats (that 13% of the campus choose to join), or merely thrashing out a play-by-play in Starbucks, you will rarely be short of a place to go on a Saturday night.

Outside Those Ivory Walls

City of Angels, La La Land, home to the stars, dwelling place of supermodels and surfers – Los Angeles will provide you with a university experience you could never get anywhere else. Whether you are rollerblading (and star-spotting) in Beverly Hills, studying marine biology on one of the beautiful Pacific beaches or catching up on some culture at the Getty Centre, you can be sure that you will accumulate more than enough stories to make your friends back home green with envy.

Anyone who is bored while at UCLA must accept the fact that life itself will probably prove a disappointment. Whatever your taste – whether it be partying till dawn, or retiring to bed after a fourteen-mile hike – you can be sure that it will be catered for here. And with an undergraduate body that beats many towns for size, you will also always be able to find people who are prepared to share the experience with you.

One of the reasons UCLA kids are always on the move is the diversity of the city they inhabit. California is one of those rare places that is able to offer beaches, mountains, cities and deserts, all in one fell swoop.

Los Angeles may not be everyone's cup of tea – the aspiring actors, constant beauty, and health regimes may drive some round the bend – but you would be hard pushed to dislike everything.

For lovers of the great outdoors, there are hiking opportunities aplenty and skiing a couple of hours away in the winter. For those who march to a rather different beat, clubs of every variety and some of the best bars and restaurants in the world can be found just around the corner (providing your credit card can keep up!). And with a great public transport system, nothing is inaccessible.

Having said that, many UCLA students find that everything they need for a successful student life is right on their doorstep. Westwood Village (like no British village you have ever seen) has more than its fair share of student hang-outs, offering a more affordable and often more friendly option to those who shun the real world. And, with most off-campus houses located in this area, this atmosphere tends to exist around the clock.

Meanwhile for those who really want to escape, UCLA is a superb launch pad for one of the must-do American experiences: the road trip. Ever fancied gambling at Las Vegas or a trip down to Central America? Find (or kidnap) a friend with a car, grab your toothbrush and off you go.

Getting In

AT A GLANCE – Application & Test Options:

– University of California application deadlines

– ACT/SAT, with Writing/essay required

– SAT Subject test requirements vary by department, so check the school's website for details

Getting in to UCLA is no walk in the park. To start with, unless you are a bone fide Californian, your chances are already slimmed to being one of the 10% of the student body that come from out-of-state. Although it is a huge student body (and bear in mind this means you stand more chance of admittance here than at UC Berkeley), this still narrows your chances considerably.

To reduce your chances even further, UCLA is also one of the most popular schools in America, frequently boasting of more applications than any other university. As the atmosphere is so competitive, top grades are a necessity as well as an ability to show a commitment to academia and other extra-curricular interests.

The SAT or ACT test is required and, in a few cases, two SAT Subject tests are as well. The SAT Subjects (if required) are often specified. For example, the Henry Samueli School of Engineering and Applied Science requires two SAT Subject tests: Math 2 plus a science.

A strong personal essay and good teacher recommendations are vital if you are to stand a chance of admission – a Californian driver's licence would stand you in even better stead. One ray of hope: your chances of being admitted are, in fact, better than those of Americans who do not live in California.

Money Matters

UCLA loves having international students (adding as they do to the diversity of the school), but it simply cannot take as many of them as its privately run contemporaries. This limitation also means there is no financial aid or even scholarships available for us poor Brits, although it is always worth enquiring.

Famous Grads

Francis Ford Coppola – Mr Godfather himself

James Dean – if only all the students looked like this

Michael Ovitz – hooray for the Disney connection!

University of Chicago

5801 South Ellis Avenue
Chicago, Illinois
www.uchicago.edu
Undergrads: 5,400
Grads: 9,800

How many University of Chicago students does it take to change a light bulb?

None – a second spent changing a light bulb is a second lost writing your thesis.

Among the academic cream of American universities – Harvard, Yale, Princeton, MIT, and the University of Chicago – it is UChicago that can most convincingly claim to provide the most rigorous, intense learning experience. Don't be put off by the famous T-shirts that proclaim that UChicago is "where fun goes to die".

The glory of a UChicago education is that not only will you get a robust, fulfilling education that will mark you out for life, but you will get a unique chance to study in the great city of Chicago, where everything is possible – and where fun goes to thrive. With the university's national recognition skyrocketing due to its connections with President Obama, and with Chicago itself prospering for much the same reason, there has never been a better time to inflict UChicago on yourself.

The Campus

UChicago occupies a little oasis of charm and serenity in the southern reaches of the "Windy City"; it's about 20 minutes by bus or "El" (the metro system) from the city centre, and a short walk to massive Lake Michigan and the beautiful beaches and parkland on its shores. The surrounding Hyde Park neighbourhood is almost a continuation of the university, full of student and faculty housing and lots of collegiate shops and cafes.

Obama's house from his days of teaching at the law school is a few blocks away, as is the room where Al Capone holed himself up (until recently it was a dorm for freshmen!)

The campus itself is centred on a large Oxbridge-esque quad, with old fashioned British-looking stone buildings covered with vines and ivy, and lush lawns and gardens filling the space between them. Beyond this area, the university expands into a series of much more modern edifices, though hardly any are unpleasant.

There is a huge, well-equipped gymnasium, and a sports stadium, famous for its home team's incredibly awful record, but the old (now unused) football field is much more exciting, because it was in a bunker underneath that the scientists of the Manhattan Project first succeeded in splitting the atom, thereby launching the nuclear age.

Students generally speak very well of their campus, though not always of their surroundings. The area is easily walkable and has good connections to other parts of the city; most of the complaints really just stem from it not being as exciting as the rest of Chicago, rather than from any big faults of its own.

Accommodation

All freshmen and most sophomores live in the dorms, which are overall very nice indeed, especially some of the newer apartments.

The accommodation system is much loved because it is arranged by "Houses" (much the same as a British public school Houses), each of which has its own community, Residential Assistants (RAs), events and competitions against other houses.

The Maroon

Students at UChicago are famous for being unbearably studious, opinionated, nerdy, and perhaps a little conceited. Outsiders believe they have seen organisms at the bottom of a pond with better social skills.

Of course, in reality the student body is full of amiable, fascinating students notable for their interest in and dedication to everything they learn about, as well as a general intensity in everything they do. Most people enjoy engaging in conversation, including heated academic debates, and they all live what they call "the life of the mind".

Certainly, the school attracts its fair share of the socially awkward, but just talk to people on campus to see that they're mostly the same fun, animated bunch that inhabits campuses across the country.

Demographically, the student body is very diverse, and more than a little international. (Don't be surprised to see people playing cricket in the quads.) This exposure to such a great range of cultures, ideas and interests is a real boon to campus life at UChicago.

Improbably, for such a work-focused university, there is a thriving Greek life at UChicago, though some consider it a more toned-down version than their infamous counterparts at the state schools. Non-Greek students don't have high opinions of their fun-loving, not-quite-as-hard-working peers in the fraternities and sororities, while the Greeks themselves hold the adamant belief that they have been cursed by fate to live the frat life in such a square college. "They're all masochists", according to a member of one fraternity, who explained: "Greek life provides sanity for people who aren't that pretentious."

It is true that when the dean of studies attempted to downgrade the difficulty of the core curriculum he was dissuaded by vociferous student protests. There does seem to be a certain twisted pride in the "where fun goes to die" image, failing sports teams and other such eccentricities.

But that doesn't mean that UChicago kids don't like to have fun sometimes. There may be a large chunk of the student body that you never see because they are permanently locked in libraries and study sessions, but many UChicago students make sure they don't seclude themselves and try to take full advantage of on-campus events and the wonders of Chicago – albeit, with their characteristic intensity.

Hitting the Books

If your top priority at university is learning as much as you possibly can, you've come to the right place. Students at UChicago go through one of the toughest, most challenging educations/ordeals (take your pick) known to mankind. But the rewards are spectacular.

UChicago has a broad, ambitious and obligatory general education known as the core curriculum, lasting the freshman and sophomore years. After this, upperclassmen get the luxury of choosing from a wide range of majors, giving them "loads of flexibility". The teaching style "focuses on the ideas" (as opposed to simple information for information's sake), and the university is careful to ensure that no one gets bogged down in wasteful obsession with grades and competition. "It's mostly big picture stuff", as one student put it, "it pushes you to become a better student".

If you have to pick the best fields on offer, though, you should definitely check out the world-famous pioneering departments of economics and social sciences, both of which have whole schools of thought named after them.

The professors teaching you are normally close to mind-blowing (only Harvard and Stanford have more Nobel Laureates on their staffs); the only complaints are that some core curriculum classes are taught by grad students who don't give much time to the pesky undergrads. Mostly, though, the faculty is superb, and they take their low-level classes as seriously as if they were your major.

Although the name "University of Chicago" may sound like a big state school, the undergraduate enrolment is closer in size to a small liberal arts college. With small, discussion-based classes guaranteeing tons of contact with superstar teachers, it might take a while to get used to everyone being leaders in their field.

"Your professor is probably famous", said one sophomore, before telling a story about meeting Prof. Obama in an elevator. Not only this, but teachers are almost always helpful and care a lot about their students' success, with lots of open-office hours available so you can squeeze out every last drop of knowledge.

The other great thing about UChicago is that being top-heavy towards graduates over undergraduates (the latter outnumbering the former almost 2 to 1) means that there are fantastic research opportunities available.

Many PhD level classes are open to undergraduates, which extends the whole plane of your education to an exhilarating out-of-the-classroom level which few other undergrads in the world are lucky enough to experience.

Still, if you're applying here for the academics – probably the best reason to come – you have to keep in mind that it's really, really tough, sometimes crushingly so. "They try and overwhelm you with lots of homework", explained one student in reference to professorial tactics. Finals week, which seems to be permanently around the corner, can be "hellish".

The other subject of much complaint is grade deflation, which students claim is endemic and designed to make you work harder than the layabouts at Harvard and Yale who get their grades handed to them on a silver plate.

Social Life

Students live their social lives as intensely as they do everything else, although there are of course those who never emerge from the library. The theory is that though social life, academics and sleeping all exist at UChicago, most students only have enough time for two of them. In the words of one student "you learn how to keep yourself sane".

There's a lot on offer, certainly something for every taste. "Some organisation is always doing stuff," stated a particularly eloquent sophomore – and all the dorm houses constantly organise events and even field trips.

The university administration is extremely supportive of student initiatives and gives groups the freedom to let their creative juices run wild. They also organise events themselves, and bring in big-name speakers to further broaden and expand the experience.

The student film society, Doc Films, is one of the oldest and most prestigious in the country, attracting huge stars and pre-premiere showings of blockbuster films. It also makes some ace documentaries. Intramural sports are another big deal, and are a lot more popular than the failing varsity teams.

Instead of game days, big campus events include the fall formal, Mardi Gras celebrations, "summer breeze", a festival of the arts and best of all, the bizarre Scavenger Hunt which is the biggest in the country and lasts 4-5 days every May.

One of the best things about living at UChicago is that there is no bubble – students live in the thick of Chicago and they take full advantage. The city centre and other cool districts scattered throughout the metropolis are within easy reach.

Bear in mind, however, that the university is only a short distance from some of the most run down areas of Chicago's infamous South Side (though this does mean you can experience some great gang-history!).

Students report that safety is not an issue – you simply avoid the bad parts and trust in UChicago's private police force, which is the largest of any university in the States and the fourth largest private security body in the world.

Outside Those Ivory Walls

Chicago is the perfect antidote to those hard-workin' blues. The city has honed its capacity and flair for having fun over the entire course of its relatively brief history, having come to fame as the epicentre of all things evil and tempting during the roaring twenties, when Prohibition pushed alcohol consumption into the speakeasies and led to gang warfare.

It still has a reputation for corruption, especially among its politicians: not so long ago, former state governor Rod Blagojevich (Blag-oy-o-vich) was discovered to have attempted to "sell" a seat in the Senate.

Chicago is the basis for the legendary Gotham City of Batman fame, and residents enjoyed watching Heath Ledger and Christian Bale in the streets making the recent Batman films, complete with stunts and explosions.

In reality, Chicago is not quite as dark and foreboding as its fictional counterpart – but it has some similarities. The first skyscraper was built here, and hulking, grimy, monolithic buildings still dominate the skyline. One of them, the Willis Tower (formerly known as the Sears Tower), is the tallest building in the country, although several buildings in Asia have now surpassed it as tallest in world. Here, you can visit Willis' new glass balcony, where you can quite literally look past your feet to the dizzying streets below.

Any kind of fun that you can possibly desire is available in lavish quantities in Chicago, from music festivals (Lollapalooza and Pitchfork are world-famous) to prestigious museums and everything in between.

Culinary delights also abound, and you have to try the deep-dish pizza that Chicago natives worship as the One True variety. The city's only real downside is the winter, when things turn hideously cold and snowy, and it's hard to avoid feeling grumpy.

Getting In

AT A GLANCE – Application & Test Options:

– Early Action, Early Decision, Early Decision II, Regular Decision

– ACT/SAT required

UChicago is, unsurprisingly, extremely competitive – only 8% applicants were admitted for autumn 2016. Admissions staff have to decide between thousands of academic brainboxes, so you're going to need an ultra standout application. Non-academic considerations are also important, so it helps if you have a well-rounded CV and can make yourself look like the motivated and successful leader that they want to fill the places.

UChicago offers Early Action, which means you can apply in November and find out early (before the winter holidays) but you don't have to go. Importantly, you can apply to other Early Action schools at the same time. And now you also have two timetables for applying Early Decision (which is binding).

Money Matters

Moneywise, UChicago is similar to most of the big-name schools in that it is ridiculously expensive and offers a lot of aid to help talented students cover the cost. International students are also eligible for this aid, which is mostly need-based, and if you are successful with your application then the university will normally cover all of what it feels you are unable to pay. Financial aid applications do put you in an even more competitive pool, though, so think about it carefully.

Famous Grads

David Axelrod – senior advisor to Obama, and chief strategist on the campaign

Philip Glass – world famous minimalist composer

Luis Alvarez, Emily Green Balch, Gary Becker, Saul Bellow, Herbert Brown, James M. Buchanan, Owen Chamberlain, James Cronin, Clinton Davisson, Jerome Friedman, Milton Friedman, Ernest Lawrence, Tsung-Dao Lee, Robert Lucas, Jr., Harry Markowitz, Robert Millikan, Robert Mulliken, Irwin Rose, F. Sherwood Rowland, Jack Steinberger, Paul Samuelson, Myron Scholes, Herbert Simon, Roger Sperry, George Stigler, Edward Lawrie Tatum, Daniel Tsui, James Dewey Watson, Frank Wilczek, Chen Ning Yang – all Nobel Laureates

University of Florida

Gainesville, Florida
www.ufl.edu
Undergrads: 32,000
Grads: 13,000

How many Gators does it take to change a light bulb?

If it'll help them win the next football game, you can have as many as you need.

The University of Florida may look from the outside like another bog standard massive state school, but it doesn't take long talking to students before you realise that their incredible enthusiasm and pride radiates from this place being something very special.

Despite nasty budget cuts following the recession which hit Florida's real-estate economy harder than most, UF continues to improve its fantastic academic reputation as a public Ivy, recruiting ever-brighter students and offering ever-more cutting-edge research programs.

Sporting opportunities are unparalleled, and not just for the few dozen athletes who make it into the top teams. With an incredibly vibrant campus life, which more than makes up for the smallish college town of Gainesville, a diverse student body and wonderful college atmosphere, UF is soaring on an upward curve. Join it before admissions become "swamped".

The Campus

With more than 50,000 students (third largest in US) and a hefty faculty, the UF campus qualifies hands down as huge. The monumental size (2,000 acres!) is complemented by an attractive red brick pseudo-European style, with lots of lovely areas for hanging out and walking or jogging.

UF even has its own stunning lake, which is apparently swarming with alligators (no one seems very concerned by this...). Perhaps this is the reason that UF students and sports teams are known as "the Gators," and that the 90,000+ football stadium (and a popular local restaurant) is known as "The Swamp".

Students speak well of their campus: everything is confined to a clearly defined area, and despite the size, most of the buildings a typical undergraduate uses on a day-to-day basis are contained within a manageable space. At peak times the campus is a crush of bustling students but, despite being hectic, it is well maintained and always provides a pleasant place to study. As with many big schools, "parking sucks", but the campus shuttle-bus system is excellent.

Accommodation

Ranked by the *Princeton Review* among the top ten schools with "dorms like dungeons", UF students affirm that on-campus residential opportunities are "gross" and "disgusting". Particularly worthy of avoidance is the notorious and overpriced "La Mancha" dorm block, where naive international exchange students often end up because of the shorter contract terms.

The advice on the street is to choose where you live carefully: don't go for the first thing you come across. The popular US website craigslist.org can be helpful for this – definitely check it out.

The Gator

The UF student body is a friendly assortment, seemingly diverse and yet full of affluent folks at the same time (the wealthiest 30% of Gators represent the wealthiest 0.5% of the country).

Unsurprisingly, with more than double the number of undergraduates of Oxford and Cambridge combined, students "run the gamut" of types and personalities. "It's like high school", explained one student, "you've got the jocks, the sorority girls, geeks, Christians, you name it." There's also a good-sized international component, which integrates well.

What's great is that UF encapsulates the diversity of Florida itself. There's a healthy mix of Southern and Northern Floridians, the former known for being laid back beach-lovers and the latter known as Southern Christian conservatives. The university is proud of its diversity, and students report an excellent level of interaction encompassing minorities and people with unusual backgrounds.

The main thing to bear in mind is that with 50,000 students in one place, no one is going to be holding your hand at UF. Things get daunting for freshmen very early on, especially when they are immediately whisked into the unfamiliar autumn football season when everyone goes nuts, before they even get a chance to familiarise themselves with the enormity of the institution.

The size is the main barrier to integration, and students earnestly recommend that you make an effort to make friends with classmates from day one to avoid marginalisation. The key to not being overwhelmed is getting a foot into the smaller groups, like sports teams or student organisations, or even fraternities if you are so inclined.

Everyone is laid-back and welcoming, and especially at the beginning of the freshmen year you're all in the same boat, so you have nothing to lose by a big social push at the outset. One thing that can help is the "Navi-Gators" program, which essentially pairs international students with locals to facilitate integration.

Although there's still a big range, Gators as a whole are rapidly becoming "more academically focused", as Florida's population expands and competition for places sharpens. "I spent twelve hours working in the library on my birthday", said one pre-med student we talked to, while her friend smirked and replied "whereas I spend all day doing nothing."

What is for sure is that you won't find anyone working on football days, and increasingly basketball days either. The Florida Gators are a big deal, and students are emphatic that "if you don't follow football, then you will follow it when you come here." School spirit is a vital part of the experience, and wearing Gator T-shirts will earn you approving remarks in surprising places around the world.

Hitting the Books

The sheer immensity of the University of Florida means that you can shape your education here into anything you want it to be. The college is a slackers' paradise, and you can feel free to sit your four years out in low-level lecture halls without concern for your grades – your experience will still be fun if unrewarding.

For those who want to learn something, however, "the school can be as academically challenging as you want it to be". Increasingly, students are choosing this option, and reaping spectacular benefits.

If you do want to get the most out of the academic side of things, then it is important to plan your classes thoroughly. Many students expect great teachers and courses to be laid before them, but in reality they have to be sought out. Too many students endure online classes or 600-strong lectures before realising that things could be better.

Finding which classes are the best depends principally on word-of-mouth, but things change rapidly as professors are switched or dropped, so pay attention. There is an online drop-out system active for the first four days of each semester – so if you don't like the look of a class on day one, change it as soon as possible.

The faculty here is equally varied, with some low-level classes taught by inexperienced teaching-assistants or grad-students, while the superstar professors only become available to the older, luckier or most persistent.

Mostly, professors (no matter how high-flying) are more than happy to help their students outside of class, and it is common to operate an "open-door policy" which means students can contact their teachers whenever they're in their office.

The best aspect of UF's academics lies in its research opportunities. The university is brimming with innovation in exciting new fields in every discipline. Graduate students benefit from this more than undergraduates, but you can still attempt to get involved – try contacting professors before arriving at the school to check out research openings: this can help you avoid the anonymity of the mammoth freshman classes and the irritation of seeing all the professors' attention going to the PhD and Masters candidates.

Stellar departments at UF include accounting, journalism, pre-med, certain engineering departments and the veterinary school. Agriculture is also very big, and actually receives more funds than any other department. Science research benefits from a nuclear reactor (though this is normally inaccessible to undergrads).

The Liberal Arts school, home of most undergrads, is "not the best", as one student put it, though anthropology has a good reputation. Unfortunately, budget cuts have hit academics hard, with lay-offs and course-cuts, and the axing of the entire documentary film institute, previously a highly respected part of the school.

Social Life

UF is often named as the official #1 party school in the country, at least so says the *Princeton Review* (of course that lofty honour is bestowed on other schools year to year – notice the Florida schools ares strong contenders most years, however). What the rankings don't tell you is that UF is also chock-full of awesome activities, some of the best sports in the country and a raving Greek life. "We're definitely not the number one party school," students laugh, insisting that the nightlife is "overblown". Instead, they say that there are loads of bars and house parties for those that want them, but that it's just as popular to get involved with the host of other activities on offer.

Whatever you do, don't expect Miami. There is nothing like the venues or attitudes of the big cities, and the sprawling oak trees and hanging moss of small-town Gainsville feels a world away from the stereotypical Florida life.

Still, it can be hard not to agree with one student's analysis that "the social life revolves around Gator football and drinking." Home games are marked by insane orgies of blue and orange, booze, thousands of supporters (not just students) and general chaos. Everyone is involved, no matter how much they may have disliked sports before coming to UF. It's infectious. (For the trivia fiends, the famous sports drink Gatorade was invented in UF to enhance the performance of the football team, a point of pride for many students.)

When there isn't a football game, however, excesses are not the norm. This doesn't dull the dynamics of campus life; with between 300 and 400 student organisations, students affirm that "you can find any club you want".

Whether it's comic books, judo, debating, community service, movies, local bands, high-profile guest speakers, academic groups, political activism, the student newspaper (7th best in the country) or the huge range of sports, there is a lot to see and do, and you should definitely "dive right into the free resources you have on campus...we have just about everything, you just have to find it."

UF students love to keep themselves fit. There are three mega-fitness centres, plus smaller gyms and every imaginable facility, all free. Intramurals are incredibly popular and very easy to get involved in, with sports competitions for everything from basketball to bean-bag tossing.

Also big are outdoors activities among the natural wonders near Gainsville, including springs, sinkholes, woods and rivers. Although UF is about as far from either coast as it's possible to be in Florida, the beach is a couple of hours away and can be a fun day-trip.

Outside Those Ivory Walls

Gainseville is a smallish student town, dominated by the university and essentially reliant on it for its economy. Your experience of the town depends on your attitude; some enjoy it as a fun, quirky little community but big city dwellers may find it claustrophobic and unfulfilling. The town is actually quite poor, leading to some clashes between locals and students, who are perceived as privileged.

Getting In

AT A GLANCE – Application & Test Options:

- Regular Decision (November 1 deadline)

- ACT/SAT required

The school is ever-more competitive, and the application success rate is now around 1 in 3. As Florida's premier state school, you will be competing with the brightest and best of the state (some of whom turn down acceptances to places such as Harvard or Duke because of good Florida scholarship programmes that give them a free ride at state unis but can only be used in Florida. Guess what their parents push for?).

Money Matters

UF has one of the largest budgets in the country, and a huge level of state funding that is now being slowly rolled back. It is rated as one of the best value universities, but unfortunately it's the in-state students who benefit most, since any needy student in Florida with the required level of SAT scores and GPA (which in recent years has been almost everyone) is automatically awarded a large scholarship, meaning their fees are almost nothing.

For international students, the options are limited to merit-based scholarships or – if you are a duel-passport holder (and one of those is from the US) – you can establish eligibility for in-state tuition rates by living in Florida for a gap year prior to application (not an automatic or uncomplicated process, but worth investigating).

Famous Grads

Wendy Thomas – Namesake of Wendy's restaurant chain

James R Thompson – NASA Director

Chris Linn – Vice-President of MTV

University of Kansas

Lawrence, Kansas
www.ku.edu
Undergrads: 19,000
Grads: 9,000

How many KU students does it take to change a light bulb?

Just one, and if you shine it from the top of the Fraser Building you can see it from the other side of Kansas.

So you think you know all about Kansas. Tornados, endless fields of wheat, schools that don't teach evolution and innocent little girls with plaits, right? Think again. While it may be true that the Dorothy State is a big, hot, empty rectangle of flatness, Kansas University is about as similar to its surroundings as a cowardly lion is to a talking scarecrow.

For a start, it's on a hill. In fact, it occupies the second highest point in the whole state, the highest being part of a large mound that is mostly in Colorado. Then there are the liberal, activist politics, the teacher who got fired for his class on intelligent design, the famous scientific breakthroughs, and of course, the town of Lawrence – which rivals Berkeley as the weirdest student community in the country. You can hardly tell you're in the centre-most American state.

The Campus

KU has a hulking great campus, spread lavishly across a prominence in the Midwestern plain, previously known as "Hogsback Ridge" but now named "Mt. Oread" to sound more prestigious. Because there's not really any ambiguity about it, most KU students call it simply "the hill".

The official reason for the university's location is that the founders wanted to make the "higher" education metaphor a bit more literal, but the truer story is that, being the only unfarmable land in the entire state, it was the sole patch that the governor was willing to donate for a public university. Whatever the reason, be prepared for some climbing on your walk to class, good sledding opportunities in the winter, and some great views of the Midwest.

The buildings are mostly modern, bricky and occasionally ugly and concrete, though there are a few nice sandstone ones too. Facilities are superb, including a library with so many books that at one point they had to put up shelves in the toilets to accommodate them all, and a massive Rec Centre complete with climbing wall and virtual golf simulator. The student union has its own bowling alley along with the usual range of eateries and performance venues.

Accommodation

Though there is ample student housing throughout the town, most freshmen and quite a few sophomores live in the on-campus dorms, most of which are newly-renovated and high-quality. They are also arranged into interesting groups, such as the "community service" block or the "creative arts" block.

There are fun, thriving communities in these blocks, but also worth considering are the "skol halls": cheap, exciting housing for fifty-or-so residents originally intended as scholarship students but actually available to anyone who's doing fairly well with their studies.

The Jayhawk

Students at KU are a mixed but universally pleasant bunch. Expect plenty of folk from the Midwest: if you've ever wanted to meet people who grew up in towns which consist of one street and a liquor store, then this is where you'll find them. That's not to suggest that KU folks are slow-paced, backward or right-wing – in fact they are the exact opposite.

KU led the way in student demonstrations during the 60s and 70s, at the forefront of the liberal wave that fought against things like Vietnam and racial injustices. The place is still full of left-wing "kooks", as non-Lawrence Kansans sometimes call them. It is very easy to get in touch with your eccentric side at

KU, and many of the people you'll meet are downright mad. This lends a certain passion to many of the goings on – and a strong intensity of focus on one's interests.

The liberal atmosphere also means that despite other indications (over 80% Caucasian, lots of Greek life) KU is a very accepting place, where you'll encounter many different and bizarre types of people and find it very easy to get on with them all.

Hitting the Books

Professors are a well-picked bunch; students feel that their teachers have their best interests at heart and are well-qualified enough to impart an excellent level of education. While you might not be having beers with them after class, professors do make an effort to be available and maintain a good contact with their students.

You may find that class sizes can be a problem in some of the introductory or popular courses, though by state university standards it's really not too bad. Besides, students tell us that the big lectures are often taught by the best professors, and they try especially hard to keep the students occupied and paying attention, so that the big classes can sometimes be the best!

Classes are normally well-taught and interesting – especially in certain standout courses (ask around to find out about the best of what's on offer) – and big name speakers are not infrequent (the likes of Bill Clinton and Madeleine Albright visited recently). The only complaint we heard is that courses can occasionally lack rigour. Expect plenty of multiple-choice tests.

This is not to say students at KU are not as clever or hardworking as their counterparts at similar universities. While they certainly leave time for other interests and socialising, there is a healthy work culture, and you'll find almost no one slacking when finals come around. One benefit of attending a big research university like KU (where helium was first isolated and the man who discovered Pluto did his experiments), is that there are lots of brilliant research opportunities available to undergraduates, who "commonly" get to take part in really interesting graduate-level work across a big range of fields.

If you're interested in studying in a different country, or just escaping temporarily to somewhere within 1,000 miles of an ocean, then you're in luck, because KU has one of the best study-abroad programs in the country, with about a third of the students participating.

Social Life

KU's social life is fairly inseparable from the town around it. There's all the usual stuff going on on campus (student groups, sports, protests), but most students are just as likely to take the 10-15 minute walk down the hill to Massachusetts Ave. (if someone asks if you want to head "down to Mass" it doesn't mean they're trying to convert you to Catholicism) as they are to visit the uber-well-equipped Rec Centre, one of the campus cafes, or the lake. In town, you'll find heaps of trendy joints, alternative culture outlets, party clubs, parks and of course student housing, with enough of interest to keep most kids entertained for years.

KU, like every state school worth its salt, is extremely competitive when it comes to sports, especially basketball. Game days are huge events, and expect to see (if not be inside) hundreds of tents in the queue to get tickets. School spirit is obligatory, and one of the first things you'll learn is the famous "rock chalk jayhawk" chant, used to intimidate opposition athletes.

It may interest some prospective applicants that KU has one of the most successful debating teams in the country, having won the National Debating Championships five times (fourth best record of any university). The debating society is open to everyone and affords excellent public speaking practice.

Getting In

AT A GLANCE – Application & Test Options:

- Regular Decision

- ACT/SAT required

- Subject tests not required

Like most state universities, KU uses its own basic application (not the Common App), which focuses mainly on your secondary school record and SAT (or ACT) test scores – good A-levels will be impressive. SAT Subject tests are not needed.

Money Matters

Financially, KU is a bargain, charging considerably less than similar level schools, even for international students. It doesn't offer much by way of needs based aid, but there are a few scholarships knocking about for international students to take a peek at.

Famous Grads

Kathleen Sibelius – Previous governor of Kansas and member of the Obama cabinet

Bob Dole – Republican Presidential nominee and Majority Leader of the US Senate

Mandy Patinkin – actor, most famously Inigo Montoya in The Princess Bride

University of Michigan

Ann Arbor, Michigan
www.umich.edu
Undergrads: 29,000
Grads: 16,000

How many students does it take to change a light bulb at UMichigan?

Ten – one to change the bulb and nine to act as the Supreme Court to affirm the decision.

Brits who are really looking to get away from the Brideshead Revisited Oxbridge experience, and who believe that East Coast America is simply not far enough, would do well to consider the University of Michigan.

You may not even know where Michigan is (think mid-West, lots of lakes), but this top public university has a reputation for being one of the best of its kind. With an excellent faculty, highly rated research facilities and a campus that numbers some 27,000 undergrads and 14,000 graduate students, UMichigan is the place to go for those who want a great education in very different surroundings.

The Campus

The geography covered by U of M is immense but once you get to the core of the campus, you'll find a traditional layout and the old character-filled buildings that are usually associated with the American college experience.

Nevertheless, the huge size of the student body can be one of the most off-putting things about the university. It is all too easy to become just one more face in a crowd, and the shy and retiring type may find the throngs of people just too much to handle.

The mass of undergraduates means class sizes (especially on the introductory level) tend to be larger than usual and students need to pick their courses with care if they are to interact with professors on a personal level.

For those who have the drive to do this, however, the benefits are many. U of M is a buzzing campus, with hundreds of options and a real student atmosphere.

Although there may be none of the hand-holding that is common at smaller liberal arts colleges, the average Wolverine (as they are known) develops an independent spirit and an ability to pursue what they want.

The U of M Student

The University of Michigan is one of the best public universities in the USA (competing with UVA and UCLA for the title of most prestigious).

As such, it has severe restrictions on who it can admit. Two-thirds of the Wolverine student body are from the state of Michigan itself. The average Brit may feel more than a little lost among all these mid-Westerners, but there can be no doubt that it will be a formative cultural experience (and your accent is sure to come in handy in striking up conversations!). Meanwhile, the magnitude of the campus means that 11,000 undergrads (more than the enrolment at a small east coast college) are from out of state – a fact that offers international students (who comprise 4% of the student body) plenty more diversity.

Hitting the Books

UMichigan is not just a school renowned for its social life (which, with its combination of frats, sports and environment is undeniably good) or even for its sporting prowess.

It is also famed for providing its students with a truly great education, offering them academic and research opportunities that many schools with an even stronger reputation cannot provide.

Prospective students apply to one of the six undergraduate schools – most of you would be looking at the College of Literature, Science and the Arts (more commonly known as LSA) although engineering, nursing, art and design, kinesiology(!) and music are also options.

Once students are admitted they can take courses across the six schools, choose from a wide variety of majors ranging from jazz studies to astronomy and even invent their own should nothing on offer appeal.

UMichigan has a huge and dedicated faculty who offer a vast number of courses – in everything from birdwatching to the history of St Petersburg. Undergraduates find themselves facing a number of requirements designed to give them a solid grounding in basics such as maths, writing and a foreign language.

Small seminars (some of them open just to freshmen) also ensure that students don't get lost among the huge numbers and offer a chance for personal interaction with some of the leaders in their fields.

Meanwhile themed semesters give students the chance to really focus on whatever offbeat topics the dean of the college has chosen for that term. Despite its size, this is a school which treats academics seriously and actively encourages you to follow your interests.

Social Life

Although many Wolverines may feel they are one among many, few of them complain they feel alienated from their school. UMichigan has some of the strongest school spirit in the US. As a proud member of the Big Ten (a group of the sporting elite), Michigan is dominated by a passion for sports and footballers (many of whom turn professional) are treated as gods.

If sports aren't your thing, the large student population naturally means there are plenty of other options – including programmes at the nationally renowned School of Music, an active theatre community and high-class journalism at the Michigan Daily.

You may want to join an intramural sports team, help out at a local charity, sing with a musical group or polish your leadership skills – or do all of the above. You have to literally be an alien not to find something to invest your time in outside of the classroom. It's one of the things that students value most about U of M.

If all this simply sounds like too much work, opportunities for leisure also abound. U of M is situated near a series of lakes – an environment that is perfect for sailing, water-sports, hiking or simply sunbathing.

Outside Those Ivory Walls

UMichigan's reputation is also made by the town in which it is situated. The lively and student-dominated Ann Arbor has become a byword for college party, referred to by students as A2 (as in A squared).

While almost all freshmen live in the on-campus residential dorms (offering a great initial bonding experience), the upperclassmen (sophomores, juniors and seniors) migrate to the many available off-campus apartments.

This off-campus living is unusual in the US and provides students with a great opportunity to experience real-world living while still benefiting from the student lifestyle.

Ann Arbor is a great place to do that in. Equipped with all the coffee shops, restaurants, bars, and general hanging-out spots that a student might need, it saves UMichigan from being just another big school in the middle of nowhere.

And for those who really feel the need for some big-city living, Detroit (home to Eminem and not the most sophisticated place in the world) is just 45 minutes away, while Chicago is four hours by the reliable Amtrak train.

Getting In

AT A GLANCE – Application & Test Options:

– Early Action, Regular Decision

– ACT/SAT, with Writing/essay required

If the University of Michigan sounds like the place for you, then make sure you get all your application material together in good time. This is one of the few colleges that operates on a rolling admissions process (first come, first served) and applying early helps your chances significantly (as does your parents moving to Michigan).

U of M remains a highly competitive school (especially for out-of-state students, for whom there's a 24% acceptance rate) so make sure your SAT or ACT scores and application essays are up to scratch (but SAT Subject tests are not required).

Money Matters

Just don't expect any help in the way of financial aid (no provision is really made for the international crew).

Famous Grads

James Earl Jones– actor (voice of Darth Vader, among other things)

Iggy Pop– rock singer

Maddona– another rock singer

Gerald Ford-President of the US

David/Scott/Alfred Worden/James Irwin– astronauts on the Apollo 15 all UM space flight to the moon

University of North Carolina

Chapel Hill, North Carolina
www.unc.edu
Undergrads: 18,000
Grads: 11,000

How many North Carolina students does it take to change a light bulb?
Fewer than those evil Duke students.

The North Carolina "triangle" – the three towns of Raleigh, Durham and Chapel Hill – is home to three world-class universities: North Carolina State (in Raleigh), Duke (in Durham) and the University of North Carolina at Chapel Hill (UNC). The three offer different educational opportunities – but while Duke normally steals the spotlight cavorting with the Ivy Leaguers up north, many feel that it is UNC that provides the best education in every area of college life.

Just talk to the students there for a few minutes and it will be immediately apparent that not only are they intelligent, sophisticated and incredibly charming, but they exude a heart-warming contentment and happiness that comes straight from their experience at school. "I only wish it were more than four years," said a tearful senior when asked what his least favourite part of the school might be.

The Campus

UNC's campus is truly lovely, and so is the beloved town of Chapel Hill. Lush, green, tree-filled quads yawn between elegant brick edifices, some of them dating back to the 1700s. UNC is the oldest state university in the country, founded by North Carolina's General Assembly in 1793 on a hill that happened to have a chapel and be roughly in the centre of the state. Students praise the "great campus setup", since the large grounds are bike-friendly and the classroom blocks are close enough together to be manageable.

In the middle of campus is a communal brick courtyard, surrounded by cafes and dining options, with an indented rectangle at the centre known as "the pit", where student organisations set up tables and the "pit preacher" makes his entreaties for passers-by to avoid eternal damnation. On the northern edge of campus is Franklin St, Chapel Hill's main drag, with loads of great restaurants and bars which are always full of students.

Campus facilities are fantastic; the libraries, for example, not only hold close to six million volumes, but are equipped with state-of-the-art computer labs and other perks for students – such as free movie rental from a huge selection of films. As with many universities, there is non-stop construction work to create new improvements and to remodel and renew outdated buildings. Students complain about the ongoing building works, but admit that end results are almost always worth it.

Accommodation

Most students live on campus, especially freshmen and sophomores, while many move out into various apartments or student housing in town by their junior year. Dorms have a reputation for grottiness, but are improving (only a tiny number suffer without central air conditioning nowadays...). There are great "themed housing" options – dorms based around sustainability, diversity, being substance-free or foreign languages, for example, all of which are popular.

The UNC Student

The student body is a wonderful thing, frequently cited as the best thing about UNC. Everyone is laid back enough to enjoy themselves but still capable of focusing on their studies and other things that are important to them. UNC kids are an extremely happy bunch – and it's not just the *Princeton Review* that says so.

Don't be daunted by the statistic that over 80% of the students are state residents – diversity is excellent, and students love the fact that they interact regularly with "people from every walk of life". UNC's size works really well with its rich community spirit – the school is apparently "big enough so that you meet new people all the time, but enough of a tight community that you can have a lot of close friends", all in a "bright, active" atmosphere which comes just as much from student attitudes as it does from the plentitude of extra-curriculars. Thus everyone can find their own niche, but still enjoy a society that is "not dominated by clean-cut cliques." Everyone is united by a sincere passion for their school.

"There are so many talented people", claims a junior, adding pointedly, "but everyone is relaxed and not cut-throat at all...unlike Duke". It seems that students have managed to purge themselves of any hatred against anyone else in the world and direct it all at their rivals eight miles away.

Talking of rivalry, sports are huge deal, especially when it's basketball, and especially when it's against Duke, NC State or the University of Virginia. Such events usually involve mutual vandalism, while victories are marked by mass gatherings and bonfires on Franklin St, which the police obligingly close to traffic despite it being Chapel Hill's main road. For the tiny minority not interested in UNC sports, this can be tough to cope with.

Hitting the Books

Teaching here is "intense, but great". Some students report "the most fantastic professors ever", while others give a more nuanced view, but it is certain that the UNC faculty has leaders in many fields, almost all of them with first-hand experience of their subject in the real world which students benefit from drawing on. Many of the best professors teach lower-level courses, not hidden away for the top students and grads like they are at most schools.

Overall, there is a "good balance" academically. Classes challenge you, but don't leave you gasping and clueless. Student attitudes to work cover the spectrum – some never leave their books, others never touch them – but most are a happy medium when it comes to tackling their studies. Science, religious studies, international affairs and pre-med courses are cited as among the best here.

Social Life

You will definitely get more out of your education at UNC if you are a proactive kind of person – there is so much here but it needs to be taken advantage of. UNC truly does have one of the most vibrant campus lives on offer; students frequently acclaim the boundless possibilities and insist that anything you want to do can be done – if a group doesn't already exist for it then it's easy to start one and find others who share your interests.

Student organisations are officially run by the Carolina Union, and receive funding from the student government from the smallish activity fee which they exact from each student. In return for this, the Union and its organisations provide the students with loads of fun events and give-aways (free food!), which creates a buzzing atmosphere of activity. At "fall fest" – a huge outdoor event on the Sunday before classes begin in August – all the organisations set up booths and advertise what they do.

As well as the awesome events hosted regularly on campus, students can attend free film showings (often before their release in cinemas), concerts (both from the hundreds of UNC bands and from outside touring groups), theatre (when we visited, the world-famous Bolshoi Ballet from Moscow was performing), and comedy.

Of course, UNC is also host to loads of typical student parties, both on and off campus, where student can let loose after...so much letting loose. Parties are hosted by every organisation, dorm block, or academic department. Cross-cultural note: Carolina (both North and South) students have, for generations, danced an easy, elegant, sliding dance innocently called 'The Shag' – just a heads up for British students approached for the first time and asked if they can shag....

Many of the big parties are run by the fraternities and sororities, which have a surprising impact on university life considering that only 18% of students are members. Like most campuses nationally (and probably internationally), UNC has not been immune to the well-publicised problems of sexual abuse and binge drinking. However, Chapel Hill is in the forefront of universities addressing issues of sexual assault, and students point to the "fantastic student-driven work to combat it".

Outside Those Ivory Walls

Chapel Hill did not exist until UNC was founded. It is the ultimate college town, and one of the coolest too. Whether you're hanging out at the great student haunts on Franklin St or heading down to the adjacent village of Carrboro, famous for its bohemian alternative culture, the town compliments the university perfectly.

Getting In

AT A GLANCE – Application & Test Options:

– Early Action, Regular Decision

– ACT/SAT required

UNC is rightly a very popular university, and not quite as big as other state schools, so admission is competitive (only about 20% of non-state applicants are currently getting in). All the academic aspects of your application are important, including test scores, recommendations, essays, class rankings and the rigour of your previous school's teaching. Interviews are not necessary.

Money Matters

Like many public universities, fees for international applicants are a lot harsher than for state residents. Still, UNC is considered very good value for money by US standards, with a limited number of scholarships available. Need-based scholarships are awarded based solely on the merits of your basic application– you don't have to submit more forms or sit an extra test or interview for those. You do have to fill out separate applications for merit-based scholarships, though – particularly the highly prestigious Morehead-Cain Scholarship and the Robertson Scholarship. Students point out that scholars regularly turn down places at Harvard, Yale, Princeton etc to come to Chapel Hill.

Famous Grads

Michael Jordan – basketball player

Thomas Wolfe – writer

Sallie Krawcheck – on Forbes' list of Most Powerful Women

David Gardner – founder of the Motley Fools

University of Pennsylvania (and Wharton)

Philadelphia, Pennsylvania
www.upenn.edu
Undergrads: 10,500
Grads: 10,900

How many students does it take to change a light bulb at Penn?

Only one – but he gets six credits for it.

Benjamin Franklin was not a man who believed in the merits of relaxation. Not content with setting up fire services, acting as international diplomat or inventing the stove, the lightning rod and bifocal spectacles, he also found the time to found one of the top academic institutions in America – the University of Pennsylvania.

Today, this thriving campus set in lively Philadelphia continues to churn out students in the Franklin mould – practical, business-minded and dedicated to public service. But UPenn has come a long way from those early Quaker roots.

If you're looking for an Ivy League education with a busy social life (that ever-elusive combination), then this could well be the place for you. And if you aim at being the next fat cat on Wall Street, then the excellent undergraduate business programme at the Wharton School should be top of your list.

The Campus

Founded in 1740, UPenn likes to lay claim to its status as the oldest university (but not college) in the United States. Situated right next to the Schuylkill River, a great location for the crew teams, the 260-acre campus provides a nice, safe, green respite from the bustling chaos of downtown Philadelphia (a mere 5 minutes away by bus).

The campus plays host to four undergraduate schools – the College of Arts and Sciences (aka "the College" – your most likely destination), the Wharton School (money, money, money), Penn Engineering (for those keen in following the founder's footsteps) and the School of Nursing (one of the best in America). Students from all of these schools live and work together on one campus along with thousands of graduate students.

Penn is a big school but the layout of the campus is easily negotiable and makes it feel smaller than it really is. Despite the age of the institution, the campus architecture does not come close to emulating the splendours of Oxford or Cambridge. Attractive stone buildings are positioned next to modern eyesores – chief among them the hideous, but extremely good, library.

Not all the architecture is a disaster, however, and Penn students take pride in the fact that College Hall provided Charles Addams (alumnus) with his inspiration for the Gothic and ghastly Addams family mansion.

Others love the fact that, despite the proximity of the big city, Penn has really achieved a rural campus feel. Whether you are sunbathing next to the statue of Ben Franklin on the Green or throwing a frisbee in the attractive Quadrangle, there is a real sense of a cohesive campus.

Accommodation

This sense of community certainly helps when nervous freshmen arrive at Penn as one among several thousand. Although it is easy to feel lost in the crowd, the freshmen residential halls swiftly dispel this feeling.

Most Penn freshmen ask to live in the Quad – a good idea as it houses most of the youngest class and a great many parties!

Sophomores, juniors and seniors have the option of living in less attractive high-rise residential buildings, their fraternities or off campus. Many choose the latter – congregating in local University City and colonizing areas around the bohemian South Street.

The Penn Student

Penn's mascot is the Quaker – a strange symbol for rousing school spirit at football games, but an appropriate representation of the school's tolerant and laid-back attitude.

Partly because of its large size and partly because of the attempts of the university administration to encourage diversity (it was the first Ivy League to have a female President), Penn is a school that offers something for everyone.

Myriad backgrounds and cultural perspectives very much define Penn these days and make it a lively and tolerant place where everyone can find a spot. And, with 10% of the student body international, even the Brit can't feel too lost.

This diversity is not to say that Penn does not suffer from the stereotypes that sadly still define many academically elite institutions. 15% of the student body are legacy kids – some of whom can probably trace their ancestry back to the days of good ole Ben.

The average Brit may not grumble about the presence of beautifully turned out, impeccably socially aware and filthily rich individuals who haunt Penn's grounds, dominate its social scene (and are only too keen to bond with Brits on the off-chance they might know Prince William).

But for others, the appearance of so many wealthy NY socialites can be a bit of a turn-off. Luckily the size of the Penn student body is such that it is easy to lose those with whom you do not see eye to eye. But, if you hold strong communist ideals or believe that fashion trends are the manifestation of the devil, then Penn may not be the place for you (turn to the Oberlin section now!)

Penn's student body is also ambitious and practically minded. While intellectualism undoubtedly has its place on campus, most people have more interest in business matters – a trend undoubtedly enhanced by the presence of the Wharton School kids.

Students here are concerned with money and many of them, from both Wharton and the College of Arts & Sciences, end up going through i-banking recruiting at the end of their senior year. This ambition leads to a strong work ethic and an intense curiosity about how the world actually works.

Penn students are constantly getting involved in different activities, taking on different internships and asking questions to which they expect concrete answers. The work ethic and sense of activity infect the whole campus and whenever something is going on (which is all the time), you can expect it to be of the highest quality. Publications, like The Daily Pennsylvanian, theatre groups and social service programmes are all prominent parts of many students' daily lives.

This work ethic should not suggest that students do not know how to have fun. Penn takes pride in its social success and offers a welcoming environment to new students. While competition may run high for the prized A in class, outside the academic sphere, people are relaxed and proud of their friendly community.

Sports matches against their long-term rival, Princeton, draw huge crowds as do such quirky traditions as Hey Day when, at the end of the school year, juniors greet their senior year by donning straw hats and canes and marching through campus (possibly the most British experience you will see in a US university).

Hitting the Books

UPenn students may love a good party, but they are also known for working as hard as they play. And in a place renowned for its academic excellence and friendly faculty, such a decision is fairly easily made. Our friend Ben was a self-taught man who believed in the merits of a thorough liberal arts education as well as the ability to apply what one learns in college in the real world. Over the centuries, Penn academia has evolved to honour both of these goals through an extensive curriculum and a plethora of classes.

Many of the stars of the academic solar system find a home at Penn and undergraduates may well find themselves in a class taught by the professor who really 'wrote the book' on the subject. Faculty members are required to teach undergrads and many of them willingly embrace the task.

But while the faculty-student ratio is extremely low (at 6:1), many students complain they find themselves in huge introductory classes where they are just one in a sea of faces.

This may be true, but there is a simple solution to the problem. Americans are by nature a little more forward (some might say pushy) than their reserved British contemporaries. If you want to talk to your professor on a one-to-one basis, you have to make the effort to seek him out, go to his office hours and prepare yourself for an intelligent conversation. If you do this, you will soon find that your working relationship goes from one among many, to an actual intellectual bond.

It is true that many of the professors at Penn are also working on their own research and that graduate students take up much of their time. But the sheer numbers of classes offered to the undergrads, and the flexibility they enjoy in selecting them, means you can really shop around until you find the faculty member who most interests you.

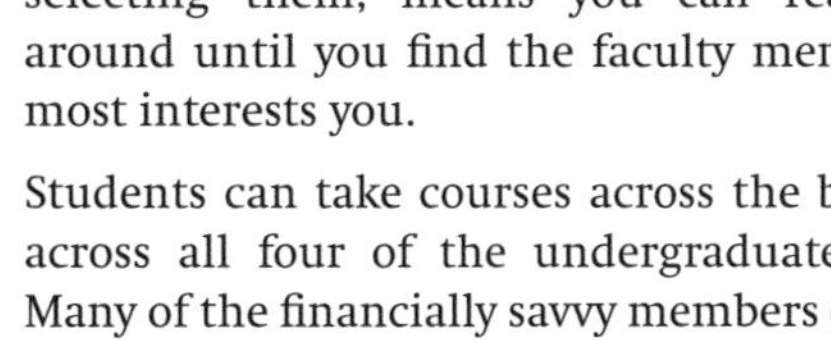

Students can take courses across the board and across all four of the undergraduate schools. Many of the financially savvy members of the college spend a lot of time taking economics classes at Wharton, while Whartonites find themselves heading back to the College for a dose of something that is not numerically inclined.

In fact, in its effort to make sure its students are well-rounded members of society, Penn insists on various core requirements. Students in the College will find themselves embracing the traditional tenets of the liberal arts education – including a stint of a foreign language, some maths and the humanities. Wharton undergrads who already find themselves taking finance, accounting, management and marketing, also face various liberal arts requirements as do their nursing contemporaries.

This mixing up of different interests and academic strengths makes for a much more interesting classroom situation. And the fact that you don't have to choose your major until the end of your sophomore year means that if one of these required courses really grabs you – you may go from being an intellectual history buff to a Wall Street wannabe after all.

The one serious complaint many undergrads have about the Penn system is its lack of advising capability. Because majors are decided upon so late, students are not assigned departmental advisors until well into their college careers.

As a result students sometimes find they make the wrong choices without anyone saying anything about it. Some like the freedom this limited support network provides but others, especially those who would rather be lazy than put in the groundwork to make a successful schedule, find it difficult.

On the whole, however, Penn students find their academic environment stimulating and absorbing – a fact that sees many of them go onto grad schools following their BA. Those of you heading to the Wharton School should also be alerted that – should you turn out to be the fiscal whiz of your class – you may have the chance to get a Masters in Business with only one additional year of studying.

This is a great and prestigious opportunity and if you're leading the pack in accountancy or economics, make sure you make enquiries about this possibility. Also, bear in mind that a degree from Wharton is the way to go if you know from the start that you want to concentrate on economics, and don't want to have to fight your way into business school at a later date.

Social Life

If you asked the average Penn student what aspect of their school they are most proud of, they would probably give you some pretentious answer about Ben Franklin's legacy or the human capital available to them on campus.

Secretly, however, they're thinking about how their party scene beats that of their Ivy League rivals into a small hole in the ground. Jealous Harvard and Dartmouth students might grouch about how Penn students never actually have to do any real work, but when it comes to college parties as the movies portray them, they are forced to admit that Penn stands alone.

Much of this social scene takes place on campus, although there are numerous options available in town for those who prefer upmarket restaurants and elite clubs. Penn itself hosts a number of fraternities and sororities whose parties attract people from all over campus.

While joining these Greek institutions may seem a bridge too far to those British students who associate fraternities with cults and initiation with Animal House madness, these parties are normally open to all and do not necessarily require that you sign your life away to Delta Kappa Gamma.

Unsurprisingly, these events attract huge numbers of socially eager freshmen – excited by the prospect of free beer (Quaker restrictions do not make evading the drinking age law in Philadelphia any easier) and drunken interaction with the opposite sex.

For those looking for a quieter life, the rowdiness of the frats is easily avoidable and the pattern of the next three years on campus settles into a quieter routine of dinner parties and smaller get-togethers. With such a large number of students around (even if we don't count the graduates), the chances are high that you'll find people to suit your pace of social life – even if said social life simply consists of sipping English Breakfast and watching the world go by.

Outside Those Ivory Walls

Nowadays the 'Streets of Philadelphia' look a great deal more cheerful than they did when Bruce Springsteen first moaned about them. This old Quaker city may have been through a rough time in the past, but it is now as vibrant and as safe as any of its East Coast contemporaries and is a great place to go to school. It also has an international airport – perfect for flights back home (or to the Caribbean if you need a little weekend break when the snow has set in for the fifth time that week).

Students at Penn can never complain about being bored. Not only do they enjoy a fun campus social life, they are also a mere 15 minutes on foot away from all the delights of the big city. Philadelphia offers all the sport, arts, culture, nightlife and shopping that any undergrad could require and the majority of students take advantage of this. Penn gives you the chance of experiencing life in a thriving city, without the manic pace of New York or the grittiness of New Haven.

For those who seek a more outdoorsy experience, the vast Philadelphia park system provides ample room for rural pursuits, while the proximity of Penn to the station gives you the option of travelling to all the hiking grounds and leisure opportunities you could desire.

For the city-minded, Amtrak is available to take you up to NY and Boston or down to Washington DC. And for those who love to shop, one of the biggest malls in the States is only a half-hour drive away. Philadelphia is one of the best-connected cities around, and it would be a short-sighted student who couldn't find anything to do there.

Getting In

AT A GLANCE – Application & Test Options:

– Early Decision, Regular Decision

– ACT/SAT required

– SAT Subject tests optional

Getting into Penn is no easy feat. Although a few years ago the application numbers for the college dipped, recent statistics have shown it is now as competitive as ever. The school may be a large one, with proportionately more places, but it also draws proportionally more students.

The admissions office estimate they accept around 9.5% of applicants. Unfortunately for international students, this number is somewhat lower. Many foreigners apply to Penn and it is estimated that only around 13% get in. As with all these traditionalist schools, it helps if Mummy or Daddy sported the Penn colours back in their day.

Penn accepts the Common Application; additional admissions requirements include an SAT or ACT test score (and two optional SAT Subject tests if you want to impress them), plus a strong personal essay designed to reveal your true self to those making the decision. This is really the chance to show yourself off on paper – so don't let your British reticence hold you back; American students will be only too proud to boast about their Junior Nobel Prize or seven Olympic medals. A non-mandatory interview is also available and is a great chance to both sell yourself and find out more about whether Penn really is right for you.

Money Matters

While some financial aid is available, international students do not share the need-blind status of their American contemporaries and any requests need to be made well in advance and may easily not be granted.

Famous Grads

Donald Trump – Bouffant blond President of the US

Charles Addams – a little twisted but very cool

Warren Buffet – he may have quit after two years but he's still doing pretty well

University of South Florida

Tampa, Florida
www.usf.edu
Undergrads: 36,200
Grads: 9,900

How many USF students does it take to change a light bulb?

Surely someone at this massive school will do it before everyone else gets home from the beach.

The Campus

To be 100% honest, USF's campus is beautiful. During orientation, this reviewer was, understandably, in a group of a lot of Americans. They were mesmerized when they were being shown around the campus and told how old the buildings were. "That one is 40 years old! This one is 50!!" This reviewer couldn't help thinking that his own mother was older than both of those buildings...

From the moment you arrive at USF, your agility will start to improve. This is due to the ridiculous number of skateboarders, or long borders as they are called here, who think they can fit through any conceivable space possible.

Also to be dodged are the preachers who, at the moment, seem to pop up everywhere blasting their beliefs at you whilst you are simply trying to get to class, and there is always one person who will take the bait and will say something stupid to these religious psychopaths and spark an argument.

That said, those are about the only things that might irk you about the campus. The buildings are wonderful, the people too. Food is available in abundance, be it at Subway or a personal favourite, a nice Chinese called Panda Express. The gym is out of this world, and it is paid for by your tuition – there are no extra fees.

Accommodation

As a "freshman" – a first year student – you'll be required to live on campus. This has all the obvious benefits that you can imagine. It allows you to meet a lot of people, get used to the layout of campus and be close to the dining halls.

You might consider Holly your first year if you want your own room and are nervous about putting your roommate selection in the hands of fate...probably your only option for a single room unless you want to live in Juniper, which is on the boring side of campus. Living at JP would be like living in the Lake District; it's nice but there isn't a whole lot going on. If you aren't the party type, Holly is again recommended – where you will rarely be woken up by loud noises.

If you are looking for a livelier dorm life, head for Beta. All the "cool kids" live in Beta. However, the Andros community is being knocked down and rebuilt – and thank goodness for that – with the proposed plans for the new area looking very impressive, so definitely to be considered. As a side note, there are plans for a new supermarket to be built close to the new community, if that tilts you in one way or another.

As for off-campus housing, your options are vast. This reviewer can personally recommend The Venue. It is situated on a road called "42nd street" on which there are many more options to choose from, including a new site which is set to be completed by August 2016. At this point in time, for one reason or another, USF's on-campus ousing is over populated, so a move off campus is strongly advised as soon as possible. The Venue also holds pool parties which are mental, but that's partly because they are in December and it is still baking hot out.

The Trojan

The population of USF is diverse, to put it mildly. There are people from all over the world, which only makes it easier to settle in. Some of the nicest people you'll meet come from the strong Caribbean contingent, a group you'll want to become good friends with because they are genuinely nice people and they have houses in the Caribbean...

Hitting the Books

If you are reading this and are sure that you are going to end up at an American university, be it USF or any other, take this advice. Do not buy all of your textbooks for your first year from the university bookstore; it will cost you a fortune and there are very accessible alternatives. If this reviewer had known this, he wouldn't have spent over $300 on textbooks for his first semester, a charge that saw his father's credit card frozen because of suspicious activity, even though the company knew he was in Florida.

Something you'll appreciate about the American university system is the range of classes that you can take. As an example, this reviewer came in as a history major, meaning seeking a degree in history. His first semester schedule included two history classes, astronomy, maths and a class called university experience. Second semester: economics, another maths class, another history class, anthropology and a music class, all the meantime still being a history major. In this same example, the reviewer's brother attends UCL in London and is doing Law, meaning he has had four tedious years of simply taking law classes. The American education gives you a break from that and puts the power in your hands.

The most popular majors at USF are either health related or engineering, but the possibilities are endless.

Social Life

There is a lot to do around USF in terms of nightlife, but the fact that the drinking age is 21 instead of 18 really is a pain. Most people's first two years are frequently spent at house parties and Ybor City. Ybor is the Latin quarter (about a 15 minute drive down the motorway or interstate) where all the nightclubs are; it's fun but also very dodgy.

In terms of sports, the Americans are far more inventive in their pre games than Englishmen. We are more than content going to the pub and having a few pints before a game. That simply is not enough for the Americans. Even though USF's American football team has not been great in recent years, the pre-games are wild. 'Tailgating' as it is termed here is a mixture of beer pong, corn hole and shotgunning beers, all things you might be unaware of before you arrive, but will have to adapt to.

If you want to play sport yourself, you might not make the varsity team, but you can definitely play on one of the club teams, which include football (British), rugby, cricket, surfing, lacrosse and tennis teams, for both males and females. USF's most illustrious club team (and we are not joking here), is their Quidditch team who have competed nationally in the past. Heads up: the first time you say "soccer" instead of "football" is not an easy experience to go through.

Outside Those Ivory Walls

Tampa has a great nightlife and the place to be is South Howard, aka Soho. The nickname alone makes you like it since it reminds you of Soho in London. Getting to the best spots will require a car or taxi but many students have cars and Uber is never far, so that probably won't be much of a problem.

The beaches here are something to behold; the two that everyone goes to are Clearwater and St. Pete, both of which are about an hour's drive, but they are well worth it. The only bad part is that it has to be over 25 degrees for a Floridian to even consider going to one. You may think this is an exaggeration but unfortunately it is not. You won't believe the number of days you will go out onto your dorm balcony and think "wow it's hot," only for one of your roommates to go "it's a bit nippy out here."

Believe me, as a Brit, you will consider the temperature here to be pretty intense. As excited as you will undoubtedly be when you first step off the plane, all this excitement might temporarily drain away when you are slammed by the wave of heat, a heat that will follow you throughout your USF career.

Much farther off campus, USF has strong connections with some British universities, such as Exeter. Every year, British students come from these places for their year abroad, and every year when informally asked if they would have preferred to come here for their entire college career, instead of just one year, the answer so far has been a unanimous "yes".

Getting In

AT A GLANCE – Application & Test Options:

– Regular Decision

– ACT/SAT required

To tell the truth, American universities love having foreign students. And it's not just because they can charge them higher rates for tuition. America has two rates for tuition, in-state and out-of-state. For example, a Floridian would pay in-state tuition to come to USF, whilst someone from California, or England, would pay out-of-state. In-state is considerably cheaper, hence universities do love out-of-state (and out-of-country) students.

Money Matters

This means that it is not overly difficult for an British applicant to get into USF, and there are scholarships available. You may well be offered one if you do well on your SATs, so do take them very seriously. The money that you save through a scholarship could effectively pay for flights and accommodation.

Also, keep in mind that A-levels can count toward college credit. For example, if you get as much as 18 credit hours for your A-levels, that would count for a whole semester, meaning your course here would only be 3.5 years, rather than 4. Although close students of the above review will be asking themselves: why would I want to leave early?

University of Southern California

Los Angeles, California
www.usc.edu
Undergrads: 18,000
Grads: 22,000

How many USC students does it take to change a light bulb?

None – they don't bother, it'll just get broken again at the next party.

The University of Southern California is where you go if you want to live like in the movies. Life here is a realisation of all the classic stereotypes of Los Angeles college life – the rich white kids, the parties, the fraternities, the drugs, the lack of work, the sun, the beaches and the beautiful girls.

The most centrally located of all the LA universities, USC enjoys a strong reputation, a huge and well-endowed campus, and one of the most dazzling (or terrifying, depending which way you see it) party scenes in America. If you want to learn something at college, it is certainly possible here, but it's not the main reason the kids apply here in droves.

The Campus

On 300 acres not far south of downtown LA, the campus at USC is little short of superb. With some incredible facilities, beautiful and well-spaced buildings and over 40 fountains, USC is so aesthetically enticing that hundreds of high-profile films, TV shows and adverts are filmed here every year.

Did you admire Harvard in Legally Blonde? Did you think Berkeley looked good in The Graduate? What about the school in Forrest Gump? All were actually filmed at USC, as were parts of The OC, the West Wing and Jeopardy.

The university benefits from huge endowments from incredibly wealthy alumni. George Lucas himself donated a fantastical 175 million dollars to the film school, one of five nine-figure sums USC has accepted. The huge wealth of the college has kept the campus in perfect condition, as well as providing for the most up-to-date learning facilities imaginable.

The 22 libraries contain about 10 million publications (over half on microfilm) including world famous collections for studying natural sciences, philosophy, international relations, Korea and Latin America. Even more noteworthy are the world's largest collection of testimonies of Holocaust-survivors (over 50 thousand), and the legendary studio archives of Warner Bros, also the largest of its kind.

The main downside of the campus is its location, bang in the centre of the sprawling urban mess of Los Angeles, the immediate surrounding district is not pleasant; some students use the term "ghetto" to describe it. The huge number of community services schemes engineered by the university involving about half the student body have helped to improve matters though.

And on the brighter side, short journeys (by car – don't count on the public transport) will take students to all corners of the city, where every kind of activity can be found.

Accommodation

Finding housing will be one of your main challenges when you arrive at USC. Campus accommodation is generally unloved by the students, but there is fierce competition to get a place in official university dorms. There are ongoing discussions about new construction to remedy this. Almost all freshmen live on campus, but the numbers drop off in the later years.

The Trojan

Students at USC – or the University of Spoiled Children as it is called by its rivals at the state-funded UCLA – are harder to categorise than you might think. Undoubtedly, a huge proportion of the student body (which itself is enormous) come from privileged backgrounds, live in California and are WASPs.

But if you look a little harder, you find that USC has the largest number of international students (almost 11,000 undergrad and grad students – over 20%) of any US university, and that hefty chunks of the student body are at the school on scholarships and come from financial backgrounds that don't involve sports cars.

Known as Trojans after the school's Trojan warrior mascot, USC students are a rapidly evolving species. With unprecedented applicant-pool sizes in recent years, the school has become more diverse, work conscious and liberal. Trojans are still united by their fierce pride in their school, but the greater variety of student backgrounds and personalities is a welcome one.

All this said, the majority at USC can still be said to conform to the Orange County spoiled child mold. Parties continue to dominate work. Greek life is important; with only 20% of students a member of a fraternity or sorority, the Greeks hold disproportionate influence over the school atmosphere – and an even greater monopoly of the good parties.

The classic Trojan is competitive – especially when UCLA is involved (sports matches are often marked by inter-campus vandalism) – but also laid-back and traditionally conservative. The school was the only one in the State that Republican Governor/movie star Ronald Reagan could visit without protection in the 70s and 80s, and indeed Republican Governor/movie star Arnold Schwarzenegger gave the graduation address in 2009.

A large number of USC alumni were in the Nixon government when it fell from grace in 1974. Yet nowadays the official USC Democrats outnumber the USC Republicans, and the majority voted for Obama.

Students often look at USC, and rightly so, as a "big club" which gives them an advantage when entering the workplace. The networking opportunities are phenomenal. Big-shot USC alumni who run major businesses like to hire fellow ex-Trojans, and ex-Trojans in turn are much more likely to secure a place for their own children at USC.

Hitting the Books

The whole spectrum is possible here. Students of certain subjects will find their work cut out; others will coast to earn their degree. Students give mixed opinions on professors, class sizes, work load and work ethic.

What is for sure is that certain schools such as engineering, architecture, business and journalism are consistently ranked among the top 20 in the country, and that students can achieve much in almost every field of the broad range available if they are willing to ignore the laid back attitude of their peers and put in the work required.

And that's just what's happening. The growth of the applicant pool has meant even more selective admissions and an ever more-work-conscious student body. This in turn has begun to attract even more distinguished professors. USC's academics seem to be on an upward curve, and they continue to base their teaching on "integrating liberal and professional education". Several professors among the giant faculty have gained international awards and recognition, including one Nobel Laureate chemist.

If you want to be a big shot in the film-industry, you'd be hard-pressed to find a better option than USC. The School of Cinematic Arts is generally recognised as among the best institutes for film studies in the world; it is certainly the oldest and largest. Originally only for the best among industry professionals, the film school finally opened its doors to the whole university in 1998, and now undergraduates can mix with the folks who run nearby Hollywood. George Lucas graduated from here, and the likes of Stephen Spielberg are regulars.

Social Life

Few dispute USC's status as a party school, and for anyone looking for the classic American Pie-type extravaganzas, you won't get much closer than here. The fraternities are especially debauched, and serious substance abuse can be an issue. Nevertheless, USC parties are the envy of other colleges, even if they often occur mid-week due to the local students' tendency to go home on the weekends.

For those who prefer a less hectic approach to socialising, it's easy to get caught up in the other activities on offer. There are over 600 student organizations, fantastic musical and theatrical productions and a generally vibrant campus life, driven by the infectious school spirit.

Outside Those Ivory Walls

USC benefits – or not, depending how you look at it – from its relative proximity to all the major attractions of Los Angeles, a city which is not particularly attractive but is exciting and extreme enough to make for a thrilling student experience. There are world-famous beaches, ideal for anything from sun-bathing to surfing, and good connections to other major cities.

The local public transport takes a lot of getting used to and is normally ignored by the students in favour of cars; a much more convenient method for crossing the second largest urban sprawl in the America.

Getting In

AT A GLANCE – Application & Test Options:

– Regular Decision

– ACT/SAT required, Writing/essay is optional

Very, very tough. The application success rate for 2016 was 17%. International students can take heart that there is a comparatively high proportion of overseas applications accepted each year but should be warned that factors such as having alumni parents can be a big advantage for locals.

A rigorous high-school academic background is very important, but the college also states that they "are particularly interested in learning about our applicants' activities outside of the classroom". Interviews are optional, and can often be conducted abroad by alumni.

Money Matters

Some people mistakenly believe that USC is part of the UC chain of California public schools, but it is in fact a private school. Overseas applicants do not qualify for needs-based aid to help with the high fees, but thanks to the school's enormous endowment, there are ever more scholarships on offer. Definitely worth aiming for one of these.

Famous Grads

John Wayne, Will Ferrell, O.J.Simpson – three of the many famous actors

George Lucas – famous director (Star Wars)

Neil Armstrong – took one small step for himself, and one giant leap for mankind

University of Texas

Austin, Texas
www.utexas.com
Undergrads: 39,000
Grads: 11,000

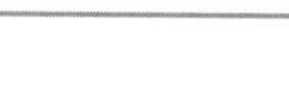

How many UT students does it take to change a light bulb?

7 – one to change it, three to choose a local rock band to play for the occasion, and three to argue about the best venue for the gig.

Like the state it represents, the University of Texas does nothing by halves. The second biggest college in the country, with a huge, ultra-liberal campus in a huge, ultra-conservative state, this public Ivy is extraordinarily capable in its academics, insanely ambitious with its party life, massively arty, massively sporty and overwhelmingly diverse.

The biggest draw is what students call "the vibe", which resonates from the incredible music scene and trendy bars of Austin as much as from the frantic or chilled activities and the wild events hosted or created by the university. If you think you have a good idea of what Texas life is like, you'll think you've been taken to the wrong airport – UT is as far removed from the Texas stereotype as it's possible to be without being in San Francisco.

So leave your cowboy hat at home and trade your banjo for an electric guitar, because this is going to be something different.

The Campus

UT sits on a large crowded campus just north of the centre of Austin. Students give almost unanimously favourable reviews, though as one student put it, the college is "lacking a bit of aesthetic quality". The buildings are packed close, while the trees and fountains struggle to lighten the atmosphere enough to instill some collegiate qualities.

There is a pleasant communal space in front of the main building (where you'll find the iconic tower from which UT student Charles Whitman massacred fourteen people with a sniper rifle in the '60s), with views over the State Capitol and downtown. There are various student centres, libraries (among the best in the country) and sports facilities (also excellent).

Parking is tricky on campus, so many students use bikes and public transport. Food is fair, with several on-campus chain restaurants as well as a fine range of dining and drinking options on the opposite side of Guadalupe Street, the western perimeter of campus.

Accommodation

Campus dorms are mediocre and overpriced according to students, with most opting for one of the student districts around the city. "West Campus" and "North Campus" are especially popular.

The Longhorn

Although about 80% of UT's student body consists of Texas locals, this statistic masks a surprising variety, and is rendered moot anyway when one remembers that for a university of UT's size (fifth largest enrollment in the country), 20% out-of-statesmen and foreigners translates to several thousand people. Students cover a wide range of demographics and personality-types, with diversity covering not just skin colour but areas like disability and sexual orientation as well. Integration is a piece of cake here, and there is guaranteed to be niche for everyone no matter how far from the mainstream they may be. Agoraphobics excepted.

There is a thriving international community, and the highly recommended Partnership for the Advancement of Language Studies (PALS) can provide good interaction with locals. Also lively is the Greek life which is easy to get involved with and even easier to stay away from. The proximity to the State Capitol, mere blocks away, means a politicised campus with a strong progressive trend: activism, especially environmental, is big here, and a certain degree of hippy spirit pervades the student body.

Hitting the Books

Students describe UT as "fairly typical" for a big school in terms of its academic demands. As ever, work load, class size and quality of professor will differ for each individual and each department, but in general UT has a phenomenal reputation. It may feel like a laid back and fun university, but there is a "serious amount of quality work" that goes on here.

As one of the biggest and best institutions in the country, UT attracts high-flying teachers and guest speakers, often leaders in their fields, and sometimes distinguished by important awards. Despite this, students report that there is no "bar" between the eminent professors and their pupils; even in the huge lecture halls the profs do a good job at making everyone feel included. Good one-to-one contact with teaching assistants helps with this.

Some students warn that UT, like many big state universities, is not always helpful in terms of hand-holding. The sheer quantity and complexity of the university machinery can be daunting and there is no way that the administration can guarantee everyone a smooth ride, either academically or socially. "If you aren't 'old' enough to take care of your own college stuff, then I wouldn't go here," advises one freshman.

Students interested in communications and Latin-American studies will be hard pressed to find a better place to study. Many graduate programs are also very strong, and the education and law schools are among the best in the country.

Social Life

The great thing about UT is that there is so much on offer. Campus life is incredibly vibrant, buzzing with student organizations (over 1000!), outreach programs, or media opportunities (several newspapers, and fantastic TV and radio stations for which any student can film/DJ regardless of previous experience). Campus events thrown by different organisations or departments are great fun and cover an unbelievable range, but are generally slightly lower key than the notorious house parties.

Playboy recently rated UT as the number two party school in the US (it's normally in the top five of this much-coveted ranking, although it dropped to – shock! horror! – number eight a few years ago). Aided by the opportunities available in Austin itself, and by an understanding police force, there are wild festivities on hand every night of the week for those who want them, and on big occasions like public holidays or one of Austin's many music festivals, the revelry can blow your mind. All this is of course entirely optional, and those with more modest tendencies will find ample social activities available to them too.

Sports are big here, and students confirm that they "live up to their reputation." The Division One varsity teams are ranked fifth in the nation, and the awesome facilities for all major sports reflect this. Football and baseball are biggest, but the swimming team is also proto-Olympic standard.

Outside Those Ivory Walls

Austin basks in the middle of the Texas desert like an oasis of hipness in a wasteland of square traditional life. Most famous for its music scene, the self-proclaimed "Capital of Live Music" is a fantastically fun city to live in, exploding with spontaneity and creative passions. Despite at least five universities, Austin is not really a college town, just a great town to live for college students.

The politics, the businesses (Apple has headquarters here, for example) and the world-famous music all make Austin very much a thriving city in its own right. Public transport is, unusually for America, cheap, easy and rapid, and the city is also cycle friendly.

Getting In

AT A GLANCE – Application & Test Options:

– Regular Decision

– ACT/SAT required

Priority is given to Texas students, and until very recently the university guaranteed spaces to the top 10% of every high school class in the state. This makes competition for international places very competitive, and excellent applications are required. It's definitely worth a try though, since in a place this size there are a still a considerable number of places open, and the university is looking to increase its out of state intake.

Money Matters

UT is rated one of the best value for money schools in the country, and by American standards it certainly is a bargain. If you live in Texas for a year prior to application, moreover, the fees become very reasonable indeed.

With one of the largest endowments across public universities in the country, UT provides plenty of financial aid, but sadly if you are neither a citizen nor a resident of the US, very little is available to you. Check with your first choice college or department to see if they have any department-specific financial aid available to international students.

Famous Grads

Laura, Jenna and Jeb Bush – wife, daughter and brother of the 43rd President

Janis Joplin – legendary blues and rock n roll singer.

J.M.Coetzee – postmodern author and Nobel Laureate

University of Vermont

Burlington, Vermont
www.uvm.edu
Undergrads: 10,000
Grads: 1,500

How many UVM students does it take to change a light bulb?

Eighteen: Fifteen to form a long distance trekking team to hike through the mountains to the nearest shop selling light bulbs, one to snowboard back with it, one to compose a country-and-western ballad about the event, and one to change it.

The biggest university in a tiny state, and one of the oldest universities in the country, the University of Vermont (UVM) is an alternative school for a certain type of alternative. Having said that, the particular niche to which this school appeals actually encompasses a very large number of people, from across the country and indeed the world.

UVM has, true to its liberal nature, often led the way in showing dedication to equality and even-handedness, being generally a champion for minority participation in higher education, and the first university to admit women or African-Americans into its Greek life. Its charter declares that the "rules, regulations, and by-laws shall not tend to give preference to any religious sect or denomination whatsoever," and it is this attitude that permeates the happy, exuberant college life here.

The Campus

The campus is a medium sized affair, with a typically New England Greek/ Romanesque central building combined with outlying groups of horrific 50s concrete. Although the main campus sits slightly apart on a hill above the town of Burlington, which in turn overlooks a huge lake that extends up to the Canadian border, it is only about six blocks to the centre, and preserves a 'townish', collegiate feel.

Burlington itself is the largest town in the state: but then the state in question is Vermont, the 49th largest in the Union by population (only Wyoming has fewer people). Considered by Americans one of the wackiest states, the little "Green Mountain State" combines the culture and intelligence of the North-East with the nature-loving, pioneering spirit of the Appalachians, and Burlington is the perfect ultra-progressive, in-the-wild example of this happy fusion.

Definitely a student town, with at least three other universities besides UVM, this beautifully situated, peaceful, attractive little settlement has got itself situated firmly on the tourist route through New England; a testimony to its charms. For those to whom such a location, with breathtaking mountain scenery and wildly-wooded countryside appeals, this is a school worth serious consideration.

For those to whom being stuck in an unruly wilderness, with no outpost that could be called a city for about 130 miles, seems a tad frightening, you will need to be very firmly attracted to UVM's other charms if you want to apply here. These charms, thankfully, are manifold.

Accommodation

On site accommodation caters for about one third of the large student body – 3,500 out of 10,500, including all first and second year undergrads – and the rest commute, without too much complaint.

The UVM Student

Students study in an exhilarating alternative atmosphere, often with excellent professors who are leaders in their field. The student body does not so much suffer from one stereotype as a whole host of vaguely related stereotypes, most of which can be bundled into one of three categories – the hippies, the snowboarders and the "Vermonters".

Hippies are charmingly traditional here – you will see real tie-dyed shirts, smell marijuana, taste over-organic foods, and hear plenty of Joni Mitchell on beat-up acoustic guitars. The snowboarders, who also include lots of skiers and general winter sportsmen, come to Vermont in droves. Attracted by the abundance of ideal mountains to practise their adrenaline-soaked activities, some snowboarders have been known to abandon their studies for significant periods of time to devote themselves entirely to their sport. "Vermonter" is a kinder term for someone who elsewhere in the States might get labelled a "hick" or "hillbilly" – they enjoy wildlife (both to shoot at and look at), "the wild", and general frontier-type, non-urban activities.

Despite these perceived groups and several other flourishing scenes, the UVM student body is a wonderfully easy place to integrate, and there is a good helping of diversity in this otherwise remote establishment.

A large chunk of the students are from Vermont or elsewhere in New England, but many are from the other 49 states, and there are plenty of foreigners for any unfortunate Brit who might otherwise feel isolated (there is even an exchange program with the University of Sussex).

The host of groups to which it is possible to belong, though internally healthy, are by no means obligatory – in general UVMers are more free-thinking than boxed-in – and social pressures are rarely if ever a complaint. Students are accommodated in themed dormitories, which can include global villages where there is a positively international atmosphere.

Hitting the Books

Study at UVM is mixed: the recent boost in student numbers has meant ever expanding class sizes and a more stretched staff, which in turn has led to cuts in some of the less popular but pleasingly diverse courses ("reggae music", for example, sadly got the axe). Mounting debt means that more budget-cuts and lay-offs seem imminent.

Nevertheless, there are over 90 majors to choose from at UVM, so the enviable range of options which has been a hallmark of the college is by no means gone.

The teachers range from world-renowned and pioneering in their field to mediocre, as do the courses available. The college has excellent politics and business schools, and the environmental department has an international reputation as one of the best and most progressive in the country, filled with exciting, forward-thinking professors and huge quantities of equally eager students. The nursing school is also very famous and extremely competitive, for anyone interested in this academic niche.

Social Life

And just because you are more or less in the middle of nowhere doesn't mean there's nothing to do there. Drinking in dorm rooms is banned (until recently it was a fully dry campus), but parties are numerous and large-scale, normally held in student housing in the town, so UVM enjoys a vibrant nightlife for those who want it. Again, students insist that such partying is only available and not obligatory, without any kind of pressure on those who prefer less hectic pursuits most nights of the week.

Day-time activities include the many clubs (over 100), societies and sports teams that spring up from the motivation and interest of the student body. UVM is almost unique in being a state university with no (American) football team, but it does excel in hockey and, of course, in all winter sports.

There are debating societies (with overseas cultural exchanges), at least two weekly newspapers, and a popular and intriguingly entitled organisation called the "UVM Outing Club".

Getting In

AT A GLANCE – Application & Test Options:

– Early Action, Regular Decision

– ACT/SAT required

US News & World Report has ranked UVM one of the nation's Top Up-and-Coming Schools, institutions that "are worth watching because they are making promising and innovative changes".

And getting in to UVM has traditionally not been too difficult (by US standards), as it has a big capacity and lots of room for interesting, if not massively qualified, individuals. As a state university, however, UVM found its application inbox overwhelmed after the 2008 economic meltdown with hard-hit students seeking slightly more manageable debts, and competition has consequently been much tougher ever since.

The process remains relatively straightforward, with the Common App plus the SAT or ACT test required – but no interviews, additional essays or SAT Subject tests.

Money Matters

Fees can be tough for non-Vermont residents, but not ultra-tough, and there are many scholarship opportunities, including occasionally for international students; check with the scholarship coordinator in the Admissions office.

Famous Grads

E. Annie Proulx – author (*Brokeback Mountain, The Shipping News*)

Ben Affleck – director, actor, director, writer (Daredevil; Sum of All Fears) [did not graduate]

Jody Williams – Nobel Peace Prize winner for action to ban landmines

University of Virginia (UVA)

Charlottesville, Virginia
www.virginia.edu
Undergrads: 15,000
Grads: 6,000

How many students does it take to change a light bulb at UVA?

Thirteen – ten to form a student committee to vote on whether changing light bulbs is a violation of the Honor Code, one to change the bulb, one to hold the keg that he's standing on, and another to attribute electricity to Mr Jefferson.

Thomas Jefferson's gravestone is decorated with his three proudest achievements. The first two, the Declaration of Independence and the Statute of Virginia for Religious Freedom remain integral parts of the great American dream. The third, his foundation of the University of Virginia, is accessible not only to those who salute the Stars and Stripes but also to lowly Brits!

The university – known to one and all as UVA (or simply "Virginia")– has possibly the most beautiful campus in the States, is situated in a quintessential Southern college town, and offers an education that, despite its public status, is nationally acclaimed. This is a school for those of you looking for a truly American educational experience, based on the doctrines of one of America's truly great men.

The Campus

'Beautiful' does not come even close to describing the campus at UVA. Anyone with an aesthetic bent who believe that nothing in America can begin to rival the 'dreaming spires' of Oxbridge, should think again. All of Jefferson's architectural endeavours were impressive (as a day trip to his home in Monticello will prove) and UVA is no exception.

Founded in 1819, the campus (or grounds as it is popularly known) has a classical feel with beautiful brick buildings with white columns, situated around vast expanses of green. Jefferson believed that a university should be akin to an academic village – scholars and faculty co-existing in a community consisting of many splendid buildings.

The showpiece of the campus is the magnificent classical Rotunda, situated at one end of the hallowed Lawn and a worthy match for rivals such as the Bodleian Library or Trinity College, Cambridge. The Lawn itself, still boasting all of the original student residences, is the central part of the UVA campus.

Living on the Lawn is a serious matter. Only the most popular and respected members of the faculty take up residence there. As for the students, living in one of these historical sites requires a whole new application process (as it undoubtedly did for Edgar Allen Poe when he lived there). A small group of individuals who are judged to be exemplary members of the UVA community are selected annually for the privilege of inhabiting this hallowed spot.

UVA has a large student body but its campus, still for the most part contained within the original boundaries, helps to provide a centre for the community. And beyond the confines of the university and the bustling town of Charlottesville, the Virginian countryside is among the most beautiful in the United States. Rife with tales of the Civil War, the rural areas are perfect for historians and nature-lovers while hikers can set off up the Blue Ridge Mountains and keep going for miles.

AND, perhaps of most importance, in Virginia the weather smiles on you. This is one of the few places in America that actually has all four seasons (most manage three at best). This may not seem the key selling point for a college, but the joys of a gorgeous spring and autumn should not be underestimated!

Accommodation

As a student you have a variety of choices regarding your accommodation. The university, leaving aside the hallowed Lawn residences, is split between the old (McCormick) dorms and the new (Alderman) dorms. There are also a number of students living in the frats and sorority residences.

Furthermore, there are residential colleges, including the recently opened International Residential College. While these may seem tempting it is, as always, recommended that you throw yourself into the 'Americanness' of things straight away. There is little point in crossing the Atlantic solely to surround yourself with your country men.

The Virginia Student

UVA is – as it states – the University of Virginia. Despite its national reputation, its focus (sharpened by the state-funding it receives) is on educating the inhabitants of the home-state. Just under 70% of the student body are locals taking advantage of the slightly easier admissions process and lower tuition. Such homogeneity will make your attendance at UVA very different from that at any other American college. You may, in fact, come home as a Virginian.

This transformation starts when those of you who thought the Civil War was over will discover...not so much. If you have not managed to glean from the British educational system what or when this nation-changing event was, prepare for a steep learning curve. Virginia was the epicentre of Civil War action – caught as it is between the North and South. As might be expected UVA – with its local student body – has some decided views on the subject. Nor should you neglect the instrumental role that Jefferson played in throwing the British out of America – spawning jokes that you may become sick of in rather fewer than four years!

Leaving history out of the equation, the homogenous aspect of UVA can be somewhat trying. Although Jefferson dreamed of an international student body, admitting the first foreign student in 1826, only a very small percentage of students are from outside the States. And even though the admissions office is flooded with applications from out-of-state individuals, the emphasis is very much on the Virginian. UVA prides itself on having a large minority population – around a third of the student body. Yet students continue to complain that, in keeping with Southern history, there is a certain amount of segregation between black and white students and the university remains dominated by upper-middle-class white Southerners. As a Brit you will probably be a source of fascination, but you may also feel a little alienated.

Yet UVAers are united around certain aspects of the campus. UVA is a school steeped in time-old traditions that bring together even the most diverse members of its community. From its own language – this is perhaps the only college in America where you will be known as a first year rather than a freshman (making Brits feel right at home) – to such peculiar customs as scrawling graffiti on bridges or streaking across the Lawn, UVA will ensnare you in its web of customs. Regardless of ethnic, national or religious background you become a product of a very individual school, marching to the same beat and singing to the same rousing football songs as every other one of your peers.

It is remarkably easy to get involved in the UVA community. This is a school where everyone likes to do everything. Societies of every possible description exist on campus and it would be tough to find nothing that captured your attention. And although some claim that student publications and radio stations are often overlooked, the reputation of the papers that do exist is very high.

For the sporting kind (and be warned, sport at UVA, as all over America, is a huge part of one's daily existence), there are a multitude of intramural and varsity sports in which you can get involved. And, good news for the Brits, our experience in football and lacrosse won't go amiss. These are areas in which UVA excels (although cricket is sadly excluded).

Hitting the Books

Honour. Honour. Honour. This uniquely Southern concept led to a culture that involved great romances, pistols at dawn and lifelong feuds and friendships. It also provided the background from which an integral part of the UVA experience was to emerge – the Honor Code. This system was designed to ensure co-operation and trust between faculty and students and was founded in 1842 following the fatal shooting of a professor by a pupil! While pistols no longer play such a vital role in academic dealings (to the relief of many unpopular faculty members), the Honor Code lives on.

'On my honor as a student I have neither given nor received aid on this exam/ assignment.' During your four years at UVA this will become a mantra that will haunt your dreams. By signing your name to this trust agreement, you earn yourself the privilege of taking exams and tests without invigilation and in any situation you like. In return you neither cheat nor take advantage of the situation.

The student-run Honor System also entitles you to local privileges – eg the writing of cheques in local shops. Such a simple code allows students a great deal of freedom and all UVAers are extraordinarily proud of this part of their heritage. Don't be tempted to cheat it. Any violation of the Code results in expulsion (you will also be expelled if you witness a violation of the code and fail to report it). Harsh treatment, but necessary in preserving one of the most historical and moral aspects of UVA.

Perhaps due to the atmosphere of trust the Honor Code creates, the relationship between faculty members and students is great at UVA. Although it is a huge school the class sizes are kept fairly small, many more intimate seminars are offered and professors are known for being extremely accessible to their students.

There is the inevitable problem of grad students teaching classes, but the professor-student ratio remains at 15:1 and most make a real effort to get involved on campus. Again it was the sainted Jefferson who extolled the importance of the faculty–pupil relationship and, as you should all have realized by now, his every word became UVA law.

UVA is officially divided into six undergraduate schools – Arts and Sciences (where in all likelihood you would head), Architecture, Engineering, Nursing, Commerce (very well-reputed), and Education. There are a huge variety of courses available and a great deal of flexibility in your selection. While the liberal arts requirements that underpin most of these American schools still exist at UVA they are measured by hours rather than course matter and are a great deal shorter as a result. Twelve hours of maths and science in four years is not really that bad!

Even deciding on a major does not limit your options. A student has to complete 120 hours of credit to graduate and while requirements vary for different subjects, only a maximum of forty-three of these that need to be in your chosen subject. Traditionally this is a great school for those interested in

English and History, but the overall course standard is very high and you would be hard pushed to find a subject here that didn't interest you. Students also benefit from the great resources (the library filled with – you've guessed it – Thomas Jefferson memorabilia) and a very efficient administration that does everything possible to make the rigours of student life easier.

You have to work hard to get into UVA and this trend continues once you have been accepted. The university takes pride in being known as 'the public Ivy' and its academic standards are often as high as those of its prestigious counterparts. Having said that, while the majority of students are pretty ambitious and push for these higher grades, it is possible for more slothful individuals to tread water for most of their academic careers.

This discrepancy of standards is perhaps encouraged by the fact that the majority of UVA students are known to be less cut-throat than their Ivy League rivals. Perhaps it is because of the faculty presence and interest in undergrads, perhaps because of the Honor Code or perhaps because of the laid-back Southern atmosphere. Whatever the reason, UVA manages to balance academic pressure and active socializing without most students slipping into either nervous breakdowns or alcoholism!

Social Life

Those of you who worry that your social life may suffer as a result of attending university in a country that often seems to positively prohibit fun, need not fear. This fate will not await you at UVA – a school that parties as hard as it works. In fact this school offers you the best of the private and the public – the academic standard and status of the former and the party reputation of the latter. Even the most hard-working of UVA students can be torn away from their desks at the weekends and the more relaxed crowd party far more regularly.

Socializing comes in many forms at UVA. The town of Charlottesville offers one option – its bars and restaurants certainly help to warm up individuals for a fun night out. The campus itself has a plethora of social opportunities – from the ever-popular football games thronged by students clad in blue and orange to events organized by the 300+ societies on campus. The UVA administration also takes students' social lives into their own hands. As a campus steeped in tradition, there are several annual events to which everybody turns out.

This is a Southern school and as such heavily influenced by the Greek scene. Fraternities and sororities thrive on campus – adding to the reputation of UVA as one of the best places to party. Around 25% of all men and women on campus are involved in these societies – opting to live in the houses situated on that social mecca – Rugby Road. The societies are very diverse and for the most part those who are not actually members do not seem to feel excluded.

Far more isolated are the notorious secret societies that live on despite the scandal that surrounds them. Of these the most renowned is 'Seven'. The pranks are seen, the reputation lingers, but the members remain unknown – although when they die, the bell tolls seven times at 7 o'clock on the seventh day afterwards while the grave is covered with flowers in the shape of (you'll never guess) a seven. Definitely the stuff of horror movies!

Outside Those Ivory Walls

If you hail from that species 'big-city dweller' who cannot walk on a street without traffic, whose lungs collapse if the air suddenly falls below the required pollution quota and who believe that Hyde Park is the country, then UVA will probably not be the university for you. Despite the beauty of the campus, and there would be few nicer places to feel isolated, this is not an urban university and cannot provide the facilities and entertainments of the big cities.

Charlottesville occasionally claims to be a city, but it maintains the feel of a charming and fun Southern town. It may not have the diversity of night clubs and bars that NYC and Boston offer, but it has good restaurants, thriving book and film festivals, cinemas, shops and a great student feel to it. Most well-known perhaps are the 'Fridays after Five' concerts given by bands at the end of each week. On other days most students head for 'the corner' – a collection of bars, coffee shops and restaurants close to the grounds.

If you are wandering further afield, the university bus service helps to facilitate movement. Although nightlife may not be the strongest feature of the town, UVA students do not, for the most part, complain. A sociable bunch, they throw their own parties, make their own fun and see Charlottesville as a great spring-board for their adventures.

The remarkable countryside outside UVA is also a great place to explore. Even those of you who shun the delights of throbbing blisters and wet canvas might be excited by the proximity of two nearby ski resorts. And if you're really feeling the need to get out then Richmond is close enough – just find a friend with a car. The national capital (Washington DC) is also just two hours away by bus.

Getting In

AT A GLANCE – Application & Test Options:

- Early Action, Regular Decision
- ACT/SAT required
- SAT Subject tests optional

This may be a public university, but it's one of the very best. Ever since *US News and World Report* began ranking public universities as a separate category, UVA has ranked either No. 1 or No. 2 – and the admissions requirements rival those of the top private schools. In the most recent years, around 31,000 students applied to UVA. Roughly 9,000 were accepted. This is about 28% – a fairly competitive environment, and much more so when you consider that 70% of them have to be from within state. Everything rests upon your application – there are no actual interviews for this university.

As always, the SAT or the ACT test is required, but SAT Subject tests are now optional. These exams need to be done by December of your final year at school – and a high academic standard is regarded as crucial by the admissions mafia.

SAT scores should be backed up by strong personal essays on the admissions form – some shorter questions and the longer 'who are you really?' type challenge. It is hard to say what else helps you to get into UVA. There is a preference given to those from Virginia – but it may be difficult to get away with that pretence! As with most universities, the children of alumni are also considered somewhat special, so if you have that in your favour be sure to mention it. There is no Early Decision option (binding) but there is something almost better – Early Action, which allows you to know your fate in December and is not binding.

Money Matters

There is no financial aid for international students unless they are also permanent residents of the United States. There are, however, a handful (literally) of scholarships available which may be worth pursuing (notably the highly competitive Jefferson scholarship).

Due to its public status, UVA's tuition is significantly less than private schools, but still high in comparison with the British system (unless you manage to get your hands on one of those scholarships).

Famous Grads

Edgar Allen Poe – spooky Southern mystery writer

Tina Fey – *Mean Girls*, writer and *SNL* presenter, Sarah Palin impersonator

Ted Kennedy – JFK's brother and US senator

University of Washington (Seattle)

Seattle, Washington
www.washington.edu
Undergrads: 31,400
Grads: 14,600

How many UW students does it take to change a light bulb?

3 – One to use Amazon to purchase the new bulb, one to make the coffee and one to put the grunge records on the turntable.

The 47,000 students at the University of Washington (UW – "U-Dub" to the locals) have life pretty good. Indeed, with a massive, leafy campus in the midst one of the coolest and most culturally interesting hubs of US society, life would be rewarding and stimulating here even if it weren't one of the best public schools in the country.

It's hard not to see the city of Seattle as the overwhelmingly best reason to choose UW as your American college experience – it is after all the home and birthplace of an improbably long list of pillars of the modern America which includes everything from Starbucks to Nirvana.

The university is the icing on the cake. With world renowned programmes in the sciences (if you want to be a high-flying dentist or psychologist, this is the place for you), UW gives excellent bang for its buck with great teaching in many subjects. Although the recession has meant devastating budget cuts from the Washington State legislature, UW remains a formidable educational institution and an unforgettable US experience, consistently ranked in the top 20 universities in the world and widely acclaimed as a prestigious "Public Ivy".

The Campus

UW sprawls across a whopping 700 acres of prime real estate in Northern Seattle, resplendent on the shores of glittering Lake Washington, across which the virgin forests and craggy Cascades mountain range can be seen to stretch into the distance. And if that's not poetic enough for you, most of the buildings are attractive – almost European in their bricky grandeur. Not far from the Canadian border, UW has a leafy and well-spaced campus in a beautiful and pioneering corner of the country. Trees are plentiful – an especially pleasant feature in spring and autumn.

The university sits comfortably just north of the main hubs of the city, Capitol Hill and downtown, and enjoys a sizzling coffee-and-laptop student environment in the surrounding mish-mash of bookstores, healthy food restaurants and alternative culture outlets, based around the famous University Way (known simply as "The Ave"), on the east side of campus. To the north lies University Village, with a reassuring abundance of chain stores for your every need.

Accommodation

About 60% of first year undergrads live on campus, in excellently located and reasonably nice dormitories, with themed housing options available. The university will also help find accommodation in other fun parts of the city if you apply too late to get a room on campus; this is usually the preferable option for students after the first year.

The UW Student

Young blood from across the country and beyond is attracted in droves to this northwestern epicentre of fine city-living, in an almost Dick Whittington-esque way. And with such a massive student body, UW wouldn't even need this diverse intake to enjoy a huge variety of personalities.

One of the less mentioned, but striking, features of students in Seattle, and indeed Seattleites in general, is how friendly they are, and this creates a very welcoming atmosphere for these newly-arrived fortune-seekers. It is not unusual for long-lasting friendships to be formed on short bus rides, and pleasant conversations with strangers are common enough for comparatively introverted Brits to feel initially overwhelmed.

Nevertheless, there is certainly more than a kernel of truth to the stereotypes of caffeine-addicted computer-and-tree-hugging vegetarian vinyl-collecting art-obsessives who go to underground music venues every night and attending marijuana legalisation rallies by day. Still, the nature of the city thrives on variety, and this produces an infectious energy on which the likes of Jimi Hendrix and Bruce Lee thrived, and which continues to inspire people of all ages and backgrounds.

UW has its fair share of yuppies, Greek life and jocks, as well as significant levels of political, environmental, and LGBT activism (with summer pride parades to rival San Francisco) and large numbers of student-run organisations. With one of the most exciting and well-known music scenes in the country, it is unsurprising that a remarkable percentage of students play in bands. There are also a reasonable number of international students, and indeed the university community is very easy to infiltrate from abroad. This is perhaps helped by the fact that UW organises the most study-abroad courses of any American university.

In general, UW students have the high levels of school pride that are common in American universities, and it is not unusual to see people wearing the all-purple uniform of the university football team, the Huskies. There is some rivalry with Washington's "other" state university, the non-Seattle-based Washington State, but less with the two other principal schools in Seattle, the Jesuit Seattle University and Seattle Pacific University.

Hitting the Books

The sciences are what make UW most famous, with cutting-edge departments in medicine, biochemistry and psychology which attract world-class professors and students. Politics and international relations are also big, and there are good programs in various areas of ecology and environmental studies, which benefit from their proximity to fascinating natural landscapes and excellent examples of geological phenomena. The college receives over a billion dollars of research funding per year, giving it one of the top five largest research budgets in the US, though new budget cuts may affect this.

UW has generally very high quality teaching staff, good academic resources (a huge library network, for example), and a great range of subjects to choose from. Despite a very respectable student:faculty ratio of 12:1, it suffers from enormous class sizes in the low-level courses (500+ is not unusual), a drag to some students and alienating to others.

Work load varies. In the most competitive and high-flying courses, especially the sciences, it can be intolerable. Yet in other areas students complain of not feeling academically challenged, even if the classes are mostly enjoyable and stimulating and much is learned.

One popular option is to use the excellent evening programme, allowing students to earn money during the day and continue their studies after work. Sensible UWers can make significant inroads into their debts this way, if they are prepared to accept the extra time pressure it entails.

Social Life

Some describe UW as a party school, others extoll the students' ability to achieve a sensible balance of work and fun, but again no generalisations can be made in such a massive university. There is definitely something for everyone here; Seattle is blessed with a constant stream of activities and events – there is always a barbecue to go to, a concert to attend, an arts show to ogle. Hard-core party goers will be overjoyed at the abundance of house-hosted events on campus as well as off.

Even without the hundreds of university-run organisations and healthy Greek life there is something always going on, and it is a disciplined soul indeed who does not get carried away with an enthusiastic urge to try everything. New friends are made as easily as purchasing a delicious chai tea from one of the ludicrously large number of laptop-filled coffee shops that swarm every block. The blood of the city flows via these coffee shops – they are the centre of most students' academic, gastronomical and social lives; they are where you work and play.

Another key extra curricular activity is sport and exercise. The university has a successful football team, The Huskies, as well as great rowing opportunities on the lake. It also provides exercise and yoga classes and excellent gym facilities (all free), and students like to stay fit by using these as well as the jogging paths both on campus and around the city.

Outside Those Ivory Walls

There are no metaphorical walls around the University of Washington, ivory or otherwise. The city is an inseparable part of the UW experience. Seattle has been on a non-stop upward spiral since its beginnings as a logging community, and its most recent incarnation has seen it pulling away from the grunge-fuelled hot-spot of the 90s and into a gleaming new haven for billionaires, dot-com boomers and Boeing employees.

But despite the corporate veneer that this has brought to the city (along with a sharp rise in house prices as people get glimpses of Bill Gates' mansions across the lake), Seattle has never lost the quirky, collegiate and arty culture that makes it so special. The fine folk of Seattle are the most educated, computer literate and well read of any city in the Union. They also drink the most coffee, and they gave the world Starbucks and Amazon.com.

Lovers of popular music would die for Seattle's scintillating music scene; the city was the centre of the world's attention during the Cobain-led explosion of garage rock and grunge in the early 90s, and since then has continued to produce some of the most innovative and exciting bands on the world stage (see Fleet Foxes, Modest Mouse or Death Cab For Cutie), in almost any genre you can name.

Brits will feel right at home in Seattle's unique climate. The mountains to the east and ocean to the west create an environment that is much more British than it is American; the seasons are temperate, with more rain and cloud cover than is typical in the US, creating less of an ice box in the winter and oven in the summer. There is nothing British about the surrounding countryside, however. Seattle is not far from incredible mountain ranges and at least two beautiful national parks that are well worth exploring.

Public transport in the city is fair, with extensive bus coverage that is affordable but often slow; development of a long awaited urban transit system in the works. Cars have a less good time of it, and some parts of the city are over-congested.

Getting In

AT A GLANCE – Application & Test Options:

– Regular Decision

– ACT/SAT usually required but not for International students

Like most state universities, UW has seen a steep increase in applications in recent years, though this has always been a competitive school. There are a large number of places available though, and the percentage of successful applications in 2016 was encouragingly around 45%.

Moreover, with an admissions emphasis placed on academic rigour at one's senior school, British students should be at an advantage. While interviews are not necessary and references count for comparatively little, the application essay(s) are very important here, so take your time on it and make sure to impress.

Money Matters

UW has always had a reputation for very low tuition fees, though cash shortages in recent years have provoked a dramatic rise in costs. As ever, the financial aid available to international students is woefully harder to come by than that for locals, but there are scholarships to be earned.

Famous Grads

Bruce Lee – iconic actor and martial arts master

Minoru Yamasaki – architect and designer of the World Trade Centre

Waldo Semon – inventor of vinyl and presumably winner of world's greatest name

Vanderbilt University

Nashville, Tennessee
www.vanderbilt.edu
Undergrads: 6,800
Grads: 6,000

How many students does it take to change a light bulb at Vanderbilt?

Two – one to call the electrician and one to call daddy to pay the bill.

You may think you know America but until you have visited the strange, strange land of the deep American South, you can never call yourself a true aficionado. Although the Civil War has long since been fought and won, the spirit of the South continues to loom larger than life. Plantation life may be over but the opinions, accents and chivalry live on. Nowhere are these more apparent than at Vanderbilt University in Tennessee.

Situated a mere five minutes from Nashville, the great country music hot spot, Vanderbilt is home to Southern belles and gents in their present form. In fact, if Scarlett O'Hara or Rhett Butler were searching for their ideal campus right now, the odds are that good ole Vandy would fit the bill nicely. With a strong academic focus, a thriving Greek life and a campus full of groomed and beautiful Southerners, Vanderbilt offers both a good education and a unique American experience.

The Campus

Vanderbilt was founded in 1873 by Commodore Cornelius Vanderbilt, a self-made millionaire who never actually visited the place but did manage to provide it with both its good Dutch name and its somewhat unusual mascot (the Commodore). The buildings are set in parkland that was recently designated a national arboretum and the campus defines southern elegance.

The spacious 380 acres are marked by old brick buildings, green quads and countless varieties of tree for shade on sunny Southern days (or shelter on the many rainy ones!). Places such as Alumni Lawn form the central focus of the campus and play host to student traditions such as the Rites of Spring – an outdoor party that embodies Stravinsky's pagan fantasies.

Accommodation

The pleasant surroundings and tight-knit community mean that most students choose to live in dorms or fraternities situated in the grounds themselves, allowing them easy access to all facets of student life at all times. In fact students have been known to refer to their campus as the Vanderbubble and are almost uniformly content to stick to the boundaries of what is, in fact, a relatively small university.

The Vanderbilt Student

Some have compared the average female student at Vanderbilt to a debutante on the evening of her first ball – with one key difference – the Vandy female is like that all the time. Certainly Southern culture, with its dictates on gentility and elegance, demands that both the Southern male and female are always immaculately groomed, well-mannered and charming. While the men who attend Vanderbilt certainly don't seem to be complaining, girls who have embraced the laddish behaviour of the twenty-first century often find it more than a little difficult to adjust to the strictures of such a life.

Many grumble that it is considered a crime to appear in public at Vandy without a full face of makeup and the perfectly accessorised outfit. Others say that such an atmosphere condones snobbery and creates problems for students who like to express themselves in other ways. At the end of the day Vanderbilt requires a certain personality type – after all the reputation of being a member of the hottest campus around necessitates a certain amount of effort.

Ironically, the British student may feel more at ease in the rarefied environment of the 'old South' than many of their North American contemporaries. The code of manners that continues to subtly influence Vanderbilt life today is akin to that which still reigns in England. Southerners are an exceptionally friendly bunch but they have an initial reserve and social protocol that has vanished in the Northern States.

British people may well find this easier to deal with, although they should be warned that this is a university with a long tradition of men asking women on formal dates to football games! While some will assuredly regard the atmosphere as verging on the cliquey and stuffy, others will find that this polite way of life makes for an enjoyable college experience. Vanderbilt is certainly one of those universities that students should visit before applying to.

Almost half the students at Vanderbilt hail from the South and there is an international student body of around 7%. As a Brit you need not worry about being accepted into the ways of American culture. The United States as a whole has a strong Anglophilic tendency, but this is particularly marked in the South. Once you are past the initial accent barrier, you will find that you and your roommates will be trading vernacular gems for years to come!

In fact you may well find it easier to fit in than many an American of a more diverse ethnic background. While Vanderbilt has made an effort to incorporate people of all backgrounds, many students note that it is a very homogenous environment.

Hitting the Books

Honourable behaviour extends from the dating game to the classroom at Vanderbilt. This university, along with other Southern schools such as UVA and Sewanee, is immensely proud of its Honor Code, which has always dictated the way in which its students behave. This Code grants students specific privileges in return for their honourable behaviour in examinations, paper guidelines and general living.

Much quoted are the words of Madison Sarratt, one time dean of the university, 'Today I am going to give you two examinations, one in trigonometry and one in honesty. I hope you will pass them both, but if you must fail one, let it be trigonometry.' Regardless of whether students take these words as free licence to fail the dreaded maths class, every Vanderbilt student is proud of the trust that exists between the student body and the faculty.

It is the quality of this relationship between teacher and pupil that will determine how much you benefit from Vanderbilt's strong academic standing. While the reputation of this smaller and less prosperous university often suffers in comparison with the academic excellence boasted of by some of its East and West Coast contemporaries, it is actually more than capable of holding its own.

The small class sizes (with a student-faculty ratio of 9:1) and the insularity of the campus offer students a real opportunity to form a relationship with their professors. While many of the faculty are genuinely interested in their pupils, the calibre of the lecturers covers a fairly wide range and students are advised to do their research before embarking on a particular course.

Vandy has long been recognized as one of the top research universities in the Southern States and it has its fair share of academic superstars who know how to inspire their classes. However it is largely up to the student to seek them out. Students who accomplish this can be assured they are getting an education that will rival any of the more prestigious schools. Those who fail to do so may well find themselves frustrated.

Vanderbilt offers the standard liberal arts education, requiring students to take a variety of core classes to broaden the base of their knowledge before they choose a specific area for concentration. These core areas include the humanities, sciences and mathematics and are covered by good introductory courses.

Social Life

Those who complain about the lack of diversity also bemoan the dominance of the Greek system within the Vanderbilt walls. In the best tradition of all

Southern schools, Vanderbilt's social scene is largely dominated by the existence of sororities and fraternities.

It is estimated that around 50% of women and 35% of men join one of these houses, often living with their sisters and brothers and confining their socializing to specific letters of the Greek alphabet.

While this may all be a little too Animal House for your liking, it is undeniable that many of these frats throw the best parties on campus and are an integral part of the Vanderbilt existence. Clever students learn how to accommodate them while refraining from sacrificing themselves on the altars of rush week. After all, there are plenty of other options available to those who are willing to seek them out and Vanderbilt's reputation as a school that knows how to have a good time was never built solely upon the members of Sigma Chi.

Outside Those Ivory Walls

Some of the lazier students moan that if you don't have a car (a crucial part of existence in the South), Nashville, while only five minutes away, is just too much effort. Yet a little exploration beyond campus confines is well worth the additional exercise or cab fare. Nashville is prosperous and lively, the home of bluegrass music, and extremely proud of its Southern heritage.

It also offers Vandy students a wonderful alternative to the occasional monotony of campus life. Visiting musicians from all over the States have ensured a plethora of restaurants, bars and concerts that combine the highest of national standards with that little bit of genuine Southern flavour. For an Britlish student whose previous experience of the South may well have been limited to drunken renditions of 'Cotton-Eyed Joe', the combination of Vanderbilt and Nashville will provide a sound cultural and academic education that would be hard to find elsewhere.

Getting In

AT A GLANCE – Application & Test Options:

– Early Decision, Early Decision II, Regular Decision

– ACT/SAT required

The merits of Vanderbilt's academics have been shown by the increasing selectivity of its admissions process over recent years (12% of 2016 applicants were admitted). As a result of this competition, would-be students need to think long and hard about their applications. The SAT or ACT is required but SAT Subject tests are not mandatory (although advised). This means that much rides on your personal essays and teacher recommendations. Early (binding) Decision is one option for those who have set their hearts on a place.

Money Matters

There are a number of merit-based scholarships open to international students that are well worth enquiring about.

Famous Grads

Ann S. Moore – former Chairman and CEO of Time, Inc

Jay Cutler – Chicago Bears quarter back

Abdiweli Mohamed Ali – Prime Minister of Somalia

Vassar College

Poughkeepsie, New York
www.vassar.edu
Undergrads: 2,400
Grads: 0

How many Vassar students does it take to change a light bulb?
Eleven – one to screw it in and ten to support its sexual orientation.

Acclaimed as one of the best liberal arts colleges in the country, Vassar College offers a tantalising mix: a gorgeous campus, academic quality on par with an Ivy League, plus the liberal views and creative student body of a smaller liberal arts school. Founded in 1861 as a women's college (and the first of the Seven Sisters – a prestigious group of liberal arts colleges all founded in the mid-1800s for women), Vassar became co-educational in the 1960s.

It has not only high standards and a sterling reputation (tracing all the way back to its founding) but also some of the happiest students around (most years placing near the top in the Happiest Student Body rankings).

The Campus

Vassar is situated on 1,000 acres in the Hudson Valley of New York state – and every inch of it is lovely. In fact, Vassar looks more like a botanical garden than a college campus. Forests, meadows, gardens, and well-manicured lawns permeate the grounds. And the academic and residential buildings – ranging from modern to Gothic – are almost all uniformly attractive.

Students can choose from several cafes on campus as well as a night club/bar that hosts weekly trivia quizzes, jazz, and themed dance nights. But the centrepiece is the library, home to the largest undergraduate collection in the United States. This, my friends, is a dreamy campus.

Accommodation

Freshman, sophomores, and juniors for the most part all live on campus – again, in beautiful buildings – and each house tends to have a unique personality that defines the lifestyle or interests of its inhabitants. The residential life is one of the best parts of going to Vassar and it provides the familial feel of a much smaller college. Apartment style accommodation is also an option if you're a junior or senior – and you don't even have to leave campus.

The Vassar Student

Though the stereotypical Vassar student is either a hipster, a strung-out genius, or a rich liberal socialist, the real Vassar student is difficult to pigeonhole. Many do encompass some of these personas but never to exclusion. The most unifying trait across the student body seems to be that Vassar students are talented and independent-minded individuals – but are also athletes, scholars, musicians, artists, tree-hugging hippies, and political activists. Plus, some who are all of the above (or none).

Relative to most small liberal arts schools, Vassar has achieved a meaningful level of diversity (even if not in political leanings) and this is considered one of the college's greatest qualities. International students (from 50+ countries) make up 8-10% of the student body. Even though there are plenty of wealthy students from influential families, there is a wide breadth of backgrounds and experiences across the student body. There's certainly a 'Vassar bubble', but this bubble contains the cream of the crop.

Hitting the Books

Students at Vassar are seriously clever and seriously motivated – it's hard to get in, and they're determined to get their money's worth. Academics are demanding and across all fields but you have a huge amount of freedom in choosing your classes (see below) and can count on a very supportive faculty (and fellow students) to get you through.

Economics and English are the most popular majors and the departments are known to be quite picky, but otherwise there is a great amount of freedom given to students to study what they like. Vassar has a fairly flexible curriculum: while each field of study has specific requirements for majors, the only universal requirements for graduation are proficiency in a foreign language (which includes sign language!), a quantitative course, and a freshman writing course.

Most classes often have no more than 25 students, so teachers figure your name out pretty quickly, and you will be expected to join the discussion. Students are surprisingly noncompetitive; although they want to do well, this does not come at the expense of others' success.

Social Life

Aside from talk of the Vassar bubble, you won't often find students complaining about the social life. The college prides itself on its busy social calendar and many Vassar students claim they rarely leave the campus (unless they need an occasional change of scenery).

It's hard to argue with this – more than 150 student organisations plus incredible visiting speakers, shows/performances, and sporting events keep the Vassar schedule full. If you prefer to hibernate in your room on the weekends or attend small parties or perform an impromptu music show, this is also considered acceptable behaviour.

There is no Greek life but there are still lots of parties – however there are more women than men and people often find themselves in dysfunctional dating situations regardless of sexual orientation. Nevertheless, it is all around agreed: it's good to be a man at Vassar College.

Outside Those Ivory Walls

The relationship the college has with nearby Poughkeepsie is not ideal and most students tend to complain about the lack of attractions in town; however as far as college towns go you will find all the necessities and a number of restaurants and cafes. Luckily, New York City is only 75 miles away and very easy to reach by train.

Getting In

AT A GLANCE – Application & Test Options:

- Early Decision, Early Decision II, Regular Decision
- ACT/SAT required
- SAT Subject tests optional

Getting in is the hard part. Vassar is placed in the top 20 liberal arts colleges in the nation and is categorised as 'most selective' and they're not kidding. Only a fourth of all applicants are admitted these days. You'll need good grades, SAT/ACT scores, activities and a great essay.

Money Matters

On the plus side, even though Vassar is expensive, it is not only for the wealthy elite - 60% of Vassar students receive some sort of aid based on need. The school will meet 100% of the full demonstrated need of all admitted students for the duration of their time at the school. However, they are not need- blind for international students, so your need for assistance can affect your admission chances.

Famous Grads

Meryl Street – multiple Oscar-winning actress

Grace Hopper – pioneering computer scientist

Mark Ronson – British DJ, guitarist, music producer

Washington University (St. Louis, Missouri)

St. Louis, Missouri
www.wustl.edu
Undergrads: 7,500
Grads: 6,000

How many Wash U students does it take to change a light bulb?

3 – one to pay too much for it, one to bring it from the East Coast, and one to put the great experience on his CV.

There's only one university currently ranked by US News and World Report *in the top 15 which is not a household name, and it's Washington University in St. Louis. But despite not (yet) enjoying the same nation-wide recognition as, say, Ivy League Cornell, which is ranked below it, Wash U more than deserves its spot among the stars.*

A middle-sized institution with tremendous academic prowess, fast-paced campus life and an ample endowment, Wash U attracts some of the finest minds from all over the country as a lesser known alternative to the all-star colleges. Though you may never have heard of the city of St. Louis (or even Missouri, a mostly unremarkable state bang in the middle of the country), it is a fantastic place to live, vying with Chicago for the best Midwestern college town award.

The only reason to hesitate before applying here is financial concerns – this is one of the most expensive schools in the world, and not just in terms of school fees – but with huge numbers of scholarships and bursaries available, this hurdle to a supreme education can be vaulted.

The Campus

Occupying a prime location at one end of the largest (and most beautiful) urban park in the US, Wash U's campus is a splendid "old-stone buildings arranged around pretty quads" affair, reminiscent of an Oxbridge college.

Like all top universities, the administration is good at keeping the campus renovated and up-to-date. New buildings and facilities abound; many (like the state-of-the-art environmental engineering department) with an increasingly energy-conscious design. Students frequently compliment the "accessibility" of the campus, and its optimal size. "You don't have to stress about half hour hikes to your next class," said one, "but it never feels claustrophobic either." The library system is excellent, and houses more books than any in other library in the state.

Accommodation

The on-campus dorms available to freshmen and sophomores are as fabulous as they come, but upperclassmen are normally more than happy to move off campus for the last two years into the equally enviable university-owned apartments nearby. Campus dining is also top-notch, if pricey, with plenty of choice in where one finds one's grub.

The Wash U Student

Folks at Wash U are involved and active, diverse and friendly, hard-working and heavy-drinking. Brits might describe the student body as a tad "public school", with a large percentage hailing from affluent East Coast families, but this is easily counterbalanced by the multi-cultural outlook of the university, which is prevalent and very inclusive. Though there is a solid party-culture as well as the usual contingent of "high-strung workaholics", students are mostly interested and engaged in their studies and campus life.

"Everyone's either outwardly a nerd or a closet nerd," said a modest junior. Segregated groups like jocks, punks and goths are rare. "A lot of people look exactly the same," reflected a senior.

Students claim that the "openness and friendliness" is such that "making friends has never been easier". Tellingly, Wash U recently gained the *Princeton Review*'s prestigious top place in the "Quality of Life" ranking. There is a "solid community" here, meaning lots of security and extra confidence for the socially awkward.

It is worth noting that Wash U has hosted more presidential debates (during the election season) than any other location in the country, and has held either a Presidential or Vice Presidential debate every election since 1992. If you'd been here in 2008 you could have seen Sarah Palin talk about mavericks with Joe Biden. However, the school as a whole is not particularly politically active (by US standards).

Hitting the Books

Big endowments and a massive reputation (at least, for those in the know) mean that Wash U can attract some of the finest professors in the world to teach undergraduates. "I got to learn genetics from the guy who wrote the book", said one enthusiastic freshman. Professors have done real field work, and try hard to pass on what they've learned from their own experiences. As well as this, teachers are accessible and attentive, and class sizes are normally contained to a minimum, meaning lots of time for close contact with the experts.

Be prepared for a heavy, challenging work load, and also for fast-paced classes. Wash U might be located hundreds of miles from anywhere you've ever heard of, but it's full of the same brainy intelligentsia that populate the very top schools in the country. One chemistry major told us that "it's incredibly hard work, especially for us science students...but not so much that you feel you're drowning."

Students here are famous for their ambitious breadth of study (according to the college newspaper, "students acquire majors about as readily as free T-shirts.") which means that if you find it difficult to narrow your interests to just one subject, you'll be in good company. The curriculum is especially designed to accommodate indecisive types, with plenty of cross-majoring and interdisciplinary opportunities available.

With the sixth largest federal research grant of any higher education institution, research plays a big part at Wash U, and undergraduates profit accordingly. Almost 60% of undergraduates are engaged in research at some level; uniquely among universities of its kind, Wash U has a policy of including undergraduates into research programs as much as possible. Moreover, research also frequently cuts through department lines and allows students with interests in several areas to engage in the kind of high-flying, in-depth study that is usually only available for those focusing on the minutiae of a single discipline

Anthropology, business and art are considered some of the best-taught subjects at Wash U, but prospective pre-med students have a good time of it too, with high-quality labs on campus and the even better off-campus medical school, one of the finest in the country, offering unparalleled opportunities for undergraduates.

Social Life

Most of your social life will centre on campus, especially for your first two years at Wash U. Students throw lots of energy at all the activities going on, the student groups, the Greek life, the events, and of course the alcohol-soaked parties.

Some of the best events are organised by the on-campus ethnic groups, fuelled by the large numbers of ethnic minority (and overseas) students and the multi-cultural atmosphere of the student body. Diwali (a two-day Asian/Indian celebration, which sells out within hours), the Latin-American-themed "Carnaval", Chinese New Year and African-American "Black Anthology" performances are all good examples of this. Non-ethnic, but equally popular is the "Vertigo" dance party put on by students in the engineering department, who design incredible light displays and dance floors to impress non-engineers.

Apart from such events and the fun to be had in the myriad, well-funded student groups that cover every imaginable interest, students like "going-out" and enjoying the neighbourhood, known to St Louis locals as "the Loop", where excellent artistic, culinary and vintage delights are to be found, including great music venues (the late Chuck Berry's own joint is here), independent cinemas and restaurants and cafes of every variety.

On campus, students find that dorms are good places to socialise, as is the "DUC" student centre, where many great campus coffee shops and diners are located. There's also "the Gargoyle" student bar which frequently hosts concerts by fantastic up-and-coming bands, though to see gigs from big name groups (Black Eyed Peas, Ben Folds) you have to go to the debaucherous and semesterly "WILD" (Walk In, Lay Down) event.

Outside Those Ivory Walls

As upperclassmen, Wash U students are more prone to moving beyond the bubble-like environment of the first two years and exploring all the delights of their lovely city. Whether you're cheering at a Cardinals baseball game, slurping "frozen custard" (much yummier than it sounds), catching a free concert under the iconic Gateway Arch, munching toasted ravioli over a game of bocce in the Italian district, or taking a stroll in the gorgeous Forrest Park, it's hard not to love St. Louis, even if "it's no Chicago", as one Wash U student put it. It's certainly worth getting to know the town and its friendly citizens properly, especially since the university provides free transport.

Getting In

AT A GLANCE – Application & Test Options:

– Early Decision, Regular Decision

– ACT/SAT required

Wash U is in the middle of the country, not on the east coast. But don't assume it's not as competitive as the Ivy League schools – only about 15% of applicants are accepted every year. Wash U has a holistic application system similar to most US colleges, where test scores, reputation of secondary school, commitment to extra-curricular activities, etc are all scrutinised. Although interviews are not required, they are recommended (by us and the university) and can be arranged with overseas alumni. Similarly, it is a very positive sign to the university if you are able to schedule a visit to look around the campus before you apply, but they will understand if this is impractical.

Money Matters

Financially, the bad news is that not only are the basic costs of attendance incredibly expensive, but everyday expenses are also bizarrely high (maybe due to some kind of micro-inflation caused by the large number of wealthy kids on campus).

The good news is that help is available. Wash U awards both needs-based and merit-based aid (and sometimes both) to international students, sometimes covering full tuition or more.

Famous Grads

William H. Webster – Director of FBI and later CIA

Peter Sarsgaard – actor (Garden State, The Man In The Iron Mask, Orphan)

Harold Ramis – actor and director (Groundhog Day, Ghostbusters)

Wesleyan University

Mlddletown, Connecticut
www.wesleyan.edu
Undergrads: 2,900
Grads: 200

How many Wesleyan students does it take to change a light bulb?

One – but he'll only change it if he can put in an energy efficient bulb.

Way back in the 1830s, the founders of Wesleyan wanted to offer something relatively unusual: an innovative and progressive education. To this day, the school is still recognised for these qualities and has a stellar academic reputation as well.

The Campus

The campus is beautiful and spacious in a traditional college way, and also very walkable. Students live on campus for all four years.

The Wesleyan Student

Wesleyan has been coined the 'Diversity University'. The campus tends to lean toward extreme political-correctness and, according to The New York Times, is "naively liberal". But don't expect to see a non-stop show of tree– hugging hippies, angry protesters and naked parties. By most measures, Wesleyan is a normal all-round (albeit progressive) college with a few bizarre frills. They even have a football team.

Hitting the Books

Open-minded, curious students flourish at Wesleyan which, along with Amherst and Williams, is one of the historic 'Little Three', a trio of prestigious liberal arts schools in New England. Much of the Wesleyan academic experience is self-directed, with the hope that students will discover what they love to do and seek further knowledge.

Getting In

AT A GLANCE – Application & Test Options:

– Early Decision, Early Decision II, Freeman Scholar Programme, Regular Decision

– ACT/SAT optional at application; however, SAT/ACT and two Subject tests are required after admission, prior to matriculating

Admission is highly selective, with about 18% of applicants admitted in recent years.

Money Matters

Costs are in line with other private liberal arts schools (ie expensive). A limited amount of aid is available for international students and is awarded on the basis of both exceptional qualifications and demonstrated need.

Famous Grads

Candace Nelson – founder of Sprinkles (the world's first cupcakes-only bakery)

Philip Abraham – film and TV director and cinematographer

Carter Bays – creator and writer of TV comedy shows

Williams College

Williamstown, Massachusetts
www.williams.edu
Undergrads: 2,000
Grads: 50

How many students does it take to change a light bulb at Williams?

The whole student body – when you're snowed in, there's nothing else to do.

Williams is one of the few American colleges that draws only two reactions from its students – either they love it or they hate it. Fortunately, for the success of this small and thriving East Coast school, the majority of its undergraduates fall into the former category.

But prospective students should be aware from the start that this is not a place for everyone. Situated in 450 acres in a tiny (as in one street) town in rural Massachusetts, Williams is an isolated college with superior academics and a small student body famed for having the nicest people around. Great for those who love skiing and sport, it could turn into a nightmare for anyone with a craving for crowds and the city lifestyle.

Since its foundation in 1793 (with the interesting objective of civilizing the local farm boys), Williams has prided itself on its unique liberal arts education. In some ways this school is more Ivy than the Ivies – in fact one of its most honoured traditions is that every graduating student plants some ivy.

The Campus

The approach to Williamstown is rural, rural, rural, rural (from all four sides) and you may start to wonder how isolated it's going to be. But the campus itself is right in town, moments from cafes and a few restaurants. In fact, students from Bennington College, just up the road, often come down to Williamstown for a night out – but that may say more about the lack of amenities in the town of Bennington than the attractions of Williamstown.

One of the oldest colleges in the country, Williams has a lot of New England charm – old stone buildings, shady walkways – but it has also added several modern buildings over the past decade, including a new student centre and a centre for theatre and dance; it's a pleasing combination of the old and new. There are five libraries, including one just for rare books and another for science. And the Bronfman Auditorium has a bigger screen than the local cinema (and offers lots of free events). Williams is also the site of the Hopkins Observatory (the oldest surviving astronomical observatory in the United States).

The school's setting at the foothill of Mount Greylock in the Berkshire Mountains is quite beautiful, allowing for walks in Hopkins Forest and skinny dipping in the Green River. If you're an art lover, you'll be happy to know the campus has a couple of great museums; the Williams College Museum of art is home to over 13,000 artworks, including work by Edward Hopper, Sol LeWitt and Louise Bourgeois. And the widely recognised Mass MOCA (Museum of Contemporary Art) is only a few minutes east of town.

The Williams Student

It used to be said that Williams is a school that attracts a certain type of preppy, wealthy and (usually) smart jock. Certainly this is a campus where you can expect to see a fair number of Brooks Brothers shirts and Abercrombie and Fitch sweaters. But diversity is creeping ever upwards (ethnic minorities now make up a third of the student body) and, while jocks still take pride of place, the predominantly WASP (white anglo saxon protestant) factor is becoming ever less noticeable.

Foreign students will find they are welcomed with open arms. Seven percent of the student body is international and Williams actively encourages its students to study abroad – ensuring the cosmopolitan perspective on campus is broader than just you. Many Brits might feel tempted to take advantage of the year abroad in Oxford programme, which truly offers you the best of both educational worlds.

Hitting the Books

This is a fairly small college with only 2,000 Ephs (as they like to be known) at any one time and hugely strong faculty-student bonds. Excellent professors are constantly on hand and interested in what you have to say.

Of course, when you are stuck in three foot of snow and you're fed up with all your roommates, tea with your professor seems like a great option and these bonds are one of the most exciting parts of the Williams' experience.

Williams operates on a term schedule that incorporates two long semesters and one month-long January semester where students can experiment by taking subjects pass/fail. The liberal arts core requirements consist of mandatory classes in the social sciences and natural sciences as well as the humanities.

There is a certain expectation that Williams' students will want to pursue a broad education and the motivation of the student body ensures that people make the most of their opportunities.

Most of the undergrads are heading for careers in finance or grad school, where they have a hugely high success rate and their early ambitions stand them in good stead. It should come as no surprise that Williams is one of the colleges with the proportionately highest number of entries in the American 'Who's Who'.

If you are not so turned on by the notion of money, consultancy or further years of education, you should also be aware that Williams offers some of the best art and music programmes in the country. It has long been noted for the mafia-like hold its alumni have over the art world, where they dominate as art critics, curators and historians.

The fantastic museums and excellent art history teaching at Williams all contribute to the success of these graduates. Similarly, the proximity of the highly rated music school, Tanglewood, offers the concert pianists of the future a great place to study while getting their undergraduate degree.

Social Life

All this success is not to say that Ephs do not know how to have fun. Although fraternities were banned in the 1960s and the 'going out' options are extremely limited, Williams has a reputation for being a beer-swilling party school. Known for the administration's willingness to turn a blind(ish) eye to alcohol consumption, on-campus parties tend to be frequent and well-attended.

And for those who want to escape the drinking culture, the plethora of groups on campus (whenever people get bored, they are said to start another one) ensures there is normally something else going on. The school's sporting prowess, which despite its size is quite remarkable, also provides a chance for constant celebrations, and the annual games against arch-rival Amherst turn out the entire student body.

Outside Those Ivory Walls

Williams is one of those places it is important to check out in advance. While reports of it are almost always favourable, everyone admits it would not suit every individual. The campus and its architecture are undoubtedly beautiful and the students are reported to be the nicest people imaginable (and an incredibly bonded community), but the isolation and the limited socializing are a turn off for many. Williams is 2.5 hours from Boston and 3 hours from New York, and on long winter days, it can feel like it.

For those who love it, however, there can be no better college experience. The long-standing affection of Williams' graduates is aptly demonstrated by the fact that its alumni society is the oldest in America. Families continue to come here generation after generation (adding to its not undeserved WASP reputation).

Getting In

AT A GLANCE – Application & Test Options:

– Early Decision, Regular Decision

– ACT/SAT required, Writing/essay optional

Williams remains popular across the States – admitting only around 15% of all applicants of which 8% were international. After all, it is amongst the best (if not 'the best') of liberal arts colleges. If you want to join this prestigious club, you need to make sure you get hold of the Common Application and take the SAT or ACT test. And remember to talk to people, and if possible visit, before you sign on that dotted line.

Money Matters

Although Williams is not need-blind for international students (only for US citizens), it has generous aid packages for admitted students and so is a great option for really talented students who are worried about paying their tuition. However, since the college prefers to save its funds for students who need financial help, there are no academic scholarships.

Famous Grads

James Garfield – President of the USA

Stephen Sondheim – composer

Dominick Dunne – gossip queen of Vanity Fair

Yale University

New Haven, Connecticut
www.yale.edu
Undergrads: 5,400
Grads: 6,800

How many students does it take to change a light bulb at Yale?
None – New Haven looks better in the dark.

Jewel. Muckheap. Two of the words that spring to mind when trying to describe Yale and its local town, New Haven. Yet while the reasons why one of the prettiest college campuses in the US ended up at the centre of one of its ugliest industrial cities remain enigmatic, the secret of the college's success are clear.

This self-proclaimed Oxbridge equivalent offers both American and international wunderkind a great academic experience, a social life that far surpasses average Ivy Leagues and a name that is respected throughout the world. And, something which even Harvard students agree on, it has one of the coolest mascots around – the British bulldog!

The Campus

While the school itself started in 1701, it was not until 1718 that Elihu Yale decided to follow in the footsteps of good old John Harvard and build a monument to his own ego. A couple of book donations later and the deal was struck.

Enter the dreaming spires of New England, brick buildings, grassy quads, an immense library (for those original books) and a smattering of Gothic architecture. Yale, the third oldest college in the nation, helped to set the well-loved pattern for many other East Coast campuses. Its grounds are both attractive and easy to navigate.

If Yale campus is the star, then New Haven is the foil by which it shines. Although intrepid and proud Yalies still swear that their surrounding metropolis is an interesting and safe place to explore, it offers few of the charms of Boston or Providence. Fortunately, for those students who crave the big city lights, New York is only an hour and a bit away by train – an easy weekend destination.

And during the week? The immediate environs of the Yale campus are stocked with enough coffee shops, bars and restaurants to satisfy all but the most demanding student.

Accommodation

Yale follows in the footsteps of the Oxbridge tradition – randomly assigning each one of its students to one of the twelve residential colleges. Each college has its own unique character and individual traditions are upheld with pride. Although most Yalies come to regard their college as the centre of their social activity, freshman year helps to establish connections across the community.

While freshmen are aware of their house affiliation from the start, most initially live in the Old Campus. This location offers the best possible entrance to idyllic campus life – a collection of Gothic buildings situated around a quad designed for sunbathing or snowballing depending on the season.

The Yalie

Both Yale and its longstanding rival, Harvard, have always considered themselves the intellectual homes of the New England elite. Since what Americans consider the year dot, and we Brits consider the eighteenth century, these colleges have been taking the brightest and the best (as well as the dimmest but most well-connected) of America's privileged families and putting them through their academic paces.

Although much-needed egalitarianism has recently broadened the college intake, there are still many legacies pacing the campus. In your first few days at Yale, you may feel that every button-down shirted individual hails from Andover, Exeter, Groton or St Paul's – the American answer to Eton and Harrow.

Do not despair. Although you may still end up with a roommate whose name reads like the Mayflower passenger list (Lowell Eliot Winthrop Adams XII, for example), Yale, along with the other elite institutions, has been forced to curtail its blue blood intake in favour of brain cell count.

The result? An extremely diverse group of students get to reap the profits provided by generations of wealthy elite. Yale today has an undergraduate student body that is 48% minorities, 11% international and 60% public (for which read state) school educated. While the legacies continue – think the Bush dynasty – the student body provides every possible cultural, ethnic and religious outlet, and does so with a minimum of discrimination.

Yalies often boast about the friendliness of their school. And it seems to be true. Despite the high pressure of academics and the distinct social groups, most students pride themselves on their sense of community. In part this may be attributed to the strong residential college programme – even in freshman year, students live within college groups. Yet, even discounting the bonds of accommodation, Yale students are a tolerant, cheerful and outgoing bunch.

There is a popular myth at Harvard that this sense of community stems from the chip that all Yalies have on their shoulder – resulting from their constant relegation to second best (in areas stemming from the football field to such coveted academic prizes as the Rhodes scholarship). Jealousy? Truth? Authorial objectivity prevents us from comment, but you have been warned!

The Harvard-Yale rivalry is at its fiercest during the annual football game (held at Yale every other year). Despite the Bulldog's recent losing streak (and the inconvenient situation of their football stadium), sport is taken very seriously at Yale and there are over thirty-five varsity teams.

In fact, Yale is known for the support it gives to extra-curricular activities. Yalies tend to be both energetic and ambitious. Whether writing for the oldest college daily, the Yale Daily News, or pioneering the most obscure club around (the Ayn Rand society, anyone?), many students devote infinitely more time to their clubs, groups and associations than to class. After all who could turn down the chance of joining an a cappella group known as the Whiffenpoofs?

Some Yale students complain their schedules are simply too hectic and they have little time to simply enjoy being students. However, most soon learn how to draw a happy medium between socializing, academics and extracurriculars. Once you have established your personal pace, Yale provides an ideal environment for fulfilling your dreams. The large endowment of the university means there is always cash available to fund student projects and the faculty is generally interested in student well-being.

Despite the prestige of the school and the pressure of their academic lives, Yale kids tend to be well-adjusted and happy individuals who benefit from the strong community that surrounds them.

Hitting the Books

Hooray for interested professors! The Yale community ethos extends to faculty as well as students. Yale recruits the brightest and the best in both departments and ensures they benefit from each other. The student-faculty ratio at Yale is under 7:1, and professors make a real effort to get to know their students. This is made much easier by the fact that Yale makes a concerted effort to keep its class sizes small – most of them under twenty students.

This creates an experience more similar to the British tutorial experience and allows for some rewarding academic relationships. As at all American schools, classroom discussion is considered to be of the utmost importance and contributes significantly to one's grade. If you are the type of student who likes to sit quietly in the back of the room and snooze, then this may not be the environment for you.

Yale consists of the undergraduate college, a grad school and ten professional schools. When all of this academic energy is combined with a 25 billion dollar endowment, some pretty spectacular resources emerge. The libraries dominate the campus, both architecturally and otherwise. Yale possesses over 15 million bound books – a far cry from the handful initially donated by Elihu and others. Students may moan about the academic pressure, but at least it is done in the most comfortable surroundings with up to the minute technology and the best professors that money (and the chance of tenure) can buy.

Yalies are spoilt for choice in their course selection, with over 2,000 options available. They also benefit from the infamous 'shopping period' – a span of two weeks at the beginning of each semester where they can test as many classes as they like. The bane of every professor's existence, this trial period helps the students to weed out the most boring speaker and hardest reading load on campus.

Harvard and Yale both share this custom along with the concept of reading week – a period before exams at the end of each semester which is allocated purely for revision purposes. This should not be underrated as a chance to catch up on that backlog of reading and to relax a little before the stress of finals.

The idea of a liberal arts education continues to form the core of Yale's attitude towards academics. The idea is that the student will teach him or herself how to learn and in so doing will form a foundation of knowledge that will prove valuable whatever the unexpected turns of life. As such there is none of the specialization of British universities. While students have a major (the most popular are History, Economics and Political Science), they are also able to double major and are required to take courses in other areas.

These distributional requirements are similar to those at other schools. A language is considered necessary (French GCSE, anyone?) as well as selections from the humanities, social sciences and maths and science. Your major has a number of requirements as well. Yale students alternatively praise and bemoan the fact that Yale insists on thirty-six credits, rather than the customary thirty-two, for graduation. While it allows more flexibility, it also adds to the work load.

Like all elite students, Yalies are not silent about these additional academic demands and competitions about who has the most work are commonplace. Yet this is after all the essence of the liberal arts education and, if you are making the trek to America, it is well worth pursuing.

Nor do you have to make the complicated decisions about which course to take on your own. All students are given freshman year advisors as well as later advisors who supervise their major. Both these and the faculty members themselves are always willing to give advice. While graduate students supervise many discussion classes, the faculty is very much present and encourages student communication.

Social Life

Yale, unlike other Ivy League schools, has woken up to the fact that 'all work and no play' makes for some very dull and unhappy students. Partly due to its strong sense of community and partly to the numerous local bars, restaurants and coffee houses, Yale students tend to enjoy a strong and diverse social life.

While there is not the strong fraternity drinking culture that dominates many American schools, Yale students do not sit alone with their maths textbooks on a Saturday night. New Haven, despite its dubious qualities, offers the best pizza in New England (some say the world) at Sally's and Pepés and a host of other cuisines to suit every taste. And after dinner, students have a variety of places to go on to – most notoriously the extremely-relaxed-on-IDs Toad's Place.

There are some clubs at Yale that are not accessible to all members of the campus. The secret societies, while not an integral part of everyone's Yale experience, are decidedly a part of its history. Dotted around the campus are huge, prison-like buildings with no discernable entrance. These are the secret societies – the most infamous of which is the Skull and Bones (the model for the 2000 film The Skulls).

Although these societies are, by default, secret, it is generally known that men such as George W. Bush and John Kerry paced these halls in their senior years. Some of these societies are accessible to both men and women and their membership numbers are kept deliberately small. Initiation rites are also mysterious, candidates are 'tapped' at the end of their junior year and after that, who knows? While not for everyone, the high-flying connections could be useful!

Outside Those Ivory Walls

For generations, Harvard students have returned from the annual football game, heaved huge sighs of relief and said, 'Thank goodness we don't live in New Haven.' Yalies, meanwhile, have fought to defend their local city, swearing that they wouldn't choose to live anywhere else.

Both sides have some validity. New Haven, an industrial city with a high crime rate and acres of low-income, ghetto-like housing that circle the stately campus is not the most pleasant of New England destinations. Yet, largely helped by Yale, it has experienced something of a renaissance in recent years, its crime rate is falling and its prosperity growing.

While the boundaries between the immediate environs of the Yale campus and greater New Haven remain pretty much insurmountable, there has been an easing of campus-town relationships. Yale remains a very safe campus (unless you count the danger of insensitive Halloween costumes). Students have no shortage of places to shop, hang out and get caffeine fixes, or even (back on campus) safe rooms to tuck away from the Possibly Offensive.

And for the more serious, there are also a number of well-respected museums – note for Brits – the Yale Center for British Art is well worth an exploration. If you need even more cosmopolitan pursuits, New Haven is well-connected to New York and Boston by both train and bus.

If you are an active person, New Haven also offers great opportunities for hiking. Sleeping Giant State Park is close by and provides a nice escape from the confines of campus. The proximity of Yale to the Long Island Sound also means the water is near – something that provides both invigorating (read cold) winter breezes and summer visits to the beach for those with cars. With all this on offer, the less salubrious parts of New Haven don't seem that bad.

Getting In

AT A GLANCE – Application & Test Options:

- Single-choice Early Action, QuestBridge, Regular Decision
- ACT/SAT, with Writing/essay required
- Subject tests are recommended, but not required

Yale and Harvard. Oxford and Cambridge. When names as renowned as these are thrown around you can be sure that the admissions process will not be a walk in the park. Yale is one of the most popular universities in America today and draws a huge number of applications.

Yale is one of the most popular universities in America today and draws a huge number of applications. For the 2016 freshman class, the school accepted approximately 2,300 students out of 33,000 applicants (6.9%), choosing those they believe will bring the most to the much-prized Yale community and make the most of its resources. The good news for Brits is that there has been a substantial attempt to internationalise the campus; students from outside the US comprise 11% of Yale undergraduate enrolment. The bad news is it's still a very difficult process.

Yale does not try to hide the fact it regards academics to be of primary importance. If your grades are poor, it is unlikely you will make the cut. Most SAT test results are in the low 700s in each area and the incoming class will be made up of students who have all been at the top of their high schools.

The SAT with essay or ACT with writing are required; the SAT Subject Tests are recommended but not required. According to the Yale website, applicants who do not take SAT Subject Tests will not be disadvantaged in the application process.

Some British students are at a big advantage here, since Yale now accepts completed A-level results as a substitute for the SAT Subjects (one A-level for each test). This is extremely good news for those students who cannot find any SAT Subject tests that suit their sixth-form subject choices. However, you need to bear in mind that the results have to be completed before application – something that, unless you are taking a gap year, will probably not have happened. Academics aside, the Yale Supplement application form also requires a few essays – your chance to show the admissions committee what you are made of.

Yale also recommends alumni interviews – available in London and other locations around the United Kingdom. While these are not essential, they come highly recommended. They allow the university to take a look at you (thus increasing your chances, unless you really irritate the interviewer) and, more importantly, they allow you to take a look at the university. This is the time to ask questions, probe the corners of Yale you might not know so well, and generally find out what you might be about to commit four years of your life to.

Finally, Yale does offer an Early Action programme which enables students to express their preference for Yale above other schools. While the Early Action programme still allows Regular Decision application to other universities, you are no longer able to apply early to anywhere other than Yale. So you need to be fairly set on the idea, and fairly organized, to follow this route.

Money Matters

GOOD NEWS! Yale offers full financial aid on a need-blind basis to international as well as American students. With the rises in English tuition fees and the crippling debt of UK student loans, these extremely generous financial aid programmes can actually make university in America a cheaper prospect. Definitely something to investigate.

Yale also takes part in a US program called QuestBridge, which helps exceptional low-income students apply to the best US colleges and universities by providing information, support and scholarships.

Famous Grads

George Bush (1 and 2) – could recent grad Barbara Bush be next in line?

Cole Porter – delicious and de-lovely

Eli Whitney – if you don't know who this is now, you will in four years' time

Also worth considering...

We are continually expanding the Guide and are already looking at the next unis we want to visit. We don't have in-depth write-ups on the following, but we think they represent value for money once you pitch up on campus, and are definitely worth a look – so we've included a little information on each.

Carnegie Mellon University

Pittsburgh, Pennsylvania
www.cmu.edu
Undergrads: 6,000
Grads: 5,000

Founded by wealthy industrialist-philanthropist Andrew Carnegie in 1900, modernistic CMU has risen to become one of the finest and most reputable universities in America. With a historical focus on science and technology, nowadays CMU has more top-ranked departments than Carnegie had railroad companies (and in fields as diverse as drama and computer science).

This means an incredible breadth and depth of study, combined with lots and lots of brilliant teachers dedicated to rousing their pupils with the same passion that they feel for their subjects. Collaboration with next-door University of Pittsburgh allows students to share classes, professors and facilities, a great boon to CMU's academics.

The Campus

Outside of the "rigorous and interesting" courses, most students find just enough time to enjoy the tradition-laced campus life and some even get their fingers into some of the delights of gritty-but-cool Pittsburgh, Pennsylvania's second city (with great public transport).

The university is home to a whopping 250 student organisations, and is well known for it's top-rate art galleries and theatre clubs. Students love the busy atmosphere and the small-but-not-too small size, which allows you to get intimate but not claustrophobic.

Accommodation

All undergrads are guaranteed housing on campus, which the majority make use of for all four years.

The Carnegie Mellon Student

Students are "focused", "quirky", "well-rounded" and "nerdy", though they can't be pigeonholed. With a relatively large number of international students (20%+), diversity is strong.

Social Life

There are some frats in operation, but if you're looking for the craziest parties, look on.

Events and societies are advertised by paintings on "The Fence", an ancient monument in the centre of campus which is closely guarded 24/7 by students to prevent others painting over their work.

Other traditions include the huge and beloved Spring Carnival and both buggy and robot racing. There is a Scottish theme at CMU, supposedly due to Carnegie's ancestry, and the university holds the intriguing distinction of being one of only two in the country to offer a degree in bagpipe music.

Getting In

AT A GLANCE – Application & Test Options:

- Early Decision, Regular Decision

- ACT/SAT required

- SAT Subject tests required for most programmes

Competition for places is tough – about 25% are admitted – with most applicants also jostling for places at all the other high-flyers in the north east.

Money matters

The financial news is not good either – CMU is expensive and does not award needs-based aid to international students.

Famous Grads

Andy Warhol – iconic pop artist

Judith Resnik – astronaut

John Forbes Nash – Nobel Prize winner (Economics) and subject of the book and subsequent film "A Beautiful Mind"

College of William and Mary

Williamsburg, Virginia
www.wm.edu
Undergrads: 6,000
Grads: 2,000

A top-notch, East Coast, very old public university, W&M can be seen as a smaller, less famous version of the prestigious University of Virginia. As the second oldest university in the country, W&M educated many of the leading figures in America's early history, including three Presidents and 16 signatories of the Declaration of Independence (including Thomas Jefferson, who went on to found the University of Virginia). It is still home to the nation's oldest fraternity.

The Campus

Surrounded by the meticulously if fanatically preserved 17th century town of Williamsburg, one of the oldest towns in the US and the 2nd capital of the British colony of Virginia, students must plow through the throngs of deeply reverent historical tourists that overwhelm their picture-perfect colonial brick campus. But no question – this is a beautiful if oh-so-quaint location for college students to roam freely.

Accommodation

Nearly 75% of students live on campus for all four years, though many of them are less than complimentary about the housing.

The W&M Student

Students are quirky, friendly, passionate and intelligent, and not ashamed to show it. They hail from an eclectic mix of backgrounds – many are North Virginians from the DC suburbs.

Hitting the Books

A so-called "public Ivy", W&M is academically hard-hitting, with uber-challenging courses and dedicated professors. The whole system is geared towards undergraduate achievement, with almost no courses taught by teaching assistants (ie they're all taught by the actual professors). The resulting quantity of learning is very satisfying, as is engagement in the vibrant campus life which is as exciting and expansive as anywhere in America.

The College offers a joint liberal arts degree program with St Andrews (two years at each), which may appeal to UK applicants. This International Honours Bachelor of Arts offers four humanities degree options (Economics, English, History and International Relations). During the first two years, students study at each university – one year at W&M and one year at St Andrews – and then, in consultation with advisors, they decide how to allocate the final two years. Graduates of this programme receive a degree awarded jointly by both universities.

Social Life

Coastal Virginia is blessed by a more temperate climate than many parts of the US, so W&M's winters aren't too severe. This is fortunate, because Christmas time is a big deal on campus, ever since college professors were the first to introduce the German tradition of decorating evergreen trees to America in the 1840s. Each year, the President of the university still dresses as Santa and recites the Dr Seuss classic "How the Grinch Stole Christmas" as part of the much loved Yule Log Ceremony.

Music is also a big part of campus life, with no fewer than 11 acapella groups and a wide range of other musical ensembles run by students. The Alma Mater, which is the unique song every major US uni sings at important college-spirit-boosting occasions, is treated with less respect at W&M, and has become something of a theme tune to be heard around campus whenever something fun or exciting happens. Comedy, dancing and sports are also popular.

Finally, W&M enjoys what some call "a culture of service" – a particularly large number of students spend their free time and holidays volunteering in various altruistic capacities both locally and further afield.

Outside Those Ivory Walls

The college and the surrounding town are more notable for their aesthetics and history than social vibe, but with lots of cool "delis" (bars), great student media opportunities, and a campus lake and amphitheatre, the attractions of the big metropolises will be hardly missed. The livelier towns of Norfolk, Va (huge military base, home of US Atlantic fleet), Richmond, Va (the capital) and Virginia Beach are accessible by car (as usual, not much in the way of public transport you'd expect in the UK).

Getting In

AT A GLANCE – Application & Test Options:

- Early Decision, Regular Decision
- ACT/SAT required
- SAT Subject tests optional

Admission is very competitive, but the process is straightforward.

Money matters

Although there is little financial aid available of any kind for international students, W&M is not as expensive as similar schools. There are two small scholarships available.

Famous Grads

Jon Stewart – comedian, host of The Daily Show

David M. Brown – astronaut

US Presidents Thomas Jefferson, John Tyler, James Monroe

Robert Gates – Secretary of Defence until 2011; previously head of the CIA

Rutgers (The State University of New Jersey)

New Brunswick/Newark/Camden, New Jersey
www.rutgers.edu
Undergrads: 43,000
Grads: 13,000

It's not clear why Rutgers is not called The University of New Jersey, because that is essentially what it is. A gargantuan state-funded institution occupying no fewer than three separate campuses, the university seems to be engaged in a non-stop struggle to make itself manageable.

It does achieve this – to an extent – but only at the price of one of the most horrifically bureaucratic administrations in the country. Each campus is divided into many "colleges", each with a unique environment and feel which creates a pleasantly self-contained sub-community.

In areas of everyday life, Rutgers exhibits most of the traits of other schools of similar immensity. There is a ridiculous number of incredible opportunities to be taken advantage of, a big range of teaching quality (some say more bad than good), and lots of intriguing research openings. The two classic pastimes of Rutgers students (officially the most diverse student body in the country for the last 12 years of rankings) seem to be inebriation and evacuation – presumably to nearby New York or Philadelphia on the weekends.

Still, campus life is exceedingly vibrant and generalization is impossible. Special mention goes to the study-abroad program, which is really top-notch. The key, as ever, is to find your niche and carpe diem: life-changing experiences and life-long friends won't come to you, but they're waiting there for you to go to them.

Getting In

Admission to Rutgers is tough but nothing like that other famous NJ college (Princeton); more than half of applicants are successful. Costs are quite high, and financial aid is not available. Some scholarships are, though.

Famous Grads

Barry Schuler – former chairman and CEO of AOL

Milton Friedman – Nobel Laureate in Economics

Mary Baglivo – Chairman and CEO of the Americas, Saatchi & Saatchi

Sewanee: The University of the South

Sewanee, Tennessee
www.sewanee.edu
Undergrads: 1,450
Grads: 80

How many Sewanee students does it take to change a light bulb?

Sewanee: Seven–the five-person Honor Council to decide if it is against the Honor Code to change light bulbs, one to find a reference in Faulkner to light bulb changing, and one to pray for the repose of the soul of the deceased bulb

Perched resplendently atop a mountain in rural Tennessee, the University of the South (universally called "Sewanee") offers an experience quite unlike any other. With a huge campus (called "the Domain") but a tiny student body, the college may be hard to reach (buses and trains don't go near – you have to fly to Chattanooga, take the airport shuttle to Monteagle, and a pre-arranged taxi from there), but the rewards are spectacular.

The academics, for a start, are exquisite –with a liberal arts curriculum thorough enough to have produced more Rhodes Scholars per capita than any other university; the campus is truly sublime; and the cultural value is completely unparalleled.

Originally founded on all the principals and bizarre traditions of our very own Oxford, and still owned by the Episcopal Church, Sewanee's isolation has kept this historical haven intact and more than a little eccentric, whilst adding a strong Southern twist.

The "Honour Code" is paramount, and taken seriously enough that theft and cheating are largely non-existent. Students leave bicycles around, and come back days later in full expectation of finding them just where they left them...or borrowed by someone but later returned to the same place. Male students attend classes in a time-honored coat and tie uniform, taught by faculty wearing gowns. Classes are small, lively and collegial, with relationships between students and faculty easy and comfortable.

The Campus

Though there is not much beyond the campus (the tiny "unincorporated town" of Sewanee is inside the university, rather than vice-versa), it does encompass the entire top of a mountain, and a beautiful mountain it is.

The Sewanee Student

The social life is vibrant and, oiled by a healthy Greek life, involves a surprising amount of booze (the Jack Daniels distillery is just down the road...). Despite administrative efforts to the contrary, the student body is homogeneous and Southern in its attitudes, and social arrangements can be cliquey.

Nevertheless, the strong community on "The Mountain" (as students call the campus) means there is room for all types – whether you want to clamber around on mountain trails, hike around caves, ravines and waterfalls, stomp around in deep woods (wild colour in the autumn), bring your horse along, party in cocktail dresses and flipflops, or, you know, study.

Students have been known to attribute unexpectedly good grades to the lack of mobile phone access (due to mountain interference) together with the snowy, foggy winters that can settle in on the campus, forcing a reduced number of entertainment options to include a closer relationship with the library.

Even though it sounds a tad isolated, many international students have made the trip – there are currently students from 20 countries enrolled.

Getting In

AT A GLANCE – Application & Test Options:

– Early Action, Early Decision, Early Decision II, Regular Decision

– ACT/SAT test-optional

Admission is not overly competitive – almost two-thirds of applicants are admitted.

Money matters

Prices are high but not as bad as they could be, and in a recent startling and smart marketing manoeuvre, Sewanee recently became one of the first unis in the US to lower their fees – because they are genuinely motivated to attract bright students without regard to income.

A significant number of merit-based scholarships are available and grants for international students can range from $5,000 to $40,000 per year.

Famous Grads

Sam Pickering– Teacher that film character John Keating was based on in 'Dead Poet's Society'

Gene Robinson– First openly gay Bishop of the US Episcopal Church

Jon Meacham– Executive Editor of *Newsweek* magazine

Syracuse University

Syracuse, New York
www.syracuse.edu
Undergrads: 14,000
Grads: 6,000

Syracuse is in many ways an ideal university, combining the good points of both big-college and small-college education along with an independent and occasionally experimental approach.

Hitting the Books

Academics are very strong, especially in areas such as public communication, architecture, life sciences, music, advertising, political science, business and even cyber security. Professors are often excellent and available, and the university gives students scope for both serious depth (plenty of great research goes on here) and an exciting breadth.

Social Life

Fairly mainstream in its social life, Syracuse has a strong frat/party culture, but also lots of alternatives and a wealth of stuff to do on campus. The basketball team is a big deal, and the college newspaper is superb. The town of Syracuse is not the most exhilarating place on earth, but the region as a whole is beautiful and perfect for outdoorsy types. Beware the horrific winters, though!

Getting In

AT A GLANCE – Application & Test Options:

– Early Decision, Regular Decision

– ACT/SAT required

Syracuse admits about half of its applicants, and only a few merit-based scholarships are available by way of financial aid for international students to help cope with the high cost.

Famous Grads

Joe Biden – Vice President of the United States under Barack Obama

Joyce Carol Oates – novelist

Shirley Jackson – novelist

University of Georgia

Athens, Georgia
www.uga.edu
Undergrads: 25,000
Grads: 9,000

As classic an experience as they come, UGA is the quintessential small-town, big-state-school US college. While competent academically, the focus here is much more on the glory of the Bulldogs sports teams, the honour of one's fraternity or sorority, and the size of the parties one is able to throw. UGA is a great place to experience the charm of the southern, beer-drinking stereotype, but also, to an extent, art-rock groups and Kafka-reading intelligentsia.

The Campus

As with all massive universities there is plenty of room to be an individual and meet very interesting people. Indeed, Athens is as cool a college town as you could hope for out in the middle of the rural South, complete with the artsy bohème of collegiate cafes and funky music scene. The campus itself is a big draw for some people, being spacious and leafy and filled with elegant buildings.

Getting In

AT A GLANCE – Application & Test Options:

– Early Action, Regular Decision

– ACT/SAT required

Money matters

Price-wise, UGA is comparatively a bargain, even for overseas appli- cants, and admission is not too competitive (just over half of applicants are admitted) but by no means assured.

Famous Grads

Emilio Pucci – fashion designer

Abdul Karim al-Iryani – Prime Minister of Yemen

Maxine Clark – founder of 'Build a Bear Workshop'

University of Miami

Coral Gables (Miami), Florida
www.miami.edu
Undergrads: 10,000
Grads: 5,000

The East Coast alternative to Orange County, UM is for those who like some sun and games with their education, but who for whatever reason didn't make it into UCLA. One of the top universities in the region, the academics are great here and getting better.

With a student:teacher ratio of 11:1 the work load will challenge you to your limits, but for many students it plays second fiddle to the exuberant night life and a devotion to all things sporty.

The UM Student

Normally parodied as cliquey, attractive, sports-car-driving, dark-shades-wearing, daddy's-wealth-relying party-maniacs, the students at Miami can be overwhelming for some, but the perfect comrades for others.

There is, however, lots of diversity here, and some worthwhile campus-life to distract you on the rare occasion that one more day perfecting your tan becomes tedious.

The palm-filled campus acts as a bubble that protects the party-life excesses of the students from the real-life poverty and race-laced politics of ever-cool Miami.

Getting In

AT A GLANCE – Application & Test Options:

– Early Action, Regular Decision

– ACT/SAT, with Writing/essay required

Admission is competitive, and attendance very expensive. Some scholarships offered, but no needs-based aid for international students.

Famous Grads

Ben Folds – pianist (Ben Folds Five)

Dwayne "The Rock" Johnson – actor and pro wrestler

Algis Budrys – science fiction writer

University of Notre Dame

Notre Dame, Indiana
www.nd.edu
Undergrads: 8,400
Grads: 3,400

A superb private Catholic school in the Middle Of Nowhere, Indiana, Notre Dame has for a long time maintained an excellent reputation for providing one of the leading undergraduate programs in the country and a legendary football team [the kind played with a pointy ball].

For anyone concerned about the Catholic side of things, fret not, because the religious bias is largely indiscernible. In fact, the university made headlines recently when it awarded an honorary degree to President Obama, who is vocally pro-abortion, pro civil-unions and pro several other things that generally upset the Vatican.

The Campus

The Notre Dame campus is gorgeous, and dominated by a huge Catholic cathedral. Students enjoy a thrilling campus life, based around big, single-sex dorm blocks which are central to the university environment. Notre Dame is famous for its "Fighting Irish" sports teams (see above), and sports in general are a big part of the community spirit. In fact, tear-jerker movies based on real players have been made about the legendary football team (eg "Knute Rockne,All American" (which starred Ronald Regan in his most famous role as "the Gipper"); "Rudy").

With fantastic teachers, great research opportunities and an engaged student body (despite some diversity problems), this is an option seriously worth considering for people of any denomination.

Getting In

AT A GLANCE – Application & Test Options:

– Restricted Early Action, Regular Decision

– ACT/SAT required

Money matters

Notre Dame is very competitive and expensive (accepting fewer than 20% of applicants, of which 8% are international, and charging close to $50,000 in tuition alone), but it provides copious financial aid, including a tiny bit for really needy international students. There are no merit scholarships.

Famous Grads

Condoleezza Rice– former US Secretary of State

Eric F. Wieschaus– Nobel Prize winner

Knute Kockne– football player

Virginia Polytechnic Institute and State University (Virginia Tech)

Blacksburg, Virginia
www.vt.edu
Undergrads: 24,000
Grads: 7,000

Although the name might now be forever associated with an awful college massacre, Virginia Tech continues to be one of the best Polytechnic schools in America, comfortably in the same ballpark as Georgia Tech, Cal Tech and even MIT. As you might expect, the engineering and science programs are scintillating, and undergraduate research opportunities are massive. There are some other good departments too, including architecture, business, and forestry. Unsurprisingly, work here is extremely challenging (but fulfilling), though students at Virginia Tech probably enjoy a much broader social life than their counterparts in Georgia or Massachusetts.

The Campus

In fact, the atmosphere is more like your typical large state school rather than a tech; Greek life and football dominate the campus life, and students are keen on making space in their hard-working schedules for lots of fun. Blacksburg, VTech's tiny college town, may be in the middle of nowhere, but this gives it the advantage of both providing an extreme community spirit, and of being close to many unbelievable sites of natural wonder, including forests, mountains and rivers.

Getting In

AT A GLANCE – Application & Test Options:

– Early Decision, Regular Decision

– ACT/SAT required

Money matters

Some scholarships are available, and take a look also at the "Presidential Campus Enrichment Grant", but in general VTech is not too expensive. More than half of applicants get an offer, but you'll need a pretty good application to stand out.

Famous Grads

Jim Buckmaster – CEO of Craigslist.org

Sharyn McCrumb – best-selling author

Roger K. Crouch – NASA astronaut

... and we can help

About Our University Consultants

If you've read this book, and you're still boggled by the whole thing and want professional help, we have just the answer. Our team of expert, hand-picked university consultants can help you.

They offer one-to-one advice on colleges and universities in the UK, United States, Europe and Asia.

They help you shorten your list of choices so you find the right "fit" for you.

They help you prepare, apply and figure out how to pay.

With long and successful track records, our consultants are equally familiar with:

- UK and US school systems.
- UK, US and international exams (e.g. A levels, GCSEs, SATs, IB, AP etc).
- US university admissions requirements and procedures.
- UK (UCAS) university admissions requirements and procedures.

Contact

The Good Schools Guide – University Advice Services

Tel: +44 (0)20 3286 6824

Email: uniadvice@goodschoolsguide.co.uk

Other Services from *The Good Schools Guide*

The Good Schools Guide Consultants Service

The Good Schools Guide Advice Service is a personal service which helps families with all aspects of educating children. Our 26 advisors are parents; all are hand-picked experts who visit hundreds of schools – state, independent, junior, senior, day and boarding.

The Good Schools Guide Consultants Service has 5 experts in SEN, a State School Service, a Scholarships and Bursaries Service and 30 years experience in all aspects of UK education. We put our expertise and wide network of personal contacts to work for you and your children.

The advice that you get from *The Good Schools Guide* Consultants Service is completely independent; unlike "agents", we take no commission from schools.

Moving abroad or back to the UK?

Whether unexpected move or planned posting, *Good Schools Guide International* advisors will share their wealth of knowledge and expertise – by phone, email or face to face – ensuring you choose the right school for your child.

Ears to the ground, *Good Schools Guide International* consultants talk to other parents, visit the schools themselves and compare schools with the best of similar schools worldwide.

GSGI advisors are ex-pats and parents themselves, and all have had years of experience analyzing and dealing with their own children's schooling across the globe. They know the international schools in their host cities, and they've ferreted out the secrets of expat survival there.

Because of their infectious enthusiasm for this nomadic life, they are exactly the sympathetic, savvy advisors parents need for educational and even cultural advice about new postings or proposed relocations.

Contact *The Good Schools Guide* or visit www.goodschoolsguide.co.uk/advice or call us on +44 (0)20 3286 6824 or email advice@goodschoolsguide.co.uk.